Siam and the League of Nations

Modernisation, Sovereignty and Multilateral Diplomacy, 1920-1940

Siam and the League of Nations

Modernisation, Sovereignty and Multilateral Diplomacy, 1920-1940

Stefan Hell

RIVER

BOOKS

First published and distributed in 2010 by
River Books Co., Ltd.
396 Maharaj Road, Tatien, Bangkok 10200
Tel: (66) 2 225-4963, 2 225-0139, 2 622-1900
Fax: (66) 2 225-3861
Email: order@riverbooksbk.com
www.riverbooksbk.com

Publisher: Narisa Chakrabongse
Editor: Stephen A. Murphy
Production: Paisarn Piemmattawat
Design: Reutairat Nanta

ISBN 978 974 9863 89 3

Printed and bound in Thailand by Sirivatana Interprint Co., Ltd.

Front Cover: *League of Nations International Opium Conference held in Bangkok in 1931
presided over by Prince Traidos Prabandh Devakul (Thai National Archives).*

Back Cover: *Delegation of Siam to the first League of Nations General Assembly, 1920.
Seated from left: Phraya Buri Navarasth, Prince Charoon, Phraya Bibadh Khosa.
Standing from left: Chuen Jotikasthira, Pan Xavier, Chuen Charuvastra,
Sidh Saukathia (League of Nations Archives).*

Frontispiece: *Delegation of Siam to the League of Nations General Assembly, 1921.
Seated from left: Phraya Bibadh Khosa, Kimleang Vathanaprida, Prince Charoon.
Standing from left: Chuen Charuvastra, Margaret Lin Xavier, Pan Xavier,
Tienliang Hoontrakul (League of Nations Archives).*

Contents

Foreword

It is a great honour for me to have been invited to contribute the Foreword to this book. Stefan Hell had introduced the subject originally in his article 'Siam and the League of Nations, 1920-1946' in 1999. It has taken more than a decade for this book, which is based on his doctoral thesis, to appear before a wider public instead of languishing in a university library archive. This might have been because Dr. Hell did not pursue an academic career but spent the intervening years in public service and did not have sufficient time to work on this academic project. It happens, but the wait has been well worth it.

Historians of Siam should be grateful to Stefan Hell for this study of a neglected aspect of Thai history. For this particular period of Thai diplomatic history, focus has largely been on bilateral relations with emphasis on negotiations to recover full sovereignty from the treaties signed in the middle of the nineteenth century with their legal and fiscal limitations on Siam's freedom and independence. The resolution of those negotiations was ultimately dependent on Thai legal reform, but parallel to the bilateral negotiations in capitals, Siam's membership and participation in the League of Nations also contributed to the successful outcome.

Siam was an original member of the League of Nations thanks to her decision to enter the First World War on the side of her erstwhile tormentors, which earned her a place as an Associated Power at the Paris peace conferences. During the League's short life, Siam was the only member from Southeast Asia and one of only three from the whole of Asia. His Majesty King Rama VI was justifiably proud and well satisfied that his kingdom had helped to found the League 'whose duty is to regulate world affairs according to the principles of right and justice'.

The League of Nations was the first permanent international organisation dedicated to multilateral diplomacy to maintain world peace in the aftermath of the bloody struggle for the mastery of Europe and the world that was the First World War. The League was not, however, Siam's first multilateral engagement, for she had been a member of the Universal Postal Union from the beginning, had joined the international Red Cross movement in 1893 and had participated in the first Hague Peace Conference of 1899.

The representatives of Siam at the League of Nations belonged to the second and third generation of Thai diplomats which had engaged with westerners. Several of their fathers and grandfathers had negotiated the very treaties in the nineteenth century which they were committed to nullify in the interwar years of the first half of the twentieth century. Many of them had been educated at the best schools and universities in England, France and other European countries. They were the elite in an elitist world. In that aristocratic and patronising environment, it stood Siam in good stead that her leading representatives had been at Eton and Harrow, Oxford and Cambridge.

Stefan Hell's book is full of wonderful and little known details. Prince Charoon's 'extremely moderate and quiet style' of diplomacy stands in contrast with his reputation for authoritarian ways which caused problems with his staff at the Paris Legation and with Thai students in France. A hint of what the Prince could have been like comes in his stout defence of his diplomatic immunity when given a speeding ticket while driving for distinguished visitors in Geneva. Things have not changed much since then. Prince Wan's later 'much more visible and outspoken presence' was an important factor in Siam's gaining the honour of hosting the first League meeting held in Asia, the Bangkok International Opium Conference of 1931, which produced the first international agreement to bear the name of Bangkok in the form of the 'Bangkok Agreement on the Suppression of Opium-smoking in the Far East' of 27 November 1931.

That Opium Control is given a chapter of its own as are Public Health and Human Trafficking gives a good overall balance to this book. These issues were new to the international agenda. The necessary multilateral diplomacy involved was a learning process for all participants, not just for Siam. The Bangkok International Opium Conference of 1931 was a bonus in that it enabled the Government to mobilise resources to make meticulous preparations both substantively and physically for the meeting. Not that it was the first time that the Kingdom had hosted an international conference, for the League of Red Cross Societies and the Siamese Red Cross had cooperated in hosting the first meeting of Far Eastern Red Cross Societies in Bangkok in 1922, and there had also been the Eighth Congress of the Far Eastern Association of Tropical Medicine in Bangkok at the end of 1930. International cooperation on public health and social issues initiated by the League of Nations was based on the creation of new international norms, which pushed domestic reform on topical issues. Peer pressure has always been important for Siam. It also laid the foundation for the modern World Health Organization, the combat against drugs trafficking, and the promotion of human rights today.

Readers of this book may be more interested, however, in the Chapter on Collective Security. After all this was the *raison d'être* of the League of Nations, for which it failed miserably. It is here that Stefan Hell is at his best in demonstrating a firm grasp and clear understanding of Thai foreign policy and diplomatic conduct of the time, the background for which can be found in the introductory chapters. It is true that Siam's membership of the League enabled her to maximise her international standing and benefits while keeping her international commitments to a minimum. This was challenged by the thorny issue of Collective Security. Dr. Hell gives a detailed account and an excellent analysis of Siam's votes on this issue in the League's Assembly. He is particularly good on Siam's abstention from voting to condemn Japan in 1933, where he clearly demonstrates that Siam's vote was on grounds of strict adherence to neutrality. Siam was the only country to abstain. The vote was exploited as pro-Japan by contemporary Japanese propaganda and has been interpreted as pro-Japanese by some historians, who read history back with hindsight whereas the policy makers of the day had no idea of what was so soon to come.

Siam's abstention from voting to condemn Japan in 1933 might have been a 'public relations fiasco' for the Kingdom at the time, but surely with only Western countries. Rather than being a 'stain' on the record of Thai diplomacy, it should be regarded more as a symbolic act of diplomatic independence. It was not just 'a reasonable policy choice' but the only viable policy option taking into consideration the domestic political situation of the day. Siam's membership of the League forced her to take a stand on international conflicts. She 'understandably avoided involvement as far as possible' for good reasons. Collective Security should have been the moral responsibility of the righteous and civilised Great Powers, whose abuse and violation of others' freedom, independence and sovereignty have always been the bane of 'small states' throughout the world. Siam went on to vote for sanctions against Italy over its invasion of Ethiopia in 1935. She again abstained from voting to condemn Japan's actions in China in 1937, but this time for different reasons. Finally, Siam voted for the expulsion of the Soviet Union from the League in 1939; those who abstained were interestingly Sweden, Norway, Denmark, Lithuania, Latvia, Estonia, Bulgaria, China, and Switzerland. Apart from the latter, proximity and the reality of Soviet power were obviously factors for consideration.

Siam's record at the League of Nations was therefore no better or worse than others. Stefan Hell has ably put it on record and set the record straight in many instances. One can agree or disagree to varying degrees with his Conclusions summarised in 'ten interlinked and overlapping systematic aspects'.

When I first joined the Ministry of Foreign Affairs in 1969, Prince Wan, who attended the League's VIII, IX, X and XI General Assembly, the latter two as Permanent Representative, was Deputy Prime Minister and in charge of the Ministry whenever the Minister, Thanat Khoman, was away. Somboon Palasthira, who attended the League's XIX and XX General Assembly from the London Legation, became my second Permanent Secretary for Foreign Affairs till he retired in 1970. His son was a close colleague at the Ministry's Information Department. Somboon Palasthira's senior colleague at the XX General Assembly, Chalee Yongsundara, also from the London Legation, was still alive and father of an outstanding international lawyer at the Ministry. Mani Sanasen, the first Thai international civil servant, who had worked at the League's Secretariat since 1925 and continued with the United Nations Organization, was a living legend in Geneva until he passed away there in 1978. The tradition of Thai diplomacy lives on as I endeavored to follow in the footsteps of my grandfather, Phraya Abhibal Rajmaitri, who attended the League's XI and XII General Assembly, and great-uncle Phraya Subharn Sompati, who was Permanent Representative and attended the XIV and XV General Assembly. My longest posting from 1990 to 1995 was as Ambassador Permanent Representative of Thailand to the United Nations Organization at Geneva, where the Thai *baht* coins placed in the foundation of the Palais des Nations in 1929 are presumably still there.

Lastly, the value of this book is enhanced by very useful Appendices, starting with a Chronology of Events, lists of Permanent Delegates of Siam to the League 1920-1939, Thai Delegations to the General Assemblies of the League, Siam's Financial Contributions to the League, Conventions and Agreements within the League's Framework, signed by, acceded to and ratified by Siam, and a name glossary. There is an excellent Bibliography, which is a testament to Stefan Hell's thorough research and scholarship.

River Books is to be applauded for publishing this book in a pleasing and easy to use format with footnotes as side-notes on each page, which is rare in this day and age and makes it so much easier to read. There are also wonderful old photographs, with one of the Palais des Nations taken from the air by His Majesty the King 'with a red filter over the lens of the camera, thus eliminating the light mist that was floating over Geneva at the time', taken from the *Standard* magazine of 7 December 1946.

Tej Bunnag
Former Minister of Foreign Affairs

Acknowledgements

This project has been with me, on and off, for over a decade and during those years I have come into contact with the most interesting individuals, who have all, knowingly or not, had a very positive influence on this study. I am honoured to thank the following, who have provided guidance, given me ample support, contributed important information and have prevented a number of mistakes: Bongojrut Bunyapukna, Nigel Brailey, Han ten Brummelhuis, Marc Frey, Franz Knipping, Paul Kratoska, Hans-Dieter Kubitscheck, J. Thomas Lindblad, Ian Nish, Bernhardine Pejovic, Prathoomporn Vajrasthira, Heiner Reber, Dietmar Rothermund, Ursula-Maria Ruser, Supit Tangwiwat, Tej Bunnag, Jeroen Touwen, and my teacher and friend Barend J. Terwiel. While their contributions were manifold, I am solely responsible for any faults in the result.

I am grateful to the staff of the following institutions for their support, without which this study would have not materialised: Leiden University and the KITLV Library in the Netherlands; in Thailand the Thai National Archives, the Thai National Library, Chulalongkorn University, the Thai Kadi Research Institute at Thammasat University, the Thammasat University Library, the Thai Ministry of Foreign Affairs, and the Siam Society Library; in Switzerland the League of Nations Archives and the United Nations Library, both at the European Headquarters of the United Nations at Geneva, as well as the Geneva Graduate Institute of International Relations; in the United Kingdom the Public Record Office and the library of the School of Oriental and African Studies in London; and in Germany the libraries of the universities of Tübingen, Passau, Freiburg and Hamburg, as well as their various relevant institutes, the State Library and the Humboldt University Library in Berlin, and the Institute of Asian Studies in Hamburg.

I wish to thank the EU-funded European Studies Programme Thailand for supporting a research stay in Bangkok in 1998 and the National Research Council of Thailand for granting me permission to conduct research in Thailand on several occasions. Last, but certainly not least, I am grateful to Narisa Chakrabongse, Paisarn Piemmattawat and Stephen Murphy at River Books for their excellent cooperation.

Stefan Hell
Beijing, February 2010

*Phraya Buri Navarasth, Delegate to first General Assembly
of the League of Nations, 1920 (League of Nations
Archives).*

Introduction

This study analyses the relations between Siam and the League of Nations from 1920 to 1940. It aims at bringing to light a cornerstone of Siam's foreign policy and an important element of Siam's domestic modernisation during the sixth, seventh and eighth reigns of the Chakri dynasty: Siam's membership in the first-ever standing international organisation with global authority, the League of Nations. Academic studies to date have examined Siam's foreign relations during the first half of the twentieth century in great detail, mainly with regard to relations with the United States, Great Britain, France, Germany and Japan. Studies of Siam's foreign policy during this period typically acknowledge Siam's League membership in passing, but do not elaborate on what this membership meant. As if League membership was merely a goal in itself in 1919-20, the path leading to it has been repeatedly described in the context of Siam's entry into the First World War and subsequent revision of its unequal treaties, but the relationship between Bangkok and Geneva during the following twenty years of the interwar period has not. This study, therefore, aims at adding a key multilateral dimension to the analysis of Thai foreign relations during the first half of the twentieth century by examining Siam's membership in the League of Nations. I will argue throughout that this hitherto obscured multilateral dimension of Thai foreign policy played an important role in modernising the country, reaffirming elite rule and regaining full sovereignty.

The League of Nations was at the centre of multilateral international relations in the 1920s and 1930s. It set, particularly during the first fifteen years of its existence, innovative rules and procedures for the conduct of national administrations in a wide array of policy areas, ranging from the classical political and security questions to very modern policy areas such as drug and public health policy, protection of children's rights, disarmament, the fight against human trafficking, international trade, or technology transfer. In short, the League dealt with all policy areas which national administrations could no longer cope with individually due to their increasingly important international dimensions. The League was thus an institutionalised expression of ever closer interaction and interdependence of societies, or globalisation. In setting these normative rules and procedures, the Western-inspired League was influenced by Western ideologies, which spanned from imperialism to liberalism and egalitarian democracy.

The Kingdom of Siam was the only territory in Southeast Asia never to have been formally colonised by any imperialist power. Surrounded by British and French colonies for many decades, Siam managed to maintain its independence amidst the turbulent times of European imperialist expansion, at the price of territorial concessions and British economic dominance.[1] Apart from benefiting from the rivalries among colonial powers, this unusual development is traditionally also ascribed to shrewd foreign policy decisions and to the broad domestic modernisation programme pursued by the Thai elite. This legacy of skilful diplomacy coupled with elite-driven domestic modernisation is firmly embedded in the collective memory of Thailand today. One of the pillars on which this legacy rests, is the involvement of Siam in the First World War and, as a direct result, Siam's membership in the world's first international organisation, the League of Nations.

Siam had indeed achieved a remarkable diplomatic feat in the course of the First World War, when it declared war on Germany and Austria-Hungary, sent troops to Europe, participated in the Paris Peace Talks after the war's end as one of the Allied and Associate Powers and ultimately, became an original member of the League of Nations alongside Great Britain, France, Japan and others. Thereafter, Siam remained a member of the League for twenty-six years, until the defunct organisation dissolved itself and handed over its responsibilities and assets to the new United Nations after the end of the Second World War. The twenty-six years of Siam's League membership were undoubtedly eventful times in the kingdom's history. The period saw four monarchs, recovery of complete sovereignty, the change from an absolute to a constitutional monarchy, a military dictatorship, war and occupation. Throughout the period, Siam's history was marked by profound modernisation of politics and society, as well as by international economic integration and rapid population growth.

The League of Nations was the first great experiment of a standing multilateral organisation with global authority. Born from the traumatic experiences of the First World War and inspired by predominantly Anglo-Saxon liberal democratic and pacifist ideas, the League stood for a new world order which it was to guarantee by facilitating peaceful resolution of international conflicts, increased cooperation among states, a broader body of international law and a new form of open diplomacy. The League of Nations was, as is characteristic for international organisations, an actor in its own right (through its decision-making and advisory bodies and its international secretariat) as well as a platform for the interaction of its member states. While the League was more than just the sum of its member states, it could also only be as much as its member states allowed it to be.

This institutionalised new multilateral framework of international politics, which Siam became a part of, provided it with opportunities to pursue its foreign policy goals on a whole new level, now sitting eye-to-eye at the same table together with the world's colonial powers. Up to the

---

1 Aldrich describes Siam as 'for a period, an integral if informal component of the British imperial system.' See Richard J. Aldrich, *The Key to the South: Britain, the United States, and Thailand during the Approach of the Pacific War, 1929-1942*, Kuala Lumpur: Oxford University Press 1993, p. 5.

mid-1920s, bilateral policies of Western countries towards Siam, which dominated the kingdom's foreign relations, were essentially conservative and aimed at preserving the status quo. This was expressed in their unequal treaties reflecting nineteenth century diplomatic practices which were advantageous to the Western powers and disadvantageous to Siam. Relations with the League of Nations, on the contrary, were progressive; they concerned matters which ultimately had the improvement of the lives of Thai people at their core. In this context, League membership allowed Siam to draw on state-of-the-art scientific and administrative knowledge in various fields, most notably in public health and medicine, and to stand at the forefront of the development of international law. In some cases, as we will see, this indeed led to tangible benefits for Siam's population.

But being a member of this new multilateral club also entailed obligations. The League exerted pressure on the Thai elite for social development and policy reforms. Siam's policy makers had to adapt domestic policies to new international standards in order to be recognised as a worthy member of the international system. The League thereby acted as an agent of globalisation, as an international body through which industrialised Western nations set new global standards – standards which they were at times enforcing on a multilateral level while still pursuing colonial policies on bilateral levels.

It is argued in this study that Siam's membership in the League of Nations was at the core of the country's foreign policy for nearly twenty years. League membership was a means for Siam to regain its full sovereignty and fiscal autonomy during the early 1920s, a means to maintain and strengthen this autonomy during the later 1920s and the subsequent decade, an important tool to modernise the country in different areas of society, and a key element in enabling the Thai elite to demonstrate and reinforce its modernity or progressiveness domestically and internationally.

This study aims to trace the membership of Siam in the League of Nations in its main aspects. It will analyse the role that League membership played for Siam and the role Siam's membership played for the League, but will not undertake to draw a general picture of international relations in the interwar period, nor will it try to give a comprehensive assessment of Siam's diplomatic relations with individual League of Nations member states. The focus is on the extraordinary multilateral dimension of Siam's foreign policy between 1920 and 1940 and, from the League's perspective, on the unique case of the organisation's only independent Southeast Asian member state. With its very wide spectrum of political, social, economic, technical and economic activities, the League of Nations functioned in a fashion very similar to the United Nations today. This study will concentrate on the most significant of these activities for Siam, besides analysing overarching policies and general features of Siam's League membership.

The concept of modernisation plays an important role in the analysis. I use the term to describe a Western-inspired concept for the transformation of Thai society, which was employed by the royal, civilian and military elites in Siam. Modernisation is thus a concept which is closely connected with imperialism and economic globalisation, with industrialisation and a notion of Western technological and cultural superiority. As a concept for transformation of society, modernisation describes the broad array of administrative, institutional, legal, social and economic changes, which were undertaken by the Thai elite from the late nineteenth century onwards; what Barend Terwiel has termed 'the politics of gradual reform'.[2] These changes served both domestic and international purposes. Domestically, they served the royal elite until the early 1930s to legitimise and reaffirm their traditional rule over the country by providing improved living conditions; equally, modernisation also served the new civilian and military elites after the 1932 coup d'état to assert their claim to power. Internationally, modernisation served as a protective shield to fend off various threats to Siam's independence until the early years of the twentieth century; after that, it served as a means to reclaim full sovereignty from Western colonial powers and to assert Siam's place in a changing international environment of states. By reforming Siam's administration and economy along Western lines, the elite was 'rewarded' by Western states with increasing autonomy and more beneficial access to markets, capital, and technology.

Two terms, which are closely related to modernisation, are the notion of progress, or of being progressive, and that of being civilised. Chris Baker and Pasuk Phongpaichit have recently described progress in Thailand in its incarnation as spread of a market economy and the resulting diversification of Thai society since the early Bangkok period.[3] Thongchai Winichakul has provided an in-depth analysis of the aspiration of the royal Thai elites to be civilised, 'Thai-ised' to *siwilai*, in order to reaffirm their superiority.[4] Both terms again refer to broadly the same Western-oriented concept employed by the Thai elites in an effort to develop the kingdom with the two-fold aim of regaining and asserting sovereignty and respect internationally, as well as domestically reasserting the legitimacy of power of these ruling elites over the rest of society in changing times.

During the period under review, Asia was largely dominated by Western imperialist states and modernisation in Thailand was thus to a large degree Westernisation.[5] The focal point or benchmark for Siam's elite-driven modernisation was the Western world, perceived as the home of economic development, technological innovation, cultural dominance, and political and military power. In response, Western-style public administration found its way to Thailand as did modern medical technology, Western architecture and clothing, Western education and beauty ideals, communications technology and etiquette. And during the 1920s and 1930s the international focal point for this Western-oriented modernisation drive of the urban Thai elite was the most

2 Barend J. Terwiel, *Thailand's Political History: From the Fall of Ayutthaya in 1767 to Recent Times*, Bangkok: River Books, 2005, p. 203ff. See also Fred W. Riggs, *Thailand: The Modernization of a Bureaucratic Polity*, 2nd ed., Honolulu: East-West Center Press, 1967, p. 368f., who defines modernisation as 'all the processes of change which result from the impact of more upon less advanced societies', while describing 'advanced' as 'the subjective evaluation by one subject or society of another.'

3 Chris Baker and Pasuk Phongpaichit, *A History of Thailand*, Cambridge: Cambridge University Press, 2005, p. 36ff.

4 Thongchai Winichakul, 'The Quest for "Siwilai": A Geographical Discourse of Civilizational Thinking in Late Nineteenth and Early Twentieth-Century Siam', *Journal of Asian Studies*, 59, 3 (August 2000), p. 528-549.

5 For a discussion of modernisation in Siam and China before the First World War, see Niels P. Petersson, *Imperialismus und Modernisierung: Siam, China und die europäischen Mächte 1985-1914*, Studien zur internationalen Geschichte, vol. 11, München: Oldenbourg, 2000, p. 13ff.

innovative experiment in international politics of the times. The League of Nations epitomised the international modernisation of different aspects of public policy: drug control, public health, measures against human trafficking, infrastructure development, education reform, administrative and legal reform.

Three additional remarks are appropriate concerning modernisation in this study. First, when describing this complex process of incorporating Western ideas, procedures and technologies, we must keep in mind that this did not imply sacrificing Siam's own culture and traditions. On the contrary, looking back at over 100 years of this process of Thai development, it is as striking as it is commonplace to point to the remarkable degree of cultural continuity in a country which has incorporated such a large number of external influences. In the words of Thongchai, *siwilai* – or we can say, modernisation – 'was a transcultural process in which ideas and practices from Europe, via colonialism, had been transferred, localised, and hybridised in a Siamese setting'.[6] Dietmar Rothermund describes this complex process in reaction to European imperialism as one of constant tension between acculturation and self-assertion.[7] Thus, this study will trace some examples of 'modernisation, Thai style' during the 1920s and 1930s, with particular emphasis on their international dimensions. Second, I do not wish to imply that modernisation of Siam was a steady, or even a predetermined process, nor that modernisation necessarily leads to a clearly defined goal. Modernisation in Siam, as the following chapters will amply demonstrate, was rather a very uneven, man-made process, which ran at varying speeds and was often characterised by rivalling goals. This aspect became most visible when the modernising policies of the traditional elite were overtaken by the modernising policies of a new elite in 1932. Third and finally, this study is positioned in a period during which perceptions of Siam in the West were changing, when colonial attitudes began to give way to more egalitarian views as a result of modernising trends within Western societies. It is a central argument of this study that Siam's membership in the League of Nations was an important factor in strengthening these trends among Western political elites on an international political-diplomatic level. In other words, the Western world, which served as the benchmark for much of Siam's modernisation, was itself not static but rapidly changing, entailing changes in the modernisation of Siam itself and in the way Siam was perceived by the West.

Although the League of Nations formally existed from 1920 to 1946, it became irrelevant for Thai policy makers – and policy makers the world over – already in the course of the late 1930s and, at the latest, during the year 1940. This decline in authority was a gradual process, which was most apparent in the League's inability to provide its core function of settling conflicts by peaceful means during the 1930s. Discredited by this failure in its core function, the League's importance for national governments in Bangkok and elsewhere then also gradually

6 Thongchai, Quest for *Siwilai*, p. 529.

7 Dietmar Rothermund (ed.), *Aneignung und Selbstbehauptung: Antworten auf die europäische Expansion*, München: Oldenbourg, 1999.

declined in its other fields of work during the years immediately preceding the Second World War. This study therefore focuses on the two interwar decades and will touch only very briefly on the final League assembly in 1946 and the Bangkok government's successful efforts to quickly revive its tradition of multilateral foreign policy by ensuring membership in the new United Nations after the end of the Second World War.

As far as the meaning of Siam's membership for the League itself is concerned, the following chapters will show that, although a relatively powerless, small member, Siam did play an important role for the League in justifying the organisation's global authority in Southeast Asia for twenty years. By the mid-1930s, when Japan had already turned its back on the League, and China was unable to play any constructive role at Geneva because it was being ravaged by Japan's occupation and civil war, Siam was the only independent League member in all of the Far East which played any constructive role at all. Surrounded by colonies throughout the League's lifetime, Siam holds the distinction of being the only independent Far Eastern state, in which the League of Nations ever held an international conference, the 1931 Bangkok Opium Conference. The resulting Bangkok Agreement was the first-ever international convention to bear the name of the Thai capital.

But it must be borne in mind throughout this study that the League of Nations suffered from severe deficiencies from birth, which resulted in a deep rift between claims and reality. Nowhere did this rift become as apparent as in the League's core task of preserving international peace by providing collective security. It is precisely for this reason that the League of Nations has been discredited ever since. However, we must also bear in mind that the League of Nations was more than a collective security arrangement and the analysis of the League's technical and social activities is precisely what leads this study to a much more balanced assessment of the League's performance during twenty years. Siam's abstention from voting to condemn the Japanese invasion of Manchuria in 1933 stands out as virtually the only event in the realm of its League membership, which has received limited scholarly attention. But being a League member meant so much more for Siam: embarking on the long path towards the abolition of legal opium consumption, raising economic sanctions against Italy, setting up a regional early-warning system for epidemic diseases, protecting women and children from trafficking, and much more. Being a member of the League of Nations meant, during the 1920s, being part of the most modern, ambitious and exciting project in international relations.

League membership played a pivotal role for the government in modernising Thai society. It provided instruments, it justified actions, it set the agenda, and it provided rewards in terms of international recognition and prestige. League membership also played an important role in reasserting national sovereignty for Siam during the first half of the 1920s. League membership and the ideals the League stood for provided officials in Bangkok and Thai diplomats abroad with a key instrument to put pressure on European governments to revise outdated treaties and grant Siam full sovereignty.

This study will, at the outset, trace how Siam became an original member of the League of Nations as a result of its domestic and foreign policies since the late nineteenth century and its involvement in the First World War (Chapter 1). Some basic features of the Kingdom of Siam will be described and an overview of the League of Nations will be given. Both spheres converged in Paris after the end of the war, when the League of Nations was created and Siam became an original member. It should emerge from this chapter that, while the Paris Peace Talks were a significant step towards the abolishment of Siam's unequal treaties, as is generally acknowledged by scholars of this period, they were much more significant for obtaining League membership. Chapter 2 will then introduce basic patterns of this membership, key actors, general organisational and financial aspects, as well as providing a brief overview of the twenty-six years of interaction between Geneva and Siam, including the final General Assembly of the League in 1946.

Among the wide range of League activities, I have chosen those four policy areas, which were the most significant in terms of the level of interaction between Bangkok and Geneva and the degree of influence the League had on policy decisions in Siam. Chapter 3 will discuss Siam's involvement in the League's international opium control activities. We will see that new international rules and changing attitudes towards drug consumption had a profound impact on Siam's domestic and international policies. This chapter will also highlight the only League of Nations conference ever to be held in Siam, the 1931 Bangkok Conference on Opium Smoking in the Far East.

Chapter 4 will trace the manifold public health activities, in which Siam's diplomats and government officials came into contact with the League of Nations. The League of Nations Health Organisation will appear in this chapter as a key partner for Siam in the improvement of health conditions of the population in areas ranging from training of doctors, improvement of hygiene, epidemic disease control, quarantine, and improvement of health conditions of the rural population.

International efforts to curb human trafficking will be discussed in Chapter 5. We will see that the Thai elite was forced to formulate policies against human trafficking because of the pressure the League was exerting, but also that Siam was one of the first countries in the world to ratify the 1921 International Convention against Trafficking in Women and Children.

One feature running through all of the above three chapters is the high degree of regional consultation and cooperation in these areas of social policy. We will see that independent Siam and the colonial administrations of Great Britain, France, the Netherlands, and Portugal worked together on issues of regional concern in Southeast and East

Asia during a period when their bilateral relations with Siam were still dominated by colonial ideologies.

Chapter 6 will analyse Siam's role in the international political conflicts dealt with by the League of Nations. The League's actions, or non-actions, in the face of Japan's aggression in China feature prominently here, and Siam's abstentions in League votes in 1933 and 1937 will be reconstructed and put into context. Less well known, but equally intriguing, are Siam's sanctions against Italy of 1935 and Siam's vote to expel the Soviet Union from the League of Nations in 1939. Overall, we will see how Siam, by and large, avoided becoming involved in the resolution of international conflicts to the best it could, thereby also avoiding taking up any responsibility resulting from League membership in this regard.

Chapter 7 will then systematically summarise the findings across the different policy fields during the entire two interwar decades. Ten distinct but interrelated aspects will be described, which make up the significance of the League of Nations for Siam. They reach, for example, from being a tool for Siam to put pressure on Western Powers to regain its sovereignty, particularly during the first half of the 1920s, to being a means for the Thai elite to demonstrate its modernity and degree of civilisation towards the international community, to having a distinct modernising impact on Thai society, to providing unique training opportunities for Thai diplomats and other officials, and assisting the governing elite in Bangkok, both before and after 1932, to consolidate its power domestically by legitimising its rule and underscoring its progressiveness towards the rest of society.

This study has a number of limitations. It is centred on foreign relations and, as foreign policy was the domain of a small group of Thai society, only reflects the attitudes and actions of the Thai elites during the 1920s and 1930s, rather than being a comprehensive study of Thai society as a whole. Furthermore, this is not a comprehensive history of drug consumption, public health development or human trafficking in Siam; rather, this is a study of the interrelations between the small, urban elite of Siam and the League in these policy areas. This study also does not undertake to draw a complete picture of the activities of the League of Nations; rather it concentrates on a limited number of policy areas, which were the most significant for relations between the organisation and its member state Siam.

The country Thailand is referred to in this text as Siam, the name used by Thais and foreigners alike in an international context during the lifetime of the League of Nations, with the exception of the years 1939 to 1945. When using the name as an adjective, I have however chosen to use 'Thai' rather than 'Siamese' and the adjective 'Siamese' is retained only when used in verbatim quotes or document titles. Thai personal names are spelled here in the English form which the individuals used themselves (for example Prince Charoon, not Prince Jarun) and by which they were referred to in the primary sources used for this study. In the case of persons who changed the transliteration of their names over time, the form they used during the lifetime of the League is used here, for example Prince Varnvaidya, or Prince Varn, not Prince Wanwaithayakorn.

Most Thai officials appearing in this study were of royal descent. For the sake of simplicity, they are referred to here in English as princes, while their princely ranks (*Mom Chao, Phra Ong Chao, Chao Fa*) are given on first mention or when they are introduced. Attention must be paid in cases where a prince is elevated to a higher rank and is conferred an honorary name. For example, Prince Devawongse's son Prince Traidos (Phra Ong Chao Traidos Prabandh) followed his father as Minister of Foreign Affairs after his death in 1923 and, in 1929, was elevated to Phra Chao Vorawongse Ther Krom Muen Devawongse Varothai, now referring to himself in English as Prince Devawongse, just like his father.

Under absolute monarchy until 1932, commoners were conferred noble titles – *Khun, Luang, Phra, Phraya, Chao Phraya* – and names when they rose up the ranks of public service. Wherever possible, the given name of the official is added in parenthesis behind the honorary title and name on first mention or when he is introduced. If the individual changed his name during the period under review, reference will be made to his previous name and title. For example, diplomat Tienliang Hoontrakul appears as member of the Thai delegation to the League of Nations General Assembly in the early 1920s and later reappears, now elevated to Phraya Srivisarn Vacha, as president of the League's Bangkok Opium Conference in 1931 and later yet again as Thai Minister of Foreign Affairs.

A name glossary of all individuals mentioned in the text is given as appendix 10.

While the common Western calendar is used almost exclusively in the text, references in this study frequently refer also to the so-called *Phutthasakkarat (P. S.)* or Buddhist Era (B. E.) calendar, which has been in use in Thailand officially since 1911. Based on the year of enlightenment of Buddha, it predates the Western calendar by 543 years. In further deviation from Western practice, traditionally the year began in Siam on 1 April and ended on 31 March; accordingly the year B.E. 2462, for example, ran from 1 April 1919 to 31 March 1920, and is expressed here as 1919-20. By government decree, the year B.E. 2483 had only nine months and, from B.E. 2484, or 1941, the year then officially began on 1 January, and since then conforms to the Western calendar.

Group photograph of some of Siam's leading diplomats in the early 20th century. Seated from left: Prince Varnvaidya Voravarn, Prince Charoonsakdi Kritakara, Prince Amoradat Kritakara. Standing from left: Phra Sarasasna Balakhand (Long Sunthanonda) Phraya Bharata Raja (Mom Luang Thotsatit Isarasena) (Thai National Archives).

1

Siam becomes a Member of the League of Nations

Siam: sketch of domestic developments and foreign relations, c.1850 to 1940

Siam was, when it became a member of the League of Nations, an independent kingdom with a territory roughly the size of France, a largely agrarian population and a feudal societal structure.[1] From the year the League of Nations first opened its doors in 1920 to the year it handed over its assets to the new United Nations in 1946, the population of Siam nearly doubled from nine to seventeen million people.[2] The large majority of the population lived in undeveloped rural areas where life was determined by traditions, religion, family and subsistence farming. Buddhism was deeply rooted in ethnically and religiously very homogeneous Siam. The Buddhist monkhood was organised as a national system and temple compounds were at the centre of rural communities providing spiritual guidance, education, medical treatment, information and entertainment. The capital Bangkok was the only notable urban centre in the country, where an internationally-oriented, well-educated and well-to-do elite of royals, commoners, and Chinese and Western businessmen dominated the political, social and economic development of the country. Towering over all subjects were the king and a small group of princes of the Chakri dynasty, who possessed almost unlimited power. The country had been undergoing profound changes since the early nineteenth century, which Terwiel has described as follows:

> The almost unlimited power of the king, the taxation system of the state, the hierarchy embedded in the *saktina* system of ranking, the names of the social classes and the system of slavery that once determined one's role, all these gave way to new organizational structures.[3]

King Mongkut and particularly his son Chulalongkorn had opened and carefully but profoundly reformed the country in response to the British-led spread of Western capitalist economy across Asia and Siam's international economic integration between the mid-nineteenth century and 1910.[4] During the last decade of King Chulalongkorn's exceptionally long rule (r. 1868-1910), the monarchy was enjoying unprecedented prestige and authority. Chulalongkorn was succeeded on the throne by his sons Vajiravudh (Rama VI), who reigned for fifteen years from 1910

1 On the modern history of Thailand during the first half of the twentieth century, domestic developments and foreign relations, see Terwiel, *Thailand's Political History*; Baker and Pasuk, *History of Thailand*; Benjamin A. Batson, *The End of the Absolute Monarchy in Siam*, Singapore: Oxford University Press, 1984; Charivat Santaputra, *Thai Foreign Policy, 1932-1946*, Thai Kadi Research Institute, Bangkok: Charoen Wit Press, 1985; Stephen L.W. Greene, *Absolute Dreams: Thai Government under Rama VI, 1910-1925*, Bangkok: White Lotus Press, 1999; Kenneth Perry Landon, *Siam in Transition: A Brief Survey of Cultural Trends in the Five Years since the Revolution of 1932*, Chicago: University of Chicago Press, 1939; Judith A. Stowe, *Siam becomes Thailand: A Story of Intrigue*, Honolulu: University of Hawaii Press, 1991; Virginia Thompson, *Thailand: The New Siam*, New York: Macmillan, 1941 (Reprint New York: Paragon, 1967); Walter F. Vella, *Chaiyo! The Role of King Vajiravudh in the Development of Thai Nationalism*, Honolulu: University of Hawaii Press, 1978; David K. Wyatt, *Thailand, A Short History*, 2nd ed., Bangkok: Silkworm Books, 1984.

2 The government conducted censuses in 1911, 1919, 1929, 1937, and 1947; see *Statistical Yearbook Thailand*, vol. 21, B.E. 2482 (1939-40) to 2487 (1944), p. 49ff. and 567ff. For Siam's population growth in a regional perspective see Ann E. Booth, *Colonial Legacies: Economic and Social Development in East and Southeast Asia*, Honolulu: University of Hawai'i Press, 2007, p. 18ff.

3 Terwiel, *Thailand's Political History*, p. 291.

4 See Kullada Kesboonchoo Mead, *The Rise and Fall of Thai Absolutism*, London: Routledge Curzon, 2004; Petersson, *Imperialismus und Modernisierung*.

to 1925, and Prajadhipok (Rama VII), who ruled as an absolutist king from 1925 to 1932 and then as the first constitutional monarch until his abdication in 1935. Prajadhipok was succeeded by his nephews Ananda Mahidol (Rama VIII) from 1935 to 1946 and then by Bhumibol Adulyadej (Rama IX), whose reign up until the present spans an astonishing 63 years and began when the League was in the last few weeks of its existence. Thus, while during the lifetime of the League, Siam accordingly had four kings, only the first two actually took part in political decision-making, while the Mahidol brothers were minors and spent most of the 1930s and 1940s studying in Lausanne, Switzerland. Kings Vajiravudh and Prajadhipok were the first Western-educated Thai kings; both were intimately familiar with upper-class English culture and spoke English fluently. They had been purposely sent to Europe by their father to train them in Western culture, language and sciences. In contrast to the reign of their father, foreign policy was largely dominated during the reign of Vajiravudh and, to a lesser extent, during that of Prajadhipok by high-ranking princes, before it then became the domain of the civilian and military administrations during the 1930s.[5]

Siam escaped the fate of being colonised like all other Southeast Asian territories by benefiting from inter-European and colonial rivalries between Britain and France during the nineteenth century, by conceding territories as well as part of its economic and legal sovereignty to the imperialist states, and by proactively modernising the kingdom along Western lines. Beginning with the Bowring Treaty between Siam and Britain of 1855, the Bangkok court agreed to enter into similar unequal treaties with nearly all major Western states and Japan in the following decades.[6] Following the precedent of the Treaty of Nanking between China and Great Britain of 1842, the treaties exempted foreign nationals from Thai jurisdiction and granted highly favourable conditions to Siam's foreign trading partners by fixing low tariffs. As Nicholas Tarling put it, Siam 'accepted voluntarily what China had been forced to concede – extraterritoriality and tariff restrictions – as the price of maintaining political independence'.[7] The commercial treaties, as Terwiel has noted, 'had a dramatic impact upon life in Bangkok', as commercial activities rapidly picked up and foreign merchants streamed into the city.[8]

During the long reign of King Chulalongkorn, Siam went through a period of profound elite-led modernisation. Faced with threats of colonial takeovers, increasing international economic integration and an inefficient and untimely mode of administration of the country by the central government, the royal elite adopted the successful European nation-states as models to provide renewed legitimacy to their power and to modernise bureaucracy and many fundamentals of society. Slavery was abandoned, Western-style government ministries were created, the education system and the country's infrastructure were modernised, state finances were overhauled, and a Western-inspired legal system was

5 See also William D. Reeve, *Public Administration in Siam*, London and New York: Royal Institute of International Relations, 1951 (Reprint New York: AMS Press, 1975); Riggs, *Thailand*; Walter F. Vella, *The Impact of the West on Government in Thailand*, Publications in Political Science, vol. 4, no. 3, Berkeley: University of California Press, 1955; David A. Wilson, *Politics in Thailand*, Ithaca (NY): Cornell University Press, 1962.

6 On the Bowring Treaty see Barend J. Terwiel, 'The Bowring Treaty: Imperialism and the Indigenous Perspective', *Journal of the Siam Society*, 79, 2 (1991), p. 40-47. See also Luang Nathabanja, *Extra-Territoriality in Siam*, Bangkok: Bangkok Daily Mail, 1924. A collection of all treaties of the nineteenth and early twentieth century can be found in Wolcott Homer Pitkin, *Siam's Case for Revision of Obsolete Treaty Obligations Admittedly Inapplicable to Present Conditions*, Supplement: Siam's Treaties, New York, 1919; see further Vikrom Koompirochana, 'Siam in British Foreign Policy, 1855-1938: The Acquisition and Relinquishment of British Extra-territorial Rights', Ph.D. Thesis, Michigan State University, 1972.

7 Nicholas Tarling, *Britain, Southeast Asia and the Onset of the Pacific War*, Cambridge: Cambridge University Press, 1996, p. 48.

8 Terwiel, *Thailand's Political History*, p. 149.

developed. Chulalongkorn was also the first Thai king to travel to Europe in 1897, where he visited thirteen countries and gathered first-hand impressions of what he desired to achieve in Siam in terms of economic, administrative and social reforms.[9]

As a result of these wide-ranging reforms, Siam on the eve of the Versailles Conference was a unified state with a functioning bureaucracy and an emerging economy, which, although surrounded by European colonies, no longer had to fear foreign invasion. In its external relations Siam was what one generally calls a 'small state', a militarily weak state largely dependent on the interests of major powers, in this case primarily of Great Britain and France, later in the 1930s of Japan. The skilful diplomacy of the Western-oriented and educated foreign policy makers in Bangkok, which featured a distinctive multilateral approach from the late nineteenth century, contributed to preserve this considerable degree of independence and territorial integrity of the kingdom between the spheres of interest of France and Britain in mainland Southeast Asia. But more than on its own polices, Siam's independence depended on a favourable international situation in Asia and Europe. Great Britain and France, in order to diffuse their potentially dangerous rivalry, divided colonial spheres of interest among them, and *de facto* established Siam as a buffer between their respective colonies India/Burma and Malaya on the one side and Indochina on the other in the Anglo-French Declaration of 1896 and the Entente Cordiale of 1904.[10] Although Siam's unequal commercial treaties of the nineteenth century played a part in averting formal colonisation, by the early twentieth century they increasingly became a serious impediment for the economic and social development of the kingdom, as they radically limited state revenue from foreign trade and forced the government to generate revenue from other sources, such as opium sales. The United States was the first to concede its privileges and sign a new treaty in 1920, followed by new treaties with Great Britain, France and others in the mid-1920s.[11]

Siam maintained diplomatic legations in European capitals since the time of Prince (*Phra Ong Chao*) Prisdang Jumsai, the first ambassador-at-large to Europe in the 1880s. The country's foreign relations were handled by Prince (*Phra Ong Chao*) Devawongse Varopakarn, a half-brother of King Chulalongkorn, for thirty-eight years from the creation of the modern Ministry of Foreign Affairs in 1885 until his death in 1923. Prince Devawongse managed Siam's foreign affairs often single-handedly and was also the key advisor to Kings Chulalongkorn and Vajiravudh on nearly all domestic matters. After his death, Prince Devawongse's son Prince (*Mom Chao*, from 1922 *Phra Ong Chao*) Traidos Prabandh, who had been sent to Harrow and Cambridge and had been groomed to succeed his father, took over the office of Minister of Foreign Affairs for the following nine years, before the 1932 coup swept princes out of senior public offices altogether.[12]

9 See Charit Tingsabadh (ed.), *King Chulalongkorn's Visit to Europe: Reflections on Significance and Impacts*, Bangkok: Centre for European Studies, Chulalongkorn University, 2000; Niels P. Petersson, 'King Chulalongkorn's Voyage to Europe in 1897', *Journal of European Studies at Chulalongkorn University*, 3, 2 (1995), pp. 1-27. The king's second visit to Europe in 1907 also served this purpose but was of a more private character.

10 See Michael Hurst (ed.), *Key Treaties for the Great Powers*, London: David & Charles, 1972, vol. 2, p. 764ff. for the text of the 'Declaration between the United Kingdom and France concerning Siam, Madagascar, and the New Hebrides' of 8 April 1904. See also Chandran Jeshurun, 'The Anglo-French Declaration of January 1896 and the Independence of Siam', *Journal of the Siam Society*, 58, 2 (1970), p. 105-126.

11 Peter B. Oblas, 'Siam's Efforts to Revise the Unequal Treaty System in the Sixth Reign, 1910-1925', Ph.D. Thesis, University of Michigan, 1974; Charles C. Hyde, 'The Relinquishment of Extra-territorial Jurisdiction in Siam', *American Journal of International Law*, 15 (July 1921), pp. 428-430; A. Berjoan, *Le Siam et les Accords Franco-Siamois*, Thèse Faculté de Droit, Université de Paris, Paris: Les Presses Modernes, 1927.

12 See M.R. Pantip Paribatra (ed.), *H.H. Prince Traidos Prabandh: His Life and Works, In Commemoration of the Centenary of His Birth*, Bangkok: Craftsman Press, 1983.

Siam gradually embraced Western technology during the 1920s and 1930s, most significantly in infrastructure and communications and, as we will see in Chapter 4, also in medicine and public health. Scientific and technological modernisation, ongoing since the late nineteenth century, was strongly focused on the capital Bangkok, which developed into a modern commercial centre during the lifetime of the League of Nations. For example, telegraph was introduced in 1874, a postal system was established in 1883, and trams ran from 1887 and were electrified from 1894.[13]

In this context, industrialisation was relatively slow to take root in Siam. During the first four decades of the twentieth century rice made up more than two-thirds of Siam's exports; rice together with tin, teak and rubber accounted for nearly 90 percent. Thus Siam's economy was vulnerable to external shocks, such as the drastic shifts in world market prices for primary products during the interwar period. The effects of the global economic crisis therefore also hit Siam, led to domestic economic and financial difficulties and helped prepare the ground for the political and social changes brought about by the 1932 coup d'état.[14] Siam's international integration into an increasingly global economy was driven primarily by Chinese and Western entrepreneurs, who developed rice, teak, tin and rubber into export commodities, while domestic industries slowly began producing consumer goods. Capital goods necessary for the nascent modernisation of the kingdom, such as electric appliances, fuels, machinery, metal manufactures and chemical products were imported. In the 1920s and 1930s machinery and equipment for railways and irrigation were imported in considerable numbers.[15] Few Westerners lived in Siam, while the Chinese, who had been migrating to Siam from the nineteenth century in increasing numbers, constituted the economically most important minority in the kingdom. Chinese immigration was marked by a high degree of assimilation during the nineteenth century as well as by the move of these immigrants and their descendants into positions of economic and political power.[16] Many of the issues discussed in the following chapters concern the Chinese population in Siam, most notably opium and human trafficking, as well as Siam's role vis-à-vis China and Japan in the armed conflicts of the 1930s.

Demonstrating the country's modernity domestically and internationally was undertaken by the Thai elite most visibly through public events in Bangkok and abroad. Siam participated in a number of world fairs from the late 1860s. The second coronation of King Vajiravudh in 1911, following a smaller-scale event in 1910, was designed as a lavish feast to impress visiting foreign royals and reassert international recognition for Siam's monarchy.[17] The year 1910 also saw the first agricultural exhibition in Bangkok which, according to Ian Brown, attracted tens of thousands of visitors.[18] The Bangkok public

13 Stefan Hell, 'The Role of European Technology, Expertise and Early Development Aid in the Modernization of Thailand before the Second World War', *Journal of the Asia Pacific Economy*, 6, 2 (2001), pp. 158-178.

14 See Sompop Manarungsan, *Economic Development of Thailand, 1850-1950, Response to the Challenge of the World Economy*, Bangkok: Institute of Asian Studies, Chulalongkorn University, 1989; Booth, *Colonial Legacies*, p. 44ff.

15 James C. Ingram, *Economic Change in Thailand Since 1850*, Stanford (CA): Stanford University Press, 1955; Somopop, *Economic Development*.

16 Baker and Pasuk, *History of Thailand*, p. 33ff.

17 On the early world fairs see Thongchai, Quest for *Siwilai*, p. 540ff.; on the second coronation in November-December 1911 see Barend J. Terwiel, *A History of Modern Thailand, 1767-1942*, Histories of Southeast Asia, St. Lucia, London and New York: University of Queensland Press, 1983, p. 294.

18 Ian G. Brown, *The Elite and the Economy in Siam, c.1890-1920*, East Asian Historical Monographs, Singapore: Oxford University Press, 1988, p. 72.

health exhibition of 1922 was then the first major publicity event showcasing the progressiveness of Siam at the beginning of the following decade, again attracting tens of thousands of visitors. Some years later, the Lumphini exhibition was designed to demonstrate Siam's progressiveness in an array of social, economic and technological areas on the occasion of the fifteenth anniversary of the king's coronation, but its opening, planned for January 1926, had to be postponed at the last minute because of the death of the king and was later called off altogether for financial reasons by his successor.[19] Beyond the realm of symbolic events and publicity, the Thai government was involved in early international cooperation in technical and political fields, ranging from the Universal Postal Union to the Red Cross movement, from the Peace Conferences at The Hague to early international opium control efforts. This international cooperation served both to demonstrate the country's progressiveness to the Western colonial powers and to form part of innovative developments for the benefit of Siam's modernisation.

Next to the reform of public administration along Western lines and the creation of a modern state revenue structure since the late nineteenth century, the process of codifying the laws was perhaps the most important development in the elite-led modernisation of Siam.[20] Drafted by Thai and European lawyers, the first penal code was promulgated in 1908, civil and commercial codes followed in 1925 and all remaining, including criminal procedural codes, were promulgated in 1935. As we will see in the following chapters, numerous Thai laws were adopted in response to international pressure exerted by the League of Nations or by proactively incorporating progressive developments in international law under the League. Legal reform was seen by the Thai elite as one of the cornerstones for the modernisation of the kingdom, as it put the country on equal legal terms with the Western states. With a Western-style legal system and public administration, Siam was organised in a way that the West could comprehend.[21] To draft new laws as well as to advise on policies in every government ministry, foreign advisers were employed to provide expertise in modernising the state and, in international relations, to enable Western states to be addressed in Western terms and in Western languages. The promulgation of a complete set of Western-style legal codes was also the precondition set by the Western states for them to abandon their extraterritorial rights during the interwar period.

After King Chulalongkorn's long reign with its profound administrative, social and economic reforms, the role and prestige of the Thai monarchy declined dramatically during the reigns of Rama VI, VII and VIII, as these sons and grandson of Chulalongkorn proved less able and communicative administrators as their father, and as later rivalling princes, civilian politicians and military strongmen fought for power and influence in the kings' name. Vajiravudh in particular was

19 The marvellous compilation, bilingual in Thai and English, designed to accompany the exhibition was published nevertheless and provides a very good picture of the intention and scope of the planned event: *The Souvenir of the Siamese Exhibition at Lumbini Park B.E. 2468*, Bangkok: The Siam Free Press, B.E. 2470 (1927); see on the postponement of the exhibition also TNA, *Bangkok Times*, 2 December 1925; Terwiel, *Thailand's Political History*, p. 249; Vella, *Chaiyo!*, p. 174.

20 See the standard work on public administration reform during the fifth reign by Tej Bunnag, *The Provincial Administration of Siam, 1892-1915*, Kuala Lumpur: Oxford University Press, 1977. See also Terwiel, *Thailand's Political History*, p. 203ff.

21 The 1908 penal code was amended in 1925, 1932, 1935, 1936, and 1946, before a new penal code was promulgated in 1956. See in detail on the development of Thai criminal law as well as for a detailed critical assessment of Western influences on Thai legal development Apirat Petchsiri, *Eastern Importation of Western Criminal Law: Thailand as a Case Study*, Comparative Criminal Law Project, Wayne State University Law School, Publication Series, vol. 17, Littleton (CO): Rothman, 1987.

not well suited to handle the day-to-day administration of the country. A shy, artistic dreamer rather than a hands-on political practitioner, he left the task of governing the kingdom largely to the senior princes. But he did contribute to the further modernisation and unification of society, mainly by sponsoring patriotic sentiments through symbolic and programmatic actions. Siam's entry into the First World War, public display of the grandeur of the court and the Wild Tiger movement – a sort of patriotic paramilitary movement inspired by the king – feature most prominently among these actions.[22] After the death of Vajiravudh in 1925, his younger brother Prajadhipok took a more active interest in government affairs. He consolidated public finances, which had suffered severely from his predecessor's lavish spending, initiated important administrative reforms, and in the early 1930s even tried to accommodate the desire for increased political participation among the non-royal elite by commissioning the drafting of a rudimentary constitution. But Prajadhipok was unable to turn the tide, which was clearly going against the House of Chakri. The bloodless coup d'état of June 1932, in which a group of civilian bureaucrats and military officers seized power from the throne and the corrupt princely elite, then led to a system of constitutional monarchy in Siam.

The 1932 coup d'état was a response to the mounting sense of dissatisfaction among an internationally-oriented new civilian and military elite with the government of the equally internationally-oriented but traditional royal elite. The coup involved only some 100 conspirators, but brought profound change to Siam by ending 150 years of absolute monarchy and transferring power from the king and a small group of royal princes to a larger group of young, urban administrators and military officers. The coup did not, however, bring about profound change with regard to the project of modernising of Siam; the old and the new elites rather shared the desire to turn Siam into a progressive and civilised state, in order to legitimise their rule over the country and to strengthen Siam's position internationally. The agents of modernisation changed, but the adherence to this project remained. For the royal and non-royal urban elite in Siam, the West served as a model for many of their aspirations; Western technological and scientific innovations were equally appealing as were Western cultural traditions, fashion, languages and rituals. Elite-led modernisation in Siam was thus a localised product of international trends.[23] Equally, the League of Nations, the modern international experiment par excellence, did not lose its attractiveness for the new elite in 1932. As we will see in the following chapters, working with the League of Nations and utilising League membership for domestic modernisation were as important policy goals in 1925 as in 1935. It was only by the late 1930s that the League lost its appeal to the Thai elite, as they, now led by the group around Luang Phibun Songkhram (Plaek Khittasangkha), were becoming increasingly

22 In describing Vajiravudh's ideas and initiatives as sponsoring patriotism rather than nationalism, I follow Barend J. Terwiel, 'The Development of Consensus Nationalism in Thailand', in Sri Kunht-Saptodewo, Volker Grabowsky and Martin Großheim (eds), *Nationalism and Cultural Revival in Southeast Asia: Perspectives from the Centre and the Region*, Wiesbaden: Harrassowitz, 1997, pp. 133-143.

23 Maurizio Peleggi has traced this process in Maurizio Peleggi, *Lords of Things: The Fashioning of the Siamese Monarchy's Modern Image*, Honolulu: University of Hawai'i Press, 2002.

militaristic and racist and led the country into armed conflicts with its colonial neighbour, into an alliance with fascist Japan and, after Pearl Harbour, to an outright declaration of war on the United States and its Western allies.[24]

The League of Nations: a revolution in international relations

The League of Nations – *Sannibat chat* in Thai, *Société des Nations* in French and *Völkerbund* in German – was arguably the most daring and ambitious project in international relations of the twentieth century. It was the first standing international organisation created to guarantee global peace and security in accordance with a commonly agreed and transparent set of rules. In addition, it served as an umbrella under which all political, social, economic and technical questions with an international dimension could be considered by representatives of member states. The League of Nations became a tangible political goal when it was spelled out by American President Woodrow Wilson in his famous address to Congress in January 1918, in which he laid down America's post-war aims in fourteen points, the last and most far-reaching of which was the creation of a League of Nations.[25]

The League of Nations grew out of the catastrophic First World War. It was a result of the Paris Peace Talks after the end of the war and emerged from the Treaty of Versailles as the first fully-fledged standing international organisation. The League was, first and foremost, the institutional expression of the desire to end armed conflicts after the traumatic experience of the First World War. But its ideological roots reached over one hundred years further back to the likes of Kant and Rousseau. Kant, in particular, had theoretically devised a state of perpetual international peace with a standing international organisation in 1795. In the realm of practical politics, the League of Nations broke with the century-old concept underlying the Congress of Vienna, which built on changing alliances among states and a so-called balance of power in international relations. The League, on the contrary, was to guarantee security collectively and replace traditional secret diplomacy with an open forum and an agreed set of rules. But the League lacked an armed force of its own and so depended on the major powers among its members to enforce its resolutions.[26] While the League relied on the political, economic and military weight of its main members – Great Britain, France, Italy, Japan, later also Germany and the Soviet Union – it had particular appeal for the large number of small states, which joined the organisation. Small states like Siam had much to gain and nothing to lose from collective security, had a greater influence on global affairs in concert with others under the League's umbrella than they could ever have alone, and could even gain a degree of international prestige.[27]

But the League of Nations was much more than an institutionalised collective security system; its objectives can be grouped into four areas:

24 For an overview of this period 1925-1945, entitled 'Restoration, Revolt and the Rise of the Military', see Terwiel, *Thailand's Political History*, p. 253ff. See also Batson, *End of Absolute Monarchy*, passim. For events surrounding the 1932 coup d'état see Stowe, *Siam becomes Thailand*, passim.

25 For detailed studies on the League of Nations see Francis P. Walters, *A History of the League of Nations*, 5th ed., London, New York and Toronto: Oxford University Press 1969; Frederick S. Northedge, *The League of Nations, its Life and Times 1920-1946*, 2nd ed., Leicester: Leicester University Press 1988; Harriet E. Davis (ed.), *Pioneers in World Order: An American Appraisal of the League of Nations*, 2nd ed., New York: Columbia University Press, 1945; D.C. Gupta, *The League of Nations*, New Delhi: Vikas, 1974; Alfred Pfeil, *Der Völkerbund: Literaturbericht und kritische Darstellung seiner Geschichte*, Erträge der Forschung, vol. 58, Darmstadt: Wissenschaftliche Buchgesellschaft, 1976.

26 On the ideological foundations of the League of Nations see Inis L. Claude Jr., *Swords to Ploughshares: The Problems and Progress of International Organization*, 4th ed., New York: Random House, 1984; p. 42ff.; Akira Iriye, *Global Community: The Role of International Organizations in the Contemporary World*, Berkley, Los Angeles and London: University of California Press, 2002, p. 9ff.

27 See William E. Rappard, 'Small States in the League of Nations', *Political Science Quarterly*, 4 (1934), pp. 544-575.

preserving international peace and security by establishing a system of collective security and by promoting disarmament; carrying out the provisions of the Paris Peace Treaties especially towards the former enemy states; establishing a forum for a new type of open or public diplomacy; and fostering international cooperation between states by facilitating joint economic, social, humanitarian and technical activities. The latter goal was based on the belief, to quote Frederick Northedge, that 'a more prosperous, better fed and educated, healthier world, free from prostitution and drug taking, would be one less riddled with war'.[28] To this end, early technical organisations had already been created since the late nineteenth century, as it became apparent that individual states could no longer devise effective policies in response to essentially international issues, such as international trafficking in humans or drugs, efforts against the spread of diseases, regulation of international communications, etc. Interestingly, a study of these technical predecessors of the League of Nations was published in 1919 by American Francis Sayre, who later played an important role as foreign affairs adviser to the government of Siam in the mid-1920s.[29] And it was chiefly in this fourth area of the League's work, that Siam cooperated with the organisation throughout the 1920s and 1930s.

Although facing strong competition from the Belgian capital Brussels, Geneva was chosen by the League's most powerful members as the seat of the new organisation. The General Assembly, in which every one of the between forty-seven and fifty-nine member states the League had during its lifetime was represented with an equal vote, constituted the League's highest decision-making body. The Assembly met at Geneva annually in autumn for its plenary and committee meetings, thereby creating perhaps one of the oldest annual traditions in multilateral diplomacy, as until today heads of states and diplomats converge annually on the seat of the United Nations, now in New York, in autumn for the General Assembly. Because of its unique role as a global plenum, the annual Assembly meetings attracted worldwide attention. As executive organ of the Assembly, the League Council was set up, on which permanent and non-permanent member states were represented. The council, dominated by the permanent members Great Britain, France, Italy, Germany (from 1926) and, as the only non-European state, Japan, usually met quarterly, but on occasion also more frequently, to address any matter of international concern, primarily in the field of collective security. As a third central organ of the League, an International Secretariat, headed by a Secretary-General as chief administrative officer, was founded to act as the permanent administration. The League's administration always remained very modest in size and never numbered more than 650 staff. These three central League bodies – Assembly, Council and Secretariat – organised work along thematic lines by setting up committees, sections or commissions for mandates, slavery,

28 Northedge, *League of Nations*, p. 166.

29 Francis B. Sayre, *Experiments in International Administration*, London and New York: Harper & Bros., 1919.

health, disarmament, opium, health, etc. Under and beside these three core institutions, a number of specialised bodies and organs with a certain degree of autonomy were created to deal with individual questions, such as the Permanent Court of International Justice in The Hague, the International Labour Organisation in Geneva or the International Institute of Intellectual Cooperation, the predecessor of UNESCO, in Paris.

The League of Nations assembled all of the roughly fifty independent states of its time as members, with the prominent absence of the United States, where Republican-dominated Congress did not ratify the Treaty of Versailles, although it was the American President Woodrow Wilson who had championed the League's creation.[30] As an essentially European or Western organisation, as far as its intellectual roots and the events leading to its creation were concerned, the League also reflected the realities of international politics in its membership structure. While it demanded word-wide authority, the League was, during its entire lifetime, dominated by its European member states, first and foremost Great Britain, France, Germany, Italy, the Scandinavian and the Benelux countries, with Japan being the only non-European member with a significant degree of global relevance. The large majority of the League's non-European member states were Latin-American republics, who joined in the wake of the initial United States enthusiasm for the League. The twenty Latin-American members as well as Canada, Australia and New Zealand can be counted with the Western group in this context. In Africa, Egypt, Ethiopia (or Abyssinia), Liberia and South Africa were represented in Geneva; in the Middle East and South Asia, Turkey, Iran, Iraq, Afghanistan and India were members. In East and Southeast Asia three states were League members, China, Japan and Siam.

At a closer look, League members in East and Southeast Asia can be grouped into four categories: Japan was the only major power in the Far East; China played a special role because of its size and the competing colonial interests of all major Western states there; the third group comprised territories which were only indirectly members of the League via their colonial motherlands: Korea and Taiwan via Japan; Indochina via France; India/Burma, Malaya, Hong Kong and the Straits Settlements via Great Britain; the Netherlands Indies; and Macao and East Timor via Portugal. Fourth and finally, Siam was the only independent Southeast Asian member state of the League of Nations. The Philippines remained the only territory in the Far East which was not in any way formally associated with the League.[31]

The League of Nations was, just as the United Nations is today, both a stage for other actors and itself an actor. The League was the grand international diplomatic stage on which Thai officials and their counterparts from some fifty other states presented their countries and

30 The League had twenty-nine original members and opened in 1920, when eighteen additional states were invited to accede, leading to forty-seven members. Membership peaked in 1934 with fifty-nine states before declining to the original forty-seven member states in 1941. In terms of geographical distribution, the League had thirty-five non-European members in total, of which eleven Latin-American members and Japan left the League during its lifetime.

31 The question of membership of the Philippines in the League of Nations (and the British Commonwealth) did, however, arise in the context of the Philippines' expected independence in discussions after the First World War; see Tarling, *Britain, Southeast Asia and the Onset of the Pacific War*, p. 34ff.

their policies to their peers from other states and interacted with their colleagues to formulate policies. The League was also an actor in its own right in international politics, formulating and enforcing policies and international laws through its own standing administration, the secretariat, and via experts it commissioned for individual tasks. It was in this latter respect that the League acted towards the Thai government with commissioners and international officials travelling to Siam for discussions, interviews and collecting surveys.

The lifetime of the League of Nations spans the period from the end of the First to the end of the Second World War. Created in 1919-20 and dissolved in 1946, the organisation went through a phase of growth, marked by widespread enthusiasm and a number of successes during roughly the first ten years, followed by a decade of difficulty and decline, during which the League failed to resolve the major international conflicts while acting successfully in technical and social fields, and finally a third phase coinciding with the years of the Second World War, during which the League was rendered irrelevant and existed on little more than paper. Contemporaries rightly judged the League by its ability to achieve its central objective, collective security, and thus discarded it by the late 1930s. With the benefit of hindsight, the scholar observes a strikingly more complex picture, in which the League indeed failed as guardian of collective security, but achieved remarkable successes in its technical and social activities.

From Bangkok to Paris and Geneva: Siam declares war, signs the Paris Peace Treaties and joins the League of Nations

Siam was among the Allied and Associated Powers during the war against Germany and Austria-Hungary. After having declared war in 1917, it deployed an expeditionary force to France, which was actually not involved in any fighting but participated in the occupation of the German Rhine territories. As a result, Thai diplomats sat at the negotiating tables at Versailles, and the country became one of the original members of the new League of Nations, which formally came into existence on 10 January 1920.

Siam had originally decided to stay neutral in the European war, in which it did not have any stake, particularly because German commercial activities played a significant role in Siam during this period. After the intensifying German submarine warfare in the Atlantic Ocean, the United States declared war on Germany on 6 April 1917, and rallied neutral states around the globe to follow their example. The American Minister in Bangkok approached the Thai government in this respect, as did his British, French, Belgian and Russian colleagues.[32] In siding with the United States, Britain and France, Thai policy makers saw an opportunity to demonstrate their equality with the West, to rid Siam of unequal treaties, have a voice in the establishment of a

32 M.L. Manich Jumsai (ed.), *Foreign Records of the Bangkok Period up to A.D. 1932*, Bangkok: Office of the Prime Minister, 1982, p. 242f.

post-war international order, and obtain material gains from the seizure of German assets in Siam.[33] Prince Charoon, the Thai Minister to Paris, was encouraged by French diplomats during the summer of 1917 to join the Allied war effort 'because she [Siam] will have a voice in the final settlement' and because 'Siam should join the future association of nations which will become reality.' Minister of Foreign Affairs Prince Devawongse in Bangkok clearly supported this position.[34] And, according to Frank C. Darling, the American adviser to the Thai government, Wolcott Homer Pitkin, also 'had considerable influence in bringing Siam into World War I on the side of the Allies'.[35]

Although the decision was not undisputed, particularly among the pro-German faction of the Thai elite, many of whom had studied at German universities or military academies, Siam declared war on Germany and Austria-Hungary on 22 July 1917. German property, including nine merchant vessels anchored in the port of Bangkok, was seized, and some 260 German and Austrian citizens were interned and later deported to India.[36] And, apart from the material gains, the declaration of war, as Terwiel points out, served an important domestic purpose for King Vajiravudh, because it 'could forge a closer link between himself and his people by personally leading them on a course towards battle'.[37]

Prince Charoon had already been enthusiastic about the declaration of war a month earlier, when he hailed it in a letter to the king as 'our real opportunity of raising the Status of our beloved country'.[38] Now that the declaration of war was formally made, he informed the king of his opinion concerning the possible consequences of this action: 'I cannot help thinking that if would enhance Siam's entry into the War if she were to take some active part or make a bit of a show (if I may be allowed to use slang)'.[39] In this correspondence of 24 July, Prince Charoon proposed to send an expeditionary force consisting of aviators, a medical corps, drivers and mechanics, all units which were designed to highlight the progressiveness of Siam's armed forces to the European states. Aviators were particularly modern and, according to Prince Charoon, their 'work suits Siamese'. 'I am certain', he continued, 'they will make a name for themselves. It does not involve such physical hardship as trench work'. Moreover, the experience pilots could gain from participating in the war would be 'enormous' for the further development of aviation in Siam.[40]

The prince's proposal was taken up by the king and Prince Devawongse in Bangkok. A Thai expeditionary force was assembled, which consisted of some 1,300 volunteer troops. After nearly one year of preparations and negotiations with French officials, the troops departed from Bangkok on 19 June 1918 under the command of Major-General Phraya Bijai Janriddhi on board a French ship and arrived in Marseilles over one month later, in late

33 Likhit Dhiravegin, *Siam and Colonialism (1855-1909): An Analysis of Diplomatic Relations*, Bangkok: Thai Watana Panich, B.E. 2518 (1975), p. 59f.; Chalong Soontravanich, 'Siam and the First World War: The Last Phase of Her Neutrality', *Nusantara*, 4 (July 1973), pp. 83-90.

34 Prince Charoon to Prince Devawongse, 20 June 1917, TNA, R6, T 15/2.

35 Frank C. Darling, *Thailand and the United States*, Washington D.C.: Public Affairs Press, 1965, p. 18. Darling misspells his name as 'Wolkot H. Pitkins'.

36 An English translation of the declaration of war can be found as enclosure in Dering to Balfour, 24 July 1917, Doc. 46, BDFA, Part II, Series E, vol. 49,. The deported prisoners of war were repatriated from India in early 1920. On the declaration of war and Siam's relations with Germany during these years see in detail Andreas Stoffers, *Im Lande des weißen Elefanten: Die Beziehungen zwischen Deutschland und Thailand von den Anfängen bis 1962*, Schriften der Deutsch-Thailändischen Gesellschaft e.V., vol. 22, Bonn: Deutsch-Thailändische Gesellschaft, 1995, p. 155ff. Six of the nine seized ships were later sold, three went to the Siam Steamship Company; see Greene, *Absolute Dreams*, p. 109.

37 Terwiel, *Thailand's Political History*, p. 243.

38 Prince Charoon to King Vajiravudh, 22 June 1917, TNA, R6, T 15.3/1.

39 Prince Charoon to King Vajiravudh, 24 July 1917, TNA, R6, T 15.3/1.

40 See Niels Lumholdt and William Warren, *The History of Aviation in Thailand*, Hong Kong: Travel Publishing Asia, 1987, who state on p. 23 that Siam indeed 'emerged from World War I with…one of the largest and best equipped air forces in Asia.' See also Edward M. Young, *Aerial Nationalism: A History of Aviation in Thailand*, Smithsonian History of Aviation Series, Washington D.C. and London: Smithsonian Institution Press, 1995, pp. 8-14.

July.[41] Upon their arrival, the ground troops were trained in Marseilles, while the Thai pilots were trained in nearby Istrès.[42] A contemporary account in the British *Daily News* acknowledged Siam's troops in a peculiar way by explaining to its readers that '[the] Siamese are particularly suited to aviation work on account of their extra-ordinarily keen eyesight, their smallness, and their daring'.[43] Thai soldiers did not actively fight enemy troops in Europe; rather, the nineteen Thai soldiers who lost their lives during the campaign were victims of accidents, not enemy fire. In 1999, the last living survivor of the expeditionary force explained in an interview that Thai troops were not involved in any fighting; a view which is supported by most international scholars.[44] But Thai troops did cross the Rhine River with French forces after the armistice was signed in November 1918, set up camp in the German town of Neustadt an der Weinstraße and spent several months patrolling the area. Thai troops later marched in the allied victory parades in Paris, London and Brussels in the course of July 1919.[45]

The thirty-two allied and Associated Powers met at Paris in January 1919 to draw up a joint peace treaty with Germany. After six months of deliberations, the Treaty of Versailles, which founded the League of Nations, was signed on 28 June 1919, and ratified by the new League of Nations on 10 January 1920. The Paris Peace Conference was dominated by the so-called Big Four: British Prime Minister David Lloyd George, French President Georges Clemenceau, Italian Prime Minister Vittorio Orlando and President Woodrow Wilson of the United States. Germany was not invited to France to discuss the treaty. As the Big Four had conflicting aims, the Treaty of Versailles was very much a compromise, which was criticised not only by Germany but also among the victors themselves. The underlying assumption for the conference and the resulting treaty was that Germany accept full responsibility for causing the war and make reparations to some of the Allies.

Within days after the armistice of Compiègne in November 1918, Minister of Foreign Affairs Prince Devawongse instructed Prince Charoon in Paris to do his utmost to ensure that Siam would be represented at the Paris Peace Conference and, more precisely, at the part of the conference which would lead to possible membership in the new League of Nations. Prince Devawongse explained that he was receiving conflicting opinions in Bangkok: on the one hand, he was receiving signals 'that when the Conference discusses the question of the League of Nations…Siam will be placed aside' and 'unless and until Siam has a representative Government (she) will not be admitted to the League of Nations'; on the other hand, that Siam would be 'sure to be requested to take part as long as (she) has a constituted Government by whatever form de jure and de facto which maintains external peace and internal order, needless to say whether it has entered into the war on the sight of Right or it has not entered into (it) at all'.[46]

41 Thais were not the only Asians sent to France in support of the Allied war effort. Some 140,000 Chinese nationals were shipped to Europe from 1916 onwards as labourers. They were employed as construction workers and in weapons factories, later also as agricultural helpers, and were accommodated in camps separate from the local population. From 1919, they were shipped back to China. According to Wyatt, some 200,000 Vietnamese from French Indochina were also shipped to France to serve as labourers; see Wyatt, *Thailand*, p. 230.

42 Keith Hart, 'The Military Participation of Siam in the First World War (1914-1918)', unpublished document, Thailand Information Centre at Chulalongkorn University Main Library, n.d., p. 3.

43 *Daily News* (London), 9 August 1918; British Library Online Newspaper Archive, <www.uk.olivesoftware.com>.

44 'The Great War Survivor': Interview with Yod Sangrungruan in *Bangkok Post*, 28 August 1999.

45 When he received news of Thai troops standing on German territory, King Vajiravudh declared it 'was the proudest day in my life'; *Bangkok Times*, 12 December 1918, cited in Vella, *Chaiyo!*, p. 117.

46 Prince Devawongse to Prince Charoon, 21 November 1918, TNA, KT 96.1/1. On the discussion regarding democratic government as precondition for League membership, which Prince Devawongse is referring to, see also Walters, *League of Nations*, p. 44.

Prince Devawongse's communication reflects both the anxiety prevailing in Bangkok over whether Siam would actually be honoured by being seated alongside the Western powers and the fact that Siam's sovereignty as a state in modern, Western terms was, in 1918, not undisputed in an international environment still dominated by colonial attitudes. Ten years after Siam had had to concede territories to France in 1907 and Britain in 1909, in order to guard its independence, the prince was convinced that, if 'Siam were to be left out by any case whatever (it) can only mean that Great Britain and France have settled between themselves the division and the destruction of Siam for their own respective benefits.' But Prince Devawongse was also hopeful that, as Siam had entered the war on the side of France and Great Britain, its neighbours were not 'capable of such German-like tricks so soon after the war.' He rightly counted on support in this regard from the United States, and he was confident that Siam would be invited to participate at Versailles because the conference was in essence no different from the Hague Peace Conference in which Siam had participated.[47]

Indeed Siam was not a newcomer to multilateral foreign policy in 1918-19. The kingdom had already been part of early international cooperation before and after the turn of the century when it joined the Universal Postal Union of 1878, participated in the First Hague Peace Conference of 1899[48], the Shanghai Opium Commission of 1909, the series of Hague Opium Conferences from 1911 and acceded to the International Telegraph Convention of 1911. We can thus assume that the idea of having Thai princes sitting at an international conference table was not completely alien to Western policy makers in 1918-19.

By December 1918 it became clear that the Big Four had decided to invite Siam to join the Paris Peace Talks. It was a matter of pride that Siam was represented not by one, but by two delegates at the conference, after having successfully argued that Siam was comparable to Portugal in the size of its population and should, therefore, be entitled to an equal number of delegates.[49] The Thai delegation to the conference was to be made up of Prince Charoon, Phraya Bibadh Kosha (Celestino Xavier) and Prince Traidos Prabandh, the Thai Ministers in Paris and Rome and the Deputy Minister of Foreign Affairs respectively. These three plenipotentiaries were assisted by eight technical experts, attachés and secretaries, bringing the total number of persons to eleven.[50] Their instructions were clear: to do their best to rid Siam of 'the burdensome provisions of the extremely antiquated treaties'. The United States had already indicated its willingness to revise its treaty with Siam, which then happened in late 1920. This left primarily Britain and France, which Thai diplomats needed to push for treaty revision at the conference. The strategy laid out by Prince Devawongse to achieve this goal in late December, was to force Western states to apply their new vision of international equality not only selectively to the Western

47 Prince Devawongse to Prince Charoon, 21 November 1918, TNA, KT 96.1/1. The same correspondence can also be found in TNA, SR 0201.29/6 (Part 1 of 3). Documentation on Siam's role at the Paris Peace Conference and general documents on proceedings can be found in TNA, SR 0201.29/6 through file 0201.29/26. On American support for Siam's participation see FRUS, 1919, vol. I: Paris Peace Conference, p. 308; FRUS, 1919, vol. II: Paris Peace Conference, p. 483, 502, 578ff.

48 Chalong Soontravanich, 'Siam and the First Hague Peace Conference of 1899', in Charit Tingsabadh (ed.), *King Chulalongkorn's Visit to Europe: Reflections on Significance and Impacts*, Bangkok: Centre for European Studies, Chulalongkorn University, 2000, pp. 31-44.

49 Office of the National Culture Commission (ed.), *The Centennial of H.R.H. Prince Wan Waithayakon Krommun Naradhip Bongsprabandh*, Bangkok: National Culture Commission, 1991, p. 61. Siam had originally been allocated one seat, but had successfully protested against this decision after the number of seats allocated to each delegation had been published in press reports; see FRUS, 1919, vol. II: Paris Peace Conference, p. 580f.

50 A detailed list of members of the Thai delegation can be found ibid., p. 53.

hemisphere and, perhaps, Japan, but also to Siam. Equality was the overriding idea. In Prince Devawongse's words,

> Siam [should] secure to herself what she deems it her right to have, that is a full acknowledgement of her position of equality with the free and progressive nations of the world and an opportunity to work out for herself in her own way and without the restrictions, which at the present time cramp and trammel her action, and impede her progress, the problems of government and of administration with which she is confronted.

Siam, so argued the prince, had joined the Allies in waging war and 'therefore, should be entitled to full participation with the Allied Nations on a basis of equality' in those parts of the conference, 'to which other than European nations are admitted'. As a logical consequence, Siam should 'naturally also be allowed to exercise freely all the rights and attributes appertain thereto, such as the right of jurisdiction, the rights of control of revenue and of [national] resources.' The subtle distinction made by Prince Devawongse is noteworthy: Siam demanded equal treatment only in those parts of the conference, to which other non-European states were invited, and had no ambition or interest in becoming involved in purely European affairs.

Closely connected to regaining full sovereignty was the question of League membership, and the Thai delegates were instructed accordingly:

> The matter of organization of a League of Nations is also of the first importance to Siam...everything that can be done in a friendly, tactful way to advance the proposal for a League of Nations, to which Siam is to be admitted on terms of equality must be done by the Royal delegates.

Prince Devawongse was by no means naïve in his understanding of equality; while he did believe 'that the nations forming the League are to be equal in every respect', he nevertheless saw it as one of the future League's key functions to 'guard the safety of the smaller nation against the greater'.[51]

The Committee for the League of Nations met for its first meeting on 3 February 1919, but Siam's delegates were not among the fifteen representatives at the meeting. In fact, the committee meetings were very much a great power event, with ten of the fifteen representatives coming from the five great powers: United States, Britain, France, Italy and Japan. As, after Belgium, Brazil, Portugal and Serbia, China was also represented on the committee, in effect Siam was the only independent Far Eastern state not to be represented. Although many smaller (European) states sharply criticised such an exclusive format for the talks, and managed to add four further states to the committee, Prince Charoon deemed it advisable 'to keep quiet [and] make no fuss',

51 Instructions by Prince Deva-wongse to the Royal Siamese Delegates to the Peace Conference, 30 December 1918, TNA, KT 96.1/1.

as Siam's delegation had no suggestions to make as to the details of the new League's statute, but only desired certain membership in the new organisation.[52] Interestingly, a week earlier, Phraya Bibadh had, in the second plenary meeting of the Conference on 25 January, called for Siam's inclusion in the list of delegations to sit on the Committee for the League of Nations, as it was, in his words, 'directly of interest' to Siam. But his request was not granted, as Wilson and his British, French and Italian colleagues wished to keep the committee as small as possible.[53]

During February it became obvious that Siam would be able to sign the covenant of the League as a contracting power. In the view of the committee members, Siam qualified in three aspects: it had not remained neutral, but had sided with the allies in the war; it had been invited to the conference, which was considered a precondition for signature; and it was considered as a state. In this last respect, Siam benefited also from the British demand to allow India to sign the covenant as a contracting power, which was ultimately accepted on the grounds that only states could be represented at the conference. India was represented and treated as a state, and not as a colony. [54]

By mid-February Prince Charoon was able to study the draft covenant. He considered many provisions therein 'most advantageous [to] small States such as ourselves' and did not have 'the slightest objection to any of the terms'. In summary, the prince found the provisions of the covenant 'much better than I expected'.[55] While the Thai delegation accepted the entire draft, it pursued its second policy goal, treaty revision, on a parallel track in bilateral diplomacy. The Thai delegation submitted a memorandum to their British and French counterparts on 22 February 1919, in which delegates made it clear that Siam should be granted full sovereignty, in order to join the League with the other 'free and independent nations.' The memorandum made the obvious connection between treaty revision and the ideals British foreign policy was propagating publicly:

> H.M. Government ... are confident that the question will be favourably examined by the British Government, [who] are at present intent upon building up a new order of right and justice, humanity and civilisation. This new order is to find a concrete expression in the League of Nations to be set up among independent states worthy of the name; and Siam feels that it cannot satisfy her desire, as an independent nation, either to become a member of that League or to sit in it with becoming dignity side by side with her associate members, unless she has previously recovered the full possession of all the attributes of international sovereignty.[56]

In essence, the revolutionary project of a League of Nations stood precisely for the principles on which Siam based its demands for treaty revision. The British Minister in Bangkok, commenting on the

---

52 Prince Charoon to Prince Deva-wongse, 4 February 1919, TNA, KT 96.1/1. On the League of Nations Committee see in detail Walters, *League of Nations*, p. 33ff.

53 FRUS, 1919, vol. II: Paris Peace Conference, p. 195.

54 Prince Charoon to Prince Deva-wongse, 18 February 1919, TNA, KT 96.1/1.

55 Ibid.

56 Memorandum for the Revision of Treaty and Tariff by the Siamese Delegation to the Paris Peace Conference, 22 February 1919, PRO, FO 371/4091 F 43379/3033/40.

memorandum, expressed 'all due sympathy to these aspirations for equity of treatment' but went on to ask, 'whether equality of treatment can safely be granted to a nation which is still far from equality in most of those attainments which are essential to stability and progress in a State.' He concluded:

> The institution of the League of Nations presumably does away with the 'gunboat' as a means for correction, but until the efficacy of measures which are to be substituted for the 'gunboat' corrective has been proved, it would be rash to submit British subjects to the insecurity arising from the process of evolution of self-government of an undeveloped oriental State.[57]

Siam found a staunch supporter of its claims in Wolcott Pitkin, Harvard lawyer and former foreign affairs adviser to the Thai government until 1917. Pitkin published a lengthy pamphlet in 1919, unequivocally entitled *Siam's Case for Revision of Obsolete Treaty Obligations Admittedly Inapplicable to Present Conditions*.[58] He listed Siam's involvement in pre-League international cooperation in great detail, from the Hague Peace Conference to international maritime agreements, and concluded that Siam was entitled to now participate in the new international cooperation 'in their ultimate fruition' and lay before the Allies its treaties for revision, which were inconsistent with the spirit of the League of Nations. This, argued Pitkin, would also help 'solidify the League and crystallise its spirit'.[59] Hailing the birth of the League of Nations – which, in Pitkin's words, 'breathes the spirit of justice and of fair dealing among the nations of the earth' – as a new era in international relations, he left no doubt that Siam's unequal treaties had to be revised and that the Paris talks were the unique opportunity to do so.[60] Describing existing extraterritorial rights in Siam, he asked: 'No self-respecting country would for a moment tolerate such a state of affairs within its borders if it could help itself. Why then must Siam?'[61]

Ultimately, as Peter Oblas has examined in detail, neither the British nor the French governments were willing to give in to Thai demands during the Paris Peace Conference. Commercial interests were interwoven with paternalistic attitudes towards non-European peoples, as expressed in a British report of early 1920, which stated that 'Siam as a modern nation is scarcely yet emerging from infancy…the moment has not yet arrived to surrender any of the extraterritorial rights which his Majesty's Government retain in Siam'.[62] Siam's League membership and skilful use of the League's ideals of equality among nations as an argument to support its demands did, however, play an important part in the subtle campaigns on bilateral and the new multilateral levels, which then led to renegotiated treaties with both European states as well as with all other treaty partners by the mid-1920s. This use of League membership and League ideals as a means to increase the pressure on

57 Lyle to Lord Curzon, 20 August 1919, PRO, FO 371/4091 F 137596/3033/40.

58 Pitkin, *Siam's Case*.

59 Ibid., p. 3f.

60 Ibid., p. 5.

61 Ibid., p. 17.

62 Annual Report on Siam for the Year 1919, Doc. 59 (F 264/264/20), BDFA, Part II, Series E, vol. 49. See also Oblas, *Siam's Efforts*, p. 110ff.

European states to revise the unequal treaties will appear in nearly all of the following chapters of this study, be it opium policy, cooperation in public health or measures against human trafficking. Time and again during the first half of the 1920s Thai officials effectively, but always careful not to act aggressively, reminded their European counterparts when dealing with specific policy issues that Siam was not free to formulate its own policy as a sovereign state because of the unequal treaties.

President Wilson expressed his sympathy for Siam's demands for treaty revision in a meeting with the Thai delegates on 19 May 1919 in Paris and told them that the matter may be put before the new League of Nations in the future.[63] As we will see in the following chapter, treaty revision was pursued on bilateral rather than on multilateral tracks, but Wilson's statement does, once again, underscore the close connection between the rationale behind treaty revision and the rationale behind setting up the League. Ironically, it was the United States which never became a League member but which first concluded a revised treaty with Siam, signed on 16 December 1920 in Washington D.C.[64]

The League of Nations Committee formally presented the draft covenant to the plenary session of the Paris Peace Conference, including the delegates of Siam, on 28 April 1919. The covenant was approved unanimously, as was the initial list of forty-two original and invited member states, the appointment of Sir Eric Drummond as first Secretary-General and the choice of Geneva as seat of the new organisation.

Prince Charoon and Prince Traidos signed the Treaty of Versailles – undoubtedly one of the key documents of the twentieth century – on 28 June 1919. Articles 135 to 137 of section IV listed the Thai demands. First and foremost, the Treaty of Versailles declared all previous treaties with Germany, and explicitly extraterritorial rights, as terminated, and all seizures of German property in Siam at the outbreak of war as justified.[65] According to the treaty provisions, a Mixed Arbitral Tribunal was set up between Germany and Siam in late 1920 to determine reparations and by 1927 this question was settled by the German government's acceptance of German assets seized by Thai authorities in 1917 as reparations under the Treaty of Versailles.[66]

As signatory state of the peace treaties, Siam was able to cancel the unequal treaties with the defeated enemy states Germany and Austria-Hungary immediately. As an Associated Power, Siam was also party to two of the three other peace treaties, the Treaty of Neuilly-sur-Seine with Bulgaria of 17 November 1919 and the Treaty of Trianon with Hungary of 4 June 1920 which bear the signature of Prince Charoon. Siam did not sign the forth of the post-war peace treaties, the Treaty of Sèvres with the Ottoman Empire of August 1920, which never came into force.

63 An American idea to somehow merge extraterritorial rights into a new multilateral treaty system under the League of Nations was already brought up in a communication by the American chargé d'affaires in Bangkok in November 1918. Asked by the State Department to report on the probable programme of the Thai delegation to the Paris Peace Conference, he suggested 'that rather than suffer our rights to lapse with time, or bargain them away for less than they are worth, provision should be made for the merging of extraterritorial privileges in a super national judicial structure of the League of Nations.' See White to Secretary of State, 14 November 1918, FRUS, 1919, vol. II: The Paris Peace Conference, p. 489ff.

64 See FRUS, 1921, vol. II, p. 857ff.; the text of the treaty can be found on p. 867ff. The meeting on 19 May 1919 is quoted by Oblas, Siam's Efforts, p. 121 and in Peter B. Oblas, "A Very Small Part of World Affairs", Siam's Policy on Treaty Revision and the Paris Peace Conference', *Journal of the Siam Society*, 59, 2 (1971), pp. 51-74, here p. 66.

65 I have used the official text of the Treaty of Versailles, as printed in French, English and German as 'Gesetz über den Friedensschluß zwischen Deutschland und den alliierten und assoziierten Mächten vom 16. Juli 1919' in *Reichsgesetzblatt*, 140 (August 1919), pp. 687-1318.

66 See Stoffers, *Im Lande des weißen Elefanten*, p. 175.

King Rama VI stated in his annual speech from the throne in January 1920:

> One of the most important points to note is that, in common accord with the Allied and Associated Powers, we have helped to found a League of Nations which would secure the reign of peace on the basis of Right and Morality. That we should be a member of the League whose duty is to regulate world affairs according to the principles of right and justice, must, in some measure, be a matter of satisfaction and pride to us.[67]

The League of Nations formally came into being on 10 January 1920. In autumn of that year, delegates from nearly 50 states came together on the shore of Lake Geneva for the first General Assembly meeting of the League. It is difficult to imagine that the Thai delegates among them were not aware of the fact that this meeting symbolically marked a new era in Siam's relations with the world.

Conclusions

Scholars of Thai efforts for treaty revision after the First World War generally acknowledge that joining the war effort did not have the desired significant impact on the willingness of Western states to renegotiate their treaties with Siam. While the United States was already willing to revise its treaty before Siam's declaration of war, it took administrations in London and Paris another half decade after the Paris Peace Conference to concede a substantial part of their extraterritorial rights and commercial privileges. But joining the Allied war effort led precisely to another desired result, that of having a say in the post-war international order. That Siam signed the Treaty of Versailles and became an original member of the League of Nations was the most significant result of the declaration of war in 1917 in the realm of foreign relations. In the case of treaty revision, Siam's demands met with largely opposed European counterparts; in the case of membership in the League, Siam's desire met with a favourable international sentiment. Of course, not only were no commercial interests at stake for France or Britain in accepting Siam in the League, but membership even underscored their sincerity towards the international public in adhering to the new ideals of equality of states.

We can assume that Siam would likely have been invited to join the League of Nations even if it had not been part of the war coalition or the Paris Peace Talks, particularly because Siam at the time already had a history of participation in early international cooperation. Although remarkable, becoming an original member of the League of Nations was not a surprising development in the context of Siam's foreign policies. While it holds true that Siam became a full member of the new international community of states barely two decades after its

67 Speech from the Throne, in TNA, *Bangkok Times*, 5 January 1920.

independence and territorial integrity were seriously endangered, League membership was in line with Siam's involvement with earlier multilateral diplomacy. As detailed above, Siam's embrace of multilateralism in 1919-20 was preceded by its involvement in earlier initiatives such as the Universal Postal Union, the various Hague Conferences and others. But it was original membership from the very first day of the League that gave Siam significant prestige internationally and boosted support for the League among the domestic elite. This difference in quality is precisely what King Vajiravudh expressed in the statement quoted above: rather then merely having been invited to join the League, Siam had 'helped to found a League'.

Sketches of Phraya Bibadh Kosha and his daughter made during the first General Assembly of the League of Nations, 1920 (League of Nations Archives).

Siam's policy makers, mainly Prince Devawongse and Prince Charoon, understood that it was best not to link treaty revision and League membership too closely, as failure in one could have also jeopardise the other. Instead, Prince Charoon rightly sensed that the general sentiment towards Siam's League membership in Paris was positive, and refrained from pushing too hard to join the exclusive League of Nations Committee which, as British and French files show, European powers were unwilling to allow. Ultimately, while treaty revision with the European states had to be postponed, Siam's original League membership came about in a remarkably non-confrontational manner. It marked one of the biggest diplomatic successes in the nineteenth and twentieth centuries for a country striving to be treated on equal terms by European colonial powers, and it opened the door for Siam to a unique experiment in international relations, which would remain constitutive for its foreign relations and domestic modernisation for nearly two decades.

2

Siam at Geneva: Attitudes, Aims, Individuals and Contributions

Attitudes and aims of Siam's League membership

❝ It is the constant aim and purpose of my Government to keep abreast of the times in every direction, so as to be worthy of their status as member of the League of Nations'.[1] This powerful statement made by King Vajiravudh in his annual speech from the throne in 1923 summarises in a nutshell the tremendous importance of League membership for the internationally-oriented Thai elite during the 1920s. Two years later, the king highlighted another facet of Siam's League membership in his speech from the throne, when he pointed out in the context of the League's efforts to curb opium trafficking that 'the League is now pursuing objects which would yield results at which we ourselves have, also, been aiming'.[2] Ten years later, after a coup led by progressive civilian bureaucrats and military officers against the absolute monarchy, the new government of Siam issued a public policy statement in December 1932, in which it proclaimed, none less powerfully than King Vajiravudh in 1923: 'As regards the League of Nations, the Government are fully alive to its importance and are always prepared to support its activities'.[3]

As we have seen in the previous chapter, Siam became a founding member of the League of Nations as a result of its engagement in the First World War and its participation in the Paris Peace Conference. Siam's objectives for League membership then changed over the following twenty-six years of the League's existence. During the immediate post-war period the League was primarily a means for Siam to put pressure on Western powers to live up to the new ideals of international politics and revise their unequal treaties with Siam. As the League of Nations was gradually filled with life, the organisation's tasks expanded rapidly and so did Siam's objectives in being a League member. The following chapters will show in detail how the League evolved from being a tool for Siam for regaining sovereignty into a force which induced changes in many areas of Siam's development before the Second World War and a forum for presenting the kingdom to the world community as a progressive and modern state.

Siam's overall policy towards the League of Nations remained unchanged over time: to minimise obligations resulting from League membership by staying out of the limelight of international political conflicts in Geneva as far as possible, but at the same time to maximise

Opposite: Prince Charoonsakdi Kritakara, Permanent Delegate of Siam to the League of Nations, 1920-1928 (League of Nations Archives).

1 TNA, *Bangkok Times*, 3 January 1923.

2 TNA, *Bangkok Times*, 5 January 1925.

3 TNA, *Bangkok Times*, 28 December 1932.

Siam's benefits from League membership in social and technical policy areas. For Siam's foreign policy makers the League of Nations was of great political importance throughout the 1920s and most of the 1930s. Thai governments during this period were, to a large degree, willing to align or subordinate their own policies in certain fields under League initiatives. Opium policy, which was a key sector of the state budget with profound social impacts, featured very prominently in this regard. As everywhere in the world, the League lost credibility in Siam in the course of the 1930s, when member states abandoned the multilateral experiment and reverted to traditional power politics and rearmament. By the time Luang Phibun tightened his grip on Thai politics at the end of the 1930s, the League played only a minor role, before becoming completely unimportant during the war years. After the end of the Second World War the League then suddenly became important once again as a legacy which Siam brought into play to gain membership in the new United Nations and to minimise retaliation for its declarations of war on Western states.

Thai diplomats used League membership repeatedly as a means to achieve the overriding goal of Thai foreign policy in the interwar period, regaining complete fiscal and juridical autonomy. The Paris Peace Conference after the end of the First World War had resulted only in the immediate cancellation of the unequal treaties with Germany and Austria-Hungary and in the revised treaty with the United States of 1920. Therefore, Siam's foreign policy objectives remained the same, abolishment of all unequal treaties. As Eldon James, who was Foreign Affairs Adviser to the Thai government between 1918 and 1923 and strongly favoured Siam's admission to the League, put it:

> Siam felt that as a modern state, a member of the newly formed League of Nations, it had demonstrated both the desire and the ability to share fully in the life of the international community. A complete revision of the old treaty system was the next logical step.[4]

During the first General Assembly meeting of the League of Nations at Geneva in 1920, the three Thai delegates, Prince Charoon, Phraya Bibadh Kosha and Phraya Buri Navarasth (Chuan Singhaseni), gave a reception for delegates and members of the new League Secretariat to acquaint them with hitherto nearly unknown Siam. As the delegates reported to Prince Devawongse, the reception served the additional purpose of propagating Siam's desire to rid itself of the unequal treaties, a purpose for which the delegates, by their own account, received much verbal support. Prince Charoon even had the opportunity to describe Siam's staunch support for the League of Nations and desire for 'collaboration of the small and great peoples [for] the salvation of the world' in an interview with the *Journal de Genève*.[5] But Britain and France were slow to accept the rules they had themselves set. Only reluctantly

4 Eldon R. James, 'Siam in the Modern World', *Foreign Affairs*, IX, 4 (1931), pp. 657-664, here p. 663; see also Pensri Duke, 'Historical Perspective', in Wiwat Mungkandi and William Warren (eds), *A Century and a Half of Thai-American Relations*, Bangkok: Chulalongkorn University Press, 1982, pp. 1-57, here p. 52.

5 See Report on the First General Assembly of the League of Nations, dated 10 January B.E. 2463 (1921), TNA, KT 96.1.3/2. A transcript of the mentioned interview on 16 December 1920 is included in the report.

did London and Paris enter into negotiations with Siam for new treaties along the American model. Thai officials, in turn, continued to remind their Western counterparts that unequal treaties were no longer compatible with the new international system represented by the League. And they made this connection not only in general terms. In 1923, Prince Devawongse wrote to the British Minister and explained that Britain's extraterritorial rights seriously limited Siam's ability to live up to its international commitments regarding opium control. To the embarrassment of the British Foreign Office, Prince Devawongse suggested that Britain give up its extraterritorial rights so that Siam could enforce international agreements to which Britain was party.[6] At the same time, however, Prince Devawongse in Bangkok and Prince Charoon in Paris and Geneva were realistic in their expectations as to what the young League of Nations could do with regard to treaty revision. They understood perfectly well, at least from the second League Assembly in 1921 onwards, that it would be counterproductive to openly put the issue of treaty revision before the League, as this would have certainly alienated the Western Powers.[7]

It was in this context of *realpolitik* that officials in Bangkok read article XIX of the League's covenant, under which the 'Assembly may from time to time advise the reconsideration by Members of the League of treaties which have become inapplicable' and, accordingly, did not put their hope in evoking it. In addition, the Ministry of Justice in Bangkok was informed by the League Secretariat in February 1923 informally that 'it was the opinion of the Director of the Legal Section that Siam could only obtain revision of her treaties by negotiating with the other signatory parties, and that the League had nothing to do with the matter'.[8] Ultimately, Siam's League membership provided additional leverage which together with the precedent of the treaty with the United States of December 1920, led to renegotiated treaties with Great Britain, France, Germany, Japan and eight further European states during the mid-1920s.[9]

As is the case in most countries at most times, foreign policy was not of general public concern in pre-war Siam; it was the domain of a small elite of society. Among this elite, the League of Nations was highly important as a cornerstone of Siam's foreign policy during most of the two interwar decades. An interesting source sheds light on this attitude; in 1924, the British Foreign Office enquired across the globe, inluding Bangkok, on attitudes of countries towards the League of Nations. The report which the British legation sent to London in reply, entitled *Report on the Attitude of the Siamese Government and People towards the League of Nations* highlights the enthusiasm with which the creation of the League was welcomed in Siam. The report explains that for Siam it was not only the guarantee of rights and independence of small nations, for which the League stood, but the fact that it meant that Siam was placed 'more or

6 Greg to Lord Curzon, 13 April 1923, Enclosure: Prince Devawongse to Greg, 10 April 1923, Doc. 159 and 160 (F 1504/421/87), BDFA, Part II, Series E, vol. 49, p. 198ff.

7 See Report by Prince Charoon and Phraya Bibadh to Prince Devawongse on the Second General Assembly of the League of Nations, dated 17 November B.E. 2464 (1921), TNA, KT 96.1.3/4.

8 Leith to Chuen Charuvastra, 16 February 1923, LNA, R 1339/22/26180/26180. For the text of the Covenant of the League of Nations see LNA, League of Nations, *Official Journal*, February 1920, p. 3ff.

9 The authoritative study on treaty revision in the 1920s is Oblas, Siam's Efforts; a collection of the revised treaties in English and French can be found in Francis B. Sayre (Phraya Kalyana Maitri) (ed.), *Siam: Treaties with Foreign Powers, 1920-1927*, Bangkok: Royal Siamese Government, 1928; see also Arnold J. Toynbee, '1. The Liquidation of Foreign Extraterritorial Privileges in Siam. 2. The Revision of the Régime along the Frontier between Siam and the French Possession and Protectorates in Indo-China', *Survey of International Affairs*, 1929, London: Oxford University Press, 1930, pp. 405-421.

less on a footing of equality with the Great Powers', which generated this enthusiasm. Although, the report continued, Thai policy makers were somewhat more sober in their expectations four years later, they continued to value and support the League. The report went on to quote at length a public speech made by Prince Varn, a prominent diplomat, which he gave to a large audience at Chulalongkorn University on 7 August 1924 and in which he emphasised the collective security system and the new, open form of diplomacy and information exchange, which the League was propagating. Prince Varn also pointed to the League's limitations and stressed that it had no armed forces at its disposal to enforce decisions, but could merely expel a member from the international community. The British Minister Johns considered Prince Varn's speech with its enthusiastic support of the League's ideals to reflect the general sentiment among the elite in Bangkok and, at the same time, pointed out to his superiors in London that it was inappropriate to speak of a general public opinion in Siam:

> The peasants are for the most part illiterate. There is practically no middle class, and few Siamese, even those of the highest rank, take any interest in foreign political or matters generally considered of world-wide interest unless brought into contact with them in the course of their official duties.

This absence of a sizeable, politically interested public in Siam was also the reason why, other than in most Western League member states and in Japan and China, no Thai League of Nations society was ever founded to promote the League's ideals and work in Siam. In Johns' view, however, 'such public opinion as there is in Siam is certainly in favour of the League of Nations'.[10]

Twelve years later in 1936, a British consular report once again evaluated attitudes of the Thai elite towards the League of Nations and came to the conclusion that Siam was, at this time, still a 'loyal member of the League', but that the League's prestige had suffered from the failures over Japan's invasion of Manchuria and Italy's invasion of Ethiopia. The report also accurately judged that Luang Pradist Manudharm (Pridi Phanomyong), then Minister of Foreign Affairs, was the foremost champion of the League's ideals of international cooperation and collective security among the governing elite in Bangkok.[11] Luang Pradist gave a policy statement that same year, in which he underlined Siam's 'principle to maintain friendliness in our relations with all foreign powers' without favouring one country over another – a policy designed with a view of shaking off the final remnants of extraterritorial rights held by foreign powers in Siam.[12]

Siam's policy towards major Western states in a League framework reflected the kingdom's general foreign policy priorities during the interwar years: general non-alignment with a bias towards Great Britain.

10 Foreign Office Circular, 24 June 1924, PRO, FO 371/10575, W 5281/5281/98; Johns to MacDonald, 25 August 1924, PRO, FO 371/10575, W 8322/5281/98.

11 Annual Report on Siam for 1936, PRO, FO 371/21053, F 1067/1067/40, p. 14.

12 'Unimpaired Balance in World Friendships is Watchword of Thai Foreign Policy', in: Siam Today, Illustrated Review, First Issue, July B.E. 2479 (1936), published by the Government Publicity Bureau, Bangkok, p. 9, in: PRO, FO 371/20300, F 6050/216/40.

Interestingly, Siam never joined together with the two other Far Eastern League members China and Japan in the League of Nations in any form of an Asian block or an Asian coalition. This policy, a consequence of the Western orientation of Siam's foreign policy in general, was clearly indicated already during the formative years of the League, as Japan and China lobbied for a stronger Asian role in the European-dominated League of Nations. They repeatedly, and unsuccessfully, pressed for something of an 'Asian quota' in League bodies and even for an amendment to the League's Covenant, laying down the equality of Asian people to those of Western countries.[13] Japan, in particular, was pressing for such a racial equality clause from early 1919 but, because of the strong opposition from Britain and France, for whose Asian colonies this would have entailed serious problems, Siam was careful not to associate itself with this proposal. After Japan's proposal was defeated for the first time, it again brought it up twice, only to see it defeated twice again. Strikingly, while for Siam League membership was to be obtained under more or less any circumstance, the repeated defeat of the racial equality proposal and the perceived position of inferiority it entailed led Japanese diplomats to even seriously reconsider joining the League of Nations at all.[14] During the League General Assembly of 1921, this movement also resounded in Bangkok, where the *Bangkok Times* noted somewhat bemused that the whole Far East was suddenly crying for equality, democracy and autonomy. Siam was, according to the paper, luckily showing 'modesty and at least avoids making herself ridiculous.'[15] But much more than modesty, Siam's striking absence from this movement reflected its traditional foreign policy focus on Britain and France, rather than on Japan and China, as well as its traditional policy of neutrality, which it would have left by aligning itself with its two Asian neighbours. Thai foreign policy during the post-war years was clearly avoiding any move which would offend Britain or France and jeopardise the overriding policy aim of revising the unequal treaties. Prince Charoon expressed his anxiety over the racial equality proposal in 1919:

> The Japanese are considering whether they will bring up the question before the full sitting of the Conference for a final vote. If so, it will be awkward for us, because as a principle for our self-respect we are bound to vote for it, but it may not be politic to do so in view of our aims.[16]

Although the situation anticipated by Prince Charoon did not arise, his note underscores the priority of Siam's foreign policy during the immediate post-war years: to avoid any action which would offend the Western Powers and make it more difficult to press them for revised treaties with Siam. Japan's failure during the formative stage of the League, despite its position as the dominant power in East Asia, served as a prime example for Siam of how not to act in the new multilateral stage.

13 See Naoko Shimazu, *Japan, Race and Equality: The Racial Equality Proposal of 1919*, London and New York: Routledge, 1998; Masatoshi Matsushita, *Japan in the League of Nations*, New York: Columbia University Press, 1929, p. 25ff.

14 Shimazu, *Japan, Race and Equality*, p. 49. Shimazu provides no evidence that Japanese diplomats approached Prince Charoon or his colleagues, and Siam is not mentioned at all in the study.

15 TNA, *Bangkok Times*, 13 September 1921.

16 Prince Charoon to Prince Deva-wongse, 17 April 1919, TNA, KT 96.1/1.

An expression of the same policy could be witnessed during the General Assembly in 1921, when Japan proposed that the League undertake a feasibility study as to whether Esperanto should be taught in League member states, a proposal which was designed to symbolically counter European cultural dominance. The proposal, which eventually disappeared from the agenda without any follow-up, was supported by all Asian member states except Siam. Again, Siam took care not to support any motion which could potentially disturb France or Britain.[17]

Siam had high hopes for the League of Nations, but Thai officials in charge of foreign policy during the post-war years were also very much realists. Prince Devawongse and Prince Charoon did not believe that complete sovereignty would be regained overnight and they quickly realised that the aims of the League's covenant and the policies of Great Britain, France and other League members were, to put it mildly, not always fully consistent. It was this realism which prevented Thai diplomats from forcing their demands for treaty revision onto the League's agenda and into the international spotlight, a move which would have likely increased the unwillingness on the Thames or the Seine to grant revised treaties to Siam. Instead, the more subtle and more quietly applied pressure was very successful and led to revised treaties within only half a decade.

As to the activities and influence of the League of Nations itself, expectations in Siam were also realistic, as Prince Varn wrote in 1932 in response to calls by idealists who expected the League to guarantee instant and lasting peace:

> No; the trouble is that we expect too much from the League: we expect it to be a panacea, to cure mankind of every ill, from war to wickedness; but if we viewed it in its historical perspective, we would perceive that the League is only in its first infancy and is the first infant of its kind. It needs to grow and develop.[18]

A similar sentiment was expressed by a *Bangkok Times* editorial in late 1933, after the League had suffered its first serious blows from the walkouts by Japan and Germany:

> It is of the utmost vital importance that the League of Nations should be able to withstand the repeated shocks which have recently threatened its stability, one after the other…Let us not necessarily assume that everything about the League is perfect and incapable of improvement, as some enthusiastic idealists are inclined to do. Let us rather admit that its machinery is sometimes creaky, sometimes inadequate and very often impotent.[19]

As mentioned above, a national League of Nations society with the objective of spreading the ideals of the League and disseminating information on League activities was never created in Siam. Although such national societies were popular in a number of League member

17 See Matsushita, *Japan and the League*, p. 51f. See also Prince Devawongse to Nitobe (League of Nations Under Secretary-General), 18 March 1922, TNA, KT 96.1/17.

18 TNA, *Bangkok Times*, 20 July 1932.

19 TNA, *Bangkok Times*, 12 December 1933.

states, and although Prince Charoon, Prince Devawongse and Prince Traidos all favoured the establishment of such a society in 1920, there seemed not to have been enough popular support in Bangkok to justify founding such an association, reflecting the small number of individuals interested in foreign affairs.[20] A particularly interesting source in this regard is an enquiry from the Japanese legation in Bangkok to the Ministry of Foreign Affairs in 1924 into how the League of Nations was being promoted in Siam and how League matters were being handled administratively by the government. Prince Traidos drafted a lengthy reply to the Japanese Minister Yada by hand, in which he explained that wide propaganda on the League was not suitable for the population in Siam because they lacked proper education and understanding. 'Any misunderstanding of the League's ideals and the League's work will', according to Prince Traidos, condescendingly, 'do more harm than good'. Propaganda for the League was therefore being limited to universities and elitist circles. At the Faculty of Political Sciences of Chulalongkorn University, a course was given twice weekly on international politics and the League of Nations, but, in the words of Prince Traidos, 'the course is naturally confined to the students of that Faculty.' However, public lectures were also organised, for instance those given by Prince Varn, and Prince Traidos expressed his belief that 'public propaganda in favour of the League will develop and enlarge itself also'.[21]

Just as there was general continuity in foreign affairs beyond 1932, the coup of 1932 did not entail immediate changes in Siam's policy or attitude towards Geneva. As mentioned above, the new government made it clear publicly in December 1932: 'As regards the League of Nations, the Government are fully alive to its importance and are always prepared to support its activities'.[22] This adherence to the principles of the League was expressed very prominently in the first Thai constitution of 10 December 1932. Article 54 of the constitution stipulated that the king had the sole right to declare war, but went on to curtail this power by stipulating that such a declaration may not run counter to the principles of the covenant of the League of Nations. Nigel Brailey has also highlighted the importance of League membership for the post-1932 governments by stating, 'the relatively idealistic Thai regimes of the 1930s had dedicated themselves not simply to the creation of a "new" Siam, but as a fully sovereign, independent state, according to the principles of the League of Nations of which it was a member'.[23]

But the gradual shifts in Siam's foreign policy which then occurred in the course of the mid and late 1930s towards Japan and away from Europe, also impacted on the view of the League among an increasing number of policy makers in Bangkok. The League was increasingly becoming discredited for having failed to guarantee collective security during these years; the report of Phraya Rajawangsan, Siam's Permanent

20 Prince Devawongse to Royal Secretariat, 6 May B.E. 2463 (1920), TNA, KT 96.1/87 (Part 1 of 3).

21 Yada to Prince Traidos, 17 September 1924 and draft letter from Prince Traidos to Yada, n.d., both in TNA, KT 96.1/22. This elitist view displayed by Prince Traidos was certainly not shared at Geneva, where the League Secretariat had, in early 1923, offered the Thai government all support in providing information on the League and on the government's cooperation with the League for the purpose of meeting public interest in Siam; see Leith to Chuen Charuvastra, 22 January 1923, LNA, R 1339/22/26180/26180.

22 The statement can also be found in: Statement of Government Policy of 4 January 1933, TKRI, United States Department of State, Consular Reports Siam, 892.01/7, p. 12.

23 Nigel J. Brailey, *Thailand and the Fall of Singapore: A Frustrated Asian Revolution*, Boulder (CO): Westview Press, 1986, p. 171.

Representative to the League, on the General Assembly of 1938 shows that the mood was already very sombre at Geneva in autumn 1938 under the grave climate of the Munich agreement and the German occupation of Czechoslovakia.[24] It does not come as a surprise therefore that the military group in the Thai government contemplated leaving the League in 1938-39, primarily for financial reasons. At the same time, however, the civilian group in the Thai government around Luang Pradist continued to adhere to the League's ideals and saw particular value in the non-political cooperation in areas such as efforts to fight human trafficking and improve public health.[25] In the context of Siam's recognition of Manchukuo in August 1941, rumours surfaced again that Siam would leave the League, which by this time had abandoned its stately headquarters on Lake Geneva because of the war raging in Europe and was virtually non-existent.[26] Ultimately, however, Siam did not retire from the League of Nations and remained a member for the entire twenty-six years of the organisation's lifetime.

The wide spectrum of contacts and cooperation between the League and Siam

This study focuses on the four most significant political areas of contact between Geneva and Bangkok – opium control, public health development, efforts against human trafficking, and collective security. But relations between the first international organisation and its only Southeast Asian member were by no means limited to these four areas, and the files available at the League of Nations Archives in Geneva as well as at the Thai National Archives in Bangkok should prove to be rich in material for future research on these other areas of work. Apart from being a member of the League of Nations proper, Siam was also a member of the two most important auxiliary organisations besides the League, the International Labour Organisation (ILO) and the Permanent Court of International Justice (PCIJ).

Siam's ILO membership, which was an automatic consequence of signing the Treaty of Versailles and becoming a League member, played a subordinate role during the interwar period in Thai foreign policy. While Siam was represented at the annual ILO conferences, the absolutist and post-1932 governments did not deem labour protection a pressing issue in a predominantly agricultural country. But international pressure from the ILO eventually penetrated Siam in the aftermath of the global economic depression, and the post-1932 governments then drew up the first legislation for labour protection.[27]

Siam's membership in the Permanent Court of International Justice, which was created by the first General Assembly of the League in 1920 and began its work in 1922, seems to have been solely motivated by the desire to appear progressive and be part of this innovative institution. Siam signed the court's 'optional clause', which obliged it to accept the court's jurisdiction if all other parties to a dispute also agreed. Never

24 Report on the 19th General Assembly of the League of Nations, dated 26 October B.E. 2481 (1938), TNA, KT 96.1.3/22.

25 See Sir Josiah Crosby's assessment to this effect in his Annual Report on Siam for 1938, PRO, FO 371/23596, F 2390/2390/40, p. 18. See, in the same sense, Crosby to Halifax, 22 March 1939, PRO, FO 371/23596, F 3219/3219/40.

26 Crosby to Foreign Office, 29 April 1941, PRO, FO 371/28135, F 3513/438/40.

27 On Siam and ILO activities see the vast files in TNA, KT 96.1.8.4/1-179; see the particularly interesting reports on labour conditions in Siam sent by Prince Devawongse to the League of Nations in 1922, 1923 and 1924 in LNA, R 1198/15/23997/16886; see also TNA, *Bangkok Times*, 25 November 1922; the only study which, to the author's knowledge, mentions Siam's ILO membership is Andrew Brown, *Labour, Politics and the State in Industrializing Thailand*, London and New York: Routledge Curzon, 2004, p. 24f. and 44f. Brown points out that this perception during the 1920s was in stark contrast to problems emerging from the developing industrial sector already before the 1930s. On the ILO during the League of Nations times see Carter Goodrich, 'The International Labour Organization', in Harriet E. Davis (ed.), *Pioneers in World Order: An American Appraisal of the League of Nations*, 2nd ed., New York: Columbia University Press, 1945, pp. 87-106; Gupta, *League of Nations*, p. 52ff.

during the twenty-six years of the League of Nations did Siam actually call on the PCIJ.[28] But when the League invited PCIJ members to a conference on the revision of the court's statute in 1929, the Thai Permanent Representative to the League of Nations, Prince Varn, was elected vice president of the conference, to the delight of foreign policy makers in Bangkok and the prince himself.[29]

One area in which Thai delegates appeared more active was the protection of minors and promotion of child welfare.[30] Another area, in which Siam adapted domestic laws and procedures to comply with new international standards, was the suppression of trafficking in obscene publications. Siam signed the League's International Convention for the Suppression of the Circulation of and Traffic in Obscene Publications in Geneva on 12 September 1923 and ratified it the following year, although – or rather, because – officials acknowledged openly that international trafficking in obscene publications to or from Siam was insignificant. Nevertheless, of the six cases, which came before court in Siam under the law against trafficking in obscene publications between 1924 and 1926, four led to convictions.[31]

A rather significant example of cooperation between the League and Siam was the important role the League played in the improvement of access to the port of Bangkok and expansion of the port itself. The entrance to the Chao Phraya River, some 35 kilometres from Bangkok, was obstructed by a sand bar, which had served the Thai capital well as protection against enemy vessels but also obstructed the increasing commercial activity, as it allowed only ships with a depth of some four meters to pass, and that only at high tide. Under pressure to boost Siam's foreign trade in the light of the global depression, the government followed a suggestion by Prince Sakol Varnakorn Voravarn, who held the position of Under Secretary of the Ministry of Agriculture and Commerce at the time, to consult an international expert for the scheme. Prince Sakol approached the Communications and Transit Organisation of the League of Nations to this end in late 1932. The advantage of a League expert was that he was likely to be more impartial and would not have to consider the interests of any firm wishing to carry out the recommended works; also, a League expert would be considerably cheaper to employ. A formal request was submitted in February 1933, and the League appointed A.T. Coode from England, G.P. Nijhoff from the Netherlands and P.H. Watier from France.[32] All three were internationally experienced water engineers and all three were working for the League's Communications and Transit Organisation. Nijhoff was dispatched to Siam with an assistant to collect the necessary information, research the technical and financial feasibility of the project, and to study the natural conditions on the spot. As a hydraulic engineer who had worked on similar studies in Poland, Persia and Argentina, he was very well suited for the task. The cost of the Nijhoff survey and the League

28 On Siam's relations with the PCIJ see TNA, KT 96.1.7/1-83; TNA, R7, T 10/15. See generally on the PCIJ Manley O. Hudson, 'The World Court', in Harriet E. Davis (ed.), *Pioneers in World Order: An American Appraisal of the League of Nations*, 2nd ed., New York: Columbia University Press, 1945, pp. 65-75.

29 See on the 1929 conference LNA, R 1988/3C/20435/18120.

30 See TNA, KT 96.1.8.1/93, 103-7, 114.

31 TNA, KT 96.1.8.1/29, 30, 41, 42, 63, 68, 78, 97. See also *The Times*, 23 September 1923. On the Act for the Suppression of the Circulation of and Traffic in Obscene Articles, B.E. 2471 (1928) see TNA, KT 96.1.8.1/55.

32 Haas to Prince Sakol, 13 January 1933 and Phraya Srivisarn to the Secretary-General, 23 February 1933, LNA, R 4269/9C/408/408.

report amounted to 70,000 Swiss francs, which was borne entirely by the Thai government.[33]

Nijhoff spent two months in Siam during summer 1933, and after his return to Europe the committee of experts drew up a detailed scheme for improved access and port expansion.[34] Nijhoff was the first expert from an international organisation to undertake a technical study in Siam and, at the same time, stood in the tradition of van der Heide, Ward, and Zimmerman, who had earlier conducted groundbreaking surveys on irrigation and rural development in Siam.[35] James Andrews' rural economic survey of 1934-35 strongly reiterated Nijhoff's recommendations and likely added to the weight of Nijhoff's report in Bangkok, in view of the desire to increase revenue from Siam's rice exports.[36] As far as the League of Nations is concerned, the Nijhoff Committee also featured prominently in contemporary accounts of the League's Communications and Transit Organisation as well as in secondary works on the League of Nations' technical activities.

During the second half of the 1930s, construction was begun on the basis of Nijhoff's plans, but, while the works were co-funded by the government of Nazi-Germany until 1945[37], it took until 1950 for construction to make serious headway, when the post-war Thai government obtained a loan of US$4.4 million from the World Bank for dredging the sandbar, deepening the river course to the Bangkok port, and purchasing loading equipment. By 1954, twenty-five years after works were begun, the port at Klong Toey was finally completed and could accommodate over twenty ocean-going vessels.

In the context of rapid infrastructure development, Siam also acceded to the Barcelona Transit Convention of 1921, which was concluded under the auspices of the League of Nations. In 1922, domestic legislation was put in place to comply with the convention, and King Vajiravudh pointed to Siam's progressiveness by so doing in his speech from the throne in 1923.[38] Already in 1919, Siam had signed the International Convention for Aerial Navigation; a step which put it at the forefront of countries developing air traffic.[39]

The effects of the worldwide economic depression of the early 1930s also hit Siam and led to a crisis in public finance. Revenue loss resulting from the drop in world market prices for Siam's export commodities, which led to a drop in tax revenue from exports, was predicted to be some 70 million baht in late 1931, and a basic restructuring of Siam's public finance system was necessary. Interestingly, the British legation in Bangkok considered the British financial adviser to the Thai government to be too involved to suggest such a fundamental restructuring; the legation proposed instead that the Thai government invite a League of Nations expert. This recommendation would have had the advantage that a League expert would be objective and could simply 'hand in his report and go'. The British Minister in Bangkok, Cecil Dormer, saw,

33 Siam transferred the amount in two equal instalments in early 1933 and autumn 1934; see LNA, R 4269/9C/408/408 and R 4269/9C/7542/408.

34 'Improvement of the Port of Bangkok and Its Approaches', Report by the Committee of Experts Appointed by the League of Nations, LNA, R 4269/9C/7542/408; see on the Bangkok port also files in LNA, COL 167/1 (Parts 1-3). Nijhoff's report was also discussed in The Times, 14 October 1935.

35 On Homan van der Heide's role in the development of modern irrigation in Siam see Han ten Brummelhuis, King of the Waters: Homan van der Heide and the Origin of Modern Irrigation in Siam, Leiden: KITLV Press, 2005.

36 James M. Andrews, Siam: 2nd Rural Economic Survey, 1934-1935, Bangkok: The Bangkok Times Press, 1935, p. 40f. and 391ff.

37 Wendler (Minister in Bangkok) to Foreign Office Berlin, 6 August 1942, suggests tungsten imports from Siam as a major motivation for the German involvement; see Auswärtiges Amt (ed.), Akten zur deutschen auswärtigen Politik 1918-1945, Göttingen: Vandenhoek & Ruprecht and Bonn: Hermes, Doc. 164, Serie E: 1941-1945, vol. II, p. 282f.; Stoffers, Im Lande des weißen Elefanten, p. 209f.

38 TNA, Bangkok Times, 3 January 1923. Files relating to Siam's adherence to the Barcelona Transit Convention can be found in TNA, KT 96.3/1 and in LNA, R 1116/14/24942/13234.

39 On the remarkable history of aviation in Siam see Lumholdt and Warren, Aviation in Thailand; Young, Aerial Nationalism.

however, that a report drawn up by a League expert would have to be published or at least circulated among League members to be in accordance with League rules, and that the government in Bangkok would certainly object to such a practice. In the end, therefore, nothing came of the plan.[40]

Four years later, when James Baxter resigned in protest over the opium smuggling scandal of 1935 (see Chapter 4), Luang Pradist, the Minister of Interior, contemplated approaching the League of Nations to ask for a suitable candidate to succeed Baxter as financial adviser. When word spread, the alarms bells at the British legation in Bangkok immediately went off, as the British government was keen to maintain its privileged position in the management of Siam's public finances through a British financial adviser. Luang Pradist indeed went to Geneva in September 1935, but he did not, as the British feared, invite the League to propose a successor to Baxter. The British Foreign Office was, however, quite concerned about the issue throughout the summer months and repeatedly enquired confidentially with Francis Walters at the League Secretariat whether the Thai government had sent any request.[41] In late November 1935, Luang Pradist was in London to negotiate the conversion of the Thai government's old 1924 foreign loan at six percent interest into a new loan at a better rate. The Bank of England made it clear during these negotiations that such a conversion would be granted only if the financial adviser would again be a Briton; and Luang Pradist, with the backing of the cabinet in Bangkok, agreed.[42] The British successor to Baxter was then found in the person of William Doll. The episode sheds light on the uniquely non-partisan role, which the League was potentially able to play with regard to providing international experts to member governments, but it also shows that, other than in the above mentioned case of Nijhoff, political interests and resulting political pressure from London were too great in this instance to allow for the appointment of an international civil servant to advise the government in Bangkok. The episode also sheds light on the high esteem in which the League was still held by Luang Pradist and others in the Thai government by the mid-1930s, not least for its function as a multilateral counterweight to the interests of individual Western powers.

Thai delegations participated in many economic, finance and trade initiatives of the League of Nations during the 1920s and 1930s, in particular the large economic conferences in Geneva and London. Thai delegates participated in international efforts to unify cheques, balances and international transfers as well as efforts to draw up international laws against counterfeiting currencies.[43] One the one hand, this allowed Thai officials to follow global financial and economic developments closely, on the other hand the League's efforts in standardising economic statistics had an impact on how economic and trade development was

40 Confidential Memorandum by Dormer on Losses of Revenue in Siamese Budget 1931-2, Enclosure in Dormer to Henderson, 21 August 1931, Doc. 34 and 35 (F 5377/9/40), BDFA, Part II, Series E, vol. 50, p. 30.

41 Relevant correspondence can be found in PRO, FO 371/19375.

42 Crosby to Hoare, 3 December 1935, Doc. 174 (F 7804/296/40), BDFA, Part II, Series E, vol. 50, p. 213f. See on Luang Pradist's meetings in Europe in 1935 also Vichitvong Na Pombhejara, *Pridi Banomyong and the Making of Thailand's Modern History*, Bangkok: Chaiwichit Press, 1983, p. 121 and 138.

43 On international economic and financial issues under the League of Nations, and Siam's participation see TNA, KT 96.1.10/1-69; on unification of cheques and balances see TNA, KT 96.1.10.1/1-6; on counterfeit currencies see TNA, KT 96.1.10.2/1-10. See also LNA, R 381/10/24309/23711; R 476/10/59581/56327; serial documents C.652.A.73.1922.II and C.360.M.151.1930.II.

recorded in Siam. In his report on the League's nineteenth Assembly in 1939, Siam's delegate Phraya Rajawangsan highlighted the utility of the League in making Siam better known to the world by providing commercial and statistical information. He emphasised in particular the beneficial role which the League's economic and financial organisations could play for Siam's development and went as far as advocating the setup of a dedicated unit in Siam's Ministry of Finance exclusively for cooperation with the League in such matters.[44]

The degree of cooperation between Siam and the League of Nations was indeed remarkable, if one considers that the 1920s and 1930s were still dominated by imperialist ideologies and policies towards non-Western states and territories. But, at the same time, Siam was not comparable to a 'modern' European state with significant political, military or economic influence. After all, global multilateral politics were, during the interwar period, still largely European politics. There were, therefore, also a number of areas of League activities, in which Siam took little interest or had nothing to contribute. First and foremost, the League's core task, maintaining world peace through collective security, must be mentioned as the most prominent area in which Siam avoided involvement as much as it could. Economic reconstruction of Europe, the system of mandates for former colonial territories, or disarmament were also important League activities, in which Siam was not actively involved.[45] Equally, intellectual cooperation, the Nansen office for refugees, European minority problems, improvement of facilities for the blind, plans for an early European union and many other fields of work were developed, understandably, without Thai participation.[46] In the case of intellectual cooperation, League activities led the Ministry of Education to draw up a detailed memorandum on education and 'intellectual life' in Siam in 1923.[47] But when the League, two years later, enquired whether a national committee on intellectual cooperation could be created in Siam, the Foreign Ministry replied that '...in the existing circumstances in this country, the time is not yet opportune for establishing a national committee on intellectual cooperation which could be of value to Siam and other countries'.[48] Prince Charoon explained to Francis Walters of the League Secretariat that his government was also unable to send, as the League requested from all its members, copies of the most significant books published in Siam because, 'these are, even if some may be classed as notable, which they generally are not, almost entirely in the Siamese language, which is practically unknown outside this country'.[49]

Quite often Thai diplomats did participate in League meetings on specific subjects, for example in the conference on establishment of radio broadcasts to promote peace in September 1936, but no action or cooperation resulted from such participation.[50] This reflects a fact of life in international relations among states, namely that a state will

44 Because of the decline of the League's overall prestige and the war in Europe, the proposal was not taken up; see Report on the 19th Assembly of the League of Nations by Phraya Rajawangsan, 20 October B.E. 2481 (1939), TNA, KT 96.1.3/22.

45 On mandates see TNA, KT 96.1.12/1-14; on reconstruction see TNA, KT 96.1.8.3/1-10; on disarmament see TNA, KT 96.1.5/1-35. Siam did participate in the major disarmament conference of 1932-33.

46 On refugees see TNA, KT 96.1.13/1-17 and LNA, R 618/11/37076/34584; Thai delegates declined to participate in the 1936 and 1938 Geneva conferences on Jewish refugees from Germany, see LNA, R5759/50/23560/23011 and R 5793/50/32361/32217; on minorities see TNA, KT 96.1.14/1-16; on intellectual cooperation see TNA, KT 96.1.8/ various files; on plans for a European Union see TNA, KT 96.1/45 and 48; on lacking facilities for the blind in Siam in 1922 see LNA, R 1097/14/19471/11407.

47 Memorandum by Ministry of Education of 1923, enclosure in Prince Traidos to Drummond, 22 January 1924, LNA, R 1054/13C/34624/25987.

48 Prince Traidos to Drummond, 7 August 1925, LNA, R 1063/13C/46072/31595.

49 Prince Charoon (in Bangkok) to Walters, 17 August 1925, TNA, R7, T 10/12.

50 On the conference to consider a draft convention on broadcasting in the cause of peace see LNA, R 4041/15B/25487/22561.

only actively participate in those multilateral activities in which it has a specific interest or from which it expects a specific beneficial result. In this sense, Siam's diplomats and ministry officials by and large acted professionally and reasonably by gathering information, joining conferences and following discussions on specific initiatives, but then choosing to follow-up only in those areas in which Siam had a particular interest.

Siam's representatives at the League of Nations

By coincidence, two Thai kings resided closer to the seat of the League of Nations than any other head of a League of Nations member state. For most of the eighteen years between 1933 and 1951, King Ananda (proclaimed king in 1935, died in 1946) and his younger brother King Bhumibol (proclaimed king in 1946) lived and studied in Lausanne on Lake Geneva, only a short car journey from Geneva itself. Several years earlier, King Vajiravudh was also able to relate personally to Geneva when the League of Nations settled there in 1920, as he himself had spent part of the summer of 1897 there, during his time as a student in England.[51] His successor King Prajadhipok even visited Geneva and the League of Nations twice, once in 1921, some years before his coronation, and again in 1934, after already having left his kingdom for good.

While these royal connections to the League and to Geneva are of little more than passing interest, the professional diplomats officially representing Siam at the League during twenty-six years reflect the importance attributed to the world's first global international organisation by the political elite in Bangkok. Siam was represented at the League of Nations by its most senior diplomats. The post of Permanent Representative to the League was attached first to the post of Minister to Paris (1920-28), later to that of Minister to London (1928-40), and during the war years the Thai representative was not accredited to any other European capital.

For the first eight years, dominating virtually the whole first decade of Siam's presence at Geneva, the kingdom was represented by its most senior diplomat in Europe, the Minister in Paris, Prince (*Phra Ong Chao*) Charoonsakdi Kritakara.[52] Prince Charoon was born in 1875 as the eldest son of Prince (*Phra Ong Chao*) Nares Vorarit, a son of King Mongkut and half-brother of King Chulalongkorn, and himself Thai Minister to London during the 1880s. With this ancestry, Prince Charoon's place in Thai society was at the centre of power. In addition, his brothers, Prince (*Mom Chao*, 1929 *Phra Ong Chao*) Bovoradej and Prince (*Mom Chao*) Amoradat also counted among the most influential individuals in Siam before the Second World War, and Prince Charoon's brother-in-law, the commoner Khuang Aphaiwongse went on to become four-time Prime Minister during and after the Second World War. Prince

51 Greene, *Absolute Dreams*, p. 2.

52 Prince Charoon's credentials can be found in TNA, KT 96.1/2. See also Charoon to Drummond, 23 December 1920, LNA, R 583/12/6787/6787x.

Charoon was among the first generation of Thai royals to be educated abroad and obtained a degree from Cambridge University. He then began his career as assistant to the office of the foreign general adviser to the Thai government, which was effectively a training programme for junior diplomats, and as an official in the Ministry of Interior. He then returned to Europe for his first stint as Minister in Paris in 1906, before again transferring to Bangkok in 1909, where he became Minister of Justice in the following year. He then moved to Paris as Minister in place of his younger brother, Prince Bovoradej, once again in 1912, as a result of a power struggle over the Ministry of Justice in which he lost out to the more senior and powerful Prince (*Phra Ong Chao*) Svasti Sophon Vatanavisishtha.[53]

As we have seen in the previous chapter, together with Prince Traidos Prabhandh, Prince Charoon represented Siam at the Paris Peace Talks and signed the Treaty of Versailles. During the 1910s and 1920s, Prince Charoon was undoubtedly the most influential foreign policy maker in Siam besides the doyen of foreign affairs, Minister of Foreign Affairs Prince Devawongse himself. Prince Charoon was instrumental in all major foreign policy decisions and achievements of the kingdom during this period, including the entry into the First World War, the Paris Peace Talks and the signature of the Treaty of Versailles alongside the major Western powers, the negotiation of new treaties during the 1920s together with Francis Sayre, and bringing Siam into the new League of Nations as an original member. Prince Charoon also gained fame as the reactionary antagonist to Pridi Phanomyong, later Luang Pradist, and the Paris group of Thai students during the mid-1920s, whom the prince considered a danger to Thai society and who, indeed, later toppled the absolute monarchy in the coup of 1932.[54]

Prince Charoon can be seen as the prototype of the Western-educated Thai royal who combined an inherent sense of superiority as a member of the elite in Siam with an acquired sense of superiority of the British upper class. This combination made the ambitious and often arrogant prince feel at home and at ease on the diplomatic stage of Europe. Educated at Harrow and Cambridge, fluent in English and French, immaculately dressed, Prince Charoon was a very suitable representative of Siam at the European courts and republican capitals. But Prince Charoon also made negative headlines, both in Bangkok and in Europe, mainly because of dubious financial dealings, which led to substantial debts and which, according to Thawatt Mokarapong, were one of the reasons behind the serious clash between the prince and Thai students in France in 1926. Moreover, Prince Charoon was brought before a French court on adultery charges by the betrayed husband of a woman with whom the prince was allegedly having an affair.[55]

Prince Charoon represented Siam at the League's General Assemblies from 1920 to 1928, with the exception of 1925, the year

53 Much of this biographical information on Prince Charoon can be found in Greene, *Absolute Dreams*, p. 21ff., 55, 59f.

54 Prince Charoon's role regarding the revolutionary students in Paris has been widely studied and acknowledged. See, for example, Batson, *End of Absolute Monarchy*, p. 33, 79f., 181; Vichitvong, *Pridi*, p. 39ff.

55 Prince Charoon complained time and again to Bangkok about his shortage of funds; see, for example, TNA, KT 96.1.8.1/30. A dispute between the Ministries of Finance and Foreign Affairs over Prince Charoon's unsettled debts became public as late as October 1934, six years after his death; see TNA, *Bangkok Times*, 16 October 1934. On the clash between Prince Charoon and Pridi see Stowe, *Siam becomes Thailand*, p. 10; on the clash between Pridi and Prince Charoon as well as on the adultery charges see Thawatt Mokarapong, *History of the Thai Revolution: A Study in Political Behaviour*, Bangkok: Chalermnit, 1972, p. 78ff.

when he returned to Bangkok on home leave. During that year, Phraya Phraba Karawongse (Wong Bunnag), the Thai Minister to the Court of St. James, stood in for Prince Charoon at the General Assembly as well as at the Paris legation.[56] Upon his arrival in Bangkok in April 1925, the *Bangkok Times* commented, 'Prince Charoon has grown grey during his absence in Europe and is handicapped by deafness. He appeared glad to be back'.[57] After his return to Europe from Bangkok the following year, Prince Charoon's health seems to have further deteriorated, but his increasing deafness did not seem to impair his authority in Paris or Geneva. Prince Charoon passed away in Geneva on 5 October 1928 at the age of fifty-three, while he was yet again attending the League's General Assembly.[58] From the reactions to his demise, it becomes clear that after nearly ten years, he was considered something of an original character in the eyes of his colleagues at the League of Nations and 'belonged' to the diplomatic scene of Geneva. Lord Robert Cecil, long-time British delegate to the League, in a letter to the editor of the *Times* called the prince 'in the highest sense a gentleman' and went on to state that '[his] loss must be a great one to his country, and it is not inconsiderable in international affairs'.[59] Sir Eric Drummond, Secretary-General of the League, sent an outright eulogy to Bangkok, in which he explained that he had 'looked upon him [Prince Charoon] as a personal friend' and that 'it is difficult for me to express how deeply we feel his loss.' Sir Eric praised Prince Charoon's 'wise judgement…and, above all, his complete uprightness and disinterested impartiality' and crowned his letter with the statement: 'Few delegates from any nation have enjoyed, to the extent to which he enjoyed, the respect and affection of all other delegations'.[60] In accordance with diplomatic custom, Prince Traidos acknowledged the letter in equally grateful words. But we can read more than just platitudes from the 'great gratification to His Majesty and His Majesty's Government to learn from such an eminently distinguished authority as yourself that the duties performed by our late representative at the League of Nations are so highly appreciated'. Indeed, this gratification was certainly sincere with regard to the pivotal role Prince Charoon played for ten years in conveying Siam's modern and civilised image on the diplomatic stage of Geneva.[61]

The files at Geneva reveal that Prince Charoon also left his mark on international diplomacy in a somewhat unusual way when he pressed the young League of Nations twice in 1921 to exercise its authority in enforcing his immunity from Swiss law enforcement and a Swiss court. The first episode involved a speeding ticket, which Prince Charoon received when he was travelling by car together with Prince Prajadhipok and Prince Chula Chakrabongse in August and which was refunded to the prince after he created quite a stir at the League Secretariat. In the second episode his car was sequestered by Swiss authorities after a dispute with a repair shop over the cost of repairs. This matter dragged

56 Phraya Phraba Karawongse was formally accredited as Permanent Representative to the League from 21 January 1925 to 30 April 1926; see relevant correspondence and credentials in LNA, R 583/XII/6787/6787x and R 1389/26/45729x/44525.

57 TNA, *Bangkok Times*, 2 April 1925.

58 A notice of Prince Charoon's death and his cremation at Geneva on 8 October can be found in TNA, *Bangkok Times*, 5 November 1928. The funeral rites took place at Bangkok on 10 December of that year in presence of King Prajadhipok. Prince Charoon's death was the first instance of a delegate passing away during a General Assembly and left the Secretariat staff at loss over what the League of Nations should do in such a case; see Memorandum Texidor, 4 November 1928, LNA, S 571/3/1928.

59 *The Times*, 13 October 1928; see also TNA, *Bangkok Times*, 12 November 1928.

60 Drummond to Prince Traidos, 9 October 1928, TNA, KT 96.1/35 and LNA, R 3567/50/7728/1787.

61 Prince Traidos to Drummond, 22 December 1928, TNA, KT 96.1/35 and LNA, R 3567/50/7728/1787.

into the following year, found its way into Geneva newspapers and was eventually settled in favour of Prince Charoon, in order to avoid a major incident, after the prince went as far as to involve Secretary-General Drummond personally. The files suggest that both cases set precedents for later immunity cases dealt with by the League Secretariat and earned Prince Charoon the distinction of being the first diplomat bringing an international organisation into conflict with Swiss law enforcement authorities – a tradition which has since been followed by generations of diplomats from virtually every country.[62] But, in spite of these episodes, Prince Charoon did leave a lasting positive impression in Geneva. Remarkably, an account of the work of the League's Opium Advisory Committee, written three years after Prince Charoon's death, still mentioned him as one of the best known late members.[63]

Prince Charoon's death in 1928 led to a major reshuffle of senior Thai diplomats. Lieutenant-General Phraya Vichitvongse Vudhikrai (Mom Rajawongse Siddhi Sudasna), who had been Minister in Washington, succeeded Prince Charoon as Minister in Paris. The position of Permanent Delegate to the League of Nations was taken over from Prince Charoon by Prince (*Mom Chao*, 1939 *Phra Ong Chao*) Varnvaidya Voravarn, the Minister in London. Until 1928, the Minister in London had also been accredited to Brussels and The Hague, but the responsibility for these two capitals was now transferred to the Minister in Paris in turn. Prince Amoradat, a brother of Prince Charoon, became the new Thai Minister in Washington.

Prince Charoon's successor as Permanent Representative was perhaps the most prominent Thai diplomat of the twentieth century. During Prince Varn's short tenure until 1930, Siam played the most active and most visible role on the League's stage. While Prince Charoon represented the extremely moderate and quiet style of Thai foreign policy at Geneva, Prince Varn's appointment heralded a significant change towards a much more visible and outspoken presence. Prince Varn took the floor and spoke in plenary meetings of the General Assembly – unheard of behaviour during the tenure of Prince Charoon. Siam invited the League to hold its opium conference in Bangkok in 1931 – an unprecedented degree of interaction and involvement. The two years, during which Siam was represented by Prince Varn in Geneva, were characterised by the careful emancipation of Siam's multilateral foreign policy from the position of a passive onlooker with a sense of inferiority to that of an active member of the League, willing to take a stand and enter into commitments, as we will see in the following chapters. A British newspaper stated, for instance, that Prince Varn, who was fluent in English and French, made a strong impression with his speeches before the 1930 General Assembly and was 'met with quite an ovation'.[64] The speeches themselves were transmitted by *Reuters News Service* and reprinted in the *Bangkok Times*.[65] Prince Varn began by

62 Both cases, including newspaper clippings and correspondence from Swiss courts, are documented in LNA, R 1280/19/17564/17564 and R 1280/19/17668/17668.

63 Harold R.G. Greaves, *The League Committees and World Order*, London: Oxford University Press, 1931, p. 227.

64 TNA, *Bangkok Times*, 10 November 1930.

65 TNA, *Bangkok Times*, 3 November 1930.

stating, 'This is the first occasion on which the Siamese delegation has taken part in the general discussion of the Assembly. Silence does not, however, imply indifference'. He then went on to praise the work of the League and to point to the numerous fields of cooperation between Siam and Geneva, before explaining to the assembled representatives of fifty-three states that Siam was a haven of tranquillity and peace – *santisukh* in Thai, as he explained – because society was rooted in Buddhism; and that it was this love of peace which Siam shared with the League of Nations. Prince Varn closed by paraphrasing Immanuel Kant's perpetual peace in stating that 'with the advent of the League, peace is not merely a passive non-combatant state, it is a positive state of understanding and friendship. That is the spirit of my country, as it is the spirit of the League of Nations'.[66] But not only did Siam become better known in Geneva during Prince Varn's tenure, during these two years Prince Varn also actively participated in shaping the League itself to a degree unheard of previously or thereafter. Be it League finances, General Assembly procedures or structure of the League's Secretariat, there were few issues on which Prince Varn did not have a clear opinion and the desire to make it known.

Prince Varn was, although his and Prince Charoon's fathers were half-brothers and both sons of King Mongkut, sixteen years junior to Prince Charoon. Born in 1896, the second son of Prince Naradhip was educated at Marlborough College, Oxford University and the École Libre des Sciences Politiques in Paris. Combined with the privileged upbringing as *Mom Chao* in the upper echelons of Bangkok royalty, this prepared Prince Varn in an ideal way for a diplomatic career. During this career, which spanned six decades, Prince Varn showed an intriguing ability to stay in favour of those in power, be it under the absolute monarchy, pre-war constitutional governments, the dictatorial rule of Luang Phibun or the changing authoritarian regimes of post-Second World War Thailand. Ambitious, eloquent and intelligent, Prince Varn, who had been working under Prince Charoon at the Paris legation during the First World War and as Deputy Minister of Foreign Affairs in charge of the Department of the League of Nations from 1924 to 1926, was an excellent choice as successor to Prince Charoon at Geneva in 1928.[67] One year before he assumed his post as Thai Minister in London in 1926, he was described in an American consular report as 'undoubtedly one of the ablest Siamese of the younger generation'; at the same time, a British report characterised him as 'almost naively preoccupied with his personal advancement and well-being' and as 'suffering from a slight attack of swelled head'.[68] Prince Varn was one of the most vocal advocates of the League of Nations in Siam and had, at the time of his appointment, already some ten years diplomatic experience in Europe and Bangkok. While Prince Charoon had somehow naturally become the first Permanent Representative of Siam

66 LNA, League of Nations, *Official Journal, Special Supplement,* no. 84: Records of the Eleventh Ordinary Session of the Assembly, Plenary Meetings, Text of the Debates, p. 71f.

67 See Office of the National Culture Commission, *Centennial of Prince Wan.*

68 Memorandum by American Legation on Personnel in Thai Ministry of Foreign Affairs, 1925, TKRI, United States Department of State, Consular Reports Siam, 892.021/6, p. 3; Greg to Chamberlain, 3 December 1925, Doc. 217 (F 78/78/40), BDFA, Part II, Series E, vol. 49, p. 284ff., here p. 286. According to another British report, Prince Varn was appointed as Minister in London to remove him from Bangkok, as he was actively working to succeed Prince Traidos as Minister of Foreign Affairs; see Waterlow to Chamberlain, 4 October 1926, Doc. 230 (F 4726/ 3715/40), BDFA, Part II, Series E, vol. 49, p. 305f.

to the League of Nations because of his position, his seniority and his work during and immediately after the war years in Europe, Prince Varn planned to take up that office as a step in his career because of the prestige and international standing attached to it.[69]

Prince Varn temporarily fell into disgrace in 1930 because of an affair with Mom Proisubin Bunnag, who was the wife of Prince Amoradat, himself a brother of Prince Bovoradej and of the late Prince Charoon. To make things worse, she was also the sister-in-law of Prince Varn's superior, Minister of Foreign Affairs Prince Traidos. As a result of the scandal, Prince Varn was recalled to Bangkok and informed Sir Eric Drummond accordingly on 6 September 1930.[70] The *Bangkok Times* quoted an unnamed English newspaper which had run a rather peculiar report on the couple's departure from the British capital: 'Many of the Diplomatic Corps came to sympathise, among them the wife of the Brazilian Ambassador and her daughter, Mlle Silvia Regis de Oliviera, a typical dark South American beauty'.[71] Prince Varn spent the following year with academic work and, after June 1932, as editor of *The Nation* newspaper. As a supporter of Phraya Phahon Phonphayuhasena (Phot Phahonyothin), Prince Varn moved back into the centre of the political stage from mid-1933, when Phraya Phahon became the country's second Prime Minister. Prince Varn became adviser to the Ministry of Foreign Affairs, a position created specifically for him alongside that of the traditional foreign affairs adviser, which was held by a foreigner, because Prince Varn was banned from becoming a cabinet minister due to his princely rank of *Mom Chao* by the constitution of December 1932. Although formally subordinate to changing ministers, Prince Varn's influence on Siam's foreign policy during the following years can hardly be overrated, to the point of being Minister of Foreign Affairs in all but name. Foreign observers during these years often linked Prince Varn's experience and professional attitude to the 'training' he had received during his term as Permanent Representative at Geneva, but continued also to describe him as 'revengeful, unscrupulous and intriguing.'[72] Sir Josiah Crosby, the British Minister in Bangkok, called Prince Varn the 'Talleyrand of Siam'.[73] In late 1935, speculations arose in some Bangkok circles that Prince Varn was indeed planning to take up the post of Permanent Representative to the League of Nations once again. But he instead went on to further consolidate his influence on Thai foreign relations in Bangkok and was so successful, that he managed to lead foreign relations during the war years as *de facto* Minister of Foreign Affairs and represented Siam at the Greater East Asia Co-prosperity Sphere conference in Tokyo in November 1943. In spite of his close relations with Luang Phibun's military regime during the war years, after the end of the Second World War Prince Varn continued his distinguished career as Thai Ambassador to the United States and Permanent Representative to the United Nations from 1947, as Thai

69 Interestingly, this was stated clearly by the British Minister in Bangkok as early as 1926; see Waterlow to Chamberlain, 4 October 1926, Doc. 230 (F 4726/3715/40), BDFA, Part II, Series E, vol. 49, p. 306.

70 See various correspondence between Prince Varn and Drummond in September 1930 in TNA, KT 96.1/39 and in LNA, R 3396/17/15114/5376.

71 TNA, *Bangkok Times*, 24 November 1930.

72 Crosby to Simon, 12 September 1934, Doc. 130 (F 6014/21/40), BDFA, Part II, Series E, vol. 50, p. 152.

73 Sir Josiah Crosby, *Siam: The Crossroads*, London: Hollis & Carter, 1945 (Reprint New York: AMS Press, 1973), p. 109.

representative to the Bandung Conference in 1955 and, as something of a crowning achievement of his multilateral diplomatic career, as first Thai President to the eleventh United Nations General Assembly in 1956.

Prince Varn was succeeded at London and Geneva by Prince (*Mom Chao*) Damras Damrong Devakul from February 1931 until March 1933.[74] A son of Prince Devawongse, brother of Prince Traidos and half-brother of Prince Pridi, Prince Damras was also a career diplomat who had been posted in various European capitals during the 1920s, among them two stints as Minister to Berlin. As chargé d'affaires at The Hague in 1924-25, he took part in the two Geneva Opium Conferences. By the time he took over the appointments in London and Geneva, the prince was already 45 years of age, only slightly younger than his brother, the Minister of Foreign Affairs, and ranked among the most senior Thai diplomats. He was, however, not held in high regard during his roughly two years of office as Minister in London and Permanent Representative in Geneva by the Bangkok Ministry. In particular, it seems he had serious difficulties in controlling Thai students studying in Britain, and this inability led to his transfer to Washington D.C. in early 1933.[75] During the time of Prince Damras as Permanent Representative to the League of Nations a number of key events took place in the realm of Siam's relations with the League: first and foremost the Bangkok Opium Conference of November 1931 and the famous Thai abstention in the General Assembly vote to condemn Japan's actions in Manchuria in February 1933. As we will see in the respective chapters on opium control and collective security, the files reveal, however, that it was mainly Luang Bhadravadi, one of Prince Damras' diplomatic staff in London, who handled these matters. Moreover, the Bangkok Opium Conference of the League of Nations was initiated not by Prince Damras but already by his predecessor, Prince Varn. In fact, Prince Damras' view of the League was rather sceptical, even negative, as highlighted in his report on the 1931 General Assembly, in which he commented laconically: 'The deliberations seemed unimportant. Sometimes the discussions made no sense at all and, finally it was agreed to postpone discussions to the following year'.[76]

In August 1932, the Foreign Ministry in Bangkok requested the League of Nations to break with the procedure established twelve years earlier and to no longer send all correspondence to the London legation, but directly to Bangkok with only a copy to London, thereby further sidelining Prince Damras. That this decision was reversed in late November 1932 seems due solely to the high communication costs this entailed and, unfortunately for Prince Damras, not due to a revived standing of the Minister in London.[77]

When Prince Damras was transferred to Washington D.C. in spring 1933, he switched positions with another career diplomat, Phraya

74 Prince Damras' credentials can be found in TNA, KT 96.1/46 and in LNA, R 3562/50/8128/488.

75 Dormer to Foreign Office, 8 February 1933, PRO, FO 371/17177, F 1721/812/40.

76 Report of the 12th League of Nations General Assembly, dated 28 January B.E. 2474 (1932), TNA, KT 96.1.3/15 (Part 1 of 2).

77 Prince Damras to Drummond, 20 August 1932; Prince Damras to Drummond, 25 November 1932; both in LNA, R 3562/50/8128/488.

Subharn Sompati (Tin Bunnag). The Cambridge-educated Phraya Subharn, who had been Minister in Tokyo previous to his posting in Washington, took over the London legation, which also entailed responsibility for Germany, as well as the post of Permanent Representative to Geneva, from 1933 until his retirement from the diplomatic service in 1935.[78] His tenure may appear uneventful, because the period from mid-1933 to early 1935 was perhaps the quietest period in relations between Siam and the League. On the side of the League this reflected the paralysis which hit the organisation after the disastrous failure to prevent Japan's expansion on the Asian mainland. In addition, the economic, financial and disarmament activities, which were at the centre of the League's work during those two years, were not of paramount concern to Siam. On Siam's side, foreign policy was definitely playing a subordinate role during 1933 and 1934, particularly after the bloody revisionist coup attempt led by Prince Charoon's brother Bovoradej and the ensuing reformation of power relations among military and civilian groups in the government.

Siam's penultimate Permanent Representative to the League, Phraya Rajawangsan (Sri Kamolnawin), on the contrary, left much more of a mark at Geneva. Born in 1886 and a career navy officer trained in Britain, he had risen up the ranks to become navy chief of staff and a member of King Prajadhipok's privy council. With the rank of vice admiral and proficient in both English and French, he was a member of the Thai delegation to the 1932 League of Nations Disarmament Conference under Prince Pridi Debyabongse. For this assignment, Phraya Rajawangsan could even look back on prior experience with the League of Nations, as he had already, when attached to the Thai Legation in Paris, and holding the rank of navy captain, been a member of the Thai Delegation to the General Assembly ten years earlier, in 1922, and had co-authored the delegation's report with Prince Charoon.[79] From the coup against the absolute monarchy in June 1932 to the coup of the junior military group among the new regime against Prime Minister Phraya Manopakorn Nitthithada (Kon Hutasinha) and the more senior, civilian and conservative faction in June 1933, Phraya Rajawangsan was Minister of Defence. In early 1933, he was one of the cabinet members who were sympathetic towards the radical economic plan presented by Luang Pradist, which then led to the eruption of the conflict between the conservative and progressive factions. He was arrested together with the Prime Minister and Minister of Foreign Affairs Phraya Srivisarn Vacha (Tienliang Hoontrakul), but escaped punishment or exile by the intervention of his younger brother, Luang Sindhu Songkhramchai (Sin Kamolnawin), a prominent member of the People's Party and close associate of the emerging new strongman Luang Phibun, who was named navy chief of staff, his elder bother's former position, in 1933. Phraya Rajawangsan was then elegantly removed from the

78 Phraya Subharn's credentials can be found in TNA, KT 96.1/58 and in LNA, S 571/3/1928.

79 Report by the Siamese Delegation on the 1922 General Assembly of the League of Nations, dated 19 January B.E. 2465 (1923), TNA, KT 96.1.3/5.

domestic political scene in August 1933, when he was named special representative of the Ministry of Foreign Affairs to prepare the forthcoming visit of the king to Europe.[80] In the words of Cecil Dormer, the British Minister in Bangkok, Phraya Rajawangsan was 'not regarded as a man of strong personality', but 'enjoys confidence'; other contemporaries characterised him more positively and considered him to be highly intelligent.[81] Phraya Rajawangsan returned to Bangkok in February 1934, and it was widely expected that he would again be offered a ministerial post. But instead he was appointed Minister in Paris later that year and, in 1935, then became Siam's Minister in London and Permanent Representative to the League, two offices he held until he passed away in February 1940.[82] In fact, Phraya Rajawangsan was transferred from the Paris to the London Legation precisely in order to take over the Geneva post and to be able to draw on London staff experienced in dealing with League matters.[83] At Geneva, where he was officially accredited from August 1935, Phraya Rajawangsan made a more significant impact than his two predecessors, but his tenure was also marked by a stronger role of the Foreign Ministry in Bangkok, which repeatedly denied his requests to be allowed to speak at League committees on the grounds that such speeches 'would involve unnecessary commitments and no real advantage would be gained therefrom'.[84] The files of the Foreign Ministry in Bangkok further suggest that only from the 1936 General Assembly onwards did the Permanent Representative Phraya Rajawangsan receive detailed memoranda on Siam's policies on the different issues on the agenda, while during the fifteen years before the Permanent Representatives possessed a much greater degree of freedom in their actions.[85]

Finally, during the years of the Second World War, Prince (*Phra Ong Chao*) Chula Chakrabongse was formally accredited to the League.[86] Born in 1908, Prince Chula was a grandson of King Chulalongkorn, the son of the former heir-presumptive to the throne, Prince Chakrabongse Bhuvanath, who passed away prematurely in 1920, and a nephew of Kings Vajiravudh and Prajadhipok. Prince Chula's mother was Russian, and he himself married an English woman, Elisabeth Hunter, in 1938. Although he had been living in England since 1921, where he took up his studies at Harrow and later at Cambridge, Prince Chula became prominent and popular in Bangkok due to his position in the royal family, his philanthropic work, generous donations to improve higher education and medical services and his successes abroad as congenial team manager and financier of his cousin's motor racing career. As early as 1921, Prince Chula attended a working session of the League of Nations during a tour of Switzerland with his uncle Prajadhipok. In 1933, rumours surfaced in British reports that Prince Chula, who was only twenty-five years of age at the time, would be appointed regent when the king would leave for Europe and the United

80 TNA, *Bangkok Times*, 18 November 1933.

81 Dormer to Simon, 14 December 1932, PRO, FO 371/17174, F 399/42/40.

82 Phraya Rajawangsan's credentials can be found in TNA, KT 96.1/71 and in LNA, R 5642/50/176/120. His credentials had to be sent from Bangkok to Geneva twice because the first set of documents was destroyed when the KLM airplane from Southeast Asia to Europe crashed on 4 May 1935.

83 Minister of Foreign Affairs to Prime Minister, 7 May B.E. 2478 (1935), TNA, SR 0201.17/7 (Part 1 of 3).

84 Luang Pradist to Phraya Rajawangsan, 5 September 1938, TNA, KT 96.1.3/22.

85 See TNA, KT 96.1.3/20.

86 Prince Chula's credentials can be found in TNA, SR 0201.17/7 (Part 3 of 3). See also Luang Phibun to Secretary-General, 9 August 1940, LNA, R 5642/50/176/120.

States.[87] Although these rumours proved untrue, they underlined the prominence and popularity of the prince. When King Prajadhipok abdicated on 2 March 1935, Prince Chula, although eligible by rank and lineage, was deemed ineligible as successor because of his Russian mother, on the basis of the Palace Law of Succession of 1924. But the prince, whom Sir Josiah Crosby characterised positively as 'strong-minded' in 1936[88], remained popular and even enjoyed something akin to celebrity status when he visited Bangkok in late 1937 together with his motor-racing cousin Prince (*Phra Ong Chao*) Birabongse Bhanudej.[89]

Phraya Rajawangsan's death in February 1940 triggered a major reshuffle among Siam's diplomatic representatives; Phra Bahidda Nukara (Suan Navarasth) was to move from Paris to London, Luang Siri Rajamaitri (Charoon Singhaseni) was to move from Rome to Paris, and Phra Mitrakarm Raksha (Nattha Buranasiri) was to become new Minister in Rome. But then Luang Phibun decided that Phra Manuvej Waitayavitmonat (Pian Sumawong) was to become new Minister in London instead. To further complicate things, the government had, in parallel, already approached Prince Chula with an invitation to take up the position as Minister in London, to which the Prince replied affirmatively, but not without stating eleven preconditions, including the construction of a new legation building. This put the cabinet in a difficult position, as it was unwilling to accept Prince Chula's conditions but hesitated to state this openly to the prince because of his high royal rank of *Phra Ong Chao*. The delicate situation was discussed at a cabinet meeting on 27 March 1940 and a number of possible solutions were brought forward. The cabinet decided that Phra Manuvej should assume the post of Minister in London while Prince Chula was to be informed, upon suggestion by Luang Pradist, that his letter had, unfortunately, been received too late. Following a suggestion by Luang Vichit Vadhakarn, Prince Chula was offered the position of Permanent Representative to the League of Nations instead.[90] While this appointment was obviously designed as a consolation prize, it was nevertheless seen by cabinet members as a reasonable appointment because of the prestige which Prince Chula would bring to the office as a high-ranking member of the Thai royal family. Prince Chula was reluctant at first, citing his lack of experience and a number of other constraints, but eventually he accepted the appointment.[91] Of course, Prince Chula's appointment remained largely academic, as the League quickly slipped into hibernation when war spread across Europe. In fact, the prince did not attend a single League meeting.[92] After the Thai legation in London was closed and staff moved to Lisbon in early 1942, the League Secretariat also sent all correspondence for Prince Chula to the Portuguese capital, while the prince continued to reside in England, where he and his wife had moved from the capital to Cornwall after the Thai declaration of war on Britain. Prince Chula and his cousin Prince Bira both joined the

87 Dormer to Simon, 13 May 1933, Doc. 96 (F 4143/42/40), BDFA, Part II, Series E, vol. 50, p. 102f.

88 Crosby to Eden, 22 June 1936, Doc. 203 (F 4620/216/40), BDFA, Part II, Series E, vol. 50, p. 256f.

89 Crosby to Eden, 22 November 1937, Doc. 260 (F 10198/1494/40), BDFA, Part II, Series E, vol. 50, p. 345f. See also biographical information on Prince Chula in his memoirs Chula Chakrabongse, *The Twain Have Met, or An Eastern Prince came West*, 2nd ed., London: G.T. Foulis, 21957; and Eileen Hunter and Narisa Chakrabongse, *Katya and the Prince of Siam*, Bangkok: River Books, 1994. Prince Chula died of cancer in 1963.

90 Minutes of Cabinet Meeting on 27 March B.E. 2492 (1940), TNA, SR 0201.17/7 (Part 3 of 3).

91 See Prince Chula to Ministry of Foreign Affairs, 30 April B.E. 2483 (1940), Direck to Prime Minister, 26 June B.E. 2483 (1940), Memorandum by Ministry of Foreign Affairs entitled 'Duties of the delegate to the League of Nations', 5 April B.E. 2483 (1940), Cabinet Secretary to Ministry of Foreign Affairs, 11 July B.E. 2483 (1940), all in TNA, SR 0201.17/7 (Part 3 of 3). The League of Nations was informed by Luang Phibun to Secretary-General, 9 August 1940, LNA, R 5642/50/176/ 120.

92 Chula Chakrabongse, *The Twain Have Met*, p. 235.

British Home Guard in February 1942, and the position of Thai Permanent Representative to the League of Nations was all but meaningless. By early 1946, the Thai legation in Berne took over League of Nations matters briefly before the legation in London again began functioning in March of that year.[93]

The above mentioned seven Permanent Representatives to the League of Nations, were supported by various legation staff in Paris and London. During the tenure of Prince Charoon, Kimleang Vathanaprida, later Luang Vichit Vadhakarn, together with Tienliang Hoontrakul, handled League of Nations issues at the Paris Legation until 1925 and took part in the General Assemblies at Geneva five times during the League's initial years from 1921 to 1925. Luang Vichit entered the diplomatic service in 1918 and worked at the Paris legation from 1921. He later described his experience at the League during these years 'as akin to attending the most prestigious university in the world'.[94] After difficulties with Prince Charoon over Luang Vichit's contacts with Pridi Phanomyong (later Luang Pradist Manudharm) and Plaek Khittasangkha (later Luang Phibun Songkhram), he was transferred to the London legation in 1926; there he worked under Prince Varn until he was transferred back to Bangkok in mid-1927 and went on to become one of the most prominent and influential Thai politicians and ideologists by the late 1930s as a close collaborator of Prime Minister Luang Phibun.[95] Soon after the post of Permanent Representative to the League was shifted from Paris to London following Prince Charoon's death, the League of Nations section at the legation was headed by the man who was to become the single most experienced individual in League matters among Thai diplomats, Luang Bhadravadi. Born as Subhavarn Varasiri in 1904, Luang Bhadravadi had lived in Paris from the age of fifteen, attended school there and went on to study law at University of Poitiers, where he obtained his doctorate in 1929. Luang Bhadravadi entered the diplomatic service that same year and was put in charge of League of Nations matters at the London legation under Prince Varn. He was in charge under varying ministers for the League of Nations section for over ten years, from 1929 until the legation was closed in 1942. During these years, Luang Bhadravadi participated in ten regular General Assemblies as secretary of the Thai delegation as well as in the extraordinary General Assemblies in 1932-33, 1936 and 1937. It was Luang Bhadravadi who, in his function as substitute delegate, raised his hand to abstain from voting to condemn the Japanese invasion of Manchuria in February 1933, arguably the single most famous act of a Thai individual in Geneva. Luang Bhadravadi also represented Siam as substitute delegate on a number of committees and commissions as well as at a number of League-sponsored conferences during these ten years. Most importantly among these, he was substitute delegate to every meeting of the Opium Advisory Committee during

93 The many changes in communications during the war years between the League Secretariat and Thai diplomats in Europe are documented in LNA, R 4900/12/2649/2649.

94 Cited by Scot Barmé, *Luang Wichit Wathakan and the Creation of a Thai Identity*, Singapore: Institute of Southeast Asian Studies, 1993, p. 42.

95 Luang Vichit looked back on his time in charge of the League of Nations while in Paris with pride, and pointed to it also in his publication in 1941; see Vichit Vadhakarn, *Thailand's Case*, Bangkok: Thanom Punnahitananda, 1941. See also Barmé, *Wichit Wathakan*.

this decade and to the League's Disarmament Conference in 1932. When the League of Nations re-emerged briefly after the end of the Second World War only to hand itself over to the new United Nations, it was again Luang Bhadravadi who handled League matters in London in 1946. The following chapters will show that Luang Bhadravadi was, particularly during the tenures of Prince Damras and Phraya Subharn during the early 1930s, in fact the individual 'running the show' in the shadow of the more prominent Permanent Representatives.

Apart from the senior post of Permanent Representative to the League of Nations, the annual General Assembly of the League provided the most exciting and visible opportunity for Thai diplomats to participate in the League's work. Accordingly, the lists of Thai delegations to the annual League Assemblies, which have been reconstructed for this study, read like a who's who of Thai diplomacy and politics. These delegations, which were led by the Permanent Representatives, usually consisted of between five to ten people from the different legations across Europe. The General Assemblies were something of a multilateral diplomatic training for which a considerable number of senior and junior Thai diplomats assembled annually in autumn on the shores of Lake Geneva. Accordingly, the reports submitted by Siam's Delegations to the General Assemblies to the Ministry of Foreign Affairs in Bangkok are very rich sources for a historian of diplomacy.[96]

The first Assemblies were attended by the 'old guard' of Thai diplomacy; led, of course, by Prince Charoon. Among the early delegates were Phraya Buri Navarasth and the illustrious Phraya Bibadh Kosha, who was born as Celestino Xavier to a Portuguese father who had come to Siam as an adviser and translator for King Mongkut, and whose career had spanned several decades by the time he passed away in late 1922. In fact, as the *Bangkok Times* recollected, he had been in the diplomatic service nearly as long as Prince Devawongse himself.[97] Phraya Bibadh attended the first three General Assemblies in his function as Minister in Rome and, as a frail man in 1921, it would have comforted him to be able to accredit three of his daughters to the League Assembly as delegation secretaries. The following year, Phraya Bibadh, now merely accompanied by one daughter to the General Assembly, passed away at the end of October 1922. Prince Chula Chakrabongse, who seems not to have been on particularly good terms with these three senior officials, visited the League in 1921 when he was a child of thirteen years, and much later remarked in his memoirs, 'At the time we had three delegates [Prince Charoon, Phraya Buri, and Phraya Bibadh] amongst whom one was deaf, one had a bad throat and could hardly speak, while the third was tortured with perpetual headaches'.[98]

Later members of Thai delegations to the General Assemblies included, for example, Phra Sarasasna Balakhand, who was a member

96 The reports on the General Assemblies from 1920 to 1938 are filed in TNA, KT 96.1.3/1 to 23.

97 TNA, *Bangkok Times*, 11 November 1922. Among Phraya Bibadh's daughters, one married the Thai Minister to Copenhagen, Phraya Visarn Bonchakich (Sudchai Toechasut), and one married Phraya Srivisarn Vacha, the later Minister of Foreign Affairs.

98 Chula Chakrabongse, *The Twain Have Met*, p. 123.

of the delegation in 1923, at an early stage of his unusual vita. Phra Sarasasna spent most of the 1920s in diplomatic service in Europe before becoming Thai Consul in Calcutta, where he won the Calcutta sweepstakes in 1928 and retired from the diplomatic service. After returning to Bangkok, he began writing pro-Japanese propaganda and went on to become Minister of Economics. In the words of Sir Josiah Crosby 'the impetuous and unintelligent' Phra Sarasasna later fled from office in 1934 to Japan and Manchukuo and became a radical propagandist for fascist Japanese policies.[99] Another prominent delegation member in 1930 and 1931 was Phraya Abhibal Rajamaitri (Tom Bunnag), then Minister in Rome, who went on to become Minister of Foreign Affairs in 1933-34.

The career of Tienliang Hoontrakul was also closely connected to the League of Nations. Born 1893 into a family of Chinese origin, the junior diplomat was posted at the legations in Paris and London from the end of the First World War. As staff of the Paris legation, he was a member of the Thai Delegation to the League's General Assemblies from 1921 to 1923 and was in charge of League matters at the legation together with Kimleang Vathanaprida, before returning to Bangkok in 1925. Elevated to Phraya Srivisarn Vacha in 1927, he was then appointed Deputy Minister of Foreign Affairs in 1928, a position he held until June 1932. Phraya Srivisarn's connection with the League was highlighted prominently when he acted as President of the landmark League of Nations' International Opium Conference in Bangkok in 1931. According to the British Minister, Cecil Dormer, 'he won golden opinions from the foreign delegates' in this position.[100] As a conservative representative of the old regime, the Oxford-educated Phraya Srivisarn was not actively involved in the 1932 coup, supposedly even acquiring a British passport as a precaution in case fighting broke out in Siam. He was appointed Minister of Foreign Affairs in December 1932 on account of his professional abilities rather than for holding progressive political views. Just before the coup, it had been Phraya Srivisarn who was, together with the Foreign Affairs Adviser Raymond Stevens, entrusted by King Prajadhipok with the drafting of a constitution. Phraya Srivisarn held the post of Minister of Foreign Affairs for only a few months, until the end of the Manopakorn government in June 1933, and during this period also took far-reaching decisions with regard to Siam's abstention at the League of Nations over the Manchurian Conflict. The royalist Phraya Srivisarn managed to stay at the centre of power during most of the decades until his death in 1968, with his official appointments including Minister of Finance, a second stint as Minister of Foreign Affairs, Privy Councillor and as late as the 1960s, under the regime of Field Marshal Sarit Thanarat, head of the National Security Council.

Besides diplomats accredited to the League, an array of prominent individuals also attended League proceedings or paid visits to the

99 Crosby to Simon, 27 September 1934, Doc. 133 (F 6034/21/40), BDFA, Part II, Series E, vol. 50, p. 157f. See in detail also Benjamin A. Batson, 'Phra Sarasas: Rebel with Many Causes', *Journal of Southeast Asian Studies*, 27, 1 (1996), pp. 150-165.

100 Dormer to Simon, 14 December 1932, PRO, FO 371/17174, F 399/42/40. See also Johns to Simon, 30 June 1932, Doc. 64 (F 5920/4260/40), BDFA, Part II, Series E, vol. 50, p. 61ff.

League's headquarters over the years. As mentioned above, in 1921, four years prior to his coronation, Prince Prajadhipok, who was in Europe for medical treatment, attended a League of Nations meeting in Geneva together with Prince Chula Chakrabongse during a tour of Switzerland. During his private trip through Europe in the summer of 1930, the iconic Prince (*Phra Ong Chao*) Damrong Rajanubhab, long-time Minister of Interior, scholar and undoubtedly one of the most influential persons in modern Siam, visited the seat of the League of Nations, while en route to Rome, where he was received by the pope.[101] In September of the same year, Francis Sayre, who had been conferred the title Phraya Kalayana Maitri for his contribution to revising Siam's unequal treaties in the mid-1920s, attended a session of the League's General Assembly.[102] Four years later, in late August 1934, King Prajadhipok once again visited Geneva on his way to England, from where he would not return to his kingdom.[103] During his tour of Europe, Luang Pradist, who was Minister of Interior at the time, attended the deliberations of the League of Nations on 20 September 1935 together with Phraya Rajawangsan and Colonel Phra Riem Virajapak (Riem Tanthanon), the Thai Ministers in London and Paris respectively.[104]

In 1928, Prince (*Mom Chao*) Sakol Varnakorn Voravarn, half-brother of Prince Varn and the key figure in public health development in Siam during the League of Nations period, visited the League Secretariat while in Europe.[105] During his visit, he met with some of the leading League experts in public health and communications, among them Ludvik Rajchman, head of the League's Health Organisation for nearly two decades and later one of the founding fathers of UNICEF, and Robert Haas, head of the Communications and Transit Organisation. We can assume that the visit strengthened Prince Sakol's determination to work closer with the League during the 1930s on a range of issues from public health through human trafficking to port and waterway development. Indeed, together with his half-brother Prince Varn, Prince Sakol became one of the foremost champions of the League of Nations among the Thai elite.

Siam and the League Secretariat

The international Secretariat of the League at Geneva, the first experiment in international administration, employed one Thai national.[106] Supported by the Ministry of Foreign Affairs in Bangkok, Mani Sanasen joined the Treasury Section of the League's administration in 1925 and worked for the League for the following fifteen years until 1940. Born in Bangkok in 1898, Mani came to Europe with his family as early as 1903. His father Phraya Visut Kosha (Phak Sanasen) was a career diplomat, had been Minister in London in 1902-03 and was, when Mani was brought to Europe, appointed Thai Minister to Germany. When his father was then transferred to once

101 TNA, *Bangkok Times*, 20 September 1930; *The Times*, 27 June 1930.

102 Report on the 11th General Assembly by Prince Varn and Phraya Abhibal Rajamaitri, 5 October 1930, TNA, KT 96.1.3/14 (Part 1 of 2).

103 TNA, *Bangkok Times*, 29 August 1934. During his extensive tour, King Prajadhipok had also met with Adolf Hitler in late July and stopped in Geneva while en route to Paris.

104 TNA, *Bangkok Times*, 3 October 1935.

105 TNA, *Bangkok Times*, 4 February 1929.

106 On the League Secretariat see Egon Ferdinand Ranshofen-Wertheimer, *The International Secretariat: A Great Experiment in International Administration*, Studies in the Administration of International Law and Organization, vol. 3, Washington D.C.: Carnegie Endowment for International Peace, 1945; Frank C. Boudreau, 'International Civil Service', in Harriet E. Davis (ed.), *Pioneers in World Order: An American Appraisal of the League of Nations*, 2nd ed., New York: Columbia University Press, 1945, pp. 76-85.

again head the London legation in 1906 the family settled in England. Mani enrolled in English schools and in 1917, entered Trinity College at Oxford, where he studied modern history and went on to obtain a law degree in 1924. Having spent virtually all his life in Europe, Mani spoke English fluently and had knowledge of other European languages; he was a typical non-royal member of the very internationally-oriented Thai elite during the first decades of the twentieth century and an ideal candidate for a position in the League Secretariat.

Herbert B. Ames, Director of the Secretariat's Treasury Section, approached Prince Charoon in the late summer of 1924 and asked whether he could recommend a junior compatriot for a newly to-be-created position in his section, after having agreed with Secretary-General Drummond to do so. The prince suggested Mani and, after a first meeting between Ames and Mani in early November 1924, the former was 'very favourably impressed'; Ames judged Mani to be 'intelligent, bright and quick', and he trusted Prince Charoon's assurance that Mani's 'moral qualifications – which are particularly important in this department [i.e. the Treasury Section] – are of as high a standard as his mental qualities'.[107]

Mani Sanasen became an international civil servant in Geneva on 5 January 1925 at the age of twenty-seven. His initial internal assessment reports during his first two years were not all positive, as he was seen to be 'suffering from a slight natural timidity in his relations with officials'. However, Mani was showing the desire to improve himself and seems to have done so quickly; another internal assessment declared, 'It would be difficult to find a more charming and more popular man'.[108] Thereafter, all successive assessments were entirely satisfactory. Mani handled a number of different financial matters of the League as well as member states' contributions. This was a very fitting task for the young Thai, as his mother country was one of the few League members with a spotless record in this regard. By all accounts Mani's work seems to have been appreciated by his superiors, and when his first seven-year contract expired, he was offered a new regular contract for another seven years. During his fifteen years of international service at Geneva, Mani's annual salary increased from 13,700 Swiss francs in 1925 to 24,900 Swiss francs in 1939.

To put Mani's employment by the secretariat into perspective, one must, however, point to the fact that by 1929 the secretariat had a total of 630 employees, of which Mani was the only Thai national. In comparison, by the late 1920s, 143 British nationals were working at the secretariat. On the other hand, as a memorandum of the Thai Ministry of Foreign Affairs showed in 1936, some thirteen non-European League members had no national on the secretariat staff at all and Francis Walters also pointed out that '[o]ver a quarter of the Members were never able to have the satisfaction of seeing a single one of their nationals

107 Memorandum Ames, 4 November 1924, Personnel File Mani Sanasen, LNA, S 874.

108 Internal Assessment Reports, Personnel File Mani Sanasen, LNA, S 874.

appointed to a post in the Secretariat'.[109] Generally it can be said that Asian member states, with the exception, perhaps, of Japan, were underrepresented, particularly when put into a wider context. According to the scholar of the League Secretariat, Egon Ranshofen-Wertheimer, Japan, China and Siam jointly contributed some twelve percent of the League budget. And while it seems true that these countries were able to provide only a small number of qualified candidates, 'taken as a whole, the number of officials from these countries corresponded neither to the political, cultural, or economic importance of these regions nor to the size of their populations'.[110]

During his years with the League, Mani proved not only to be a good administrator but also a valuable liaison person between the League and Bangkok. Unofficially, Mani provided the secretariat and various League bodies with information on Siam and explained titles, names, weights, measures, currency, etc.[111] On the occasion of the 1931 Bangkok Opium Conference, Mani travelled to Siam to participate in the conference in his function as an official of the League Secretariat.[112] Mani informally also provided important information to the Thai Permanent Representatives to the League, for example during the tense and hectic times of applying sanctions against Italy in 1935.[113] And Mani even attracted media interest when he came to Bangkok on leave in early 1927; under the header 'Siam and the League of Nations' the *Bangkok Times* informed its readers, 'It may not be generally known that the staff of the Secretariat of the League of Nations at Geneva has for some little time included a Siamese, Nai Mani Sanasen having been seconded from his duties in the Ministry of Foreign Affairs for this particular work'.[114]

By the end of 1939, the League Secretariat was in dissolution in the face of war on the European continent and all sections were drastically downsized as there was virtually no more work to be done. Among those officials asked to resign was Mani Sanasen but Prime Minister Luang Phibun, who was also holding the foreign affairs portfolio at the time, intervened. In a letter to the Secretary-General, which was diplomatically phrased but strong in its message, he urged that Mani be retained. Ultimately, this intervention only managed to postpone the request for Mani's resignation and in the summer of that year Mani suffered the same fate as nearly all League Secretariat employees; he tendered his resignation on 7 July 1940.[115]

Mani returned to his old home in London, while the remaining small core secretariat was evacuated to Princeton, New Jersey. He then planned to return to Bangkok to work for the ministry but was instructed while en route to Bangkok via the United States by the Thai Minister, Seni Pramoj to stay in Washington and support him at the legation. Mani stayed in Washington until April 1942, when he returned to London to become liaison officer between Seni Pramoj and the Free Thai Movement in England, as he knew a number of British officials

109 The same memorandum also pointed out that other League members which paid the same 6 units in annual contribution also had only one (Cuba) or two (Portugal) nationals working at the League Secretariat; see Memorandum by Ministry of Foreign Affairs, 17 December B.E. 2479 (1936), TNA, KT 96.1/73. For the quotation by Walters see Walters, *League of Nations*, p. 131.

110 Ranshofen-Wertheimer, *Great Experiment*, p. 360. By the late 1920s, five Japanese nationals were working at the Secretariat, all of whom held rather high positions.

111 See, for example, files in LNA, R 741/12A/19026/18661 or R 5642/50/176/120.

112 See TNA, *Bangkok Times*, 3 and 5 November 1931.

113 The files show that Mani and Phraya Rajawangsan discussed the possibility of Siam exempting ships ordered by the Thai navy in Italy from the sanctions; see Phraya Rajawangsan to Phraya Srisena, 23 October 1935, TNA, KT 96.1.6.1/8. See also chapter 6 for further details on sanctions and exempted navy contracts.

114 TNA, *Bangkok Times*, 28 January 1927.

115 Luang Phibun to Secretary-General, 22 January 1940, Personnel File Mani Sanasen, LNA, S 874.

from his work in Geneva and his time in London. According to John Hasemann, Mani, together with Sanoh Tanboonyuen, then directed the Free Thai movement in England.[116] In 1944 Mani returned to Bangkok, but after the end of the war again travelled to Washington, where he briefly worked once more at the Thai legation, before finally moving back to Geneva, where he joined or, in a sense, rejoined the Secretariat of the new United Nations until his retirement, and where he lived until his death in 1978. Mani Sanasen was the first international civil servant from Thailand and began a tradition which led, in 2002, to Supachai Panitchpakdi becoming the first Director-General of the World Trade Organisation from a developing country and, since 2005, Secretary-General of the United Nations Conference on Trade and Development (UNCTAD).

Very nearly a second Thai person could have worked at the League's secretariat, albeit only as an intern. Mani informed Prince Damras of this possibility in spring 1931, explaining that such an appointment would be within the Secretariat's Information Section and that the cost would have to be shared between the member government and the League. Prince Damras suggested nominating a Thai student on his way back to Bangkok after completion of his studies in Europe, and the matter was supported by the Ministry of Foreign Affairs in Bangkok, which also approached the Ministry of Education in this regard. But the officials involved doubted that the qualifications of the available candidates would meet the requirements of the League. The three candidates the Ministry of Education had in mind were Mom Luang Pin Malakul, Chai Unipan, and Mom Luang Manich Jumsai. In the end, the initiative resulted in nothing and no candidates were put forward to the League.[117]

In 1936-37, another chance arose for a second Thai on the secretariat staff when the League announced a vacancy in the secretariat's Social Section. Minister of Foreign Affairs Luang Pradist encouraged Luang Bhadravadi to apply for the position.[118] The Foreign Ministry in Bangkok was particularly keen to have a Thai national in the Social Section or the Opium Section of the League Secretariat because those sections were in charge of matters, as we will see in the following chapters, which were particularly relevant for Siam.[119] Phraya Rajawangsan, the Permanent Representative, also supported Luang Bhadravadi's application in a letter to the League's Secretary-General, but the position was ultimately filled by another candidate and Mani Sanasen remained the only Thai person to ever work in the League Secretariat.[120]

The question of League Council membership

During the twenty-six years of the League's existence, Siam was never a member of the League Council, the executive body of the General Assembly. This absence of Siam from the Council was primarily an

116 John B. Hasemann, *The Thai Resistance Movement During the Second World War*, Bangkok: Chalermnit, n.d., p. 34. See on biographical details and Mani's role in England during the war also Puey Ungphakorn, 'Temporary Soldier', in Thak Chaloemtiarana (ed.), *Thai Politics, Extracts and Documents, 1932-1957*, Bangkok: Social Science Association of Thailand, 1978, p. 407ff.

117 See all correspondence regarding this matter in TNA, KT 96.1/52.

118 The League's vacancy notice of 14 November 1936 and Luang Pradist to Phraya Rajawangsan, 29 December B.E. 2479 (1936), TNA, KT 96.1/73.

119 Memorandum by Prince Varn, 28 December B.E. 2479 (1936), TNA, KT 96.1/73.

120 Phraya Rajawangsan to Secretary-General, 19 January 1937 and application by Luang Bhadravadi, same date, TNA, KT 96.1/73. The letter of the League Secretariat's Director of Personnel and International Administration to Phraya Rajawangsan, informing that Luang Bhadravadi had not been selected, dated 29 July 1937, can also be found in TNA, KT 96.1/73.

expression of the kingdom's policy of neutrality in international conflicts and its general reluctance to take on responsibilities in potentially controversial security issues. The League Council was made up, similar to today's UN Security Council, of permanent and non-permanent members. Britain, France, Italy, Japan, and, from 1926, Germany were permanent members. They were joined by four and from 1922 by six non-permanent members. Although not formalised, it was widely accepted that the composition of non-permanent members should follow geographical divisions. In 1926, when Germany joined the League and was granted a permanent seat on the Council, the number of non-permanent seats was increased from six to nine and one seat was still considered to be earmarked for a second Asian member besides Japan.[121] During the 1926 process of Council reform, Siam took a clear position; in coordination with the government in Bangkok, Prince Charoon wrote to the League that 'Asia does not now have sufficient voice in the Council having regard to its vast populations and the growing importance of its relations with the rest of the world.' He pointed out that the 'fact that several European permanent members have large territories and interests in Asia makes it all more essential that the views of the independent Asiatic peoples should be given greater weight'.[122] Siam stood a good chance to be elected, and Prince Charoon lobbied strongly to obtain the agreement from Bangkok for such a candidature. In Bangkok, Siam's desire for a non-permanent Council seat even made the newspapers, but King Prajadhipok decided that Siam should not stand for election to the Council, as it would be too awkward a position in case there was disagreement between Britain and France and Siam would be forced to take sides.[123] Prince Charoon accepted the instructions but reported bitterly to Bangkok that he was even unable to give any reason to his colleagues as to why Siam was not standing for election, particularly since the unequal treaties had just been revised and Siam now enjoyed nearly full sovereignty.[124] This response from Paris motivated Prince Traidos to write a detailed letter to Prince Charoon on 22 September 1926, in which he laid out the rationale behind the refusal to stand for election. He explained that the French Minister in Bangkok had signalled France's support for a candidature during an informal discussion with Prince Traidos and Prince Varn. The Minister had pointed out that if Siam were a Council member, this could boost its support for France's anti-communist policies in Asia. The two American advisers on foreign policy, Francis B. Sayre and Raymond B. Stevens, were also consulted by Prince Traidos and they also supported Siam's candidature. But, ultimately, Prince Traidos felt that the disadvantages outweighed the benefits of a Council membership. He had no illusion about French support and pointed out that it was mainly motivated by the conviction that Siam would follow the French lead in Council decisions. This would inevitably lead to frictions with

121 From its entry in 1934 to its expulsion in 1939, the Soviet Union was the sixth permanent Council member. For a very comprehensive memorandum on Council composition, changes, elections procedures, regional groupings, and members for the period 1920 to 1936 see the document drawn up by the General Assembly's Committee on the Composition of the Council, 20 April 1936, LNA, R 5213/14/35649/13477.

122 Prince Charoon to Drummond, 4 June 1926, LNA, R1441/27/50909/50424.

123 Prince Traidos to Prince Charoon, 6 August 1926, TNA, KT 96.1/33. See also a cutting from the *Bangkok Times* of 21 April 1926, TNA, KT 96.1/33.

124 Prince Charoon to Prince Traidos, 3 September 1926, TNA, KT 96.1/33.

Britain and put Siam in an undesirable position, as it was not strong enough in economic and military terms to take independent decisions on the Council. Apart from the issue of relations with European colonial states, Prince Traidos also saw potential difficulties arising from the fact that disagreements with China on the Council could have domestic repercussions among the Chinese population in Siam.[125]

Siam received one or two votes on a number of occasions in the annually recurring elections of non-permanent Council members, but was only once determined to actively stand for election, when China's term as a non-permanent member ended in 1928 and Persia and Siam were eligible successors to the 'Asian' seat.[126] As it was widely expected that Persia would not stand for election, Prince Varn and Prince Charoon already received indications from a number of delegations during the 1927 General Assembly that Siam should take over China's Council seat in the following year. Prince Charoon and Prince Varn sent a joint memorandum to Bangkok in October 1927, in which they pushed for a candidature and expressed their belief that 'there seems to be very little doubt that Siam's candidature next year will be successful, for Siam, with her complete sovereignty, will be preferred to Persia.' The princes set out the reasons for a non-permanent Council membership in this memorandum. Apart from the obvious gain in prestige for Siam, they explained that Council membership would allow Siam to establish contacts with leading statesmen in Europe, which 'would be a great asset for future settlement of important questions with foreign Powers.' At the same time, the princes acknowledged that the reservations of 1926 still held true and that Siam could 'contribute nothing of real use' to the Council.[127] In Bangkok, Foreign Affairs Adviser Stevens agreed with the two princes that the rivalry between Britain and France was no longer a serious impediment for a candidature and summarised:

> There would be a distinct advantage to Siam in the election to the Council. Siam at present is little known to the world at large. In view of her rapid progress and her liberal and successful Government, she is entitled to wider recognition. No form of recognition would be more valuable or confer more prestige than election to the League Council...It seems, therefore, that His Majesty's Government...might wisely, at this time, decide to be a candidate.[128]

Meanwhile in Europe, Prince Charoon intensified the lobbying and hosted a lunch in honour of the Council president and a number of Council members in February 1928, during which the Council president V. K. Wellington Koo, the Chinese Minister in Paris pledged his support and vowed to try and secure Japan's support for Siam's candidature. Prince Charoon had high hopes during these months that the candidature would be successful, 'If success can be obtained it will be a fitting climax to our having obtained autonomy, it is a sort of decoration

125 Prince Traidos to Prince Charoon, 22 September 1926, TNA, KT 96.1/33.

126 The election history of Siam for a non-permanent seat on the League Council was as follows: Assembly of 1920: 0 votes; 1921: 0; 1922: 1; 1923: 0; 1924: 2; 1925: 2; 1926: 2; 1927: 1; 1928: 6. See George Ottlick (ed.), *Annuaire de la Société des Nations, 1920-1939*, Geneva: Editions de l'Annuaire de la Société des Nations, 1920-1939.

127 Confidential Memorandum by Prince Charoon and Prince Varn, 5 October 1927, TNA, KT 96.1/33.

128 Memorandum Stevens, 17 January 1928, TNA, KT 96.1/33.

bestowed on a country – a honorific one it is true, but greatly [enhancing] the prestige of the country's public point of view'.[129] In March, the king and the cabinet council agreed that Siam should declare its candidature for the League Council, a momentous step indeed, as a successful candidature was certain to entail involvement in international disputes, responsibility for their settlement, and numerous further international commitments which could not be anticipated. The decision to stand for election to the Council in 1928 can, therefore, be seen as a significant step away from the traditional Thai policy of international neutrality, a step triggered by the wish to increase Siam's international recognition and prestige during a time when the League of Nations was itself at its height of prestige and success.[130]

Prince Charoon made it clear that he would, in the event of Siam's election, only ceremonially attend the first Council session and then hand over to Prince Varn on account of his deteriorating health and deafness. For Siam's frail and ageing senior diplomat the attendance of a session of the League Council as a full member would, without doubt, have marked the pinnacle of his professional career.

But there was a problem. Against earlier expectations, Persia was also interested in being elected to the Council. Both countries' delegations therefore began lobbying big and small League members.[131] Prince Charoon and Prince Varn hosted a number of lunches at Geneva, London and Paris for this purpose, but support from key members such as Britain, France, the Netherlands or Spain seemed half-hearted. In parallel, both princes competed to position themselves in the event that Siam would actually be elected as Council member. While Prince Charoon proposed to the Ministry of Foreign Affairs in Bangkok the creation of a new position of Minister to the League of Nations with a seat at Geneva in the event of Siam's election, a posting which he 'himself would be willing to take', Prince Varn suggested that he take over the position of Permanent Representative to the League as Minister in London from Prince Charoon in Paris. But while Prince Varn was already debating benefits and drawbacks of this or that secretary for his assignment on the League Council with the Ministry in Bangkok, it transpired that Siam would be unable to rally the necessary support during the summer of 1928 and would lose out to Persia. In particular, Persia was able to secure votes of the South and Central American League members, which gave it the clear advantage over Siam. When the General Assembly met in September, the situation was so bleak that Siam even dropped its candidature, as it was sure to lose. Persia made the race for the 'Asian' seat with forty votes, while Siam still received six votes, in spite of not officially standing for election.[132] Although Siam lost out to Persia, it was never as close to becoming a Council member as in 1928. In a dramatic coincidence, the health of Prince Charoon, who had dreamt of representing his country on the Council for many years,

129 Prince Charoon to Prince Traidos, 21 February 1928, TNA, KT 96.1/33.

130 See on the decision to stand for election also Prince Traidos to Prince Charoon, 13 March 1928, and Prince Traidos to Prince Charoon, 24 March 1928, TNA, KT 96.1/33.

131 Prince Charoon to Prince Traidos, 16 May B.E. 2481 (1928), TNA, KT 96.1/33.

132 See Prince Varn to Prince Traidos, 11 September 1928, TNA, KT 96.1/33; Report on the 9th Assembly by the Siamese Delegation, TNA, KT 96.1.3/11; see also Report on the 9th Assembly of the League of Nations, 26 November 1928 Doc. 19 (W 11286/8660/98), BDFA, Part II, Series J, vol. 1, p. 70; Prince Varn to Prince Traidos, 11 September 1928, TNA, KT 96.1/33.

worsened during the days of the Assembly and he passed away three weeks after Persia, and not Siam, was elected to the Council.

After the failed candidature in 1928, Council membership was never again an issue for the makers of foreign policy in Bangkok. Siam generally supported Asian candidates during the following years, in spite of repeated lobbying by other states, such as Ireland in 1929 and 1930.[133] Thai officials did not even stand for election in 1934-35 when the Council was for the first time in fifteen years without a Far Eastern member state and chances for a candidature would have been excellent. In his instructions to Phraya Subharn, Minister of Foreign Affairs Phraya Abhibal referred cryptically to 'certain political reasons in the East' as the reason for not standing for election, but it can safely be assumed that in the aftermath of the Manchurian Conflict any intentions in Bangkok of becoming a Council member had been spoiled for good.[134] In fact, nearly sixty years passed before Thailand first sat on the Council, by then of course the United Nations Security Council, as a non-permanent member during the 1985-86 term.

Siam's financial contribution to the League of Nations

Membership in the League of Nations entailed a serious financial commitment for Siam. The League, as the United Nations today, funded its operations as well as its administration largely by raising annual contributions from its members. The contribution of each League member was based on a key developed by the Universal Postal Union, which was annually adjusted according to the budgetary needs of the organisation and fluctuations in its membership structure.[135] According to this key, Siam contributed between three and ten out of between 500 and 1,000 units to the budget of the League of Nations and the International Labour Organisation. In general terms, Siam's financial contribution to the League gradually increased during the 1920s as the League assumed more and more tasks and grew into a fully-fledged international organisation; the funds annually transferred from Bangkok to Geneva then gradually decreased during the 1930s as a result of the League losing important members and having to scale down some of its operations, while the government in Bangkok simultaneously pressed for reductions. In absolute terms, Siam's contribution peaked in 1932, when the kingdom contributed nearly 300,000 Swiss francs to the League.[136] The year 1929 may serve as an example to put Siam's contributions into perspective. In that year, the total League budget was around US$5.2 million, or £1.0 million. The budget was divided into 986 units of US$5,289, or £1,086. Great Britain was the largest contributor with 105 units, followed by France and Germany with seventy-nine units each and Italy and Japan with sixty units each. The ten largest contributors were completed by India, China, Spain and Canada.[137] At the opposite end of the scale were twenty-five League members who contributed between

133 See on the efforts of Ireland to secure Thai support Prince Varn to Prince Devawongse, 6 February B.E. 2482 (1929), TNA, KT 96.1/33; see also Michael Kennedy, *Ireland and the League of Nations, 1919-1946: International Relations, Diplomacy and Politics*, Dublin: Irish Academic Press, 1996, p. 139f.

134 For relevant correspondence between Phraya Subharn and the Ministry of Foreign Affairs see TNA, KT 96.1/33. The possibility of standing for election was indeed even discussed by the cabinet in early September 1934, but was decided negatively. See also relevant correspondence in TNA, KT 96.1/69.

135 For an overview of the League's budget from 1920 to 1938, see League of Nations Information Section (ed.), *Essential Facts about the League of Nations*, 9th ed., Geneva, 1938, p. 110.

136 The League budget and member states contributions were calculated in gold francs, an imaginary currency which, until September 1936 corresponded to the Swiss franc. A comprehensive list of Siam's contribution to the League can be found in TNA, KT 96.1.1/19.

137 China, with its national finances in disarray, unstable governments, civil war and foreign occupation, time and again defaulted on its financial obligation towards the League; see Walters, *League of Nations*, p. 130.

one and five units, among them European states such as Austria, Greece, Portugal, and Hungary. By contributing nine units, in monetary terms US\$47,600 or £9,781, Siam was spending close to 0.7 percent of its public budget, contributing about one percent to the total League budget and was on par with Cuba, Norway and Peru.[138] In the Thai government budget, the annual contributions to the League were classified as contractual payments, similar to payments to 'Lao Chiefs' and 'Forest Royalty' under ordinary expenditure, and paid not from the budget of the Ministry of Foreign Affairs but from the general state budget.[139] For a tabular listing of Siam's annual contributions to the League of Nations between 1919 and 1946 see appendix 4.

During the first League Assembly in 1920 Prince Charoon skilfully connected the issue of member states' contributions with that of Siam's limited fiscal autonomy, reminding Western states that it was difficult for Siam to meet increasing financial demands from Geneva as long as its hands were tied in Bangkok with regard to revenue from foreign trade. Indeed, he made a rather compelling argument in which he singled out 'a large number of foreign subjects who by their treaty rights do not contribute at all to the expenses of the administration of the state, in which they enjoy a stable government' and concluded that as long as 'Siam is placed in such circumstances, the Siamese Government is compelled to reserve the right to limit the amount of its contribution to an amount within its means'.[140] Nevertheless, Siam went on to hold a very positive payment record at Geneva. Different from many other League members, Siam was never in arrears between 1919 and 1939. This fact was pointed out in Bangkok as well as abroad by government officials with a justified sense of satisfaction; and the *Bangkok Times* stated, very much to the point in 1936, 'Siam has always paid promptly'.[141] Following the financial crisis of the early 1930s, however, the Thai Foreign Ministry tried almost every year until the end of the decade to obtain a reduction of its annual contribution to the League of Nations. By so doing, Siam was in the company of a majority of League member states, who, although League bureaucracy was kept to a minimum, all voiced concern over their contributions to Geneva. India, for example, also pressed for a reduction of its contribution during the first half of the 1930s, as Dina Nath Verma has shown, and then obtained reductions by two units for 1936 and again for 1937, and by four units for 1938.[142] Siam's contribution was reduced twice during the decade, from nine to six units for 1935 and from six to five units for 1940. In addition to this, the annual contribution had already been reduced for 1925, without any efforts by the Thai government, from ten to nine units when the admission of Germany led to financial restructuring of member contributions. The 1925 reduction from ten to nine units was equivalent to 22,000 gold francs, or nine percent, the 1935 reduction meant 92,100 gold francs, or thirty-three percent, and the 1940 reduction meant

138 After consolidation of the League's annual budget for 1929, the real amount paid by the Thai government was US\$44,399.

139 *Report of the Financial Adviser in Connection with the Budget of the Kingdom of Siam for the Year B.E. 2480 (1937-1938)*, p. 42, LNA, R 5286/17/12732/2276.

140 See Report on the First General Assembly of the League of Nations, dated 10 January B.E. 2463 (1921), TNA, KT 96.1.3/2.

141 TNA, *Bangkok Times*, 27 May 1936. During the early years of the League international money transfers were still a somewhat complicated procedure; see LNA, R 1475/31/2271/2271. See also the contemporary account by Sivaram Madhvan, *The New Siam in the Making: A Survey of the Political Transition in Siam, 1932-1936*, Bangkok: Stationer's Printing Press, 1936 (Reprint New York: AMS Press, 1981), who states on page vii: 'In its relation with the League Siam has the distinction of being one of the few member states whose subscriptions have never fallen into arrears.'

142 Dina Nath Verma, *India and the League of Nations*, Patna: Bharati Bhawan, 1968, p. 131f.

savings of 40,800 gold francs, or thirty percent. Let us now look at the efforts leading to the two reductions in the 1930s in greater detail.

By the year 1934, Siam was feeling the effects of the global economic and financial crisis. Like a number of other League members, Siam therefore pushed for a reduction of its annual contribution to the League.[143] To this end, Phraya Subharn began lobbying among representatives of League member states and among League officials in summer 1934, while the Ministry of Foreign Affairs in Bangkok submitted a detailed aide-mémoire to the League in early October.[144] In this paper, the ministry made a very reasonable case for a reduction not only by pointing to the severe economic effects caused by the drop in rice prices for Thai exports and the resulting sharp decline in state revenue, but also by comparing Siam's population size, national wealth, and foreign trade with countries such as Norway, Portugal, Cuba or Greece, which were all paying less to the League than Siam in relative terms. The aide-mémoire also pointed to the fact that state revenue from opium sales had dropped by over fifty percent since 1928 and made it clear that this was caused by Siam's 'scrupulous execution of International Opium and Drug Conventions'. While initial reactions from League officials had been very discouraging, due also to the fact that a large number of League members were in arrears with their contributions, Siam's case seemed increasingly reasonable to them during the summer months.[145] The reduction from nine to six units was decided by the League Assembly's committee on allocation of expenses in late October 1934.[146] But it was not at all smooth sailing at the committee's meeting, as Mani Sanasen, who was present, informed Phraya Subharn confidentially. According to Mani, all committee members would have been willing to agree to a reduction by two units but the demand for a reduction by three units caused such a heated discussion that the meeting even had to be interrupted. Later, an equal number of committee members voted for and against the reduction, and Siam's demand was accepted only because of the French chairman's casting vote.[147]

In 1938, when the League had lost much of its credibility around the globe as the guardian of collective security, some members of the Thai cabinet advocated a withdrawal from the organisation. This proposal, brought forward by the military faction in the cabinet, was motivated mainly by financial concerns, as a withdrawal would have meant saving the annual contributions to the League's budget. At a cabinet meeting in preparation for the League's General Assembly of 1938 on 22 August, the Minister of Finance pressed for a reduction of Siam's contribution to the League. Luang Vichit Vadhakarn echoed this call and expressed his dissatisfaction with the amount of Siam's annual contribution to the League in relation to the single Thai national working at the League's Secretariat. If Siam were expected to continue paying the present contribution, Luang Vichit argued, then it should at least have

143 The formal letter of request is Phraya Abhibal to Secretary-General, 24 July 1934, LNA, R 5286/17/12732/2276.

144 Notes on Phraya Subharn's lobbying as well as the Thai aide-mémoire can be found in LNA, R 5286/17/12732/2276. The aide-mémoire can also be found in TNA, SR 0201.17/15.

145 Phraya Subharn to Minister of Foreign Affairs, 11 October B.E. 2477 (1934), TNA, SR 0201.17/15.

146 Avenol to Ministry of Foreign Affairs, 12 November 1934, TNA, SR 0201.17/15. See also Phraya Subharn to Minister of Foreign Affairs, 23 October B.E. 2477 (1934), in which he informs that Mani Sanasen was also involved in the decision, and Minister of Foreign Affairs to Prime Minister, 24 November B.E. 2477 (1934), all TNA, SR 0201.17/15.

147 Phraya Subharn to Minister of Foreign Affairs, 26 October B.E. 2477 (1934), TNA, SR 0201. 17/15.

an additional staff member in the League Secretariat in return. But Luang Vichit also admitted that it would be difficult to find a qualified individual for such a position.[148] As we have seen above, Luang Bhadravadi, arguably the most qualified Thai national besides Mani Sanasen, had already applied unsuccessfully for a staff position at the League Secretariat in 1936-37. As a result of the cabinet meeting, Minister of Foreign Affairs Luang Pradist sent a letter to the League, in which he cited his country's difficult financial situation and requested a reduction of Siam's contribution. The request was supported by attaching the latest report of the financial adviser, which was intended to demonstrate the difficult export situation for Thai rice.[149] In parallel, Phraya Rajawangsan was instructed to carefully, without angering European delegates, sound out League members on the allocation committee whether there was support for the proposal.[150] British support for the proposal was sought by the Minister of Foreign Affairs via the British legation, and it was understood among British diplomats in Bangkok that a reduction of the annual contribution was seen by the Thai government as a condition for continuing League membership.[151] The British Minister in Bangkok, Sir Josiah Crosby, in particular realised the political significance of this financial issue, and British support in the League's Council for the Thai proposal was eventually secured. In May 1939, Siam was then granted a reduction in annual contribution by one unit from six to five units for the following year, a reduction which effectively led to a net reduction of some thirty percent in 1940.[152] The demand for an additional Thai national at the secretariat, however, proved unrealistic, as secretariat staff was, by late 1939, already being reduced because of the outbreak of the war in Europe and the deterioration of the League. Nevertheless, the bargain had paid off for Siam. All the League could credit itself on was not having lost yet another member during these turbulent years.

In this episode, the pro-League civilian faction in the cabinet, headed by Luang Pradist, prevailed once more over the military officers only months before the outbreak of the Second World War in Europe finally pushed the League to the sidelines of international politics and Siam abandoned the discredited idea of collective security. Chao Phraya Sridharmadhibes (Jit na Songkhla, Phraya Chinda), Deputy Minister of Foreign Affairs in 1938, explained to Sir Josiah Crosby in March 1939, after having in the meantime, taken over the foreign affairs portfolio from Luang Pradist, that he and the other advocates of League membership in the cabinet acknowledged the League's continuing importance as an international clearing house and for its work in the fields of fight against drugs and human trafficking. Nevertheless, advocates of the League of Nations were, from 1940, no longer influencing Thai foreign policy.

Siam did not pay its League contributions between 1940 and 1945,

148 Minutes of Cabinet Meeting on 22 August B.E. 2481 (1938), TNA, SR 0201.17/7 (Part 2 of 3); see on the issue of an additional Thai staff in the Secretariat also a report by Phraya Rajawangsan on a discussion with a Secretariat official in Phraya Rajawangsan to Ministry of Foreign Affairs, 1 November B.E. 2481 (1938), TNA, KT 96.1.3/22.

149 Luang Pradist to Secretary-General, 9 September 1938, LNA, R 5286/17/12732/2276 and TNA, SR 0201.17/15.

150 Luang Pradist to Phraya Rajawangsan, 9 September B.E. 2481 (1938), TNA, SR 0201.17/15.

151 See the comprehensive memorandum by Crosby to Halifax, 22 March 1939, PRO, FO 371/23596, F 3219/3219/40.

152 Phraya Rajawangsan to Ministry of Foreign Affairs, 10 May 1939, TNA, SR 0201.17/15.

in common with most other League members, including Great Britain and France. The League Secretariat sent payment requests and reminders, but the Foreign Ministry in Bangkok decided not to respond. On the other hand, the Ministry also deemed it opportune not to resign from the defunct League, which would have ensured that dues would not have to be paid retroactively one day. The reason not to leave the League, as a Foreign Ministry memorandum of early 1944 plainly put it, was that Japan had so far not pressed Siam to do so, and it was considered to be more prudent to wait and see what would become of the League after the end of the war.[153] Indeed, in 1946 the Thai government then agreed to pay its dues to the League of Nations, in order to maintain a spotless financial record with a view to obtaining UN membership.[154] By late 1946, the League's board of liquidation and the Thai government found a compromise according to which Siam paid fifty percent of its contributions for the years 1940 to 1944 and one hundred percent of the contributions for 1945 and 1946. The total net amount, after deduction of a proportional amount from the League's reserve fund, was 604,000 Swiss francs.[155] And this outstanding contribution was indeed paid, although only in March 1947, as the government in Bangkok was facing a dramatic shortage in foreign currency.[156]

The sound payment record Siam held during the twenty-six years of the League of Nations reflects the conservative and sound overall financial policy pursued by Thai governments under the influence of their British financial advisers during this period. But it is, at the same time, noteworthy that the financial contributions to the League were indeed a significant expenditure. Foreign Ministry files in Bangkok often point to limited financial means as reasons for certain policy decisions. Siam was not only financially unable and unwilling to open a permanent delegation to the League at Geneva, but it also, at times, limited travel of its diplomatic staff from Paris or London to the Geneva meetings.

And there were additional expenses and contributions outside the annual contributions to the League's general budget. In 1920 Siam responded to an appeal by the League to support the fight of a typhoid epidemic in Poland by making £1,000 available from the king's own funds.[157] Siam also answered a call from the League in 1930 to contribute to the construction of a designated building at Geneva for the international press covering the League's work by making available 5,000 Swiss francs.[158] Siam contributed 2,500 baht annually to the budget of the League's Far Eastern Bureau in Singapore from 1926, which came from the funds of the Ministry of Interior. In addition, the Thai government contributed in varying degrees to expenses for commissions of enquiry visiting the kingdom, paid for its participation in the two Bandung conferences, for training of medical staff in Singapore and, of course, the expenses for its delegations in Geneva.

153 Files relating to outstanding payments in 1940-1944 and Memorandum by Ministry of Foreign Affairs, 1 March B.E. 2487 (1944), TNA, KT 96.1.1/ 19.

154 Luang Bhadravadi to Ministry of Foreign Affairs, n.d. (between 27 July and 7 August 1946), TNA, SR 0201.17/15.

155 See all details in TNA, KT 96.1.1/19. See also Lester to Minister of Foreign Affairs, 3 October 1946, TNA, SR 0201. 17/15.

156 See details relating to the payment and the difficulties involved in TNA, SR 0201.17/15.

157 Extensive documentation on this financial contribution is found in LNA, R 813/12B/6298/1719 and in TNA, KT 96.1.11/2 and 3 (Parts 1 and 2). This episode is also mentioned in Arthur Sweetser, 'The First Year and a Half of the League of Nations', *The Annals of the American Academy of Political and Social Science*, 96 (1921), pp. 21-30, here p. 25.

158 For details see TNA, R7, T 10/ 17; Prince Varn to Drummond, 18 October 1930, TNA, KT 96.1/47.

The landmark Bangkok Opium Conference of 1931 came with a significant price tag of close to 150,000 Swiss francs attached for the Thai government.

But there were limits; when an increase of the League's budget for the benefit of expanding the technical assistance to China was discussed during the General Assembly in autumn 1937, the Ministry of Foreign Affairs was clearly opposed to the idea. That this strict opposition did not become public was due to Foreign Affairs Adviser Prince Varn, who instructed the delegates not to state this position openly at Geneva 'because it might unnecessarily offend China' in the light of the deliberations on renewed Japanese attacks ongoing at Geneva at the same time.[159]

On a final note, it is worth mentioning a different contribution Siam made to the League by sending a wooden book cabinet in elaborate traditional Thai style as a gift to adorn the new Palais des Nations in the mid-1930s, which remains in the United Nations' possession until today.[160]

The final Assembly of the League and Siam's admission to the United Nations

The League of Nations remained largely dormant during the Second World War. The Secretary-General resigned, the Secretariat staff was laid off or evacuated from Geneva to England and the United States, and the impressive Palais des Nations was locked down. The Thai legations in London and Paris were closed in 1942, and the few remaining League matters were addressed to the Thai legations in Lisbon and Berne. The Berne legation also received the letter by the last Secretary-General Sean Lester in October 1945, in which he requested the formal approval of Siam as well as of all other League members to hand over all assets of the organisation to the new United Nations. The Thai government did not respond to this request which according to the procedure, meant approval.[161]

It had been a central objective of Siam's foreign policy to be present at the birth of the League of Nations after the First World War, but it seems that the government of Siam had no interest in attending the League's funeral at the end of the Second World War. Accordingly, no Thai representative participated in the final Assembly of the League of Nations, which had the sole task of dissolving itself and handing over its assets and responsibilities to the new United Nations.[162] As an original member, Siam had been invited to participate but did not reply.[163] The files consulted at the Thai National Archives are not conclusive on the issue of Siam's absence from the final General Assembly. The League's formal invitation letter, which was sent out on 4 February 1946, carries a date stamp suggesting it was received only on 24 July, well after the Assembly meeting. Equally, the annotated provisional agenda of the Assembly meeting seems to have been received only on 2 July. Whether

159 Memorandum by Prince Varn, 4 October 1937, TNA, KT 96.1.6.2/12; see also TNA, KT 96.1.11/19.

160 The book cabinet was shipped from Bangkok in December 1934 and arrived at Geneva the following February, only to be put in storage for ten years before damage it had suffered during shipment was repaired by a local carpenter in 1944; the cabinet was put on display at the League's small museum in 1946. Documentation regarding the book cabinet, including sketches, can be found in LNA, R 5399/18B/3005/199. See also TNA, KT 96.1/56. See *The Times* of 3 September 1934 for an article on the gifts presented to the League for its new edifice by various member states, which did not fail to mention the 'carved bookcase in Siamese style'.

161 Lester to Siamese Legation Berne, 18 October 1945, LNA, R 5812/50/43262/43262.

162 Thompson to Foreign Office, 26 April 1946, PRO, FO 371/ 57112, U 4602/24/70.

163 A thin file on the final League Assembly can be found in TNA, KT 96.1.3/23. Therein is the invitation letter, dated 4 February 1946. A first invitation had been sent on 20 September 1945, see LNA, R 5256/15/43545/40199, but this letter could not be traced at the TNA; the League Secretariat had difficulties in determining the addressee of the invitation, as it was unclear which Thai legation was still operating in Europe; see LNA, R 5256/15/ 40199/40199. Ultimately, Siam was one of six countries which did not reply to the invitation, the others being Bulgaria, Ethiopia, Iran, Iraq, and Liberia; see LNA, R 5259/15/ 43598/43454.

the Foreign Ministry deliberately did not reply to the invitation or whether it received it too late, in both cases it can be assumed that Thai foreign policy makers had no strong interest in participating in the funeral of the League; they were already focused strongly on becoming a member of the new international organisation, the United Nations. In the end, in the words of George Egerton, mainly 'the principle luminaries of the League gathered in Geneva for a requiem assembly to mark the formal death of the League'.[164] The *Thai Newsmagazine*, in an appraisal of the League of Nations spanning many pages, described the atmosphere of the final session, which took place in Geneva from 8 to 18 April 1946:

> Geneva, who watched over the League's cradle, has seen it safely to its grave. But although the session had something ghostlike about it, the whole process has been conducted with all due pre-war formalism and scrutiny. And the slight mist of melancholy which hovered around, together with past memories, was soon dispelled by the brilliant sunshine, the gorgeous flowers, the ever kindly welcome of the Swiss people, and the unchanging beauty of Geneva and its lake and mountains in the early spring.[165]

The thirty-four member states present unanimously voted to abolish the League from 19 August 1946.

The League was dead but the problems remained. When the weapons finally fell silent in 1945, in many ways the world found itself where it had been after the end of the First World War; once again there was a widespread desire to establish a collective security system as well as an acknowledgement of the essentially international dimension of many of the world's problems. But not only was the League of Nations discredited by its failure to prevent the conflicts of the 1930s and the war, but also by the absence of the two most important post-war powers, the United States and the Soviet Union. As a result, a fresh start seemed the best way forward to the Western allies. The Atlantic Charter (1941), the United Nations Declaration (1942), the conferences of Moscow (1943), Dumbarton Oaks (1944) and Yalta (1945), and the San Francisco conference in June 1945 marked the path to the establishment of the new United Nations, well before the defunct League of Nations was formally abolished. The United Nations came into being on 24 October 1945 and thereafter developed a much improved collective security system. Nearly all of the League's areas of work – drugs, human trafficking, intellectual property, protection of minors, refugees, health, mandates, economic cooperation, etc. – were taken up by the new UN and developed into programmes or specialised organisations under the UN system (WHO, UNICEF, ECOSOC, UNHCR, UNESCO, UNDOC, WTO, UNDP, UNIDO, UNDCP, FAO, UNCTAD, etc.).

164 George Egerton, 'Collective Security as a Political Myth: Liberal Internationalism and the League of Nations in Politics and History', *The International History Review*, 4 (1983), pp. 496-524, here p. 517.

165 TNL, *Thai Newsmagazine*, 3 November 1946.

166 TNL, *Thai Newsmagazine*, 21 July 1946; see also TNL, *Thai News-magazine*, 25 August 1946. See also Songsri Foran, *Thai-British-American Relations during World War II and the Immediate Post-war Period, 1940-1946*, Thai Kadi Research Institute Paper no. 10, Bangkok: Thammasat University Press, 1981.

167 FRUS, 1946, vol. 1, p. 372f., 381, 388ff., 457f, 458f.

168 Direck to Lie, 20 May 1946 (copy), PRO, FO 371/54387, F 9091/10/40. See also the interview given by Direck to *The Standard* on 20 July 1946, in TNL; and see Direck's detailed account of the war years in Direck Jayanama, *Thailand im Zweiten Weltkrieg, Vom Kriegsausbruch in Europa bis zu Hiroshima, Ein Dokument zur Zeitgeschichte Asiens*, Tübingen and Basel: Erdmann, 1970, p. 267ff.

169 Direck to Lie, 21 July 1946 and Lie to Prince Varn, 16 December 1946, both in TNA, (3)SR 0201.7.2.1/1. See also the detailed study by Pracha Guna-Kasem, 'Thailand and the United Nations (1945-1957)', Ph.D. Thesis, Yale University, 1960.

170 Ministry of Foreign Affairs of Thailand (ed.), *Statements by Chairmen of the Delegations of Thailand at the 2nd-40th Sessions of the United Nations General Assembly (1947-1985)*, Bangkok: Ministry of Foreign Affairs, B.E. 2529 (1986), p. 22ff.

171 On early UN organisations and Siam see TNA, KT 75.1/1 through 75.1/20; see also United Nations Information Service (ed.), *United Nations in Thailand*, Bangkok: ECAFE, 1971; United Nations Information Service Bangkok (ed.), *United Nations and Thailand*, Bangkok: United Nations Information Service, 1964; United Nations Information Service, ECAFE (ed.), *Thailand and the United Nations*, Bangkok: United Nations Information Service, 1966; Darmp Sukontasap, 'The Third World and the United Nations Security Council: The Thai Experience, 1985-1986', Ph.D. Thesis, Fletcher School of Law and Diplomacy, Tufts University, 1993, p. 85ff.

For Siam history also repeated itself somewhat: Nearly thirty years after the country successfully strove to become a member of the new League of Nations, Siam's overriding foreign policy goal after the end of the Second World War was once again to preserve its independence and sovereignty in the face of British and French claims and, to this end, to become a member of the new United Nations. UN membership was considered in Bangkok as nothing less than a 'vital interest of the nation'.[166] As early as 1945, members of the Free Thai movement were discretely establishing contacts with the emerging United Nations and already in spring 1946, the US Department of State was strongly in favour of admitting Siam to the UN.[167] The Thai Minister of Foreign Affairs, Direck Jayanama, emphasised the kingdom's 'earnest desire' to join the United Nations in a letter to the newly-appointed Secretary-General, Trygve Lie, in May 1946 and explained:

> Siam has been a faithful member of and a fervent believer in the former League of Nations, of which it had the great honour to be an original member. The regrettable failure of the League, in no way, lessened our firm conviction in the absolute necessity of an international organization to insure peace and security of the world.[168]

Direck sent Siam's official application for United Nations membership to Secretary-General Lie on 21 July 1946, and Siam was formally admitted to the United Nations on 12 December 1946 as the organisation's fifty-fifth member. It was once again Prince Varn who played a key role in bringing about this key foreign policy success and who put his signature under the UN Charter for Siam.[169] Prince Varn also went on to become Siam's first Permanent Representative to the United Nations from 1947 and, as mentioned above, President of the UN General Assembly in 1956, ten years after the League of Nations ceased to exist.[170]

Bangkok quickly evolved as the Southeast Asian base for many UN agencies. The Economic Commission for Asia and the Far East (ECAFE) was established in 1947 in Shanghai but moved its headquarters to Bangkok in January 1949. The name ECAFE was changed in 1974 to UN Economic and Social Commission for Asia and the Pacific (UNESCAP) to reflect both the economic and social aspects of development and the geographic location of its member countries. The headquarters of UNESCAP remain in Bangkok until today.[171]

Conclusions

This chapter has sketched a number of overarching features of Siam as a small member state of the League of Nations. The special position of Siam among League members as an independent state surrounded by European colonies has become apparent, as has Siam's special position in Geneva as a non-Western member state amidst delegates, some of whom represented European governments which continued to pursue imperialist policies towards their Asian colonies and the colonies' indigenous populations.

The League of Nations has been described in this chapter as a means for Siam's policy makers to regain full sovereignty from Western states during the first half of the 1920s, as a training ground for a substantial number of Thai diplomats, and as a stage on which the kingdom could present its modernity and degree of civilisation to the world. We have also seen that Siam had a geographical handicap by being so far from Geneva, which at times prevented it from becoming involved in League activities to the degree which would have been possible if the journey to Geneva had not been so cumbersome. On the other hand, as has become apparent in the context of the two half-hearted and unsuccessful Council membership bids, Thai governments were often unwilling to become involved in League activities to the degree that would have been possible. Council membership must, in this regard, be seen as the place where, first and foremost, international political conflicts were dealt with; and chapter 6 will examine in detail how Siam generally preferred to stay as removed from this field of the League's work as possible, in order to avoid potential conflicts with other states. Hypothetically, we can assume that, if one of Siam's two Council bids would have been successful, Siam's foreign relations, not only regarding the League, would likely have developed very differently as the Thai government would have been intimately involved in and responsible for the mediation of the major global conflicts of the time.

Thai delegation negotiating new treaties with Western states in 1925. From left: Luang Srivisarn Vacha, Phraya Prabha Kara-wongse, Phra Bahidda Nukara, Francis B. Sayre, Luang Prasert Maitri (Courtesy of Paisarn Piemmattawat).

สมเด็จพระปรมินทรมหาประชาธิปก พระปกเกล้าเจ้าแผ่นดินสยาม ผู้เป็นเอก-
อัครพุทธศาสนูปถัมภก, ขอประกาศให้ทราบทั่วกันว่า

ด้วยเหตุว่า ในภาคต้นแห่งสัญญาสันติภาพ, กรุงสยามได้ตกลงกระทำปฏิญญาณ
ตั้งสันนิบาตชาติขึ้น. เพราะฉะนั้น เพื่อปฏิบัติการให้เป็นไปตามมาตรา ๓ แห่งคำปฏิญญาณ
นั้น, เราจึงตั้งโดยประกาศนี้ให้

มหาเสวกตรี หม่อมเจ้าดำรัสดำรงค์ เทวกุล องคมนตรี ซึ่งได้รับเครื่องราช
อิสสริยาภรณ์อันเฉลิมเกียรติยศยิ่ง ประถมาภรณ์มงกุฎสยาม. เครื่องราชอิสสริยาภรณ์อันเป็น
ที่เชิดชูยิ่ง ทวีติยาภรณ์ช้างเผือก, สมาชิกแห่งเครื่องราชอิสสริยาภรณ์สำหรับตระกูล
จุลจอมเกล้า อัครราชทูตพิเศษผู้มีอำนาจเต็มประจำราชสำนักเลนดุเจนส เป็นผู้
แทนกรุงสยาม.

ให้มีอำนาจเต็มในการที่จะเจรจา. หารือ, และตกลงข้อความใด ๆ ด้วยสมาชิกอื่น ๆ
แห่งที่ชุมนุมสันนิบาตชาตินี้ ณเวลาใดเวลาหนึ่งสุดแต่จะมีโอกาสขึ้นที่จะต้องกระทำ
เช่นนั้น.

โดยประกาศนี้เรารับรองว่า ข้อความใดอันผู้แทนของเราจะได้ตกลงตามมอบไป.
โดยอำนาจอันเราให้ไว้นี้. และได้โดยอนุโลมตามคำสั่งของเรา ดั่งปรากฏอยู่ในที่นี้ ถ้า
เป็นการสมควรเราจักเห็นชอบด้วย.

เพื่อเป็นพยานในการนี้ เราได้ลงพระปรมาภิไธย และประทับพระราชลัญฉกร
สำหรับแผ่นดินไว้, ณพระราชวังดุสิต, กรุงเทพมหานคร, วันที่ ยี่สิบเจ็ด ธันวาคม
พุทธศักราช สองพันสี่ร้อยเจ็ดสิบสาม, เป็นปีที่หก ในรัชชกาลปัจจุบัน.

*Credentials of Prince Damras Damrong Devakul as Siam's Permanent
Delegate to the League of Nations in 1930, bearing the signature and seal of
King Prajadhipok (League of Nations Archives).*

The Thai elite appointed its most able diplomats to represent the kingdom at the League of Nations. In particular, Princes Charoon and Varn stood out during the 1920s, as did as Phraya Rajawangsan and Luang Bhadravadi during the 1930s. By and large, their work was judged positively by the court, the Foreign Ministry and the occasional press report. For example, the *Bangkok Times*, assessing Siam's changing image abroad in early 1925, looked 'particularly at her representations at the constantly recurring conferences in Europe' under the aegis of the League of Nations and highlighted Siam's efficient representation abroad, 'which in a quiet way has caused this country to be respected and the people to be considered shrewd and well informed'.[172] Mani Sanasen stands out as Siam's first-ever international civil servant, who worked for the League Secretariat for fifteen years. Over the course of two decades, the list of individuals who came into contact with the League's work in one way or another, be it in Geneva or in Bangkok, reads like a who's who of Thai diplomacy and government.

While Siam chose to remain in the shadow of other, more vocal League member states on most occasions, it held a commendable record for paying its financial contributions throughout the League's lifetime. This record is not tarnished by the efforts to reduce Siam's contributions to the League during the 1920s, as such policy was common to virtually all League member states, and it is, moreover, a feature of nearly every administration's policy regarding every international organisation since the League's days. Siam's financial record must also be appreciated in the light of the profound changes affecting the kingdom's economy and public finances both in the 1920s and the 1930s, and thus emphasises the importance League membership had for the Thai governments.

The low profile Siam cultivated in Geneva with the remarkable exceptions discussed below also proved very successful with regard to Siam's foreign policy goals during the dawn of the League and the advent of the United Nations. Siam was able, after the Second World War, to bring its League membership into play in an entirely positive light, when lobbying for UN membership. Ultimately, the governments of Thailand during the second half of the twentieth century were able to further intensify cooperation with the UN and reap further benefits for the development of the country in the tradition of their predecessors who pioneered Siam's multilateral foreign policy during the times of the League of Nations.

The following three chapters now focus on specific policy areas, in which the League of Nations and Siam came into contact in manifold ways and with significant consequences for the government and people of Siam as well as for the multilateral political system.

172 TNA, *Bangkok Times*, 28 February 1925.

1 An earlier, short version of this chapter was published in German as Stefan Hell, 'Diplomatie gegen Opiumhöhlen: Siam und die Bemühungen des Völkerbundes zur internationalen Opiumkontrolle', *Periplus 2000, Jahrbuch für außereuropäische Geschichte*, pp. 154-175.

2 Siam's policy with regard to international efforts to control other dangerous drugs besides opium for smoking, such as heroin and cocaine, will also not be analysed, as these substances rapidly became popular in Thailand only after the Second World War while the habit of opium smoking declined. On opium production, trade, consumption and opium suppression during the era of the League of Nations and beyond see William B. McAllister, *Drug Diplomacy in the Twentieth Century, An International History*, London and New York: Routledge, 2000; Carl A. Trocki, *Opium, Empire and the Global Political Economy, A Study of Asian Opium Trade*, London: Routledge, 1999; Martin Booth, *Opium: A History*, New York: St. Martin's Press, 1996; Kathryn Meyer and Terry Parsinnen, *Webs of Smoke: Smugglers, Warlords, Spies, and the History of the International Drug Trade*, Lanham (MD): Rowman & Littlefield, 1998; Christopher P. Spencer and V. Navaratnam, *Drug Abuse in East Asia*, Kuala Lumpur: Oxford University

No.

IMPORT CERTIFICATE.

International Opium Convention, 1912.

<u>Certificate of Official Approval of Import.</u>

I hereby certify that the Ministry of Finance, of the Government of Siam, being the Ministry charged with the administration of the law relating to Opium for smoking purposes, to which the International Opium Convention of 1912 applies, has approved the importation by

    (a) The Director General, Opium Department, Bangkok, Siam,

of (b) ......chests (................) of Opium for the month of ...., 19....

from (c) ....

and is satisfied that the consignment proposed to be imported is required for the purpose of smoking under Government restriction, pending complete suppression, and that it will not be re-exported.

        Signed on behalf of the Ministry of Finance,

          By order of the Minister of Finance.

              Under-Secretary of Finance.

Bangkok,

    Date.....................

                        Tawee.

Opium Import Certificate issued by the Government of Siam in accordance with League of Nations Regulations. (League of Nations Archives).

3

Opium Control[1]

For 100 years, from the 1850s to the late 1950s, addicts in Siam could legally consume opium. They were able to purchase the drug legally from the state, which sold it to them first indirectly, and later directly at opium shops. Opium consumption was put on the agenda of international politics around the turn of the century, and when the League of Nations appeared on the international scene it was entrusted with suppressing opium production, trade and consumption. The League's anti-opium activities rapidly became one of its most important tasks and the single most important area of relations between the League of Nations and its member state Siam. This chapter will analyse Siam's policy vis-à-vis the League in the field of opium control, while limiting itself to issues related to opium smoking. Accordingly, this chapter will not touch on the League's efforts to control the international trade of opium for medical and scientific purposes, as its relevance for Siam during the interwar period was in comparison almost negligible.[2]

Opium in Siam and Southeast Asia

Opium has been known in China and Southeast Asia since times immemorial where it was used primarily as medicine. Opium smoking began in the seventeenth century, when European sailors brought the habit of smoking tobacco from America to Asia. It is commonly thought that the practice of mixing opium with tobacco spread through Asia from Java. From this time, opium was primarily smoked in East and Southeast Asia, while the habit of eating opium was widespread on the Indian subcontinent. Soon opium was smoked without mixing it with tobacco and primarily by employing opium pipes. This so-called prepared opium for smoking could be produced from raw opium in a fairly simple procedure of boiling, straining, fermentation, and evaporation. The resulting product is a thick black paste weighing some thirty percent less than the used raw opium.[3] Opium became a major trading commodity in the eighteenth century when British firms took over control of the international trade, massively expanded opium production in India, and standardised production, packaging, distribution and price.[4] China was the main market for opium from British India, and the habit of opium smoking then spread into Southeast Asia on a large scale in the wake of the waves of Chinese emigration during the nineteenth century.

Press, 1981; William O. Walker III., *Opium and Foreign Policy: The Anglo-American Search for Order in Asia, 1912-1954*, Chapel Hill (NC) and London: University of North Carolina Press, 1991; Kettil Bruun, Lynn Pan and Ingemar Rexed, *The Gentlemen's Club: International Control of Drugs and Alcohol*, Studies in Crime and Justice, Chicago and London: University of Chicago Press, 1975; Bertil A. Renborg, *International Drug Control, A Study of International Administration By and Through the League of Nations*, Washington D.C.: Carnegie Endowment for International Peace, 1947; Stanley H. Bailey, *The Anti-Drug Campaign: An Experiment in International Control*, London: P.S. King, 1936; Albert Wissler, *Die Opiumfrage: Eine Studie zur weltwirtschaftlichen und weltpolitischen Lage der Gegenwart*, Probleme der Weltwirtschaft, vol. 52, ed. by Bernhard Harms, Jena: Institut für Seeverkehr und Weltwirtschaft an der Universität Kiel, 1931.

3 For the chemical, medical, and technical aspects of opium production and consumption see Matthias Seefelder, *Opium, Eine Kulturgeschichte*, 3rd ed., Landsberg: Ecomed, 1996.

4 Trocki, *Opium, Empire and the Global Political Economy*, p. 58 and 169.

5   See the treaty texts in Pitkin, *Siam's Case*, Supplement, p. 11 and 18. On opium in Siam in the eighteenth and nineteenth centuries, also in the context of the Opium Wars between Great Britain and China, see Terwiel, *Thailand's Political History*, p. 121ff.

6   For details see Memorandum on Opium in Siam by the Ministry of Finance, 8 March B.E. 2463 (1921), TNA, KKh 0301.1.6/17. The system of revenue farming was also applied to the indirect taxation of land ownership, transit of goods, alcohol, salt, and gambling; see generally John Butcher and Howard Dick (eds), *The Rise and Fall of Revenue Farming: Business Elites and the Emergence of the Modern State in Southeast Asia*, London and New York: St. Martin's Press, 1993; see on Siam in particular Constance M. Wilson, 'Revenue Farming, Economic Development and Government Policy during the Early Bangkok Period, 1830-92', in: Butcher and Dick, *Rise and Fall of Revenue Farming*, pp. 142-165; Ian Brown, 'The End of the Opium Farm in Siam, 1905-7', in: Butcher and Dick, *Rise and Fall of Revenue Farming*, p. 233-245. See also James R. Rush, *Opium to Java: Revenue Farming and Chinese Enterprise in Colonial Indonesia, 1860-1910*, Ithaca (NY) and London: Cornell University Press, 1990; Eric W. Van Luijk and Jan C. van Ours, 'The Effects of Government Policy on Drug Use: Java, 1875-1904', *Journal of Economic History*, 61, 1 (2001), pp. 1-18; Eric W. Van Luijk and Jan C. van Ours, 'The Effects of Government Policy on Drug Use Reconsidered', *Journal of Economic History*, 62, 4 (2002), pp. 1122-1125.

7   Speech from the Throne on 21 September 1908 on the Opium Question, in Memorandum on Opium in Siam by the Ministry of Finance, 8 March B.E. 2463 (1921), in TNA, KKh 0301.1.6/17.

8   Three departments in the Ministry of Finance shared competencies with regard to opium, namely the Opium Department, the Department of Indirect Taxation, and the Customs Department. This system was then streamlined during the following decades for the benefit of greater efficiency.

In the course of this Chinese emigration opium smoking also found its way to Siam. Under King Rama III efforts were made already during the first half of the nineteenth century to fight this new habit, and Siam's treaties with Great Britain of 1826 and the United States of 1833 expressly outlawed opium imports into Siam.[5] But these efforts proved ultimately futile, and during the reign of King Mongkut political and economic pressure led to the issuance of licenses to rich merchants, often of Chinese origin, by which they were granted the right to sell opium on behalf of the state. These state concessions were usually granted for a limited period and a limited geographical area and were auctioned off to the highest bidder, as the government in Bangkok was unable to directly administer opium sales throughout the kingdom. This system of revenue farming for indirect taxation, an early form of outsourcing, became common practice in many Southeast Asian territories during the latter half of the nineteenth century and was not limited to opium sales.[6] But King Mongkut, nevertheless, tried to limit opium consumption to the Chinese population in Siam and, in 1871, outlawed imports of raw opium into the kingdom, except when licensed by the state. A complete import ban on opium was no longer possible at this time, as Great Britain had established its right to export Indian opium to Siam in the Bowring Treaty of 1855. The revenue farming system was then improved as part of the wide-ranging administrative reforms during the reign of King Chulalongkorn around the turn of the century, mainly by reducing the number of concessionaries, tightening government control, and increasing state revenue.

Only a few years later, in 1908, the revenue farming system was abandoned for financial reasons, and the state reverted to direct control of its important revenue sources. The state now handled the import, processing, and wholesaling of opium, and only the retail sale of prepared opium to addicts remained in the hands of concessionaries. These changes, which were made possible by strengthening the Bangkok government's control of the country through wide-reaching administrative reforms, led to a steep increase in revenue from opium sales, mainly because profits which had to be conceded to middlemen under the revenue farming system could now be reclaimed by the state. The creation of the Thai opium monopoly was marked by a speech from the throne on 21 September 1908, on the occasion of the king's 55th birthday, in which King Chulalongkorn devoted a substantial section to opium. He declared that, while it was 'unquestionable that the drug has evil effects upon its consumers; and casts degradation upon every country', the 'great hindrance' in the way of suppressing opium smoking was 'the considerable shrinkage in the State revenue to be faced'. The administrative reforms in view of a state opium monopoly were, he explained, in line with the king's desire 'not to neglect Our people and allow them to become more and more demoralised by indulgence in this noxious drug.' In fact, through the monopoly 'the spread of the opium habit among Our people shall become gradually lessened until it shall be entirely suppressed'.[7]

Control of the state opium monopoly was in the hands of the Ministry of Finance[8] and followed a pragmatic rationale, as outlined by King Chulalongkorn above. As it was not possible to effectively stop opium consumption in Siam, it could at least be regulated, and the state could increase its revenue from opium sales at the same time. The government monopoly also had a positive effect on opium smuggling, as legalisation undermined the business of smugglers by withdrawing many of the buyers. The opium monopoly was organised along the lines of those operating in the European colonies surrounding Siam. In French Indochina, for example, an opium monopoly was set up in 1881, in the Netherlands Indies from 1894 and in Malaya and the Straits Settlements in 1910.[9] Of all Southeast Asian territories, only in the Philippines was opium trade and consumption outlawed by the American colonial administration in 1908. In Siam, state revenue from the opium monopoly rapidly became an important element for further administrative and economic modernisation during the early twentieth century.[10] Between 1908, the year the opium monopoly was created by King Chulalongkorn, and 1919-20, revenue from opium more than doubled from some 11.2 million baht to over 23 million baht, and revenue from this substance contributed more than a quarter of total state revenue. This structure of public finances was not unique to Siam but could be found in similar forms in all European colonies in Southeast Asia at the time.[11]

During the nineteenth century opium was predominantly consumed in Siam by immigrant Chinese who worked as labourers in Bangkok and the provinces. Opium offered these addicts, almost exclusively men, a craved-for relief from the hardships of heavy physical labour, for example in railway construction or tin mining. According to Carl Trocki, opium smoking strengthened these labourers' ability to work more than impeding it, as it enabled them to endure the often very harsh working conditions. In addition, the amounts consumed seem to have been fairly small, so that workers were more likely to lose their ability to work or their lives from the work itself rather than from smoking opium.[12] A memorandum by the Thai Ministry of Finance of 1921 explained, 'The Chinaman's usual method of enjoying himself, when in funds, is to meet his friends and smoke opium, even though he may not be addicted to the drug – much in the same way as Europeans meet and partake of alcohol'.[13] Jacques M. May, a French doctor, who became well-known for his work as a physician in Hanoi, was practicing in Bangkok during the early 1930s and gave this detailed account:

Alongside the Ministry of Finance, it was the obligation of the Ministry of Interior to enforce legislation regarding opium, while the Ministry of Foreign Affairs was responsible for international aspects of the opium trade. An inter-ministerial permanent opium commission was created in 1925, which largely followed a proposal by Francis B. Sayre of 1924; see Memorandum by F.B. Sayre, 28 June 1924, TNA, KKh 0301.1.6/18. See also Ian G. Brown, *The Creation of the Modern Ministry of Finance in Siam, 1885-1910*, Basingstoke and London: Macmillan, 1995.

9 For details on the establishment of the state opium monopoly see Brown, *Ministry of Finance*. King Chulalongkorn sent a representative to Java in 1908 to study the efficient and profitable opium monopoly there; see Rush, *Opium to Java*, p. 232.

10 Trocki, *Opium, Empire and the Global Political Economy*, p. 158, explains: 'In fact, herein lies one aspect of the real importance of opium and the opium farming system. It supplied the necessary framework within which the new state structures of Southeast Asia were erected.'

11 See, for example, the case of French Indochina as studied by Chantal Descours-Gatin, *Quand l'opium finançait la colonisation en Indochine, L'élaboration de la régie générale de l'opium (1860 à 1914)*, Collection Recherches Asiatiques, Paris: L'Harmattan, 1992; and Philippe Le Failler, *Monopole et prohibition de l'opium en Indochine: Le pilori de Chimères*, Collection Recherches Asiatiques, Paris: L'Harmattan, 2001; on British Malaya see Derek Mackay, *Eastern Customs: The Customs Service in British Malaya and the Opium Trade*, London and New York: Radcliffe, 2005; on Burma see Ronald D. Renard, *The Burmese Connection: Illegal Drugs and the Making of the Golden Triangle*, Studies on the Impact of the Illegal Drug Trade, vol. 6, Boulder (CO) and London: Lynne Rienner, 1996.

12 Trocki, *Opium, Empire and the Global Political Economy*, p. 170.

13 Memorandum on Opium in Siam by the Ministry of Finance, 8 March B.E. 2463 (1921), TNA, KKh 0301.1.6/17.

14 Jacques M. May, *A Doctor in Siam*, London: Cape, 1951, p. 66.

15 Trocki, *Opium, Empire and the Global Political Economy*, p. 149.

16 Opium Questionnaire, 1921, p. 12, LNA, R 724/12A/15181/12437. The same estimate can be found in Memorandum on Opium in Siam by the Ministry of Finance, 8 March B.E. 2463 (1921), TNA, KKh 0301.1.6/17. See also TNA, *Bangkok Times*, 6 December 1922.

17 To obtain the figure of 88,921 smokers in 1930, the League's commission of enquiry asked the Thai government to count all persons smoking in all opium houses on one day. Such a count was made from 6 a.m. on 15 January 1930 to 6 a.m. the following morning. Of the recorded number of opium smokers, 1,096 were women; see LNA, S 194/3, Document 8. For the 1939 figure see Kenneth P. Landon, *The Chinese in Thailand*, New York: Russell & Russell, 2nd ed., 1975 (Revised Issue of New York: Institute of Pacific relations and Oxford University Press, 1941), p. 22.

18 For details on raw opium imports see TNA, KKh 0301.1.1.6/1, 2 and 14 (Parts 1 and 2); Thompson, *Thailand*, p. 728.

19 Chests were the common unit in the trade of raw opium. One chest corresponded to roughly 65 kilograms. By the time the League of Nations came into existence, the Bangkok opium factory had a capacity of boiling and preparing 1,800 chests of raw opium annually and of packing around 60 million tubes of prepared opium; see Memorandum on Opium in Siam by the Ministry of Finance, 8 March B.E. 2463 (1921), TNA, KKh 0301.1.6/17.

20 Various documents regarding the phasing-out of Indian opium exports to Siam, including a detailed schedule listing amounts of raw opium to be exported annually until 1935, can be found in TNA, KKh 0301.1.1.6/25. See on India's opium policy M. Emdad-ul Haq, *Drugs in South Asia: From the Opium Trade to the Present Day*, Basingstoke and London: Macmillan, 2000.

Under the influence of opium a hungry man does not feel his hunger. An aching man forgets his pain, a tired man can work again. This is the basic reason for opium addiction in the Far East. This is why, under present conditions, opium is a comfort. As a substitute for food it is popular mainly because it diminishes the need for costly calories. I have often seen in my hospital men who had lived on a handful of rice a day but still able to carry enormous loads thanks to the help of the black smoke which dissolves the toxic deposits of fatigue. For a few cents in an opium den a man can smoke himself to rest and oblivion. For hours after that he does not feel the need for food and saves the price he would have to pay for it. To reach a similar degree of comfort by the absorption of food would probably cost him three times as much. Opium is food for the poor and drink for the rich.[14]

While Chinese immigrant labourers continued to make up a large part of opium consumers in the twentieth century, the number of ethnic Thais who became addicted had been on the rise since the second half of the nineteenth century, particularly in Bangkok and central Siam.[15] An official estimate given by the Thai government to the League of Nations in 1922 mentions a total number of 200,000 opium addicts, of which 50,000 were ethnic Chinese.[16] In addition, a third, smaller group of opium consumers established itself among the ethnic minorities in the inaccessible northern border regions of Siam. According to a report by a League of Nations commission of enquiry of 1929, the number of smokers of legal opium declined to 89,000 and in 1939, ten years later, according to Kenneth Landon, the number decreased further to 60,000.[17] As we will see below, this reduction in numbers was a result also of the cooperation between the Thai government and the League of Nations.

The Thai government imported raw opium during the first two decades of the twentieth century from British India, first by participating in the Calcutta opium auctions, and from 1918 on the basis of a bilateral agreement between the two governments. In addition, smaller quantities of opium were imported from the Chinese province of Yunnan, but this practice was stopped in 1922.[18] Siam's monthly requirement during this period was an average of 200 chests of raw opium, or around 1.3 tons, from which prepared opium was then produced, since 1912-13 at a central government-owned opium factory in Bangkok.[19] After the British government had already agreed in 1907 to reduce opium exports to China, by far the most important export market for Indian opium, by ten percent annually, it decided in 1926 to phase out all opium exports for non-medical purposes until the year 1935.[20] What effect this change in British opium policy, which was again a consequence of, among other factors, the work of the League of Nations, had on Siam will be described below.

Opium as an issue of international law

As states were increasingly searching for multilateral solutions to different political and social problems around the turn of the century, the international opium trade and the habit of opium smoking, which by then had spread to nearly all of Southeast and East Asia, were also put on the new international agenda. The initiative for the first intergovernmental conference on opium in 1909 came, on the one hand, from religious and humanitarian interest groups, who were being formed in Great Britain and the United States and, on the other hand, from the Chinese government, which tried to limit the amount of opium it was contractually obliged to import from British India. Following an initiative by American religious circles led by the bishop of the Philippines, Charles Brent, the government in Washington convened a conference in Shanghai.[21] Governments of twelve states, among them Siam, accepted the invitation[22], and the thirteen government delegations of this so-called Shanghai Commission discussed issues relating to opium trade and consumption on a multilateral level for the first time in February 1909, but stepped short of agreeing on binding steps to reduce production, trade, or consumption. The resolutions listed in the final act of the conference were therefore limited to general suggestions and vague goals, rather than containing binding commitments, a result also of the fact that the representatives at the Shanghai Commission did not have a mandate to agree on legally-binding measures.[23] The importance of the commission lay in its pioneering role, as it was the first step in putting opium on the international agenda. In Shanghai, Siam's opium policy earned the recognition of the American delegate Hamilton Wright, who observed that Siam had tried 'to put their house in order so as to appear before the Commission with clean hands'.[24] Public statements as well as confidential documents reveal that the Thai government was, indeed, already at this time seriously committed 'to ultimately suppress the use of opium'.[25]

Under the influence of pressure groups in the United States, which was dissatisfied with the results of Shanghai, the American government immediately began with preparations for a follow-up conference which would no longer be focused exclusively on Asia and which would lead to concrete results. These renewed American preparations were also seen in Siam as 'greatly in advance of those which led to the Conference at Shanghai'.[26] This leading role of the United States administration, which was to continue during the following decades, was not only a result of effective lobbying by pressure groups but also of a claim to moral authority in American foreign policy and of the fact that the United States did not earn any revenue from an overseas opium monopoly.[27] In late 1911 this second conference convened in The Hague with the stated goal to draw up the first legally binding international opium convention.[28] And the eleven government delegations, among them once again a delegation from

21 See on Siam's participation in the Shanghai Commission the 'Confidential Instructions to Delegates to Joint Opium Commission to be held at Shanghai, n.d.' and 'Statement by the Siamese Commission', both TNA, KKh 0301.1.1.6/5. See in detail on the Shanghai Commission and the Hague Opium Conference Peter D. Lowes, *The Genesis of International Narcotics Control*, Geneva: Librairie Droz, 1966.

22 Apart from the United States and Siam, eleven further governments took part in the conference: Great Britain, France, the Netherlands, China, Japan, Persia, Portugal, Germany, Austria-Hungary, Italy, and Russia. Siam was represented at Shanghai by three officials of the Ministries of Finance and Foreign Affairs, see TNA, KKh 0301.1.1. 6/5.

23 See the text of the Shanghai resolutions in Lowes, *Genesis*, p. 199f. and in 'Resolutions adopted on the 26th February, 1909, by the International Opium Commission, sitting at Shanghai, China', TNA, KKh 0301.1.1.6/5. See also Syamal Kumar Chatterjee, *Legal Aspects of International Drug Control*, The Hague, Boston and London: Martinus Nijhoff, 1981, p. 43.

24 Lowes, *Genesis*, p. 130.

25 Quotation from 'Confidential Instructions to Delegates to Joint Opium Commission to be held at Shanghai, n.d.', TNA, KKh 0301.1.1.6/5. See also Speech from the Throne, 21 September 1908, TNA, KKh 0301.1.1.6/5.

26 Memorandum by Financial Adviser W.J.F. Williamson, 11 November 1909, TNA, KKh 0301.1.1.6/8.

27 On the role of the United States, which, in 1900, had an opium-addicted population of 250,000, more than Siam, in the international opium suppression efforts see David R. Bewley-Taylor, *The United States and International Drug Control, 1909-1997*, London and New York: Pinter, 1999.

28 All participants in the Shanghai Commission were represented at The Hague, except Italy, a delegate of which was present at a single session only, and Austria-Hungary. See on the conference at The Hague Lowes, *Genesis*, p. 176ff.

Siam[29] indeed succeeded, in spite of serious differences, in adopting the first basic document of international law on opium, the Hague Opium Convention of 1912. The convention was the first-ever legally binding international document to state the long-term goal of completely eradicating opium smoking, but still stepped short of detailed measures to this end or of setting a timeframe. On the other hand, while it aimed at eradicating opium smoking, the convention also welcomed the Asian state opium monopolies as an effective measure against illicit opium trade and as a means to improve government control of opium matters. The Thai government supported this standpoint, which was in line with the instructions given to its delegate at The Hague:

> His Majesty's Government is not inclined to surrender any of its powers of control over the opium administration, since it needs all the powers and wisdom that it can command in order to deal successfully with the matter...To repeat, the fiscal, commercial and moral interests involved are of great magnitude. Any hasty action is to be deprecated, because it might involve grave results.[30]

As will be seen below, this strong position was given up ten years later for a much more conciliatory and open position when the League of Nations appeared on the international scene. But during the following years, only a few signatories of the Hague Opium Convention deposited their ratification instruments; in particular Great Britain and Germany blocked the convention from coming into force, the former because of the great fiscal importance of opium exports from British India, the latter because of the flourishing pharmaceutical industry. Two further conferences at The Hague in 1913-14 also failed to significantly speed up the ratification process, before the outbreak of the First World War brought it to a complete halt. However, Siam was among the countries which ratified the convention as early as 10 July 1913. The Hague Convention came into force after the end of the war when it was incorporated as article 295 into the Treaty of Versailles.[31] In parallel, the conference in Versailles entrusted the new League of Nations in article XXIII(c) of its covenant with the task of international opium control. Thus, for the first time in history, a standing international organisation was charged with drug control. An official account of the League of Nations, written some fifteen years later, evaluated this task as follows:

> The supervision of the traffic in opium and other dangerous drugs is perhaps the most important social and humanitarian activity undertaken by the League, in view of the considerable interests at stake, the extent of the evil to be overcome, and the natural anxiety of the public, which cannot endure that the world should stand by while hundreds of thousands of persons, and even whole races, are physically and morally ruined.[32]

29 For details on Siam's participation in the conference at The Hague, see 'Confidential Instructions to Delegates to the International Opium Conference, to be held at the Hague', n.d., 'Memorandum on The International Opium Conference at The Hague, December 1911', by William J. Archer, 29 December 1911, 'Second Memorandum of the International Opium Conference at The Hague', 29 January 1912, by William J. Archer, as well as various correspondence and official invitation letters, all in TNA, KKh 0301.1.1.6/8 (Parts 1 and 2).

30 'Confidential Instructions to Delegates to the International Opium Conference, to be held at The Hague', n.d., in TNA, KKh 0301.1.1.6/8.

31 The Hague Convention became an integral part of the Treaty of Versailles, which meant that ratification of the Treaty of Versailles implied *ipso facto* the ratification of the Hague Convention. Similar clauses were also included as article 247 in the Treaty of St. Germain, article 230 in the Treaty of Trianon, article 174 in the Treaty of Neuilly, and as article 280 in the Treaty of Sèvres. See also Wissler, *Opiumfrage*, p. 193.

32 League of Nations (ed.), *The Aims, Methods and Activity of the League of Nations*, Geneva, 1935. p. 175. For the text of the Covenant of the League of Nations see LNA, League of Nations, Official Journal, February 1920, p. 3ff.

Siam and international opium control, 1920 to 1940

The League's activities with regard to opium control during the 1920s and 1930s can be summarised in the following steps. At the outset, the League aimed at creating an awareness of the opium trade and consumption as a problem among its member states' governments by encouraging discussions and publishing relevant information. In a second step, the League aimed at collecting reliable data on production, trade and consumption of opium for the first time and, to this end, put a mandatory reporting system in place for its member states. On the basis of this data, it then became possible to try to separate licit from illicit opium trade, and the League thus developed a standardised import certificate system, which member states were encouraged to adopt under their national legislation. In parallel, the League expanded its activities from opium to other dangerous drugs. In a next step, the League tried to limit illicit opium trade and limit global opium production to the quantity required for legal use. The final goal of all these steps was clear, opium trade and consumption, except for medical and scientific purposes, should be eradicated globally.

The League's central body for opium matters was the Advisory Committee on the Traffic in Opium and other Dangerous Drugs, commonly called the Opium Advisory Committee (OAC). The OAC formulated the League's opium policy, served as the main discussion forum for opium matters, prepared meetings and conferences and drafted conventions. Furthermore, the OAC had the task of collecting information and statistical data on opium from League members and supervising international opium trade as well as implementing the Hague Convention and other international agreements. Siam and seven further states, which possessed colonies in which opium smoking was legal, were invited to join the OAC when it was created by the League's General Assembly in 1920.[33] The OAC, which met annually, normally in or around May, was not made up of independent experts but of the diplomatic representatives of member state governments.[34] This ensured that not only desirable goals were formulated by the committee, but goals which were politically feasible, as the committee's legal authority was very limited, and any decision on the implementation of the OAC's recommendations was in the hands of member state governments. Of particular significance was the participation of the United States as an observer from 1923 because, although not a member of the League of Nations, it was often the United States which pushed the OAC's work ahead during the following years.[35] In contrast to other international bodies, members on the OAC seem to repeatedly have lost their diplomatic countenance. In the words of Francis Walters, the OAC meetings were 'the scene of violent language and hasty action to a degree unknown among other organs of the League', an expression of the controversial nature of opium issues.[36] In similar fashion the *Bangkok*

33 LNA, R 710/12A/11489/103 46. At the outset, Great Britain, France, the Netherlands, India, Japan, China, and Portugal were represented on the OAC next to Siam. The number of OAC members then increased steadily over the following two decades and reached twenty-eight in 1939. See on the early years of the OAC also LNA, COL 307/Box 103/File 1/12A/20403/20403. See on Siam's participation TNA, KT 96.2.5/1 (Parts 1 and 2). The vast files in TNA, KT 96.2.3/1 to 94 cover Siam's participation in and evaluation of each and every OAC meeting from 1921 to 1940. See also on the OAC Greaves, *League Committees*, p. 222ff.; Renborg, *International Drug Control*, p. 31ff. and 177; Meyer and Parsinnen, *Webs of Smoke*, p. 3ff.

34 See Herbert L. May, 'The Evolution of the International Control of Narcotic Drugs', *UNODC Bulletin on Narcotics*, 1 (1950), <http://www.unodc.org/unodc/en/data-and-analysis/bulletin/bulletin_1950-01-01_1_page003.html>.

35 On the American participation on the OAC see FRUS, 1923, vol. I, p. 89ff.

36 Walters, *League of Nations*, p. 185.

Times commented on the 1923 OAC meeting by stating, 'Geneva has been having quite an orgy on opium'.[37]

Siam's membership on the OAC did not come about automatically. In fact, at the outset in 1920, the European members did not envisage Siam being an OAC member, it was the active lobbying of Prince Charoon, Phraya Buri and Phraya Bibadh, which resulted in Siam's membership on the OAC. They anticipated that Siam would be strongly affected by the OAC's decisions and deemed it crucial to be part of the committee.[38] The delegates of Siam, most prominently Prince Charoon and Prince Varnvaidya, by and large acted in a very cooperative manner during the annual meetings of the OAC and managed to present their country as a staunch supporter of the cause of international opium control. One contemporary observer highlighted the prominence which Prince Charoon gained on the international diplomatic stage through his work as vice chairman of the OAC during the 1920s.[39] 'Siam was found on the right side', as was remarked in Bangkok with no small degree of satisfaction.[40]

The OAC functioned, with continuous Thai participation, for twenty years, from 1921 to 1940.[41] It was supported by the League Secretariat's Opium Traffic and Social Questions Section, which was headed for over ten years by Dame Rachel Crowdy and then successively by the two Swedes Eric Einar Ekstrand and Bertil Renborg.[42]

That the League's first objective with regard to opium control was essential, namely creating an awareness of the opium trade and consumption as a problem among its member states' governments, and that this already posed a formidable task, is illustrated by the statement by the delegate of India in the 1922 League Assembly:

> …that in certain Eastern countries, including India, there was a legitimate and general use of opium...opium was the Indian parallel to alcohol in the West...It was a good thing that efforts were being made to prevent the abuse of opium, but, however desirable it might be, it was none the less difficult, in the course of daily life, for everybody to be philanthropists all the time. It was the abuse and not the legitimate use of opium which constituted the danger.[43]

Such patronising, colonial attitudes were, especially in the 1920s, still widespread among Western government officials and diplomats. Thai diplomats at Geneva were well aware of these attitudes. Prince Charoon and Phraya Bibadh reported to Bangkok from the 1921 General Assembly that it was obvious that the colonial powers were unwilling to forsake opium sales in their Asian colonies because of their financial importance and because of their desire to keep the indigenous population addicted: only Siam and China were sincere in their wish to rid their countries of opium, and their delegates were the only ones able to look all other OAC members 'straight in the eye without shame'.[44]

37 TNA, *Bangkok Times*, 13 June 1923.

38 Report on the First General Assembly of the League of Nations, dated 10 January B.E. 2463 (1921), TNA, KT 96.1.3/2.

39 Greaves, *League Committees*, p. 227.

40 TNA, *Bangkok Times*, 28 June 1921.

41 The final meeting of the OAC, its 25th, was held on 13 May 1940, and was attended by Phra Bahidda Nukara, Thai Minister in Paris, and Luang Bhadravadi, Chargé d'affaires in London; see TNA, KT 96.2.5/92. Preparations were made for the 26th meeting in May 1941, but this never came about because of the war; see TNA, KT 96.2.5/94.

42 William McAllister, who reports that the office of Head of the Opium Section was also colloquially known as the 'Poppy Throne', provides very colourful biographical descriptions of these officials as well as of all prominent individuals involved in international opium suppression in the twentieth century; see McAllister, *Drug Diplomacy*, passim.

43 Confidential Report of the British Delegates to the 3rd Assembly, 1922, Doc. 106 (-/-/-), BDFA, Part II, Series J, vol. 1, p. 376. On "the role of India in the drama of international traffic in opium [as] that of a notorious villain" see Verma, *India and the League*, p. 215ff.

44 Report by Prince Charoon and Phraya Bibadh to Prince Deva-wongse on the Second General Assembly of the League of Nations, dated 17 November B.E. 2464 (1921), TNA, KT 96.1.3/4.

One of the OAC's key activities then was the collection of information on the extent of the opium problem, as only on the basis of reliable information could effective action be planned. To this end, member states were instructed to submit detailed annual reports on opium production, trade and consumption as well as on any relevant domestic developments. Member states were also required to report in detail on seizures of smuggled opium and on the implementation of national opium legislation. The files in Geneva and Bangkok reveal that Siam met these reporting requirements with remarkable diligence throughout the 1920s and 1930s.[45] At the outset of its work in 1921, the OAC sent a very detailed questionnaire to League members and fifteen other states, and the replies to this questionnaire then formed the bulk of the material basis on which the OAC set out to suppress opium. The League's questionnaire triggered the compilation of a memorandum on the opium situation in Bangkok in 1921, which represented the most comprehensive account of developments since the mid-nineteenth century and remains remarkable for the amount of detailed information it contains on various aspects of opium in Siam.[46] This memorandum then led to a series of newspaper articles, which described the historical development of Siam's opium policy as well as policies prevailing in 1922 in detail.[47] Furthermore, the establishment of the OAC and its system of information collection from member governments led to the collection of quantitative information in Bangkok in accordance with modern statistical standards during the first half of the 1920s. Siam's delegates, chiefly among them Prince Charoon, were able to convey a very positive image of the country's opium policy during these first years of the OAC. In 1922, a *Bangkok Times* editorial remarked:

> This country has reason to view the proceedings of the Opium Commission of the League of Nations with some complacency... One might almost suppose that the Opium Commission has in effect taken Siamese legislation on this question as the model for universal application.[48]

But Siam's opium policy from 1920 was marked by a fundamental conflict. On the one hand, Siam cooperated with the League in the international efforts to suppress opium trade and consumption, on the other hand, opium constituted a major source of state revenue. At the outset of the League's work, the Thai government argued it could not do without revenue from opium because the Bowring-type unequal treaties with European states of the nineteenth century, denied Siam tariff autonomy by fixing import tariffs at a maximum of three percent of the value of the goods. This compelling argument had already been made during the Paris Peace Conference in 1919:

> The Government realises that the opium traffic must be done away with. And it intends to do away with it at the earliest moment

45 A good overview of which reports were received by which League member state during the League's first decade can be found in LNA, League of Nations, *Official Journal*, no. 6 (June 1930), p. 756f.

46 Memorandum on Opium in Siam by the Ministry of Finance, 8 March B.E. 2463 (1921), TNA, KKh 0301.1.6/17. This memorandum then formed the basis for the government's reply to the League of Nations, which was received in Geneva on 30 August 1921; see LNA, R 724/12A/ 15181/12437. The League's questionnaire can be found in LNA, R 724/12A/12437/12 437.

47 TNA, *Bangkok Times*, various issues 2-7 December 1922. The memorandum and newspaper articles were met with great public interest, also because of the conference of the Oriental Congress of the League of Red Cross Societies, which was being held in Bangkok that month and which also discussed opium smoking; see the Red Cross conference in chapter 4 of this study.

48 TNA, *Bangkok Times*, 2 May 1922.

compatible with Siam's financial safety. But it realises too that that moment has not come and that, until the [Western] Powers grasp the situation and undo the evil which they have unwittingly done to her [i.e., through the unequal treaties], Siam is helpless.[49]

Siam's annual reports on opium to the League constantly repeated this argument until the mid-1920s and indeed, a steep drop in opium revenue during these years would have had a seriously adverse effect on Siam's state budget. The annual opium reports to the League were, therefore, a useful tool for the Bangkok government to put pressure on European governments, over and beyond the realm of international opium control to revise the unequal treaties. The *Bangkok Times* also adhered to this view in 1922 by stating that Siam 'is now in a position to use the general desire to reduce the consumption of opium as a means to bring pressure to bear on the great Powers in order to induce them to concede fiscal autonomy. Truly everything has its uses.'[50] Apart from the lack of fiscal and tariff autonomy, the reports did not fail to mention Siam's difficulties in enforcing its national opium legislation towards citizens of Western countries residing in Siam. The report for the year 1922-23 explained, for example:

> The same difficulties in regard to the application and enforcement of the laws in connection with raw and prepared opium...still exist, i.e. that the control of opium resulting from the extraterritorial jurisdiction still possessed by the subjects of certain foreign powers. Unless these foreign states... are willing either to make regulations providing for the enforcement of the law among their own nationals, or to allow the Siamese authorities to enforce the law, there seems to be no way of escaping the present difficulties.[51]

The background of this argument was that foreign citizens in Siam could expect drastically milder sentences for drug offences from their respective consular courts than from Thai courts. And that foreign citizens were, indeed, committing drug offences in Siam, is illustrated by this rather colourful report on a police raid in Bangkok in 1924:

> On Monday a police officer accompanied by officials of the Opium Department and representatives of the Netherlands and Japanese Legations went on a little expedition in Bangkok. First they called upon a Netherlands protégé at Tapan Han, where they seized about a tamlung of illicit opium...The next visit was to another Netherlands protégé in Chesua Niem lane where they got two tamlung of the stuff that had not been bought from the Government... The party then went on to a private smoking divan at Talat Mai kept by a Japanese subject. Six or seven Siamese smokers were arrested there. The police also seized two tamlung of the illicit drug, seven pipes and other accessories.[52]

49 Pitkin, *Siam's Case*, p. 26.

50 TNA, *Bangkok Times*, 2 May 1922.

51 Report on the Traffic in Opium and Other Dangerous Drugs for B.E. 2465, p. 4, LNA, R 741/12A/19026/18661. This file also holds the opium traffic reports submitted by the Thai government for the years 1921 to 1924. All Thai reports for the 1920s and 1930s can also be found in TNA, KT 96.2.3 and KT 96.2.7.

52 TNA, *Bangkok Times*, 10 July 1924.

Siam's cooperation with the League in opium matters as well as in other areas thus made its awkward position readily apparent to the international political public in Geneva. On the one hand, Siam was bound to the international agreements to which it had become party as a sovereign League of Nations member state, on the other hand, Siam was not able to fully enforce its domestic laws also towards foreign citizens residing in the kingdom. And Siam's strategy of utilising its League membership for its broader policy goals indeed reached the intended addressees, as a report from the British Minister in Bangkok to his government of 1923 shows:

> The situation in which the Siamese Government finds itself as a result of the extra-territorial privileges...is somewhat embarrassing and I venture to think that there is much to be said in favour of the proposal made by His Royal Highness [Minister of Foreign Affairs Prince Devawongse] to the effect that with the responsibility created by the international conventions and membership in the League should go to the power to give practical effect to international obligations, even were this to infringe in some measure on these same extra-territorial rights and privileges.[53]

Nevertheless, the British government was at this time not yet willing to give up its extraterritorial rights in Siam, not least because it feared that this would strengthen Chinese demands to the same end.[54] But during the second half of the 1920s, when new international treaties granted Siam fiscal and tariff autonomy[55], state revenue from opium sales indeed declined, as the government implemented measures for stricter opium control. This trend continued into the first half of the 1930s and was later reversed towards the end of that decade in the course of the fundamental shifts in Siam's domestic and foreign policies.

But not only Siam's policy towards opium suppression was marked by conflict, the same was true for the other governments assembled on the OAC, as Prince Charoon stated very much to the point already after the very first OAC meeting in 1921:

> Besides the material question, I suspect there is also a political aspect underlying the reluctance of countries having colonial possessions in the Far East to give up the monopoly. For so long as their subjects are addicted to the opium habit, they must...remain degenerate and, consequently, would be far less likely to cause any trouble. The same may be the reason in regard to China, a country [in] which it is to the interest of Japan as well as the European Powers to keep perpetual disorder and schism.[56]

A direct consequence of the coming into force of the Hague Convention as part of the Treaty of Versailles and of Siam's membership in the new League of Nations was Siam's Opium Law of 6

53 Greg to Lord Curzon, 13 April 1923, PRO, FO 415, F 1504/421/87, reprinted in Great Britain, Foreign Office (ed.), *The Opium Trade 1910-1941*, 6 vols., Wilmington and London: Scholarly Resources, 1974, here: document no. 43, part XIX, vol. 5.

54 Foreign Office to Home Office, 18 May 1923, PRO, FO 415, F 1504/421/87, *The Opium Trade*, no. 44, part XIX, vol. 5.

55 See the collection of treaty texts in Sayre, *Siam: Treaties with Foreign Powers*.

56 Confidential Report by Prince Charoon, 11 May 1921, TNA, KKh 0301.1.1.6/18.

57 The text of the Opium Law and Ministerial Regulations can be found in TNA, KKh 0301.1.1.6/17. See also the comments by the Thai government given in response to the League's opium questionnaire in 1921, LNA, R 724/12A/15181/12437; the original Thai text of the Opium Law was also submitted to the League; see LNA, R 741/12A/19026/186 61.

58 Speech from the Throne by King Vajiravudh in TNA, *Bangkok Times*, 5 January 1922.

59 See Mackay, *Eastern Customs*, p. 138ff.

60 'Interview by the League of Nations Commission of Enquiry into the Control of Opium-smoking in the Far East with William Mundie', 11 December 1929, LNA, S 194/4.

61 In order to better control opium sales and prevent substitution of licit with illicit opium by the retailers, opium pots were substituted from 1913 in Bangkok and from 1915 throughout the kingdom 'by collapsible tin tubes of different sizes similar to those used for artist's colours, but sealed with a brass eyelet and a Government mark, instead of being closed with a screw cap. As, after use, the tubes become destroyed, the retail dealers will not be able to again fill them with opium and they will thus be prevented from in any way participating in the sale of smuggled opium. In addition to this it will be a simple matter for Government to know the exact consumption of the drug.' See 'Confidential Instructions to Delegates to the International Opium Conference, to be held at the Hague', n.d., TNA, KKh 0301.1.1.6/8. See also Memorandum on Opium in Siam by the Ministry of Finance, 8 March B.E. 2463 (1921), TNA, KKh 0301.1.6/17. How advanced the production of tin tubes for opium was, is underlined by the fact that, for example, in Singapore opium was sold for another fifteen years in bamboo leaves or paper before a production plant for tin opium tubes was opened in 1930; see Mackay, *Eastern Customs*, p. 137f.

January 1921.[57] King Vajiravudh made it clear in his speech from the throne that the promulgation of this law was done 'in accordance with the policy pursued hitherto by the Siamese Government and in compliance with the desires of the League of Nations'.[58] This law limited legal opium consumption to opium houses, with the exception of few wealthy or chronically ill opium addicts who could apply for special licenses to smoke at their homes, and even forbid the possession of opium pipes. In addition, the law provided for the registration of all opium consumers. Once registration was completed, no new licenses were to be issued to opium consumers, and the amount of opium provided by the state to registered consumers was to be rationed. But the timing for implementation of this wide-reaching registration and rationing scheme was left open due to three factors; first of all, the government deemed itself unable to bear the financial losses this scheme would have entailed in the light of its lack of fiscal autonomy during the early 1920s; secondly, a comprehensive registration of opium smokers would have been impossible in the early 1920s because foreigners in Siam could not be forced to register and because the central bureaucracy did not possess the necessary means to carry it out; and finally, the government was aware that registration would have stayed ineffectual as long as no effective measures could be undertaken against opium smuggling into Siam from Burma. The registration and rationing scheme was, although put into national legislation as early as 1921, postponed again and again and was ultimately never implemented during the League's lifetime, mainly because when Siam did regain full fiscal and legal autonomy, the illegal opium trade had reached such startling levels that the government rightly judged the scheme inoperable. In this regard Siam was in a much more difficult position than, for example, the British Straits Settlements, where smuggling could much better be checked and where, accordingly, a registration scheme of opium smokers was introduced during the 1930s.[59] William Mundie, editor of the *Bangkok Times*, put it bluntly in an interview with the chairman of the League of Nations commission of enquiry on opium in late 1929; when asked whether he thought that the government had been doing everything in its power to control opium smoking, Mundie replied:

> Of course not. The machinery is there but the law is not enforced. There is no registration of opium smokers. That has not been done and unless Geneva compels it will not be done simply because then smuggling becomes the main source of supply.[60]

As mentioned above, opium could only be smoked legally in Siam, with the mentioned exceptions, in opium houses, also called opium shops, dens or divans. In these establishments, opium portions were sold in sealed tin tubes and the consumer was handed a pipe.[61] After smoking, the consumer had to return the pipe with the remaining opium dross, the residue which still contained morphine. The standards and hygiene levels of opium houses varied according to the social status of their patrons. Author W. Somerset Maugham must have visited one of the more pleasant opium houses during his stay in Bangkok in 1922, which he described as follows:

> It was a cheerful spot, comfortable, home-like, and cosy. It reminded me somewhat of the little intimate beer houses of Berlin, where the tired working man could go in the evening and spend a cheerful hour. Fiction is stranger than fact.[62]

More often, however, opium houses were filthy and uninviting establishments, or, in the words of one observer, 'bare and dingy places...not social centres in any way'.[63] The number of opium houses was reduced from 3,100 in 1917-18 to 1,028 in 1920-21; and by 1925 only 946 official opium houses existed in the kingdom.[64] Not only Siam pursued this policy of reducing the number of smoking establishments; a parallel development could be witnessed in British Malaya.[65] But by the mid-1920s, the government realised that if it were to seriously curb smuggling, it had to provide opium where consumers were, and consequently new opium houses were opened in rural areas.[66] The retail price of legally prepared opium was constantly increased during the 1920s, in order to make it less attractive to addicts. During the second half of the decade, the price for a month's supply of prepared opium, one *tamlung* or 37.5 grams, was 15 baht in Bangkok, while it was much cheaper in some border areas and as little as 5 baht in Siam's north where opium smuggling was thriving. A coolie earned about 1 baht per day during this period and, consequently, spent around half of his monthly income on his addiction. In stark contrast, a month's supply of illicit opium was available for a mere 7 baht in Bangkok and as little as three or even 1 baht near the northern border.[67]

The Thai government aimed at controlling the entire process from opium import to the retail sale to the consumer from the early 1920s. Therefore, it was began to substitute licensees who had hitherto managed retail sales at opium houses with employees of the state opium monopoly. These state employees received a fixed salary and therefore had no financial interest in the amount of opium they sold. Licensees, in contrast, made their profits by re-selling opium dross, the residue remaining in the opium pipe after smoking which still contained morphine and which could be smoked once more or eaten. In this way, licensees earned from each tube of prepared opium they sold. But, yet again, the implementation of this new policy was slow, as suitable infrastructure and employees as well as additional funds were lacking. A memorandum by the Ministry of Finance pointed out in 1924 that 'not less than ten thousand employees would be required for the existing 946

62 TNA, *Bangkok Times*, 3 November 1922.

63 'Evidence given by Dr. Henry O'Brien, Chiang Mai, to the League of Nations Commission of Enquiry into the Control of Opium-smoking in the Far East', December 1929, LNA, S 194/4. See also another description of a cheap opium den in Bangkok in May, *Doctor in Siam*, p. 62f.

64 Memorandum on Opium in Siam by the Ministry of Finance, 8 March B.E. 2463 (1921), TNA, KKh 0301.1.6/17; see also TNA, *Bangkok Times*, 2 December 1922; Westel W. Willoughby, *Opium as an International Problem: The Geneva Conferences*, Baltimore: Johns Hopkins Press, 1925, p. 100; and 'Instructions to the Siamese Delegates at the First International Conference on Opium to be held under the auspices of the League of Nations at Geneva in November 1924', August 1924, TNA, KKh 0301.1.6/22.

65 See Mackay, *Eastern Customs*, p. 135.

66 TNA, *Bangkok Times*, 21 March 1923.

67 'Interview of the League of Nations Commission of Enquiry with Prince Viwatchai, Deputy Secretary of State for Finance', 10 December 1929, LNA, S 194/3.

shops – that is, an average of about ten persons per shop' and, after a series of meetings, 'it was thought quite impracticable'.[68] In spite of these shortcomings, Siam had implemented international agreements regarding opium control to the limits of its capability, and notably without a domestic pressure group against opium as in Great Britain or the United States; Virginia Thompson pointed out that while 'Siamese public opinion is certainly against smoking, if not against smuggling', opium suppression was, to a large degree, a project of a small, internationally-oriented urban elite.[69] Thai government sources paint a detailed picture of continuous efforts to comply with new international legal requirements, particularly those coming from the League's OAC.[70] Siam's delegates could, therefore, travel to Geneva with a self-confident attitude in late 1924 to participate in the League of Nations' two major opium conferences.

The two Geneva Opium Conferences of 1924-25[71]

Following an initiative by the OAC, and by the United States delegation in particular, the League of Nations invited all concerned member states to Geneva for two conferences. The first, for Siam the more important Geneva Opium Conference, chaired by the Belgian W.G. van Wettum and the unanimously elected vice chairman Prince Charoon, aimed at strengthening measures against opium smoking in Asia.

During the long run-up to this First Geneva Opium Conference, Siam in 1923 received welcome support in its efforts to use opium control as a means to push for treaty revision from Elizabeth Hamilton Wright, the American observer on the OAC. Clearly aware of the connection between the fiscal importance of opium for Siam and Siam's lack of complete fiscal autonomy, she saw a chance to get Siam to improve opium control in exchange for US support for treaty revision. As Mrs. Hamilton Wright wrote to Prince Charoon in July 1923, the US would be willing to support Siam's case at the planned conference, 'I feel that Siam through opium has a very extraordinary opportunity to get rid of influences which have in many ways handicapped her in the past'.[72] Mrs. Hamilton Wright visited Prince Charoon in Paris early that month and the Prince was quite enthusiastic about her suggestion; he reported to Prince Traidos in Bangkok, 'Our voice in the Council of nations has very little weight. If a great power like the United States advocates our case, we have a better chance of the treaty powers listening and taking heed'.[73] But the government in Bangkok chose not to follow up on the American offer by formulating a strategy for combining opium issues with treaty revision at the Geneva Opium Conferences, firstly because by the time the conference convened in late 1924, Francis Sayre and Prince Charoon had already concluded negotiations with the French government and the Foreign Office in London had already signalled its willingness to also conclude a new treaty, and secondly because the

68 'Note on Meetings at the Ministry of Finance regarding the Opium Question', 13 March 1924, TNA, KKh 0301.1.6/18.

69 Thompson, *Thailand*, p. 741.

70 The 'Note on Meetings at the Ministry of Finance regarding the Opium Question', 13 March 1924, TNA, KKh 0301.1.6/18 is a very good example, as it considers OAC recommendations in great detail.

71 The meeting protocols of the First Geneva Opium Conference can be found in LNA, R 776/12A/40174/28626; the final documents of the First Geneva Opium Conference are in LNA, R 3159/12/819/819. Documents relating to the Second Geneva Opium Conference can be found in LNA, C.760.M.260.1924.XI. See also Raymond L. Buell, *The International Opium Conferences with Relevant Documents*, World Peace Foundation Pamphlets, vol. VIII, no. 2-3, Boston: World Peace Foundation, 1925; Willoughby, *Opium as an International Problem*, passim.

72 Hamilton Wright to Prince Charoon, 5 July 1923, TNA, KKh 0301.1.6/21.

73 Prince Charoon to Prince Traidos, 7 July 1923, TNA, KKh 0301.1.6/21.

government preferred to maintain its, ultimately successful, line of quiet and non-offensive diplomacy on the multilateral stage towards the European treaty powers. Prince Charoon was accordingly instructed to make the connection between opium policy and fiscal autonomy clear at the conference, but not to go as far as to publicly offend Great Britain or France because there was, in the words of the Foreign Ministry in Bangkok, no longer any 'necessity...of making use of the Opium question in any way as a lever for effecting the abolishment of extra-territoriality'.[74]

Prince Charoon, who described himself in a letter to Prince Traidos as 'only an amateur' in opium matters[75], acted exactly as instructed and used the conference to point to his government's inability to prosecute opium offences committed by foreign nationals because of European states' extraterritorial rights in Siam.[76] He further argued that his government was unable to effectively implement the planned registration and rationing scheme because the unequal treaties forced Siam to rely heavily on revenue from opium sales.[77] But Prince Charoon stepped short of demanding the abolition of treaties or otherwise forcefully putting pressure on his fellow diplomats from Europe. Furthermore, Prince Charoon did express his hope that it would be possible for the government in Bangkok to implement the comprehensive registration of opium smokers within three years.[78] This commitment seems not to have been authorised by the government in Bangkok and could not be fulfilled.[79] As long as opium smuggling could not be checked effectively, opium rationing plans seemed fairly pointless, as consumers could conveniently revert to illicit opium when the state reduced the amount it made available. In the final agreement of the First Geneva Opium Conference signatories agreed to strengthen the certificate system for the international opium trade and the state opium monopolies in Asia; two recommendations which Siam already fulfilled to a large degree. The 'Agreement concerning the Suppression of the Manufacture of, Internal Trade in, and Use of, Prepared Opium' was signed on 11 February 1925, came into force on 28 July 1926 and was ratified by Siam on 6 May 1927.[80]

Siam also participated in the much larger Second Geneva Opium Conference of 1924-25. In parallel to the first conference, this meeting, in the words of its president 'the most difficult in the history of the League of Nations', attempt to regulate the production and trade of all harmful drugs, such as heroin and cocaine, as well as opium, the raw material for many of these harmful drugs.[81] But a global restriction of opium production to the amount required for medical and scientific purposes, as propagated by the United States, could not be agreed upon and in the end, the American and Chinese delegations walked out of the conference. The resulting International Opium Convention, which nevertheless imposed stricter control measures on the basis of new statistical reporting standards, established the Permanent Central Opium Board as a

74 'Instructions to the Siamese Delegates at the First International Conference on Opium to be held under the auspices of the League of Nations at Geneva in November 1924', August 1924, TNA, KKh 0301.1.6/22.

75 Prince Charoon to Prince Traidos, 21 March 1924, TNA, KT 96.1.3/7.

76 'Instructions to the Siamese Delegates at the First International Conference on Opium to be held under the auspices of the League of Nations at Geneva in November 1924', August 1924, TNA, KKh 0301.1.6/22.

77 'Report of the Delegates on the First Opium Conference', 30 April 1925, TNA, KKh 0301.1.6/22; see also Buell, *International Opium Conferences*, p. 59.

78 'Report of the Delegates on the First Opium Conference', 30 April 1925, TNA, KKh 0301.1.6/22.

79 'Instructions to the Siamese Delegates at the First International Conference on Opium to be held under the auspices of the League of Nations at Geneva in November 1924', August 1924, TNA, KKh 0301.1.6/22; see also Annual Report on Siam for 1925, PRO, FO 371/11719, F1122/1122/40, p. 13.

80 For the text of the Geneva Opium Agreement see document C.82.M.41.1925.XI. in LNA, R 3159/12/819/819.

81 Frederick Llewellyn-Jones, *The League of Nations and the International Control of Dangerous Drugs*, Cambridge: W. Heffer & Sons, 1931, p. 28.

supervisory body and set new standards in the international opium and drug trade. It was signed on 19 February 1925, came into force on 25 September 1928 and was ratified by Siam on 11 October 1929.[82] The two Geneva Opium Conferences did not achieve the establishment of a comprehensive control regime for international opium trade, but further strengthened the provisions of the 1912 Hague Convention and the League's control mechanisms. At this point in time, Siam stood in the front row of progressive states avid for reform in opium matters.[83] Therefore, King Vajiravudh was able to state in his speech from the throne with regard to the Geneva Opium Conferences that 'the League is now pursuing objects which would yield results at which we ourselves have, also, been aiming'.[84] Siam's policies and the long-term goals of the League of Nations matched in this regard. In the light of political, social and economic realities, neither Geneva nor Bangkok aimed at an immediate ban of opium smoking but rather at a gradual suppression of the habit. And the reasons behind this policy were also judged similarly in Bangkok and Geneva, namely the economic importance of the opium monopolies for governments in Southeast Asia and the close connection with the problem of opium smuggling. Underlining these matching long-term objectives, Francis Sayre, General Adviser to the Thai government, summarised the outcome of an inter-ministerial meeting in Bangkok on opium matters in 1924, some months prior to the Geneva Conferences, as follows:

> It was agreed that the complete abolition of opium smoking must be effected, not simply because of foreign pressure brought through the League of Nations, but primarily because the ultimate welfare of Siam imperatively require it.[85]

This sentiment was echoed by Prince Charoon, who, after he had attended a meeting of the League's General Assembly at Geneva in 1926, in which the Indian delegate announced the phasing-out of opium exports for smoking until 1935 to the world, reported to Bangkok: 'So it behoves us to put our house in order to meet the situation'.[86] In the context of raw opium exports for smoking, a crucial matter of concern of the two Geneva Opium Conferences of 1924-25 was the implementation of the international import certificate system for raw opium, which was being applied by Siam already since 1923.[87] Certificates for legal imports of raw opium to Siam for the purpose of preparing opium for smoking were issued by the Ministry of Finance. If opium alkaloids or raw opium for medical purposes were imported, the Department of Public Health under the Ministry of Interior was the issuing agency of the certificate. This innovative system certainly marked one of the most important steps in international opium control. In the words of one contemporary commentator it was 'in fact the *sine qua non* of international [opium] control'.[88] It ensured that legal opium imports

82 On Siam's ratification see LNA, R 3160/12/4150/1148.

83 A similar judgement is expressed in an editorial in TNA, *Bangkok Times*, 23 May 1925: 'Siam marches in the front rank of the reformers, and can point to the fact that she is carrying out the terms of the Convention in effecting a reduction in the amount of the drug consumed in this country.'

84 Speech from the Throne, TNA, *Bangkok Times*, 5 January 1925.

85 Memorandum by F.B. Sayre, 28 June 1924, TNA, KKh 0301.1.6/18.

86 Report on the 7th Assembly, 30 September 1926, p. 22, TNA, KT, 96.1.3/12.

87 Prince Charoon to Drummond, 26 December 1922, LNA, R 736/12A/19025/16685; see also 'Cooperation of Siam in the Work of the League for the Control of the Traffic in Opium', enclosure in confidential letter Leith (League Secretariat's Information Section) to Chuen Charuvastra (Thai Ministry of Justice), 16 February 1923, LNA, R 1339/22/26180/26180.

88 Arthur Woods, *Dangerous Drugs: The World Fight against Illicit Traffic in Narcotics*, New Haven (CT): Yale University Press, 1931, p. 112.

The League of Nations commission of enquiry on opium smoking with Prince Viwatchai Chayant, Deputy Minister of Finance (fifth from left), Bangkok, December 1929. Others present include commission chairman Eric Ekstrand (sixth from left); commission members Bertil Renborg (third from left), Jan Havlasa (fourth from left) and Max-Léo Gérard (ninth from left) (courtesy of Paisarn Piemmattawat).

could be clearly identified and separated from illicit trade. Concerned authorities in the exporting and the importing country were informed on the details of the shipment, and standardised documentation accompanied the shipment itself. In accordance with this system, Siam imported raw opium from India, Persia and Turkey and regularly submitted reports on its opium imports to the League of Nations. The League carefully scrutinised the annual reports and the Secretariat did not hesitate to enquire with Siam or other concerned governments in the case of non-corresponding export and import figures.[89]

A new Opium Law was enacted in Siam in late 1929, which went beyond the old law by expanding state control on opium dross, as the OAC and the two Geneva Opium Conferences had demanded. While licensed operators of opium houses had hitherto resold the dross to addicts for some thirty percent of the price of prepared opium, the opium monopoly now bought back the opium dross at a fixed price from the licensees and then resold it to consumers. These dross consumers had to register in the course of one year to obtain a license, after which no new licenses for the purchase of dross were issued. With this step, the Thai government implemented, albeit only for dross and not for prepared opium itself, the registration system which the League of Nations was promoting and which the government itself had been considering since 1921. New administrative procedures for the opium houses, especially concerning dross, had already been issued by the Ministry of Finance in 1927, and the lack of effective legal guidelines for dross sales had become the object of frequent newspaper articles in Bangkok and the region during that year.[90] But the new opium law was only enacted in anticipation of the visit of the League of Nations commission of enquiry on opium, to which the Thai government wished to present itself as conscientious in the national implementation of international agreements. As the financial adviser to the Thai government, Sir Edward Cook, pointed out towards the Ministry of Justice in mid-1929:

89 See, for example, the case of the annual report on traffic in opium submitted by the Thai government for the year 1927, which, because of inaccurate calculations, listed less opium as imports from India than India reported as exports to Siam. The League confronted the Thai government with this inaccuracy in early 1929, which led to an extensive exchange of notes within the Ministry of Finance and ultimately, in the words of Sir Edward Cook, to a 'peccavi' reply to the League; TNA, KKh 0301.1.6/35.

90 Finance Circular of 22 February B.E. 2469 (1927), TNA, KKh 0301.1.6/29. The same file contains clippings of various newspaper articles on the issue of the government's inadequate policy regarding dross, e.g. *Siam Observer, Bangkok Times, Straits Times*.

91 Cook to L'Evesque, 17 July 1929, TNA, KKh 0301.1.6/37. See also Mackenzie to Secretary of State, 14 January 1930, TKRI, United States Department of State, Consular Reports Siam, 890.00 P.R./17. An English version of the Thai Opium Act B.E. 2472 can be found in LNA, S 209.

92 See LNA, R 3318/14/6286/ 1502 and R 3201/12/6245/ 6245 for documents regarding the British initiative; see also Confidential Memorandum by Prince Varn and Prince Vipulya, 27 September 1928, TNA, KKh 0301.1.6/37; and Doc. 20-22 in BDFA, Part II, Series J, vol. 1, p. 75ff.

93 Confidential Memorandum by Prince Varn and Prince Vipulya, 27 September 1928, TNA, KKh 0301.1.6/37.

94 See various documents relating to preparations in Siam for the visit of the commission in TNA, KKh 0301.1.6/37; see also the speech by Prince Varn before the League Council on 13 December 1928 in Lugano, LNA, League of Nations, Official Journal, no. 1, January 1929, p. 35; and LNA, R 3318/14/8424/1502. Prince Charoon had originally been invited to participate in an earlier Council meeting on the same subject on 31 August but was already too ill to attend at the time; see various correspondence in LNA, R 3318/14/6286/1502 and R 3201/12/6245/6245. The Thai government contributed 13,650 Swiss francs to the expenses of the commission; see financial files in LNA, R 3203/12/11288/6245 and R 3203/12/8618/6245. On the composition of the commission of enquiry see Drummond to Prince Devawongse, 27 May 1929, LNA, R 3203/12/11288/ 6245; besides Ekstrand, it was formed by Belgian Max-Léo Gérard, Czech Jan Havlasa, Bertil Renborg of the League Secretariat and a shorthand stenographer.

95 Note by Opium Department on 'Visit of League emissaries for the study of opium problem', 10 November 1928, TNA, KKh 0301.1.6/37.

96 Prince Varn to Drummond, 1 June 1929, Enclosure: Note by the Ministry of Finance, LNA, R 3203/12/11288/6245. A detailed programme of the visit can be found in TNA, KKh 0301.1.6/37.

...a League of Nations Commission...will arrive in Siam in the coming autumn...You will appreciate therefore that it will be most unfortunate if Siam has to confess that she has not yet given legal sanction to the provisions which she undertook to enforce. It is the opinion of this Ministry and of the Ministry of Foreign Affairs that the sooner the Law is promulgated the better; even at the best we shall have to make what excuses we can for having been so long about the business.[91]

The League of Nations commission of enquiry on opium smoking

In 1929 the League of Nations appeared in Siam not only indirectly via international agreements but in person through the members of a commission of enquiry on the opium situation in the kingdom. The commission had been appointed following a British initiative the previous year, to collect for the first time, first-hand and reliable information on the opium situation in Asia for the League of Nations.[92] In Geneva, Prince Varn and his colleague Prince (*Mom Chao*) Vipulya Svastiwongse Svastikul, Thai Minister in Copenhagen, speculated, however,

> ...that the real object of the British proposal is to find out and to expose bad conditions concerning the control of opium smoking in the Far East including, if possible, the Philippines, so that the results may be brought up before the Opium Conference which it is proposed to hold in 1929, in order that India may possibly find excuses for not being able to carry out the terms of the Hague Convention and the Geneva Agreement in regard to Opium.[93]

Nevertheless, the commission, chaired by the Swedish diplomat Eric Ekstrand, former Swedish Minister in Argentina, and made up of five persons in total, travelled to nearly all Southeast Asian territories and Japan between September 1929 and May 1930. The government in Bangkok welcomed the appointment of the commission and actively participated in the practical and financial preparations.[94] The Opium Department in the Ministry of Finance felt confident that it had done all in its power to comply with international opium agreements and suggested an extensive itinerary for the commission, including a visit to the northern border 'where illicit opium is grown and smugglers make their entrance into Siam'.[95] The commission members arrived in Bangkok on 30 November 1929 and stayed a fortnight before travelling on to Saigon on 15 December. For its enquiry on the ground the commission was given full freedom; the four commissioners conducted 35 interviews, surveyed opium houses, the government laboratory, opium depots, administrative offices of the opium monopoly and port facilities.[96] The visit was organised by the Thai government as if it were an official state visit; dinners were hosted for the commissioners by the

Minister of Finance and the Minister of Foreign Affairs, a soirée was held in their honour by Prince Damrong, they signed visitor's books in no less than five different royal palaces, they were given sightseeing tours of all spectacular sights of Bangkok and Ayutthaya, and at the end of their visit the commission members were received by the king at Bang Pa-in. The commission was lodged at the Phya Thai Hotel close to the Grand Palace, 'drinks, ice, soda, spirits, beer, wines, and cigars [were] sufficiently provided', and all costs were borne by the Thai government.[97] The visit also received extensive press coverage, giving an indication of its importance for Bangkok's urban elite.[98]

The commission conducted a key interview on 4 and 10 December with Prince (*Mom Chao*) Viwatchai Chayant, Deputy Minister of Finance, and Phraya Bibadhanakorn (Chim Besayanu), Director-General of the Opium Department, which Prince Viwatchai opened by stressing that 'we are at your service for as long as you can bear to listen to us'.[99] The records of the interview reveal a very frank exchange, in which the Thai government representatives provided an accurate and very detailed picture of the situation as well as of the limitations of the government's policies. The transcript of the interview suggests that the Cambridge-educated Prince Viwatchai was an ideal interviewee from both the perspective of the Thai government and of the commission, as he possessed a great deal of international experience from his participation at a number of the League's international financial conferences. In fact, Prince Viwatchai, born in 1899 and a grandson of King Mongkut, went on to represent Siam at the annual conferences of the League's Economic and Financial Organisation until 1935, was later the first governor of the Thai central bank from 1942, played a key role in post-war peace negotiations and remained closely connected to the League's successor, the United Nations, until his death in 1960.

The commission also interviewed the Thai government's inter-ministerial opium commission which, set up in 1925, was chaired by Prince (*Phra Ong Chao*) Kitiyakara Voralaksana of Chandaburi, long-time Minister of Finance and later Minister of Commerce, and assembled Thai and foreign representatives of different ministries.[100] Furthermore, the commission interviewed Phraya Komarakul Montri (Chuen Komarakul na Nagara), Minister of Finance; Prince Sakol Voravarn, Director-General of the Public Health Department in the Ministry of Interior; Alec Malcolm, the British chairman of the international Chamber of Commerce; William Mundie, editor of the *Bangkok Times*, as well as officials of the opium monopoly, police officials, abbots, doctors, missionaries, representatives of the Chinese community, managers of government opium shops, mining and railway officials. The Ministry of Finance even issued a communiqué inviting anyone to give evidence to the commission.[101] In its interviews and inspections, the commission was very thorough, on occasion astonishingly so; the manager of the Bombay

97 See various memoranda and correspondence regarding practical preparations for the visit of the commission in TNA, KKh 0301.1.1.6/37.

98 See various issues of TNL, *Siam Observer* and TNA, *Bangkok Times* between late November and mid-December 1929.

99 The detailed minutes of all interviews conducted by the commission of enquiry can be found in LNA, S 194/3 and 4. See also Memorandum on the Interview of 4 December 1929, TNA, KKh 0301.1.6/37.

100 On the creation of the permanent opium commission see 'Report by the Government of Siam for the Calendar Year 1925', LNA, R 755/12A/56100/18661.

101 The *Bangkok Times* commented favourably on this government initiative to call for opinions but remarked: 'It is difficult to see what more a Government could do to secure an expression of public opinion. But as far as we know there has been no or practically no response to this invitation.' TNA, *Bangkok Times*, 31 October 1929.

Burma Corporation in Siam was asked by commission chairman Ekstrand whether he thought elephants could become opium addicts, to which the interviewee could only reply dryly, 'I hope not'.[102]

The commission evaluated Siam's opium policy as serious and effective, and was particularly impressed by the factory, in which the monopoly prepared raw opium for smoking. According to one commissioner, this factory was particularly well organised and 'one of the best in the Far East'.[103] In a confidential letter to the League Secretariat, Bertil Renborg, a member of the commission of enquiry, reported extensively on the very cooperative attitude displayed by representatives of the Thai government.[104] He judged the opium houses for the sale and consumption of opium as particularly effective; and in its landmark report the commission of enquiry later recommended the adoption of the Thai system of opium houses in all of Asia.[105] Renborg, like the Thai government, also saw the disadvantages resulting from the high retail price for legal opium and informally recommended that it be lowered. He summarised the attitude of the government on the financial aspects of opium as follows:

> ...as long as opium smoking is permitted, it is better that the Government gets revenue than that that profit goes into the pocket of the smuggler, but on the other hand the Government is quite prepared to sacrifice its revenue when they can assure complete suppression of opium smuggling.

In the same confidential letter, Renborg also made two interesting general remarks which shed light on his preconceptions of Siam and his experiences on the spot:

> I have the impression that the Siamese Government is seriously concerned with the spread of the habit among the Siamese and there is no doubt that the Government is willing and desirous of improving the situation...It was very interesting to make the enquiry in an Oriental country ruled by its own people and that was to be expected. It would seem that the Government took a more paternal interest in the opium problem than in other countries ruled by European powers.[106]

The commission of enquiry submitted its final report to the Council of the League of Nations in November 1930.[107] The report reaffirmed the policy of a gradual suppression of opium smoking over an immediate ban in recognition of practical feasibility. While Siam received a generally positive assessment, the report was critical about the degree of state control. It pointed especially to the fact that only 51 of the 972 opium houses in the kingdom were operated by state employees who received a fixed salary. All other houses were still operated by licensees who had an interest in selling as much opium as possible because they earned their profit from reselling dross to the state monopoly.[108] In spite

102 LNA, S 194/3.

103 Johns to Henderson, 23 December 1929, PRO, FO 415, F 581/545/87, *The Opium Trade*, no. 13, part XXVI, vol. 6.

104 Renborg to Crowdy, 15 January 1930, LNA, R 3203/12/14411/6245. See also an interview given by Eric Ekstrand to the *Siam Observer* on 15 December, in which he spoke highly of Siam's opium policy and the government's cooperation with the commission of enquiry: TNL, *Siam Observer*, 16 December 1929.

105 Commission of Enquiry into the Control of Opium-smoking in the Far East, Report to the Council, p. 142f., LNA, C.635. M.254.1930.XI.

106 Renborg to Crowdy, 15 January 1930, LNA, R 3203/12/14411/6245.

107 Commission of Enquiry into the Control of Opium-smoking in the Far East, Report to the Council, LNA, C.635.M.254. 1930.XI.

108 Commission of Enquiry into the Control of Opium-smoking in the Far East, Report to the Council, p. 79, LNA, C.635. M.254.1930.XI.

of the criticism, the Thai government was, rightly, pleased with the report and commented favourably on it to the League.[109]

The report by the commission of enquiry remains an outstanding achievement in the history of international opium control until today.[110] With hindsight we can see that its recommendations were well ahead of its times; only in the 1960s and 1970s did Thailand try to implement many of the report's recommendations.[111] Nevertheless, the Thai government had reason to feel generally reassured in its opium policy by the report when it was published in 1930.

The Bangkok Opium Conference of 1931

With the report by the commission of enquiry, the League now had a comprehensive assessment of the opium situation in Southeast Asia, on the basis of which the failures and achievements of ten years of international opium control could be evaluated and future steps could be planned. To this end, the follow-up conference envisaged in article twelve of the Geneva Opium Agreement of 1925 was planned for the year 1931. Siam seized the initiative and extended an invitation to the League Council to hold this conference in Bangkok.[112] Already during the visit of the commission of enquiry to the kingdom, Eric Ekstrand had suggested that the follow-up conference be held in Siam, and Prince Traidos submitted the suggestion to the king in September 1930. He explained that such a conference would be a 'unique chance to glorify Siam' and that the cost involved would be greatly outweighed by the benefits. King Prajadhipok deemed it 'most proper' to organise the conference, and Prince Traidos instructed Prince Varn to officially invite the League of Nations on 22 September 1930.[113] The acceptance of this invitation by the League and its member states was seen by the Bangkok elite, in the words of King Prajadhipok, as 'a signal honour conferred on Siam'.[114] Holding this international diplomatic conference in an Asian country was as much a first for the Thai government as it was for the League of Nations itself. Discussions in the League Secretariat during 1930 acknowledged the logistical difficulties and financial implications but ultimately judged: 'If one takes a long view of the League's work in this field [opium control], one cannot avoid the conclusion that the holding of the Conference in the Far East is highly desirable'.[115]

While delegates and League representatives bore their travel costs, the Thai government committed 150,000 Swiss francs to the organisation of the conference.[116] The logistical preparations in Bangkok were extensive, and they were taken very seriously by the Thai government. Sahadaya Hall in the palace grounds was prepared, staff was assigned, mail, telegram and telephone connections were set up for the delegates, and hotel rooms were reserved at various hotels in town, including the Phya Thai Hotel, the Oriental, Royal and Trocadero Hotels. Not only in-town transport was arranged but also railway transfer

109 Secretary-General to Minister of Foreign Affairs, 28 February 1931 and Observations by the Siamese Government on the Report by the Commission of Enquiry, n.d. (1931), TNA, KKh 0301.1.6/40; see also Prince Devawongse to Drummond, 29 May 1931, Enclosure: Observations by the Siamese Government on the Report of the League of Nation's Commission of Enquiry into the Control of Opium-smoking in the Far East, LNA, R 3203/12/11288/ 6245.

110 Spencer and Navaratnam, *Drug Abuse in East Asia*, p. 15, shared this assessment in 1981: 'The 1930 report of the League of Nations Commission is an extensive, painstaking, and informed document which...provides a picture of drug abuse in the region...which had never been attempted before, or achieved since.'

111 Spencer and Navaratnam, *Drug Abuse in East Asia*, p. 22.

112 See the extensive documentation in LNA, R 3159/12/819/819. On the Council decision see LNA, League of Nations, *Official Journal*, no. 2, February 1931, p. 197. See also TNA, *Bangkok Times*, 23 January 1931.

113 Prince Varn to Prince Devawongse, 9 September 1930; Prince Devawongse to Royal Secretariat, 17 September B.E. 2473 (1930); Note by King Prajadhipok, 19 September B.E. 2473 (1930); Prince Devawongse to Prince Varn, 22 September 1930; all in TNA, R7, T 10/16.

114 Speech from the Throne, TNA, *Bangkok Times*, 27 February 1931.

115 Memorandum Duncan Hall, 6 August 1930, LNA, R 3406/ 17/17336/16866. The League conference establishing the Singapore Bureau of the League's Health Organisation was held in the British colony in 1925 and was the only prior League conference in Asia.

116 On financial issues relating to the Bangkok Conference see LNA, R 3159/12/7220/819. In the end, the amount contributed by the League was 15,500 Swiss francs, while the Thai government paid some 76,000 Swiss francs to the League.

from Penang port to the Thai capital. For transport within the city, each delegation, as well as Mr. Ekstrand, was provided with one automobile for the duration of the conference, and it was arranged for conference participants to access the Chitlada Golf Club as well as the Royal Bangkok Sports Club.[117] Prince Varn was busy welcoming delegates during the days preceding the conference, as he was personally acquainted with many of them from his time at Geneva until the previous year. Invitations were extended to all conference participants for a royal garden party at Dusit Palace on the second day of the conference, 10 November, on the occasion of the king's birthday.[118] Preparations for the event seem to have occupied a considerable part of the government elite, including a number of senior princes, members of the royal household and even King Prajadhipok himself, who, for example, worried whether the mask dancers would have enough time to rehearse before performing for the conference participants.[119]

Given the importance of the event, conference preparations were marked by rivalries between the Ministry of Finance and the Ministry of Foreign Affairs over which would take the lead role. Prince Viwatchai, Director-General of the Opium Department, demanded that the Ministry of Finance be in charge of all instructions to Siam's delegation: 'my opinion is that the opium question is our question, and this Ministry must uphold its dignity'.[120] In the end, instructions to the Thai delegates were drawn up jointly by the Ministries of Finance and Foreign Affairs, and while they generally recommended to support the League's policies as far as possible, they did remain sceptical of certain far-reaching measures, such as the comprehensive registration of smokers, opium retail exclusively by government employees, provisions for anti-opium education or medical treatment of opium addicts.[121] And, on the opening day of the conference, additional instructions were issued with regard to the controversial issue of what to do with opium dross, and delegates were told to avoid the issue as far as possible.[122]

The conference opened in the grounds of the Grand Palace on 9 November 1931 and lasted until 27 November.[123] Prince Damrong attended the opening session, and the king sent a royal message, in which he acknowledged the conference as a contribution to 'the better welfare of the world at large and in the sole interest of humanity'.[124] In his opening statement, Prince Traidos expressed the government's gratitude,

> …that this particular Conference should be discussing the question of opium. Siam has always been a firm supporter of the League of Nations and I feel certain that the present Conference will make the League better known to the people of this country and will inspire them with even greater confidence in its strength and its future.[125]

117 On logistical arrangements see Phraya Srivisarn to Ekstrand, 10 July 1931, and Ekstrand to Phraya Srivisarn, 23 July 1931, both in LNA, R 3159/12/819/ 819.

118 Note, n.d., TNA, R7, T 10/16.

119 Note by King Prajadhipok, 26 October B.E. 2474 (1931), TNA, R7, T 10/17.

120 Prince Viwatchai to Minister of Finance, 23 July B.E. 2474 (1931), TNA, KKh 0301.1.6/40.

121 Instructions to Delegates at Opium Conference to be held in Bangkok in November next, n.d., TNA, KKh 0301.1.6/40.

122 Supplemental Instructions, 9 November 1931, TNA, KKh 0301.1.6/40.

123 The conference protocols, minutes and the final agreement are found in LNA, C.577. M.284.1932.XI and in TNA, KKh 0301.1.1.6/41 (Parts 1 and 2), 42 (Parts 1 and 2). See also LNA, R 3196/12/33815/3865 and the November and December 1931 issues of TNA, *Bangkok Times*, which cover the conference proceedings in great detail.

124 Royal Message, 7 November 1931, TNA, KKh 0301.1.6/40.

125 Opening Speech, 7 November 1931, TNA, KKh 0301.1.6/40.

Cecil Dormer, the British Minister in Bangkok, remarked, 'It was a most representative gathering and testified to the importance which the Siamese attach to the fact that it is the first international conference to meet in Siam under the League of Nations'.[126] Next to the host government, delegations from Great Britain (including delegates from Hong Kong, Straits Settlements and Federated Malay States), India (Burma), France, Japan (including a delegate from the administration of Taiwan), the Netherlands (including delegates from the Netherlands Indies) and Portugal (Macao) took part in the conference, and the United States (including a delegate from the Philippines) sent a delegation with observer status. Significantly, the Chinese government declined the invitation to participate, as it was clear that they would be accused throughout the event as the main source of opium smuggling in Asia.[127] Among the delegations which did participate were some of the 'grand old men' of international opium control, some of whom had sat on the OAC for a decade, and the Netherlands' delegate who had even been a member of the Shanghai Commission as far back as 1909. The head of the Thai delegation to the conference, Deputy Minister of Foreign Affairs Phraya Srivisarn Vacha, was elected conference chairman as a matter of custom and courtesy. The Thai delegation was further made up of Prince Viwatchai, the Director-General of the Revenue Department in the Ministry of Finance, Phraya Bibadhanakorn, Director-General of the same Ministry's Opium Department and member of the inter-ministerial opium commission and as secretary to the delegation, Phra Manjuvadi, who was head of the League of Nations Section in the Ministry of Foreign Affairs. Phraya Srivisarn Vacha, later Minister of Foreign Affairs, who had intimate knowledge of the League of Nations and international opium control from his time as diplomat in Europe during the 1920s, had been carefully chosen for his ability to chair the conference, which he was said to have done with great skill. Sir Malcolm Delevingne, British delegate at the conference and perhaps the single most prominent advocate of international opium control during the interwar decades, called him 'an admirable president' in a confidential report.[128] Eric Ekstrand, who had chaired the League's commission of enquiry, acted as the conference's secretary-general, supported by Mani Sanasen, the only Thai national employed by the League, and Bertil Renborg, both of the League Secretariat.[129] The delegates spent the first week on the exchange of detailed information on the opium situation in the European colonies in Southeast Asia and in Siam. Thereafter, in closed session, problematic issues such as smuggling and illegal opium production were debated. In one of these three 'secret meetings', Prince Viwatchai presented the situation in Siam with regard to opium smuggling; he stated clearly that some sixty percent of smuggled opium was estimated to be brought in from the Burmese Shan States and more than twenty percent from French

126 Dormer to Simon, 14 November 1931, PRO, FO 451, F 7515/172/87, *The Opium Trade*, part XXVIII, vol. 6. no. 25; see also the report by Eric Ekstrand in Ekstrand to Drummond, 9 November 1931, LNA, R3159/12/33455/819.

127 See on the 63rd session of the Council, during which it was decided to invite China, LNA, R 3159/12/819/819.

128 Delevingne to Foreign Office, 23 December 1931, PRO, FO 415, F 418/225/87, *The Opium Trade*, part XXIX, vol. 6, no. 1; see also Dormer to Simon, 14 December 1932, PRO, FO 371/17174, F 399/42/40. On the role of Sir Malcolm Delevingne see Meyer and Parssinen, *Webs of Smoke*, p. 24f. and 33. On the selection of Phraya Srivisarn see also Prince Damras to Prince Devawongse, 13 July 1931, TNA, KKh 0301.1.1.6/40 (Part 1 of 2).

129 Ekstrand insisted that Mani travel to Bangkok in his capacity as an official of the Secretariat to support him, see Ekstrand to Mani, 12 August 1931, LNA, R 3159/12/7220/819. Bertil Renborg left a particularly negative impression on the Thai delegates, who reported that he was 'the most unpopular man with both the Secretariat officials and with the delegates. He has an insolent and conceited air about him…The situation was unpleasant, as Mr. van Wettum, the Vice President of the Conference, practically hated both Ekstrand and Renborg.' See Report by the Siamese Delegation on the Bangkok Conference, 18 December 1931, TNA, KKh 0301.1.6/42.

Indochina, much of it originating in the Chinese province of Yunnan.[130] At the heart of all discussions, however, were the recommendations contained in the report by the commission of enquiry of the previous year. But the delegations could not agree on far-reaching measures, too deep were the rifts between them on individual issues. Sir Malcolm in particular repeatedly attacked delegates from France, Portugal and Japan with regard to their ineffective monopolies or their lack of proper import procedures. The Thai government, in contrast, came out of the conference with a rather untarnished image with regard to its opium policy. In the end, and in spite of the differences, the conference participants managed to agree on improved measures with regard to opium dross control along the lines of the measures already being implemented in Siam and to agree on improved measures for the protection of minors against opium consumption.

Accordingly, although the results of the Bangkok Conference were modest or, in the words of the London *Guardian*, 'very meagre', no one had realistically expected a more dramatic outcome.[131] For all participating delegations the main problem remained the large amount of opium – over three quarters of the estimated global production, which was illegally produced in China, and a substantial part of which then found its way along the smuggling routes into Southeast Asia. The Chinese government was named as the main culprit several times during the closed sessions by the British and French delegates, while the Persian government was also blamed for encouraging poppy cultivation. In the opinion of the Thai government as well as the European colonial governments in Southeast Asia, until the large-scale illicit opium trade could be effectively checked, individual control measures by states or colonies would remain largely ineffective.[132]

The conference ended with the signing of the 'Bangkok Agreement on the Suppression of Opium-smoking in the Far East' of 27 November 1931, the first multilateral agreement in international law which was associated with the name of the Thai capital. The Bangkok Agreement marked an improvement over the first Geneva Opium Agreement in that it demanded complete control by the state monopolies of opium from its import to its retail sale by state employees at a fixed price and in that it forbid opium sales to persons under twenty-one years of age. The agreement also encouraged closer cooperation among Asian administrations against the illicit opium trade. Siam ratified the agreement on 19 November 1934 after Great Britain, France, Portugal and the Netherlands had already done so. India's and Japan's ratifications did not follow until 1937, and the Bangkok Agreement consequently came into force on 22 April 1937.[133]

Irrespective of the long ratification process, a new opium law was enacted in Siam already on 31 March 1934. The so-called 'Opium Act B.E. 2472 Amendment Act B.E. 2476' implemented the recom-

130 Provisional Minutes of Second Secret Meeting held on 12 November 1931, TNA, KKh 0301.1.6/40.

131 *Guardian*, 28 November 1931, LNA, R 3159/12/33800/819.

132 See Report by the Siamese Delegation on the Bangkok Conference, 18 December 1931, TNA, KKh 0301.1.6/42; see also TNA, *Bangkok Times*, 26 August 1924, 30 September 1926, and 21 September 1929.

133 The text of the agreement can be found in LNA, R 3159/12/33007/819. On ratifications see LNA, COL, Box 115, Files 136 through 141. See also Bailey, *The Anti-Drug Campaign*, p. 32.

mendations of the Bangkok Agreement by strengthening the state's control of opium dross, raising the minimum age for opium consumption from eighteen to twenty-one years of age and increasing police competencies in the fight against opium smugglers. In the following year, the maximum punishment for opium offences was raised to ten years of imprison-ment.[134] Siam had once again demonstrated its seriousness to the world in transforming an international agreement into domestic legislation and W.D. Reeve, foreign adviser to the Bangkok excise department, expressed what can be taken as at least a partial motivation of the administration in implementing the Bangkok Agreement, 'I feel we must make the biggest "show" possible so that we can write colourful reports to Geneva'.[135] But the government's problem with regard to opium dross remained, namely that it was unable to export the dross bought back from the opium shops for morphine production in Europe or the United States, as the international opium control system did not allow any international trade in opium dross.[136]

Immediately after the end of the conference, the Thai government landed a coup by convincing Sir Malcolm Delevingne to travel to the northern border, where 'he was able to see for himself the nature and extent of the land frontier bordering on the Shan States and Indo China'. Accompanied by Prince Viwatchai and Phraya Srivisarn, the situation on the ground must have made quite an impression on Sir Malcolm, and he not only acknowledged the difficulties which originated from the virtually uncontrolled opium production in the Shan States, but confidentially suggested that the government in Bangkok buy opium produced by the hill tribes in the border region. 'In this way it was hoped the question of smuggling would be greatly improved and the hill tribes would become friendly and law abiding'.[137]

How does the balance sheet of the Bangkok Opium Conference present itself? First and foremost, a success not to be underestimated is that the conference took place at all, especially during times of economic depression and when the attention of the international political public was absorbed by the rapidly unfolding Manchurian Conflict between Japan and China. The meeting was a success for the movement towards better international opium control because, once again, representatives of nearly all concerned Far Eastern states and colonies met to search for possible solutions to the problems and, at least modestly, improved the set of international rules on opium. The conference was also a success for the League of Nations, as it was visible as a living organisation in Siam. In the words of Eric Ekstrand during the closing session of the conference, 'the spirit of international co-operation – so often referred to as the League spirit – was not only confined to Geneva, but was found also in this country so far away from the seat of the League'.[138] The press played an important role in facilitating this visibility in Bangkok by covering the proceedings of the conference in great detail on every single day.[139]

134 TNA, *Bangkok Times*, 17 April 1934 and 23 November 1935.

135 Reeve to Baxter, 15 November 1932, TNA, KKh 0301.1.6/40.

136 This issue had been raised time and again since the late 1920s, not only within Thai government ministries, but also by Thai delegates to the OAC in Geneva; see various memoranda and correspondence in TNA, KKh 0301.1.6/40.

137 Report by the Siamese Delegation on the Bangkok Conference, 18 December 1931, TNA, KKh 0301.1.6/42.

138 Minutes of the Bangkok Conference, p. 107, LNA, C.577. M284.1932.XI.

139 See the extensive coverage, which in some issues spreads over several pages, in TNA, *Bangkok Times*, 3 November through 1 December 1931, and 29 December 1931. While the bulk of the published material follows minutes of meetings, it also contains commentaries, both positive and critical on the work of the conference.

And it was, finally, a particular success for the Thai government and the Thai elite. For it was the only time in pre-Second World War history that Siam did not simply participate in an international political meeting, but actually hosted it in its own capital. For the Thai elite, the conference was a grand opportunity to demonstrate its progressiveness and underline its legitimate demand for complete sovereignty towards Western governments. They managed to impress delegates as generous hosts and, by organising an event in accordance with the international standards of the time, further contributed to the changing perceptions of Siam in the West as an increasingly civilised and modern country which was to be taken seriously. Ekstrand reported to Secretary-General Drummond, 'The Siamese Government has made excellent arrangements for the Conference, which includes a very good conference hall and the necessary offices for the delegates, the Press and the Secretariat.'[140] Prince Viwatchai and Phraya Bibadhanakorn summarised:

> What has Siam gained by the Conference?…Our honesty of purpose has been acknowledged and accepted. We have been able to enlist the sympathy of those whose opinion is entitled to international respect in the matter of opium.[141]

The importance which the Bangkok Conference had for the ruling elite was further underlined by King Prajadhipok in February 1932, when he wrote in a message on the occasion of his coronation anniversary, 'It has been a matter of gratification to Myself and to My Government that the Council of the League of Nations decided to convene the last opium Conference in Bangkok'.[142] It was to be not only the most important but also the last gratifying international event to take place in Bangkok for King Prajadhipok before a coup d'état swept away the absolute monarchy four months later.

Opium smuggling

Opium smuggling into Siam increased steadily once Siam put its raw opium imports under the League of Nations' new import certificate system during the mid-1920s, and particularly from the mid-1930s, when India stopped exporting opium for smoking to Siam. Siam's inaccessible northern border was particularly vulnerable to smuggling activities, and opium was brought into the kingdom along routes from Burma and Yunnan. The border was, and remains to a certain extent still today, impossible to police effectively as an American missionary from Chiang Mai told the League's commission of enquiry in 1929, 'The border is an absolute sieve, mountainous and wooded country most of it. If that border were policed properly, it would take all the resources of the Siamese Government'.[143] Some years earlier, the British consul in Chiang Mai, W.A.R. Wood, had already acknowledged that 'it is an absolute

140 Ekstrand to Drummond, 9 November 1931, LNA, R 3159/ 12/33455/819.

141 Report by the Siamese Delegation on the Bangkok Conference, 18 December 1931, TNA, KKh 0301.1.6/42.

142 TNA, *Bangkok Times*, 27 February 1932.

143 'Interview of League of Nations Commission of Enquiry into the Control of Opium-smoking in the Far East with Dr. Edwin Cort', 9 December 1929, LNA, S 194/4. The *Bangkok Times* was full of reports on opium smuggling during the 1920s and 1930s; see, for example, TNA, *Bangkok Times*, 6 June 1922; 20 August 1922; 20 April 1928; 1 July 1929; throughout 1930; 30 August 1932; 1 May 1933; 3 November 1934; 1 July 1935; 24 August 1935. On opium production in Burma and smuggling into Siam see the two outstanding articles by Robert Maule: Robert B. Maule, 'The Opium Question in the Federated Shan States, 1931-36: British Policy Discussions and Scandal', *Journal of Southeast Asian Studies*, 23, 1 (March 1992), pp. 14-36; Robert B. Maule, 'British Policy Discussions on the Opium Question in the Federated Shan States, 1937-1948', *Journal of Southeast Asian Studies*, 33, 2 (June 2002), pp. 203-224. See also Renard, *Burmese Connection*.

impossibility, in view of the length of the frontier (about 300 miles), and the nature of the country, to prevent, or even considerably to limit, smuggling'.[144] According to Virginia Thompson, at least 1 million *tamlung* (or 37.5 tons) of opium were smuggled into Siam this way annually during the 1930s, far exceeding the amount of licit opium available in the country and generating an estimated 3 million baht in profits. State-confiscated illicit opium was so large in quantity that, for instance, between 1932 and 1935 the government did not even need to import any opium legally to meet domestic demand. The extent of smuggling activities is also illustrated by the high number of recorded drug offences, largely smuggling, which peaked in 1937 with 11,809 cases.[145]

Opium smuggling became such a lucrative enterprise for cross-border criminal networks and such a pressing problem for officials that the government in Bangkok repeatedly approached the neighbouring colonial administrations during the 1920s and 1930s to sound out joint measures.[146] British authorities, who had established a system of indirect rule in parts of Burma, exercised little control over opium production and smuggling in the so-called Federated Shan States. A report submitted to the League's commission of enquiry in late 1929 even mentioned the exact location of an opium factory only 5 kilometres beyond the border with Siam, which was 'ostentatiously situated on the roadside, containing a spacious building, with a daily output of 700 *tamlung*, or 26 kilograms, of prepared opium and an ever ready stock of sale'.[147] In fact, British colonial authorities in Burma showed little willingness to act effectively against opium smuggling into Siam throughout the League's lifetime. The ethnic minority peoples in Siam's north also produced opium and, although they consumed much of their crop, increasingly large amounts of this home-grown opium illegally found its way to addicts in the central and southern parts of the kingdom.

The ominous connection between opium smuggling and corruption among government officials in Siam became dramatically apparent in 1935. In that year a spectacular smuggling operation came to light through an article in the *Straits Times*, in which the British financial adviser to the Thai government, James Baxter, who had resigned from office over the affair, wrote, 'This is probably the largest single contraband operation that has ever taken place even in the luridly chequered history of opium'.[148] What had occurred? In January 1935 the unusually large amount of 250,000 *tamlung*, or 9.3 tons, of prepared opium was 'smuggled' on trucks from the Burmese Shan States to Siam, an amount which easily covered one third of Siam's legal annual requirement of prepared opium. It then emerged that law enforcement officials had left Bangkok already two weeks earlier, in order to 'intercept' the vehicle convoy and to 'confiscate' the opium. In fact, this particular opium deal had been agreed upon already in April 1934 when Luang

144 Wood to Greg, 21 January 1926, TNA, KKh 0301.1.1.6/26.

145 See Thompson, *Thailand*, p. 731ff., also more generally on law enforcement activities. The same figure is given in TNA, *Bangkok Times*, 24 December 1937.

146 Waterlow to Chamberlain, 5 September 1927, PRO, FO 451, F 8042/1302/40, *The Opium Trade*, part XXIV, vol. 6, no. 11; Delevingne to Foreign Office, 23 December 1931, PRO, FO 451, F 418/225/87, *The Opium Trade*, part XXIX, vol. 6, no. 1. On contacts between the British administration in Burma and the Bangkok government regarding opium smuggling into Siam between 1919 and 1920 see also Memorandum on Opium in Siam by the Ministry of Finance, 8 March B.E. 2463 (1921), TNA, KKh 0301.1.6/17. That smuggling was a major problem for all territories in the region is shown, for example, by Eric Tagliacozzo, *Secret Trades, Porous Borders: Smuggling and States Along a Southeast Asian Frontier, 1865-1915*, New Haven (CT): Yale University Press, 2005, p. 186ff.

147 Report by Phraya Phiphat, 9 September 1929, TNA, KKh 0301.1.6/37. Various reports on drug seizures submitted by the Thai government to the League of Nations up to late 1941 can be found in TNA, KT 96.2.3/3, 5, 6, 9, 12, and 28 to 40. See also Renard, *Burmese Connection*, p. 27ff.

148 James Baxter, 'Siamese Opium Scandal, The Full Facts', *Straits Times*, 31 October 1935, PRO, FO 371/19375, F 6961/25/40. The scandal is documented in detail in TNA, KT 96.2.3/14 through 27; and in PRO, FO 371/19375; see also TNA, *Bangkok Times*, 16 and 19 November 1935, and Maule, The Opium Question in the Federated Shan States, 1931-36, p. 38ff. Reeve in 1951 already pointed to the temptation which profits from opium smuggling had for parts of Siam's public administration before the Second World War in Reeve, *Public Administration in Siam*, p. 63.

149 The departments of opium, excise and revenue were amalgamated in 1932 and were headed by one director-general; see Annual Report on Traffic in Opium by the Government of Siam for 1932, TNA, KT 96.2.5/6.

150 See various correspondence between Baxter and Phraya Phahon in PRO, FO 371/19375; see also Foreign Office to Bank of England, 27 June 1935, PRO, FO 371/19375, F 4128/25/40; Memorandum by Prince Varn, 1 February B.E. 2477 (1935), TNA, KT 96.2.3/14. Baxter fell ill and had to postpone his departure from Siam to 31 July 1935; see The Times, 14 August 1935.

151 The quarterly reports by the Thai government to the League of Nations are collected in LNA, R 4821/12/951/388. See also the annual figures given for opium seizures between 1925 and 1937 in the Report of the Financial Adviser in Connection with the Budget of the Kingdom of Siam for the Year B.E. 2480 (1937-1938), p. 21, LNA, R 5286/17/12732/2276.

152 James Baxter, 'Siamese Opium Scandal, The Full Facts', Straits Times, 31 October 1935, PRO, FO 371/19375, F 6961/25/40.

Narubesr Manit (Sa-nguan Chudatemiya), Director-General of the Excise Department and cabinet member, visited the Kengtung Sawbwa.[149] During this visit the Sawbwa apparently offered to supply as much as 400,000 tamlung of prepared opium annually. As it was not possible to purchase and import the opium legally in light of the League of Nations system of international opium control, the deal was disguised as a smuggling operation gone wrong and involved a very elaborate payment scheme, whereby an 'informant', a relative of the Sawbwa, was to receive 2.50 baht reward per confiscated tamlung of prepared opium. As one tamlung sold for less than 1 baht in Kengtung, this ensured the producer a handsome profit, and part of the reward was presumably to wander into the pockets of the involved Bangkok officials. But the profit scheme did not end here, as the confiscated prepared opium was intended for sale by the opium monopoly to consumers at the legal retail price. At first, neither the Thai government nor the parliament were willing to appoint an independent commission to investigate the matter, although parliament did debate the matter in February 1935, and James Baxter and the British legation in Bangkok intervened to no avail. When it became clear that the government had already authorised the payment of 300,000 baht in reward money, roughly half of the total reward, in late May, Baxter decided to resign from his post as financial adviser on 21 June 1935 because of this blatant misappropriation of public funds.[150]

The potential international ramifications of this scandal at Geneva were readily apparent to concerned circles in Bangkok. In fact, this whole affair, which constituted one of the gravest political scandals of the young constitutional government in Siam in the 1930s, was only initiated because of the existence and functioning of the League of Nations system of international opium control. To appreciate the enormous amount of prepared opium concerned, one need only consult the quarterly reports on opium seizures which Siam submitted to the League of Nations during these years. On average, some 50 to 200 tamlung of illegal prepared opium were seized in each police action, with seven particularly large amounts during the years 1934-36 as big as two to six thousand tamlung each, all completely negligible amounts in comparison with the nearly 250,000 tamlung in question.[151] Appropriately, Baxter stated in the above-mentioned Straits Times article that 'Siam now holds the record in illicit traffic in opium'.[152] As early as 22 January 1935, officials in the Ministry of Finance contemplated including a remark on 'increasing quantities of opium produced in British Territory', i.e. British Burma and the Federated Shan States, in the annual report on illicit opium traffic to the League of Nations for 1934, in order to anticipate that the huge 'recent transaction in opium…will have to be reported in the 1935 report'. But Baxter judged such an effort of 'forestalling possible comments in the Advisory Committee' as futile 'because owing to the excessive quantities of opium involved, the case would undoubtedly evoke comments, no matter what explanation is made before hand by way of excuse'.[153]

In Bangkok the Ministry of Finance was coming under increasing pressure over the incident and, in September 1935, the government finally decided to set up a special committee of enquiry after all, under the chairmanship of Prince Varn, with representatives of the national assembly as well as the public prosecution office and the criminal investigation department. When Baxter's spectacular article appeared in the *Straits Times* the following month, the Thai government, of course, denied '*in toto* the ugly suggestions made'.[154] The person at the heart of this scandal was clearly Luang Narubesr Manit, who was not only a cabinet member but also a political ally of Luang Pradist. His statements before the committee of enquiry were highly inconsistent and were contradicted by a number of other individuals.[155] Luang Narubesr resigned his cabinet seat in 1935 but was eventually let off the hook. He returned to the cabinet table in 1937 for a further five years, during three of which he also held the post of Deputy Minister of Finance, and after the war he briefly reappeared as Minister of Industry in the short-lived 1946 Pridi government.

Luang Pradist, when in Geneva en route to London in September 1935, gave Phraya Rajawangsan, Siam's Minister in London and Permanent Representative to the League of Nations, 'only an outline of the case' and asked Mani Sanasen of the League Secretariat to enquire informally whether Great Britain had already informed the OAC of the incident as part of its regular reporting requirements concerning India and Burma. Mani replied that no report had been submitted by the British government, which led Luang Pradist to recommend to Prime Minister Phraya Phahon to quickly prepare a report to the League and 'not wait till we have become the accused'. Mani also stated that he had been visited by Sir Malcolm Delevingne, the British representative on the OAC, who had given him to understand that the gravity of the affair might even lead to a discussion in the League's General Assembly.[156] But the report which was then submitted to the League the following month was as brief as it could possibly be. On one page and a half it reported that some 248,904 *tamlung*, prepared opium had been seized by the Sai River close to Chiang Rai, marking the border between Siam and the Shan States, on 9 January 1935, after a tip off had been received in late December 1934.[157] The Head of the Secretariat's Opium Section, Eric Ekstrand, was clearly unsatisfied with this appallingly brief report and twice demanded more detailed information from Phraya Rajawangsan. As the next session of the OAC was approaching in May 1936, he made it clear that:

> …there are bound to be discussions in the Seizures Sub-Committee and in the Advisory Committee in regard to this case which, as you know, has received considerable attention, not only in Siam and the

153 Memorandum by Ministry of Foreign Affairs, 22 January 1935, TNA, KT 96.2.7/10.

154 TNA, *Bangkok Times*, 7 October 1935.

155 Details on the committee of enquiry can be found in TNA, KT 96.2.3/20 to 27. See also Report communicated by the Government of Siam to the League of Nations on 21 May 1936, TNA, KT 96.2.3/27.

156 Luang Pradist to Phraya Phahon, 11 September B.E. 2478 (1935), TNA, KT 96.2.3/21; Phraya Rajawangsan to Minister of Foreign Affairs, 14 September 1935, TNA, KT 96.2.3/14. Thai officials in Geneva and Bangkok were relieved when the session of the fifth committee of the League's General Assembly closed without any mention having been made of the opium smuggling scandal; see Phraya Rajawangsan to Phraya Srisena, 20 September 1935, TNA, KT 96.2.3/14.

157 The Report can be found in TNA, KT 96.2.3/14.

Far East generally but also in Europe and the United States of America.[158]

James Baxter, who had returned to London after resigning as financial adviser to the Thai government, met for lunch with Phraya Rajawangsan in early February 1936 and sent a shockwave through the Thai legation, which spread as far as Bangkok, by announcing to the Minister that he had been asked by the British Foreign Office to prepare to stand as a witness before the OAC when it discussed the scandal. Clearly, the British government was trying to put pressure on Bangkok and to distract from the fact that the nine tons of prepared opium originated in the Shan States. At the same time, in March 1936, the Foreign Office in London received a memorandum from Sir Josiah Crosby, the British Minister in Bangkok, putting much of the blame for the affair on the British administration in Burma. He strongly urged the government to put an end to the rule of the *Sawbwa* of Kengtung, in order to allow Britain to live up to its international agreements regarding opium control.[159]

But the OAC postponed discussion of the matter, as the League of Nations was occupied with the move to its splendid new building overlooking Lake Geneva in the spring of 1936, and as both the Thai and the Burmese administrations promised detailed enquiries. The matter stayed with the League for a full year before it was brought up at the next regular meeting of the Seizures Sub-Committee of the OAC on 20 May 1937. For this meeting, the OAC had in hand two detailed reports on the incident.[160] The Thai and the Burmese reports both clearly implicated Luang Narubesr and his subordinates, but, perhaps also because nearly a year and a half had passed since the incident, the OAC was willing to drop the case, as Phraya Rajawangsan was pleased to report to Bangkok. Luang Bhadravadi, who represented Siam at the meeting, refrained from making any statement and was met with a very friendly and cooperative attitude by the British representative, who had no interest in adding fuel to the fire.[161]

The whole incident was a blatant violation of Siam's international obligations, which banned any import of prepared opium and allowed raw opium imports only under the import certificate system. Not only does the affair shed light on corruption and smuggling in Siam, but it highlights the fact, by no means limited to Siam, that upright advocates of opium suppression always faced interest groups in official positions willing to profit from opium addiction. In the words of Virginia Thompson, the affair was 'probably chiefly the work of third-class functionaries who wanted, in addition to lining their own pockets, to spare the country the expense of buying opium from abroad by so cheap a device as confiscating contraband opium'.[162] The uncovering of the smuggling scandal, Baxter's resignation and the international attention it received did not have any measurable effect on smuggling

158 Ekstrand to Phraya Raja-wangsan, 23 October 1935 and 8 February 1936, both in TNA, KT 96.2.3/14.

159 Phraya Rajawangsan to Minister of Foreign Affairs, 2 February B.E. 2478 (1936) and 13 March B.E. 2478 (1936), TNA, KT 96.2.3/14. The possibility of Baxter giving evidence before the OAC was anticipated as early as June 1935 in a confidential letter from Prime Minister Phraya Phahon to James Baxter of 25 June 1935, PRO, FO 371/ 19375, F4567/25/40. On Crosby's criticism see Crosby to Eden, 13 March 1936, Doc. 192 (F 2194/2194/40), BDFA, Part II, Series E, vol. 50, p. 236.

160 Report communicated by the Government of Siam to the League of Nations on 21 May 1936, Report communicated by the Government of Burma to the League of Nations on 19 June 1936, both in TNA, KT 96.2.3/27. The permanent Sub-Committee on Seizures was established by the OAC in 1931.

161 Report by the Sub-Committee on Seizures on the Work of its Ninth Session, LNA, League of Nations, Official Journal, no. 12, December 1937, p. 1123ff. (O.C./ S.C.S.1-13). See also Phraya Rajawangsan to Minister of Foreign Affairs, 22 and 23 May 1937, TNA, KT 96.2.3/27.

162 Thompson, *Thailand*, p. 736.

163 TNA, *Bangkok Times*, 23 November 1935.

164 See chapter 2 for further details.

activities, although the government, in reaction to the affair, again raised the maximum punishment for opium-related crimes in 1935, only one year after it had been raised in response to the Bangkok agreement.[163] The fallout from the 1935 opium scandal also included Luang Pradist's flirtation with the idea of ending the tradition of British appointees as financial advisers and instead requesting the League of Nations to appoint a successor to Baxter, a possibility which triggered frantic actions by British officials and which was only averted when Luang Pradist was pressured during his visit to London with the possible refusal of the Bank of England to accept renegotiated loans to Siam.[164]

Siam and the other League members had achieved the aim of distinguishing the licit from the illicit opium trade but, as the 1930s showed, this was not nearly enough to effectively counter opium smuggling. The League and Siam therefore intensified their efforts against smuggling from the mid-1930s. In Siam, the maximum punishment for opium offences was again increased and on an international level the League focused on limiting opium production and on coordinating anti-smuggling activities of member states.[165] Already in 1931 the League of Nations invited member states to another international opium conference in Geneva, the so-called Geneva Limitation Conference, which aimed at fixing the legitimate global requirement of opium and other drugs and pressing opium-producing countries to ban any production exceeding this amount.[166] But in spite of these efforts, drug smuggling continued to flourish during the remaining years before the outbreak of the Second World War in Siam as well as in the surrounding European colonies, and the final Geneva conference on opium and other drugs in 1936, which was even exclusively devoted to the smuggling problem, was unable to generate a significant impact.[167] The Bangkok government, unable to curb opium smuggling effectively, during the second half of the 1930s then reverted to increasing the number of licensed opium houses and reducing the retail price for opium in an effort to draw consumers away from illicit opium. But more noticeable success in the fight against smuggling over the northern border could only be achieved in Thailand during the 1970s, not least because of continued financial interests of government and military officials in this illicit trade.[168]

The financial development of Siam's opium monopoly

In the founding year of the League of Nations, the Thai state collected 23 million baht in revenue from opium sales, which contributed twenty-five percent of total state revenue. The opium monopoly was, thereby, the single largest revenue source in the state budget. This percentage dropped continuously from the year 1919-20 onwards and reached its lowest level by the mid-1930s when it was between seven and a half and nine percent of state revenue. In financial terms this represented a drop from 23 million to 9 million baht.[169] This downward trend is particularly

165 Illegal opium production in China remained at the heart of the problem of opium smuggling in East and Southeast Asia until the late 1940s. While India and later Turkey held the position of main legal exporter of opium during the interwar period, the amounts they exported were almost negligible compared with the amount of opium produced illegally in China. After opium production had been curbed with some success during the closing years of the Chinese empire and after Great Britain even agreed to end opium exports from India to China, opium production underwent a renaissance during the civil war years of the Chinese republic. Various warlords promoted opium production, particularly in Yunnan and Manchuria, on such a massive scale that more than an estimated three quarters of global opium production took place in China. Although, according to Meyer and Parsinnen, by 1935 some twenty percent of the total Chinese population of 400 million people consumed opium, vast amounts of the drug found its way as contraband into Siam and Southeast Asia. See Meyer and Parsinnen, *Webs of Smoke*, p. 3.

166 Siam adhered to the resulting Convention for Limiting the Manufacture and Regulating the Distribution of Narcotic Drugs of 13 July 1931 on 22 February 1934. The convention came into force on 9 July 1933; see LNA, C.509.M.214.1931. XI; see also on the conference in detail Bailey, *The Anti-Drug Campaign*, p. 62ff.; May, Evolution, passim.

167 Phraya Rajawangsan and Luang Bhadravadi represented Siam at the conference at Geneva. On Siam's participation see LNA, R 4975/12/ 22023/22023 and R4975/12/ 23585/22023. The conference protocols from 8 to 24 June 1936 can be found in LNA, R 4976/12/ 24359/22042. The conference resulted in the Convention of 1936 for the Suppression of the Illicit Traffic in Dangerous Drugs, signed on 26 June 1936. The convention did not come into force during the lifetime of the League of Nations and Siam did not sign or adhere to it. See also Booth, *Opium*, p. 184. Renard, *Burmese Connection* p. 39f., points to increased smuggling from Burma into Siam after 1938.

168 See details in Walker, *Opium and Foreign Policy*, p. 189ff.

169 Data from *Statistical Yearbooks of Siam/Thailand, B.E. 2470, 2480, 2482*; *Report of the Financial Adviser in Connection with the Budget of the Kingdom of Siam for the Year B.E. 2480 (1937-1938)*, LNA, R5286/17/12732/2276.

remarkable in light of the strongly fluctuating state revenues during this fifteen year period; overall revenue increased sharply when Siam was able to reclaim tariff autonomy from the mid-1920s and fell dramatically when the global depression sent the world market price for rice – by far Siam's primary export commodity – tumbling during the early 1930s.

The steady decline in opium revenue was due to a number of factors. It was first and foremost due to a change in policy which was triggered by Siam's membership in the League of Nations and which implied a willingness to reduce income from opium sales. Minister of Finance Phraya Komarakul Montri was able to state to the League's commission of enquiry into opium control in December 1929:

> [When] I say that Siam can now face the gradual loss of the opium revenue I do not imply that the money is of no consequence to us, neither are we exactly burning to lose this revenue. On the contrary, the loss of this revenue will entail an appreciable sacrifice. We are a young country, and it is only recently that we have had money to spare. There are a good many necessary things we want to spend money on – not only on material development, but on education, on public health, and others…I beg to emphasize that the loss will be a sacrifice, but Siam is willing to make it for humane reasons and for the good of her people, provided, of course, such sacrifice is effective, i.e. that there is a *real* end of opium smoking, otherwise, it would not be any good either to the nation or to the cause of opium restriction.[170]

Tighter control of opium matters by the state also led to a reduction in the number of consumers of legal opium in Siam during the two interwar decades, a trend which was amplified by the opium monopoly's policy of repeatedly increasing the retail price of opium to suppress consumption. This policy indeed led to reduced annual amounts of prepared opium provided by the monopoly but it also drove many addicts to look for alternative illegal sources. During the 1930s opium smuggling became so rampant that the government had no choice but to reduce the retail price of opium again, in an effort to make it more attractive to consumers.[171] At the same time, the price of legally available raw opium on the world market also fell rapidly as demand declined in the wake of the economic depression and in the face of more effective international controls.[172] As Thai authorities were confiscating increasing amounts of opium during this period and, around the mid-1930s, hardly had to import any raw opium legally to satisfy domestic demand, the reduction of the retail price did not lead to a drop in overall opium revenue to below the above-mentioned 9 million baht annually. But, in spite of the falling trend in revenue, the opium monopoly remained, alongside import duties, land tax and revenue from railways, mining and timber concessions, one of the most important sources of revenue for the Thai government throughout the 1920s and 1930s. Carl Trocki, who has studied the economic relevance of the Asian opium trade in detail,

170 'Statements made by Phraya Komarakul Montri, Acting Minister of Finance, Siam, on the 6th December, 1929 to the Chairman and Members of the League of Nations Commission of Enquiry into the Control of Opium-smoking in the Far East', LNA, S 194/4.

171 TNA, *Bangkok Times*, 7 April and 24 December 1937.

172 'Historical Survey', *UNODC Bulletin on Narcotics*, 3 (1953), <http://www.unodc.org/unodc/en/data-and-analysis/bulletin/bulletin_1953-01-01_3_page003.html>.

describes opium in European colonies in Asia in a way which is also valid for Siam, namely as:

> …vital, both to the capitalist transformation of the local economies as well as to the finance of the colonial administrative structures which protected those economies…Opium created pools of capital and fed the institutions that accumulated it: the banking and financial systems, the insurance systems, and the transportation and information infrastructures.[173]

Siam abandons international opium control before the Second World War

While opium smuggling was increasing, the withdrawal of India as the main global supplier from the early 1930s led Siam and the British, French and Dutch colonies in Southeast Asia to search for new sources for their legal requirements for raw opium. They found new suppliers in Turkey and Persia, who were only too willing to step in for India. Turkey already held the dubious distinction of being the largest exporter of raw opium in 1930.[174] But by the late 1930s it became increasingly difficult to legally import sufficient quantities of opium to Siam because of the above-mentioned decline in legal global production. Confidential negotiations were begun with British administrations in Burma and Afghanistan in 1940, and the following year Siam imported raw opium from Afghanistan to supplement declining shipments from Persia and Turkey.[175] In addition to raw opium imports, the Thai government for the first time officially authorised opium production in the north of the country in late 1938.[176]

Already during the Bangkok Conference of 1931 Sir Malcolm Delevingne had suggested that Siam authorise opium production on a limited scale to counter the influx of smuggled opium from Burma.[177] By 1933 financial adviser James Baxter openly supported the idea and considered the international implications, clearly with the League of Nations in mind:

> There seems to be a good case for allowing the cultivation of opium in the North…Just how much deference the Government should pay to possible criticism outside Siam of this departure from present policy, is a matter for consideration. My own view is that a goodish case can be put up. Siam has been so virtuous up-to-date in opium matters that the delinquency proposed would hardly smirch the virginal purity of her opium reputation.[178]

But it took until 1938 for the scheme to be officially adopted, and it was then branded an experiment to underline its non-permanent character. The League Secretariat's Opium Section was watching these events from Geneva and was well informed via the British legation in Bangkok and the drugs branch in the British Home Office. The

173 Trocki, *Opium, Empire and the Global Political Economy*, p. 173.

174 See Jan Schmidt, *From Anatolia to Indonesia: Opium Trade and the Dutch Community of Izmir, 1820-1940*, Leiden: Nederlands Instituut voor het Nabije Oosten, 1998, p. 176. Siam already began importing raw opium from Persia in 1929.

175 The British Foreign Office ultimately decided against the sale of opium from Kengtung because of the ramifications this could have had in Geneva. On this decision and on raw opium imports from Afghanistan in 1940-41 see TNA, KT 96.2.3/41 and 42; PRO, FO 371/24747, F 3077/416/87 and F 3740/ 416/87.

176 See Landon, *Chinese in Thailand*, p. 94. Much earlier sources on opium production in northern Thailand can be found, for example, in TNA, *Bangkok Times*, 4 May and 6 June 1922. In 1908-09, a confidential memorandum of the Ministry of Finance acknowledged opium poppy cultivation 'by the distant hill-tribes in the North for their own consumption, yet the quantity is so small that no steps have been taken to interfere with this cultivation.' See 'Confidential Instructions to Delegates to Joint Opium Commission to be held at Shanghai, n.d.', TNA, KKh 0301.1.1.6/5. The possibility of purchasing domestically grown opium was also discussed between the Ministry of Finance and Prince Damrong, Minister of Interior, in 1912; see Minister of Interior to Minister of Finance, 26 April 1912, TNA, KKh 0301. 1.6/8. Siam's opium purchases from Persia were monitored by the League of Nations as late as summer 1940 and an extensive correspondence between Luang Bhadravadi and Bertil Renborg was still possible on the subject in spite of the war in Europe; see LNA, R 4939/12/ 7810/7810.

177 Home Office to Foreign Office, 23 December 1931, PRO, FO 415, F 418/225/87.

178 Memorandum Baxter, 24 July 1933, TNA, KKh 0301.1.6/40.

Bangkok government, while to the League it had officially denied rumours to this effect until 1937 amidst an array of newspaper reports to the contrary, now justified the scheme as an effort against opium smuggling, because the opium in question, which was now declared to be legal, would have hit the domestic market illegally anyhow.[179] By March 1940, the government declared the experiment a success and announced that it would expand legal opium production. For this expansion, large consignments of poppy seeds, enough to plant 16,000 acres, were imported from India in mid-1941.[180]

In a somewhat ironic coincidence, the OAC suggested that the League call another international conference on opium, particularly to limit further global opium production through even stricter control measures and reporting requirements, in the same year that Siam began sanctioning domestic opium production.[181] The Thai Foreign Ministry welcomed the suggestion in a letter to the League in early 1939, but pointed out that, as it considered itself as an opium-producing country now, it should be included in the list of worldwide legal producers. After nearly twenty years of cooperation between Siam and the League of Nations in the field of opium control, this letter of 1939 also contained the sober statement, that if the League of Nations did not manage to check global opium smuggling,

…the work of control of the [Opium] Advisory Committee, so far as the illicit traffic in Siam is concerned, cannot possibly be met with the results which are not unreasonably to be expected of it, and it will be difficult for the Siamese Government to explain to the people of Siam what utility of a positive and concrete nature to this country is derived from its participation in the work of the Advisory Committee.[182]

Because of the outbreak of hostilities in Europe the conference ultimately did not materialise and the increasingly authoritarian Thai government turned further away from the League's efforts to control opium. Instead it further expanded domestic opium production during the early 1940s, increased the number of licensed opium houses, and approached the government of Burma with an offer to purchase opium in an effort to tap into the ever-increasing smuggling in the north of the country.[183] In abandoning the system of international opium control, Siam followed the global trend brought about by the League's failures in political and security matters. During the following years, state revenue from opium sales then reached unprecedented heights which even dwarfed the spectacular figures of the 1920s.

Conclusions

During and after the Second World War, Siam reverted to opium as a prime revenue source and in 1950 the opium monopoly generated

179 Various correspondences between Bangkok and Geneva and between London and Geneva, memoranda and numerous newspaper clippings on poppy cultivation in Siam during the period 1934-1939 in LNA, R4942/12/11853/8069. See also Jon Boyes and Piraban S., *Opium Fields*, Bangkok: Silkworm Books, 1991, p. 31.

180 TNA, KT 96.2.3/44.

181 See LNA, C.L.192.1938.XI and R 5017/12/35907/35907.

182 LNA, O.C.1751(c) of 20 February 1939, p. 4f., LNA, R 5017/12/35908/35907. That this marked a fundamental shift in Siam's official opium policy towards the end of the 1930s is illustrated by a Thai proposal of 1931, in which the Bangkok government had advocated measures to keep non-opium producing states from beginning production. See Prince Devawongse to Drummond, 29 May 1931, Enclosure: Observations by the Siamese Government on the Report of the League of Nation's Commission of Enquiry into the Control of Opium-smoking in the Far East, p. 2, LNA, R 3203/12/11288/ 6245; the same document can be found in TNA, KKh 0301.1.6/ 40.

183 Direck to Crosby, 13 April 1940, TNA, KT 96.2.2/41.

some 110 million baht in revenue.[184] Because the Japanese occupation of Southeast Asia cut off the trade routes with Turkey and Persia, opium production in Siam's north intensified, as did the smuggling of opium from the Shan States, and, as a result, the 'continued availability of substantial amounts of inexpensive opium for addicts in Thailand meant that the country came through the war years with her enormous addict population intact'.[185] In fact, during the Japanese occupation of Southeast Asia the opium monopolies in the occupied territories were even encouraged to expand, reinforced by Japan's own large-scale opium production in Manchukuo. After the new communist government in China successfully eradicated opium production as part of its land reform, by employing draconian punishments around the year 1950, Thailand became the global centre for drug production during the following two decades.[186] According to Spencer and Navaratnam, from the end of the war to 1962, opium production virtually exploded from seven to 100 tons annually.[187] Legal opium consumption had become an anachronism in the post-war world and was finally outlawed in 1959, not least due to pressure by the international community through the United Nations.[188] Interestingly, the League of Nations became active in this regard once again during its brief resurgence after the end of the war. Bertil Renborg, who had meanwhile been promoted to head the League Secretariat's Opium Section, in January 1946 asked Mani Sanasen, who was at the Washington legation at the time, to do whatever he could to pressure the government in Bangkok to abandon legal opium smoking in conformity with surrounding colonial territories because it 'would certainly have a favourable influence on Siam's international position'. While the legation in Washington, spurred by Renborg's letter, indeed urged the government in Bangkok to act accordingly, it took another twelve years before the monopoly was finally abolished.[189] In Indochina, Malaya, Singapore, Hong Kong, Macao and Indonesia, opium consumption had already been banned after the end of Japanese occupation during the late 1940s or early 1950s, with only Burma maintaining a partial opium monopoly until 1965. The number of opium consumers in Thailand declined after the end of the state monopoly and became increasingly limited to the ethnic minorities in the north. But, countering this trend, the number of heroin addicts increased rapidly during the second half of the twentieth century.[190]

The League of Nations handed over responsibility for international drug control to the new United Nations in 1946, while the tasks of the OAC were passed on to the United Nations Commission on Narcotic Drugs.[191] Guided by the United Nations, efforts for international drug control were continued with agreements in 1948 and 1953, until the UN Single Convention was concluded in 1961, which encompassed all agreements of the preceding fifty years from The Hague onwards, also including the Bangkok Agreement of 1931. A new international

184 Data from Ingram, *Economic Change*, p. 185. The first Thai government after the end of the Second World War announced a ban on opium in 1946 but did not stay in office long enough to pass legislation to this effect or to enforce the ban; see Walker, *Opium and Foreign Policy*, p. 185.

185 Spencer and Navaratnam, *Drug Abuse in East Asia*, p. 36.

186 Ibid., p. 24. On Japan's opium policy see John M. Jennings, *The Opium Empire: Japanese Imperialism and Drug Trafficking in Asia, 1895-1945*, Westport (CT) and London: Praeger, 1997.

187 Spencer and Navaratnam, *Drug Abuse in East Asia*, p. 21.

188 The act outlawing opium was passed in December 1958, and the closure of all opium dens was to be completed by June 1959. At the same time, a first detoxification centre for drug addicts was set up. See ibid., p. 36.

189 See relevant correspondence in early 1946 between Bertil Renborg, Mani Sanasen and W.H. Coles of the British Home Office in LNA, R 5006/12/43533/31213.

190 By 1976, an estimated 400,000 people in Thailand were addicted to heroin; see Booth, *Opium*, p. 262.

191 On international drug control since 1945 see Bruun, Pan and Rexed, *The Gentlemen's Club*; Booth, *Opium*, p. 188ff.; Alfred W. McCoy, *The Politics of Heroin*, New York: Lawrence Hill, 1991.

convention aiming to curb drug smuggling was adopted in 1988, and states continue to the present day with their efforts to limit drug abuse, production and trafficking.

In the light of this brief outline of further developments, the balance sheet of cooperation between Siam and the League in the area of international opium control between the two world wars remains positive. From the perspective of the League of Nations the net effects were certainly positive. Of course, drug trafficking existed throughout the twentieth century and will stay with us in the twenty-first, but the pioneering work of the League was of great importance as it placed opium and other dangerous drugs firmly on the international agenda. The goal was clearly defined, namely the suppression of illegal and legal opium smoking. The legal opium trade was standardised by use of the certificate system and made clearly distinguishable from the illicit one. The first steps were made to limit opium production and the first international measures against drug smugglers were developed. The League of Nations was the first global forum able to address these issues in their whole international scope, and the League's activities regarding the collection of information and the supervision of the international drug trade were innovations which formed prerequisites for the efforts undertaken by of the United Nations after 1945. In the words of Bertil Renborg, who was in charge of opium control in the League Secretariat,

> In fact, in the short span of 20 years – 1920-1940 – the League brought order where there was chaos, blazed a new trail in international law, created a veritable international administration and established practically universal co-operation among States.[192]

That Renborg's positive assessment was by no means unique, is illustrated by the authoritative study by Bruun, Pan and Rexed, who wrote in 1975, 'The late 1920s and early 1930s constituted the peak era of international drug control'.[193] And it was also in this era that the perception of opium changed fundamentally in the West as well as among parts of the Thai elite. Opium was no longer seen as simply another commodity which could be traded and sold, but rather as potentially harmful to individuals and societies, and its trade for non-medical or non-scientific purposes was seen increasingly as immoral and incompatible with modern societies.

Two structural factors were, however, responsible for the modest degree of success of the League's efforts. On the one hand, international organisations are, of course, dependent on the political will of their member states for the implementation of any new international rules. And since the League's member states were unwilling to support radical changes in the area of opium control, the implementation of the League's far-reaching goals remained fairly

192 Bertil A. Renborg, 'The Grand Old Men of the League of Nations', *UNODC Bulletin on Narcotics*, 4 (1964),<http://www.unodc.org/unodc/en/data-and-analysis/bulletin/bulletin_1964-01-01_4.html>; see also Renborg, *International Drug Control*, p. 220ff.

193 Bruun, Pan and Rexed, *The Gentlemen's Club*, p. 277. Writing in 1975, the authors stated with regard to the activities of the United Nations on p. 160: 'All key organs have their forerunners in the League of Nations. The League's traditions are still strong.'

Opium house in Bangkok, taken from the League of Nations Report on Control of Opium Smoking in the Far East, 1930. (League of Nations Archives).

vague. On the other hand, the means which the League had at its disposal to enforce its aims must be considered, namely international public opinion and the instruments of international law. The former was, of course, not nearly as powerful in influencing political decisions seventy years ago as it is in today's era of mass media; the latter were during the League's times not equipped with sanctioning mechanisms which could have been used to force member states to implement international agreements. Nevertheless, the remarkable achievement remains that the League of Nations managed to bring together sixty-seven states, among them Siam, in a political process which ultimately led to the worldwide abolition of legal opium smoking.[194]

As far as Siam is concerned, a number of different factors influencing opium control have been discussed in this chapter. The diplomatic efforts in Geneva clearly contributed to a change in perception of opium as a problem in Bangkok, but international political pressure was not strong enough before the Second World War, as in the case of the European colonies surrounding Siam, to lead to an abolishment of legal opium sales to addicts. This chapter has identified two factors as the most significant reasons for this, the tremendous importance of opium for the state budget during the 1920s and the rampant and uncontrollable smuggling activities across the northern border during the 1930s. It would certainly be unrealistic in a historical context to expect Siam to unilaterally sacrifice its opium monopoly while its neighbouring territories all maintained similar monopolies, and, as seen above, the maintenance and even strengthening of opium monopolies was very much in line with the League of Nations' recommendations. But the Thai government was, nevertheless, willing to sacrifice a considerable

194 This point is strongly emphasised by Herbert L. May, 'Dangerous Drugs', in Harriet E. Davis (ed.), *Pioneers in World Order: An American Appraisal of the League of Nations*, 2nd ed., New York: Columbia University Press, 1945, pp. 182-192, here: p. 187.

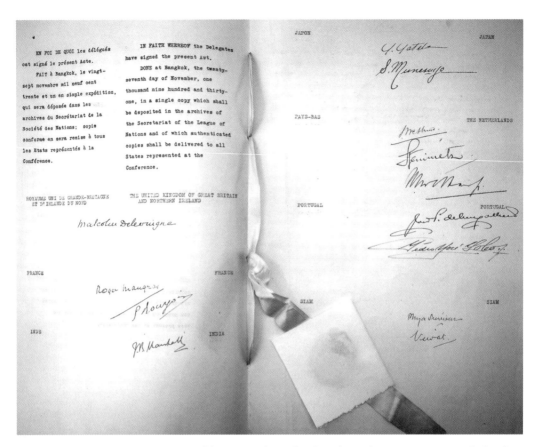

EN FOI DE QUOI les délégués ont signé le présent Acte.

FAIT à Bangkok, le vingt-sept novembre mil neuf cent trente et un en simple expédition, qui sera déposée dans les archives du Secrétariat de la Société des Nations; copie conforme en sera remise à tous les Etats représentés à la Conférence.

IN FAITH WHEREOF the Delegates have signed the present Act.

DONE at Bangkok, the twenty-seventh day of November, one thousand nine hundred and thirty-one, in a single copy which shall be deposited in the archives of the Secretariat of the League of Nations and of which authenticated copies shall be delivered to all States represented at the Conference.

ROYAUME UNI DE GRANDE-BRETAGNE ET D'IRLANDE DU NORD

THE UNITED KINGDOM OF GREAT BRITAIN AND NORTHERN IRELAND

FRANCE

FRANCE

INDE

INDIA

JAPON

JAPAN

PAYS-BAS

THE NETHERLANDS

PORTUGAL

PORTUGAL

SIAM

SIAM

Original signature page of the Final Act of the Bangkok Conference on Opium-smoking in the Far East of 27 November 1931. This is the first international agreement known as 'Bangkok Agreement' (League of Nations Archives).

part of its revenue by seriously trying to improve state control of opium consumption. According to the figures given by Constance Wilson, the number of convictions for offences against opium and excise laws in Siam increased from 2,985 in 1920-21 to 25,234 in 1935-36.[195] Furthermore, Siam's participation in the international opium control efforts in Geneva led to changes in Siam itself. The government in Bangkok implemented the international agreements as national laws, both with regard to the opium trade and opium smoking. Thus the League of Nations directly influenced Thai law and practice. The degree of importance this cooperation with the League had among policy makers in Bangkok became particularly apparent during the visit of the League's commission of enquiry in 1929 and the Bangkok Opium Conference of 1931. Furthermore, Siam's cooperation with the League of Nations in opium control also contributed to the government's overarching policy goal of regaining complete sovereignty. Its diplomats skilfully demonstrated the link between full sovereignty and an effective opium control policy to their European counterparts during the 1920s. And Siam's elite was repeatedly able to demonstrate its progressiveness in the area of opium control internationally and domestically during the interwar years.

195 Constance M. Wilson (ed.), *Thailand: A Handbook of Historical Statistics*, Reference Publication in International Historical Statistics, Boston: Hall, 1983, p. 290f.

However, the League did not only influence Siam. Thai diplomats and officials also influenced the League's work and the evolution of international opium control in general, for example by actively contributing to the work of the OAC, by cooperating with the commission of enquiry, by hosting the Bangkok Opium Conference and, last but not least, by serving as a model in the transformation of League recommendations into national legislation, as seen, for example, with the import certificate system or the system of opium houses.

By the mid-1930s, Siam had implemented the majority of the international agreements to suppress opium consumption, had established a workable system for the import and distribution of opium, and state revenue from opium sales had hit a historic low. That the Bangkok government then refrained from continuing on this path by further limiting the number of smokers and the amount of opium through a system of registration and rationing was certainly due to the problems resulting from smuggling and to administrative difficulties. But it must also be seen as part of a much wider global trend of turning away from the League of Nations and the international system. In addition, it was due to the ever-present groups of Thais, Chinese and Westerners who did not see opium as a vice to be suppressed but rather as an appropriate Asian substitute to alcohol, or simply as 'a stimulant of energy'.[196] The fact that the Thai government went as far as sanctioning domestic opium production before the Second World War underscores the loss of influence the League and its ideal of international cooperation suffered during these final years. Nevertheless, the late 1930s and early 1940s do not discredit the seriousness with which Thai politicians, diplomats and government officials cooperated with the League of Nations for at least a decade and a half. The political, economic and social situation in Siam and Southeast Asia did not allow a comprehensive ban of opium smoking before the Second World War. But Siam's cooperation with the League did trigger a long-term change in the kingdom's opium policy.

State opium monopolies, which seem strangely antiquated from today's perspective, are long gone, but drug abuse and the illicit drug trade remain among the most pressing problems of international politics. As the *Bangkok Post* pointed out in 2000:

> By all evidence and statistics, the demand for illicit drugs in Thailand is greater than ever. Millions of Thais, literally, have used narcotics and, recently, speed pills. Perhaps as many as one million of the 60 million Thai people use illegal drugs regularly. Opium and heroin remain a major threat to our nation...Drug traffickers exploit the weak members of the Thai nation, and that will continue.[197]

As a member of the United Nations, Thailand remains involved in the international efforts to deal with these problems.

---

196 TNA, *Bangkok Times*, 28 April 1937.

197 *Bangkok Post*, 3 August 2000.

Prince Sakol Voravarn (Courtesy of River Books collection).

4

Public Health

While Thai princes participated in the Paris Peace Conference and tried to convince Western governments to abandon the unequal treaties, the influenza pandemic of 1918-19, which was ravaging across Europe, also claimed some 80,000 victims in Siam. Similarly, when Thai diplomats were participating in the formative steps of the new League of Nations in Europe, a cholera epidemic led to 10,000 deaths in Siam in 1919-20.[1] Such figures were by no means exceptional, epidemics were a recurring menace and improvements in public health, sanitation and the fight against communicable diseases were a dire necessity in Siam in these years. This chapter aims to reconstruct the wide range of contacts between Siam and the League of Nations in the field of public health, which began in 1920 and lasted for two decades, and which played an important role in improving public health for the urban and rural population in Siam as well as in ensuring the reach of the world's first international organisation to Southeast Asia. This chapter will again attempt to demonstrate how a concrete field of activity within the League of Nations, in this case public health, was utilised by the governing elites in Siam to develop the country according to their Western-inspired concepts of modernisation.

Indeed, Siam's membership in the League's Health Organisation was a very important stimulus for the development of public health in the kingdom before the Second World War.[2] Efforts in which Siam cooperated with the League included the fight against leprosy, malaria and cholera, pharmaceutical standardisation, the training of public health managers and medical practitioners and the establishment of an international warning system for epidemics and of the first-ever international office in Asia. The League repeatedly sent medical experts to Siam to investigate the situation and to assist local public health authorities. The Thai government sent doctors to the League's Singapore bureau for training and participated in international conferences on public health issues. But for these events to take place during the 1920s and 1930s, public health had first to become an issue of international relations.

Public health as an international issue and a task of the League of Nations

Public health became an issue of international concern in Europe in the course of the nineteenth century when the mobility of the population

---

1 *The Directory for Bangkok and Siam, A Handy and Perfectly Reliable Book of Reference for all Classes*, Bangkok: Bangkok Times Press, 1922, p. 5.

2 TNA, *Bangkok Times*, 12 November 1925. For an overview of the League's activities see Martin D. Dubin, 'The League of Nations Health Organisation', in Paul Weindling (ed.), *International Health Organisations and Movements*, Cambridge: Cambridge University Press 1995, pp. 56-80.

increased through railways and steam navigation, and waves of communicable diseases, first and foremost cholera, swept across the continent as a result. The very first international sanitary conference took place as early as 1851, but progress in coordinating national efforts against epidemic diseases remained very slow, in spite of some ten follow-up meetings during the subsequent fifty years. The first international agreement on health, the International Sanitary Convention, was adopted in 1892, while the first international institution in the field of health, the International Sanitary Bureau, was established by the republics of the Americas in 1902 in Washington D.C. and went on to become the Pan American Sanitary Bureau in 1923. This trend towards the internationalisation of health management was complemented by the foundation of the International Red Cross in 1863. Medical science made a number of important discoveries with regard to cholera, plague and yellow fever, which became generally accepted by the late nineteenth century, and in 1907 the Office International d'Hygiène Publique (OIHP) in Paris was created by twelve states (Belgium, Brazil, Egypt, France, Italy, The Netherlands, Portugal, Russia, Spain, Switzerland, Great Britain and the United States). Originally a predominantly European institution, the OIHP grew to include nearly sixty countries and colonies by 1914. It was concerned with epidemic diseases in general and also with the special case of the annual pilgrimage of Muslims to Mecca and Medina, the Hajj.[3] The First World War was a landmark in the development of international public health in that it left disastrous pandemics in its wake. The influenza pandemic of 1918-19, the deadliest disaster of the twentieth century, took an estimated 15 to 20 million lives across the globe and in 1919 cholera then claimed nearly 250,000 lives in Poland and some 1.5 million in the young Soviet Union. These disasters overburdened the OIHP, and the new League of Nations was therefore entrusted with the task of coordinating international public health work.[4]

Before the First World War international public health in Asia was 'a narrow, defensive arrangement intended to protect European and American enclaves from epidemics of plague and cholera endemic in other regions'.[5] With the creation of the League's Health Organisation, a clearing house for public health matters existed, which took up issues across the globe, including Southeast Asia. The League's Health Organisation dealt with nearly all the then prevalent epidemic diseases such as cholera, malaria, typhoid fever, leprosy, hookworm, smallpox and so forth. In addition, it also dealt with social health conditions, nutrition, as well as with cancer research, with biological and pharmaceutical standardisation – in short, with the whole range of public health issues relevant at the time.

The League of Nations was entrusted with the promotion of public health through international cooperation on the basis of article XXIII(f) of its covenant. National public health issues were to be dealt with only

3 On the OIHP and the series of fourteen international sanitary conferences held between 1851 and 1938 see Milton I. Roemer, 'Internationalism in Medicine and Public Health', in Dorothy Porter (ed.), *The History of Public Health and the Modern State*, The Wellcome Institute Series in the History of Medicine, Amsterdam and Atlanta: Editions Rodopi, 1994, pp. 403-423. The English text of the Agreement on the Establishment of an International Office of Public Health of 9 December 1907 can be found in: Franz Knipping, Hans von Mangoldt and Volker Rittberger (eds.), *Das System der Vereinten Nationen und seine Vorläufer*, vol. II: 19. Jahrhundert und Völkerbundszeit, ed. by Franz Knipping, München: C.H. Beck and Berne: Stämpflie & Cie, 1996, p. 276ff.

4 Although it would have been logical to integrate the OIHP into the much larger League of Nations structure, this was not possible because the United States wished to remain an OIHP member but was, tragically, not a member of the League. The OIHP, therefore, continued to exist alongside the League's Health Organisation.

5 Dubin, League of Nations Health Organization, p. 73. See also League of Nations, *Aims, Methods and Activity*, p. 147.

when the League was requested to do so by national governments. A Health Section was first set up in the League Secretariat together with a Permanent Epidemic Commission, from which the League of Nations Health Organisation evolved in 1923. The Health Organisation, which received significant budgetary support from the American Rockefeller Foundation, went on to encompass the Permanent Health Committee of the League's General Assembly, the permanent commissions on malaria and biological standardisation, the Singapore Bureau from 1925 and the International Centre for Leprosy Research in Rio de Janeiro from 1934 onwards. The rationale for the League's intervention was that 'disease is no respecter of frontier, and epidemics spread from country to country with disconcerting rapidity, as mankind has long since learnt by painful experience'.[6] Under its energetic, controversial and visionary director, Dr. Ludvik Rajchman, a Polish bacteriologist, the Health Organisation developed into one of the most important and sustainable activities of the League of Nations.[7]

Public health in Siam: issues, management and early international cooperation

As a tropical country, Siam had, and still has, a particular public health situation. Tropical diseases have always been prevalent, first and foremost malaria. Some diseases, such as smallpox and cholera, occurred as epidemics and followed seasonal or annual patterns. Traditional Thai and Chinese herbal medicine was commonly used by the urban and rural population, and traditional healers were consulted in the event of illness. Western medicine was first introduced to Siam by American missionaries in the 1830s.[8] Terwiel has shown that while the first vaccination campaigns against smallpox during that decade relied on vaccines imported by Western doctors, namely by the American missionary Dan Beach Bradley, but that they were driven by a progressive royal elite.[9] By the late nineteenth century this elite generally acknowledged a responsibility for the health of the population, the desire to redefine society as modern and civilised also required the population to be healthy. Of course, the elite turned to Western medicine as the tool for this modernisation, as the medical and technological innovations introduced by missionary doctors seemed strikingly superior to traditional Thai medicine and healing. Medical and sanitary reform became an important part of the general administrative reforms during the the reign of Rama V around the turn of the century. The first systematic primary health care initiatives in Siam began in the 1870s in Bangkok with sanitation measures and were then slowly expanded to rural Siam. In 1909, the government began setting up health centres and clinics in small towns and rural communities. The central government paid the salaries of the health workers and nurse-midwives who staffed the health centres while the communities provided materials, labour, and funding for their construction.

6 See League of Nations, *Essential Facts*, p. 245ff. For the text of the Covenant of the League of Nations see LNA, League of Nations, *Official Journal*, February 1920, p. 3ff.

7 This assessment is shared by Dubin, League of Nations Health Organization. Dubin gives details on Rajchman's biography and career and his extensive involvement in China. Rajchman (1881-1965) headed the Health Organisation until 1939 and can be rightly regarded as one of the founders of international public health.

8 See in detail on the introduction of Western medicine in Siam Davisakd Puaksom, 'Of Germs, Public Hygiene, and the Healthy Body: The Making of the Medicalizing State in Thailand', *Journal of Asian Studies*, 66, 2 (May 2007), pp. 311-344. See also a case study by Herbert R. Swanson, 'Advocate and Partner: Missionaries and Modernization in Nan Province, Siam, 1895-1934', *Journal of Southeast Asian Studies*, 13, 2 (September 1982), pp. 296-309.

9 Barend J. Terwiel, 'Acceptance and Rejection: The First Inoculation and Vaccination Campaigns in Thailand', *Journal of the Siam Society*, 76 (1988), pp. 183-201.

The first modern Thai hospital, Siriraj, had been opened in Bangkok some years earlier, in 1888, with 44 beds. The first public dispensary was established in Bangkok in 1890 to sell Western medicine to government officials and the general public. In the same year the country's first medical school started training physicians for Siriraj Hospital at what was to become the Royal Medical College in 1901. But the level of training and equipment was poor. In 1916 Dr. Victor Heiser of the Rockefeller Foundation, which played a very prominent part in early medical and public health development in Siam, paid a visit to the college and afterwards informed King Vajiravudh, 'I have visited medical schools all over the world…I regret to say that Your Majesty's Royal medical School is the poorest I have ever seen'.[10] The following years then saw efforts to improve medical education, for which the Rockefeller Foundation provided support between 1922 and 1934 in the form of infrastructure, hardware, scholarships and salaries. The college was amalgamated with Chulalongkorn University in 1918 and became the faculty of medicine, which later formed the core of the new medical university founded in 1943.[11]

The *Red Unalom Society* was founded in Bangkok in 1893 but its name was changed to the Siamese Red Cross Society in 1910, and it was incorporated into the International League of Red Cross Societies, which was itself only two years old at the time, in 1921. One year earlier, in 1920, a public health section of the society was created. The section worked together with the Rockefeller Foundation, which supported the government and the Red Cross Society by promoting public health education and supporting anti-leprosy work. From 1917 to 1928, the Rockefeller Foundation also supported a successful programme to eradicate hookworm in Siam.[12] The Red Cross Society began sending small teams to villages, where they first lectured on diseases, then encouraged inhabitants to be examined, stopping short of treatment, however, and finally undertook a sanitary inspection of the village.[13] The gravity of the hookworm problem is illustrated by a report of 1924, which stated that out of some 243,000 people tested, fifty percent had hookworm.[14] An important part of the campaign was the promotion of latrines, which, however, had to deal with entrenched habits, as the following statement by a Thai farmer illustrates:

> You American people are strange. In the past, when I wanted to excrete, I would go find a quiet place in the field where there is a nice view with a nice wind. Now you tell me what I have eliminated is very harmful and that I should be as far away from it as possible. Then you tell me to dig a hole and say we should leave this harmful thing in the hole. This means I must get much closer to that thing – and not just mine but also those of other people. I prefer the field to this hole, which has no view and a bad smell.[15]

10 Heiser recalls this statement in his long article entitled 'Hustling the East' in TNA, *Bangkok Times*, 15 May 1937.

11 The medical university has been named Mahidol University since 1969 after the father of King Ananda and King Bhumibol. See on the Rockefeller Foundation's public health work in general also John Farley, *To Cast Out Disease: A History of the International Health Division of the Rockefeller Foundation (1913-1951)*, Oxford and New York: Oxford University Press, 2004.

12 The Rockefeller Foundation pulled out of Siam in 1929 due to disagreements with the government over programmatic and financial issues; see TNA, *Bangkok Times*, 15 May 1936.

13 TNA, *Bangkok Times*, 4 December 1922.

14 Report by the Department of Public Health and the Health Board of the Rockefeller Foundation, quoted in TNA, *Bangkok Times*, 18 July 1924.

15 John J. Hanlon, *Principles of Public Health Administration*, St. Louis: Mosby, 1950, quoted in *The Nation*, 14 August 2002. See also TNA, *Bangkok Times*, 4 December 1922 for an account of the campaign by the director of the public health section of the Siamese Red Cross Society.

In spite of such views, the number of households with latrines increased from ten per cent in 1917 to seventy-six percent in 1928. From 1923, when the initial programme was completed, the Department of Public Health under the Ministry of Interior took over the implementation of the anti-hookworm campaign from the national Red Cross Society.[16]

Siam was also represented in early regional initiatives, namely the congresses of the Far Eastern Association of Tropical Medicine (FEATM). This association, founded in 1904 Manila as an American initiative, held ten medical congresses in different Asian countries between 1910 and 1938. The eighth congress was held in Bangkok in 1930 and was generally considered by observers and government administrators as 'an event of national importance'.[17] To sum up, international cooperation of parts of the Thai elite before the League's creation with the League of Red Cross Societies, the Rockefeller Foundation, and the FEATM were important and had positive impacts on the modernisation of public health in Siam, but from 1920 the width and depth of international public health cooperation changed, and by 1922 national authorities clearly affirmed the new League of Nations as the 'one supreme and authoritative body to deal with the whole subject of international health in its many and varied aspects'.[18]

Public health in Siam from 1920: national and international developments

In 1920 international observers complained that the sanitary situation in Bangkok was in dire need of improvement, but that nobody in the government seemed to take an interest in public health issues.[19] Indeed, the public health situation in Siam was not good in the early 1920s, particularly in the provinces. The great majority of Siam's population continued to live in basically the same sanitary and medical conditions as they had for generations. Foreigners residing in Bangkok put pressure on the Thai government to improve public health conditions throughout 1921 and the spring of 1922. In November 1922, Siam's landmark first public health exhibition opened its gates at Saranrom Palace. The exhibition, which aimed to educate the public in matters of disease prevention, was jointly organised by the Department of Public Health and the Red Cross Society. The exhibition, which lasted from 25 November to 9 December, coincided with the Oriental Congress of the League of Red Cross Societies in Bangkok and the visit to Bangkok of the League of Nations commission of enquiry on leprosy, which we will discuss below. The exhibition was such a spectacular success that, according to the *Bangkok Times*, the almost unbelievably large number of nearly 90,000 visitors was counted during the first six days.[20]

The sanitary situation in the capital was already beginning to improve slowly, as the Bangkok waterworks had been providing the capital with clean drinking water since 1914 and were generally

16 TNA, *Bangkok Times*, 3 January 1924.

17 TNA, *Bangkok Times*, 9 December 1930. On the FEATM congresses and early colonial cooperation on medical issues see Karine Delaye, 'Colonial Co-operation and Regional Construction: Anglo-French Medical and Sanitary Relations in South East Asia', *Asia Europe Journal*, 3 (2004), pp. 461-471. See also TNA, *Bangkok Times*, 31 August 1921; 29 August 1923. Details on Siam's representation at FEATM congresses can also be found in Department of Public Health (ed.), *Report of the Department of Public Health, Including the Report of the Office of the Medical Officer of Health*, Bangkok, Bangkok: Department of Public Health, 1922, p. 43.

18 Ibid., p. 41.

19 TNA, *Bangkok Times*, 25 November 1920.

20 TNA, *Bangkok Times*, 9 November, 29 November and 1 December 1922.

considered a true engineering marvel by local and foreign residents. The system had 62 miles of piping and 390 street fountains, from which the population could draw clean water free of charge and by the 1920s, the pressure in the pipes was sufficient to bring water to the first floor of houses.[21] The waterworks were a major step towards the gradual elimination of waterborne diseases, such as cholera. One observer stated by the end of that decade, 'Bangkok to-day is a healthy port with a death-rate which compares favourably with Singapore. That it has become so is very largely due to the excellent town water supply, which is available free in copious quantities to all its inhabitants.'[22]

By the mid-1920s, sanitary conditions had already improved remarkably. The *Bangkok Times*, which had been very critical of the public health situation in previous years, stated in November 1925, just two weeks before the death of King Vajiravudh: 'Nothing greater perhaps has been achieved in the reign than the progress in regard to sanitation and public health'.[23] A few months later, in June 1926, the new British Minister gave this account of conditions shortly after his arrival in Bangkok:

> Bangkok is not unhealthy, and has coped successfully with the cholera epidemic that was at its height when I arrived. It is provided with most of the amenities of civilization, including tolerable roads, electric light, electric trams and an admirable water supply; but excluding drainage.[24]

But, in spite of obvious improvements in sanitary conditions, it is important to contrast such statements with the uneven spread of improvements between the urban centre and rural Siam as well as between different ethnic and social groups, as a colourful description by Kenneth Landon of Chinese-run hotels in Siam in 1939 illustrates:

> The hotels that abound in every market centre are a definite menace to health. They are run by Chinese and are usually unscrubbed, smelly from sewage, urine, and pigs, and over-run with prostitutes. The average room is equipped with a double bed, having a thin mattress on a wooden bottom, a pillow, a bolster, a mosquito net that was bought and hung when the bed was new...The guest walks around in wooden shoes to keep off the floor, avoids shaking the bed when crawling in so that not too much dust will settle on the face, and cringes as he waits for the 'zing' that proves that the local mosquitoes know where the cracks are between bed and netting. The nets are seldom long enough to tuck in under the mattress, but are draped around the edge of the bed. Their chief office is to hinder the paying guest from getting in and out of bed too easily, and to conserve all tuberculosis germs from the guests of former years.[25]

21 Thompson, *Thailand*, p. 524ff; *The Siam Directory, The Only Complete and Up-to-date Hand-Book of Siam*, Bangkok: Siam Observer Press, 1922, p. 119. A British report of 1920 marvels at the water-works and its effect on public health: 'Bangkok has in the past depended for its water supply upon the river and the numerous canals and waterways intersecting the district. Befouled with vegetable matter and sewage, the Bangkok water is of a most poisonous quality, and outbreaks of cholera are of frequent occurrence. By a scheme entrusted for political reasons to French engineers in 1909...the River Menam has been tapped by a special canal 25 miles north of Bangkok, and the water brought by this means to Bangkok is forced through a series of filters before being distributed. The principle portion of Bangkok lies to the east of the river, and this district is now served with this purified water to the incalculable benefit of the public health.' See Annual Report of Siam for the Year 1919, Doc. 59 (Enclosure in F 264/264/40), BDFA, Part II, Series E, vol. 49, p. 59.

22 C.H. Forty, *Bangkok: Its Life and Sport*, London: H.F. & G. Wither-by, 1929, p. 16.

23 TNA, *Bangkok Times*, 14 November 1925.

24 Waterlow to Chamberlain, 30 June 1926, Doc. 221 (F 3158/78/40), BDFA, Part II, Series E, vol. 49, p. 293.

25 Landon, *Siam in Transition*, p. 159. Landon also provides an interesting analysis of the health situation of Chinese in Siam in the 1930s in Landon, *Chinese in Thailand*, p. 83ff.

Next to sanitation, the second major public health issue in Siam was epidemic diseases. Smallpox was one of the paramount infectious diseases in both the nineteenth and the beginning of the twentieth century. But when a smallpox epidemic broke out in Bangkok in autumn 1923, compulsory vaccination of the city's twenty-five inner districts was introduced and the epidemic was quickly brought under control.[26] One reason for this swift action was that vaccines were produced in Siam by this time. Operated by the Red Cross Society since 1911, the Bangkok Pasteur Institute produced vaccines, sera, and anti-venoms. By the early 1920s, the institute was housed in new purposely-built, spacious premises and prepared enough smallpox vaccine to meet the needs of the entire country, besides producing vaccines for plague, cholera, typhoid, gonorrhoea, anthrax, etc.[27]

Modern pharmaceutical development was at an early stage in the 1920s and 1930s. In Siam, herbal Thai and Chinese medicine was widely available at market places and remained the medicine of choice for the majority of the population. Available potions included 'Potent water', 'Murder' or 'Motive Power Powders'.[28] But Western pharmaceutical development before the Second World War equally gave room for somewhat interesting medicines, as a 1922 advertisement in the *Bangkok Times* for the well-known drug Chlorodyne illustrates:

> The original & only Dr. J. Collis Browne's *Chlorodyne*; acts like a charm in Diarrhoea and is the only Specific in Cholera and Dysentery. Checks and arrests those too often fatal diseases, fever, croup, ague; the best remedy known for coughs, colds, asthma, bronchitis; effectively cuts short all attacks of spasms; is the only palliative in neuralgia, rheumatism, toothache.[29]

In other words, Chlorodyne was a true wonder drug that would cure virtually any disease; in fact it was mainly a mixture of an alcoholic solution of opium, cannabis, and chloroform, and, indeed, readily lived up to its claims of relieving virtually any pain. But, Chlorodyne and others aside, Western medical science had been developing rapidly since the late nineteenth century and served to underscore Western superiority towards colonised and non-colonised Asians, not least through major innovations in vaccine development and microbiology; in other words, Western medicine claimed global authority. During the decades around the turn of the century, enlightened scientists, doctors and health administrators in the West, in colonised Southeast Asia and in Siam shared the conviction that diseases could be eradicated by medical science; and it was this confidence which led to the modernisation of medical and public health practice, laws and administration in Siam before 1920 and after.

26 Greg to Lord Curzon, 9 January 1924, Doc. 175 (F 412/412/40), BDFA, Part II, Series E, vol. 49, p. 220; TNA, *Bangkok Times*, 5 September 1923.

27 TNA, *Bangkok Times*, 4 December 1922. See also Landon, *Thailand in Transition*, p. 140.

28 Landon, *Chinese in Thailand*, p. 84.

29 TNA, *Bangkok Times*, 4 December 1922.

Medical and public health developments in pre-Second World War Siam have become strongly associated with individual members of the royal family through Thai historiography. According to this traditional narrative, Prince Mahidol and Prince Rangsit almost single-handedly modernised the Thai medical and public health systems. While it is true that the two half-brothers, both sons of King Chulalongkorn, made significant contributions to health development, there were other individual and institutional forces at work, both national and international. Prince (*Phra Ong Chao*) Rangsit Prayurasakdi of Jainad was one of the early directors of the Royal Medical College and its Siriraj Hospital and first Director-General of the Public Health Department from 1918 to 1926. Prince (*Chao Fa*) Mahidol Adulyadej, father of Kings Rama VIII and Rama IX, studied public health and medicine at Harvard University and was involved in medical education and practice in Siam before his untimely death in 1929.

Public health management was spread over different government agencies until King Vajiravudh ordered it to be concentrated in a newly to-be-created Department of Public Health in the Ministry of Interior in 1918. In reality however, rivalrous ministries and lack of leadership by the king kept this administrative change from becoming truly effective for several years. Stephen Greene has reconstructed this process as an example of King Vajiravudh's inability to effectively control the administration.[30] The reorganisation meant shifting the Department of the Medical Health Officer from the Ministry of Local Government to that of Interior and combining it with the Department of Public Welfare. Three years after the king's instruction, still nothing had happened. According to Greene, 'the King had forgotten about the matter in the meantime. His memory was jogged by the news that a committee of the League of Nations was coming to Bangkok the next year to discuss the problem of public health in Asia.'[31] Because of this forthcoming visit by Dr. Norman White to enquire into sanitation and port health, the issue of administrative reform in public health was back on the table. Although the haggling between the Ministries of Interior, Finance, and Local Government over funds and influence continued, this episode shows that the wish to appear in a favourable light before the League of Nations commission of enquiry gave the reorganisation of public health management in Siam an important boost in 1921. From 1922, the two Ministries of Local Government and Interior were merged, greatly facilitating the effectiveness of the new Department of Public Health. Nevertheless, it had taken Siam ten years longer than, for example, its neighbour to the south, British Malaya, to set up a unified health service.[32] During the lifetime of the League, public health issues were dealt with administratively by this department, which was situated in the Ministry of Interior and which was headed until 1926 by Prince Rangsit.

30 Greene, *Absolute Dreams*, p. 147f.

31 Ibid., p. 147.

32 Lenore Manderson, *Sickness and the State: Health and Illness in Colonial Malaya, 1870-1940*, Cambridge: Cambridge University Press 1996, p. 15.

The beginnings of modern public health administration in Siam are closely connected with Prince Sakol Varnakorn Voravarn, elder half-brother of Prince Varnvaidya. Both brothers were grandsons of King Mongkut and held a strong belief in the value of international cooperation in the development of their country. While Prince Varn entered the diplomatic service and went on to represent Siam at the League of Nations headquarters at Geneva, Cambridge-educated Prince Sakol entered the public health service in Bangkok and later represented Siam in receiving visiting League officials and attending League of Nations conferences in Singapore and Bandung. Born in 1888, he began working in the field of public health from 1915 and, in 1926, succeeded Prince Rangsit as Director-General of the Public Health Department, a position which he held until the coup in June 1932.[33] The first permanent constitution of December 1932 banned him from holding a senior position in Siam's public administration because of his princely rank of *Mom Chao.* But, as in the case of his brother Prince Varn, the post-1932 constitutional governments continued to rely on the expertise of Prince Sakol and, after briefly holding the position of Deputy Minister of Agriculture and Commerce, he became adviser to the Ministry of Interior, just as his brother became adviser to the Ministry of Foreign Affairs. In this function as adviser, Prince Sakol was able to continue propagating his pronounced liberal views, to continue the Western-style modernisation of Siam's public health services and also to represent his country in contacts with the League and third governments. Prince Sakol developed profound expertise in international issues relating to Siam's development and can be described as the single most influential official in Siam's public health development during the two interwar decades. Indeed, the questions on which his advice was sought were not limited to matters of public health. Thus it was Prince Sakol who represented Siam at the League of Nations-sponsored Bandung Conference on Trafficking in Women and Children in 1937. He also earned the nickname 'red prince' after 1932, when he, as a member of the committee to investigate Luang Pradist's economic plan, showed sympathy for the socialist-inspired ideas of the revolutionary. After the Second World War, Prince Sakol continued to represent Siam internationally and as early as October 1946 he served as delegate to the international labour conference in Montreal, where he was said to have given 'probably one of the finest speeches of the conference.'[34]

Together with the modernisation of public health administration, the government also cast procedures and policies into a Western-style legal framework by passing numerous laws and acts. The public health report of 1922 gives a detailed summary of laws enacted to that date.[35] In 1923 the new Medical Law was promulgated, which followed the earlier Decree for the Prevention of Venereal Diseases of 1908, the Infectious Diseases Law of 1913 and the Vaccination Law of 1914.[36]

33 One may add as an *aperçu* that the two princes not only devoted their professional lives to public health, but, in another parallel, both Prince Rangsit and Prince Sakol happened to marry German women, and both Princes passed away at the age of 65.

34 TNL, *Thai Newsmagazine*, 17 November 1946. The ILO had moved to Montreal from Geneva in 1940 because of the war in Europe.

35 Department of Public Health, *Report for 1922*, p. 46ff. On earlier decrees relating to sanitation and public health see also Davisakd, Medicalizing State, p. 317ff.

36 It is systematically relevant in this context that English translations and Thai original texts of these laws were sent to the League of Nations, together with some one hundred other legal texts between the 1920s and the early 1940s. The decrees, acts, laws, and codes served to demonstrate to the Western world the degree of civilisation and progressiveness of the Thai government. The laws can conveniently still be found at the United Nations European Headquarters at Geneva today.

It is fair to assume that the visit of the League's Leprosy Commission to Bangkok and the Red Cross Congress in 1922, both of which are discussed below, functioned as catalysts for the Medical Law of 1923. The new law established a medical council to oversee medical practices and their modernisation. The Health Regulation of 1929 then led to a separation of traditional and modern medicines, whereby the latter was given clear priority. In 1930, the medical law was amended once again and it was only now that the Public Health Department had full authority to enforce sanitary measures throughout Siam.[37] In the course of the 1930s, the legal framework for public health was further improved through the 1934 Local Organisation Act as well as the 1935 Public Health Act and Communicable Diseases Act. As the healthcare situation in Bangkok had reached an acceptable level by the mid-1930s, emphasis was increasingly put on providing better healthcare in the provinces through the decentralisation of public health services. This shifting of emphasis from the centre to the periphery was highlighted on an international level in 1937 when Siam participated in the League of Nations Rural Hygiene Conference in Bandung.

The promotion of midwifery became an important issue for the public health authorities in the late 1920s because of the rapid population growth in Siam. Prince Sakol even called better midwifery 'our primary and most urgent need' in a lecture he gave at the *Samaggi Samagom* in London in 1929.[38] But compared with the region as a whole, infant mortality remained very high in Siam and was considered excessive by officials throughout the period under review in this study. In 1938, over 46,000 infants died at birth or within the first twelve months, a fact which did not go unnoticed by the international community in Siam.[39] However, by that year the infant mortality rate in Siam already compared well regionally. In fact, according to the Public Health Report for B.E. 2481 (1938-39), it was lower than that of all British colonies in the region and even than that of Japan.[40]

In addition to midwives, training junior or assistant doctors for rural areas was also promoted by Prince Sakol during the 1920s, as a result of the acute shortage of fully trained doctors. The situation was vividly described by French doctor Jacques M. May, who worked in Bangkok:

> Siam, just emerging from the dark ages with the help of scores of European and American advisers, had, in 1932, a medical picture which was not too bright. There were some eight to ten European doctors in Bangkok, all busy with private practices in their own communities – French, English and German. In addition there were a few dozen Siamese who held the degree of bachelor of medicine, but they were employed for the most part in the public health service, the army or navy. The rank and file of the people were taken care of by persons who were listed as 'healers'...[41]

37 The organisational structure of the Department of Public Health in 1933 can be found in TNA, *Bangkok Times*, 4 May 1933; the organisational structure in 1937 is detailed in the 'National Monograph contributed by the Siamese Delegation to the Rural Hygiene Conference, 1937', TNA, KT 96.1.11/17, insert after p. 5.

38 TNA, *Bangkok Times*, 4 February 1929. A school of nursing and midwifery was founded in Bangkok in 1896 and upgraded in 1906.

39 Greg to Chamberlain, 2 December 1925, Doc. 217 (F 78/78/40), BDFA, Part II, Series E, vol. 49, p. 287. Greg makes this observation when reporting that King Prajadhipok was the 76th son of King Chulalongkorn, and that the majority of his older brothers had likely died as infants.

40 On infant mortality rates in Malaya, 1901-1937, see Manderson, *Sickness and the State*, p. 44 and 55ff.

41 May, *Doctor in Siam*, p. 104.

However, as we will see below, it took until the late 1930s for the number of junior doctors to reach a significant level.

Apart from preventive and curative measures, medical training and sanitary work, the Department of Public Health also promoted public health education. Newspaper campaigns were organised on specific public health subjects, while booklets on different diseases were printed in 1922 in Thai but also, partially funded by a philanthropic society in Shanghai, in Chinese. Western educational films on hookworm and malaria were shown in rural Siam during the 1920s. And, of course, the public health exhibition of 1922 proved a magnet for visitors. Educational measures were considered 'indispensable to satisfactory advance in nearly all lines of public health work' and were continued throughout the 1920s and 1930s.[42]

By 1930, Siam was considered by observers to have made 'wonderful advance in one generation' in the field of public health: 'Siam has set herself to educate her people in these matters, and has taken more pains over the work than most countries do'.[43] After the overthrow of the absolute monarchy in 1932, the new government issued a policy statement, in which public health issues featured prominently. Apart from reorganising the local sanitary board, the government planned to carry out an extended disease prevention and hygiene programme as well as to establish more hospitals and local health centres throughout the kingdom. Furthermore, the new government committed itself to an increased effort in the control of malaria, leprosy, and tuberculosis.[44] The necessity of such policy priorities is highlighted in a comment by the British Minister in Bangkok:

> Public health measures are as urgent as any in this country, as was brought home to me shortly after reading the Government programme, when I saw two drowned oxen and a dog, obviously very dead, floating about in a canal along the highway into which they had been thrown. Within a few yards people were washing and bathing contentedly, and doubtless imbibing much water.[45]

Before analysing in detail the cooperation between Siam and the League in public health, it is useful to point once more to the colonial environment, in which this cooperation took place. One the one hand, we have seen above how innovative trends led to the creation of the first international structures in response to threats posed by epidemics and even pandemics. On the other hand, when the League of Nations was created, public health in the Asian colonies of European states was still largely neglected and was only an issue in as far as it was necessary to protect Europeans in the colonies and to maintain an indigenous labour force. As Dorothy Porter points out regarding British India, 'even when an obligation to apply health reforms to the entire Indian population was theoretically acknowledged by the British, neglect, parsimony and bigotry about oriental "backwardness" prevented progress'.[46] We must

42 Department of Public Health, *Report for 1922*, p. 51. Department of Public Health (ed.), *Report for B.E. 2481 (1938-39)*, Bangkok: Department of Public Health, B.E. 2485 (1942), p. 150ff. provides an interesting comparison of public health education twenty years after the first report.

43 TNA, *Bangkok Times*, 9 December 1930.

44 Policy statement cited in Dormer to Simon, 30 December 1932, Doc. 85 (F 691/42/40), BDFA, Part II, Series E, vol. 50, p. 89. Preparations for a tuberculosis control scheme were begun in cooperation with the Far Eastern Bureau of the League's Health Organisation in 1938; see Memorandum of Ministry of Interior, n.d. (1938), TNA, KT 96.1.11/17.

45 Policy statement cited in Dormer to Simon, 30 December 1932, Doc. 85 (F 691/42/40), BDFA, Part II, Series E, vol. 50, p. 90.

46 Dorothy Porter, 'Introduction', in Dorothy Porter (ed.), *The History of Public Health and the Modern State*, The Wellcome Institute Series in the History of Medicine, Amsterdam and Atlanta: Editions Rodopi, 1994, p. 1-44, here p. 21. See also the excellent study on colonial Malaya: Manderson, *Sickness and the State*, passim.

keep these preconceptions and policies in mind when analysing how Siam, the only territory in Southeast Asia governed by Asians, acted on the international stage regarding public health.

League of Nations commissions of enquiry in Siam

One of the novel tools in international relations which the League of Nations had at its disposal was the commission of enquiry.[47] As we can observe in the case of Siam, the impact and importance of some of these commissions went far beyond simple fact-finding missions. They often boosted developments in their area of concern, even to the point of triggering new laws, regulations and practices and they were often used by the Thai government to present itself as modern and civilised towards its own population and towards the outside world. League of Nations commissions were dispatched to Siam to investigate issues relating to opium control, public health, and human trafficking. In the field of public health, five commissions of enquiry visited Siam between the early 1920s and the late 1930s. They were concerned with epidemic diseases and port health (1922), leprosy (1930), malaria (1931), rural hygiene (1936), and cholera (1937).

Commission of enquiry 1: epidemic diseases and port health, 1922

Dr. Norman White, a medical and sanitary expert serving the League, visited thirty-four ports throughout Asia on a marathon tour between November 1922 and July 1923.[48] Resulting from a Japanese initiative at Geneva, his enquiry provided important preliminary work for the establishment of the League's Singapore Bureau in 1925 and the setup of an Asian 'epidemiological intelligence service'.

White, who was Deputy Director of the League Secretariat's Health Section and the League's Chief Epidemic Commissioner, both bodies being predecessors of the League's Health Organisation, which came into existence in 1923, was specifically assigned to collect information on epidemic diseases occurring at ports and thereby posing an international threat. White examined the sanitary standards of ports and on ships as well as quarantine and medical facilities. His itinerary was discussed with concerned delegates, who were in Geneva for the General Assembly in September 1922. Public health officials in Bangkok were already keenly interested in the League's new role, albeit still limited to Europe, in international epidemiological surveillance, as the public health report of 1922 shows.[49] Accordingly, Prince Charoon was very supportive of White's planned visit to Bangkok, but disagreed with the proposed itinerary. Instead of White visiting Bangkok in March 1923 – according to Prince Charoon 'the worst month of the year, not only from the climatic point of view, but also from the fact that nearly everyone will be absent', the Prince suggested White visit Bangkok in November

47 While the League's commissions of enquiry were novel tools in different respects, they were, of course, not an exclusive domain of the League. As far as medicine and public health is concerned, for example, the Liverpool School of Tropical Medicine undertook an enquiry in several British and non-British territories in Asia in 1935; see ibid., p. 225.

48 'The Prevalence of Epidemic Disease and Port Health Organization and Procedure in the Far East. Report Presented to the Health Committee of the League of Nations by F. Norman White, Geneva 1923', LNA, serial document no. C.167.M.43. 1924.III. See also LNA, R 843/12B/31957/23230.

49 Department of Public Health, *Report for 1922*, p. 43.

1922. He suggested that Dr. White attend the health conference, which was to take place at the end of November in Bangkok under the auspices of the League of Red Cross Societies, and that he do so in his official capacity as a representative of the League of Nations. The League of Red Cross Societies had already invited the League of Nations to send a representative, in order to participate in the discussions on issues related to opium. The Opium Advisory Committee, however, was unable to fund a mission of an expert to Bangkok, and Prince Charoon now pointed Secretary-General Drummond to the convenient synergy arising from Dr. White's mission, for which funding had already been secured by the League Council. Prince Charoon also saw an additional advantage in combining Dr. White's visit with his attendance of the health conference in that the League's 'existence and activities on questions of humanity should be brought home to the people of my country'. In other words, in the person of Norman White the League would become visible for the first time in Siam.[50] Drummond, although supportive of the prince's proposal, was sceptical as to its practicality. However, on 27 September, a sub-committee of the League Assembly's Health Committee decided at a meeting in Paris to take up Prince Charoon's suggestion, which had meanwhile been reinforced by an official letter from the Foreign Ministry in Bangkok.[51]

Dr. Norman White embarked at Marseilles on 3 November and, via Singapore, arrived in Bangkok on 28 November, the first stop of his extensive tour. White inspected the Bangkok port, conducted a number of interviews and participated in the conference of the League of Red Cross Societies. But his visit to Bangkok was very brief, and his report did not go beyond an overview. In fact, White originally intended to revisit Siam at the end of his tour through Asia, but his schedule later prevented this. Nevertheless, White did try to provide more than just information about the sanitary conditions of the Bangkok port and gave a more comprehensive assessment of the public health situation in Siam in 1922, including the prevalence of smallpox, cholera and plague, and of public health administration.[52] White described the quarantine station on Phra Island as clearly inadequate, but acknowledged that the Bangkok port had a designated anchorage site for ships with infected passengers.

White spent some two weeks in Siam as a guest of the Thai government and left the kingdom on 8 December 1922.[53] His letter to Prince Devawongse, written a day before his departure, was sure to please his hosts, 'I should like to express…the pleasure I have experienced in witnessing the well directed energy and enthusiasm now being devoted to public health problems in Siam, by the Red Cross Society and Government departments alike'.[54] The visit of Norman White can be considered the first in a long line of successful 'public relations' exercises on the part of the modernising Southeast Asian kingdom, for which it made use of its League membership to

50 Prince Charoon to Drummond, 18 September 1922, LNA, R 843/12B/24288/23230.

51 See various correspondence regarding White's itinerary in LNA, R 843/12B/24288/ 23230. See also Lenore Manderson, 'Wireless Wars in the Eastern Arena: Epidemiological Surveillance, Disease Protection and the Work of the Eastern Bureau of the League of Nations Health Organisation, 1925-1942', in Paul Weindling (ed.), *International Health Organisations and Movements*, Cambridge: Cambridge University Press 1995, pp.109-133, here p. 110f.

52 White's report can be found in LNA, R 843/12B/24288/ 23230. An in-depth report on the Red Cross conference can be found in TNA, *Bangkok Times*, 4 December 1922. White's report was later considered useful but led one commentator to state that the issue of port health should not be overstated, as only three disease outbreaks in Bangkok had been triggered by passengers on incoming vessels during the previous sixteen years. See TNA, *Bangkok Times*, 3 May 1923.

53 For details see TNA, KT 96. 1.11/7.

54 White to Prince Devawongse, 8 December 1922, TNA, KT 96. 1.11/7.

demonstrate its progressiveness and underscore its sovereignty vis-à-vis the international community. White's visit also provided authorities in Bangkok with an up-to-date assessment of port facilities and recommendations of an international standard on which they could base plans for future port developments; White's visit, as those of all other League commissions of enquiry, was thereby a means for the transfer of Western knowledge to Siam, for which the Thai elite was highly receptive in its eagerness to modernise the country.

Commission of enquiry 2: leprosy and the meeting of the League of Nations leprosy commission in Bangkok, 1930

When the League came into existence, leprosy was endemic in Southeast Asia and Siam. Estimates put the number of lepers in Siam in the 1920s and 1930s at between 15,000 and 20,000.[55] Lepers were treated in two leprosaria run by Western missionaries and by the late 1930s also in three institutions run by the government. However, all leprosaria combined provided space for only two thousand lepers.

In 1930-31, the League of Nations conducted an enquiry into leprosy in East and Southeast Asia. This followed an earlier League enquiry into the situation regarding leprosy in Latin America and was the result of a Japanese initiative in 1928, as Japan was facing a serious leprosy problem and desired, ultimately unsuccessfully, to work with the League in setting up a research centre for leprosy under League auspices in Japan. The proposal by the League's Health Committee to dispatch a commission of enquiry on leprosy to Siam was met with full-hearted approval by the government in Bangkok. Prince Sakol replied to Dr. Rajchman that 'the problem of leprosy in Siam is one of considerable importance, and since it is only too easy to make mistakes in dealing with this problem, the health authorities in Siam are keenly interested in the investigations carried out by your Commission'.[56]

The Health Organisation decided in October 1930 that the members of the Leprosy Commission should meet in Bangkok and hold a formal meeting there, to coincide with the eighth congress of the Far Eastern Association of Tropical Medicine, which was also to be held in the Thai capital. This meeting of the leprosy commission of the League of Nations Health Organisation took place in the grounds of Chulalongkorn University from 8 to 12 December 1930. It marked the first time that Siam hosted an official meeting of an international organisation. The meeting was presided over by the German Dr. Bernhard Nocht, Director of the respected Hamburg Institute of Tropical Diseases and later an international expert at the League's International Centre for Leprosy Research in Rio de Janeiro. In addition, six representatives of five countries and territories participated. Representing the United States, India, South Africa, Japan, and the Philippines, all the experts were medical researchers or representatives of

55 See, for example, The Far Eastern Association of Tropical Medicine, Executive Committee of the 8th Congress (ed.), *Siam: General and Medical Features*, Bangkok: Bangkok Times Press, 1930, p. 301ff.

56 Letter Prince Sakol to Rajchman, 12 May 1931, in: LNA, R 5892/8A/6659/6651. For the visit of the Leprosy Commission see also TNA, KT 96.1.11/15. On both the FEATM Congress and the Leprosy Commission see also TNA, R7, M 7.2/2. On leprosy in Siam see also the report of 1925, quoted at length in TNA, *Bangkok Times*, 28 December 1925.

public health services. In addition, the League itself was represented by Dr. Etienne Burnet, Secretary of the League's leprosy commission, Dr. Raymond Gautier, Director of the Far Eastern Bureau of the League of Nations Health Organisation, and the Australian Dr. Charles Leslie Park, who was at the time on the staff of the League Health Section and who succeeded Gautier in Singapore in 1932.

The commission mainly discussed issues relating to leprosy prophylaxis, for which they tried to lay down general guidelines. The meeting called on responsible authorities to standardise terminologies, treatment and statistical documentation. The commission also dealt with technical issues pertaining to the International Centre for Leprosy Research in Rio de Janeiro and the similar centre, which the Japanese government intended to establish. Prince Sakol made a strong impression on the commission by attending every single session of the meeting, 'thus demonstrating his interest in the questions under discussion and the importance which his country attaches to the League's work'.[57] But the commission's strongest and most fundamental recommendation to national health administrations in Asia, that lepers were to be strictly isolated from the healthy population, was obviously, not practical in Siam. However, in response to this recommendation, the Department of Public Health did initiate a scheme under which mobile units were set up to provide medical treatment to lepers in their homes, if they could not be treated at a leprosarium.[58]

After the meeting, the commission members accepted an invitation by the Thai government to visit the Phra Pradaeng leprosarium south of Bangkok, and some members travelled to Chiang Mai to visit the leprosarium run by American missionaries. The members of the commission then left Bangkok for Manila, where they took part in the conference of the 'Leonard Wood Memorial for the Eradication of Leprosy' in January 1931. Dr. Burnet submitted his twelve-page report on 'The Principles of the Prophylaxis of Leprosy' to the League's Health Committee in April 1931 after his return from Asia. The report reflects the discussions held in Bangkok and Manila and gives a condensed picture of the situation regarding leprosy in the region, from the standpoint of international medical hygiene.[59]

In conclusion, the Bangkok meeting of the League's leprosy commission was, together with the FEATM Congress, a big success for the Thai government. The congress and the visit of the commission both featured prominently in the king's speech from the throne on the fifth anniversary of his coronation on 25 February 1931, and the London *Times* noted that Siam had 'made a surprising advance [in public health] in the course of the last generation'.[60] Not only had Bangkok emerged as a centre for the modernisation of public health in Asia, but members of the Thai elite had also managed to impress the visiting public health specialists with their hospitality and their professionalism. Ludvik

57 Draft Memorandum of Leprosy Commission on the Bangkok Conference, LNA, R 5930/8A/30632/29090.

58 Rural Hygiene in Siam: National Monograph contributed by the Siamese Delegation to the Rural Hygiene Conference 1937, p. 24, in TNA, KT 96.1.11/17.

59 LNA, R 5887/8A/13191/4621 and R 5930/8A/30632/29090. The report entitled 'The Principles of the Prophylaxis of Leprosy', dated April 1931, can be found in: LNA, R 5887/8A/26044/4621.

60 TNA, *Bangkok Times*, 27 February 1931; *The Times*, 6 January 1931.

Rajchman, Director of the League Health Organisation and one of the pioneers of modern public health, congratulated Prince Sakol and Major-General Phraya Damrong Baedyagun, Director of Chulalongkorn Hospital, in personal letters:

> In addition to my personal thanks I am to convey to you the congratulations of the Health Committee for the brilliant success of the 8th Congress of the Far Eastern Association of Tropical Medicine, and at the same time to thank you on its behalf for the valuable help which you accorded to the Leprosy Conference.[61]

The visit of the commission of enquiry led to a continued exchange of information between the League's leprosy commission and authorities in Bangkok during the following years. For example, Geneva regularly received updated statistical data on leprosy from the Department of Public Health beginning from 1932.[62]

Commission of enquiry 3: malaria, 1931

The League's Health Organisation had set up a malaria commission in 1923 to deal with the malaria epidemic in Eastern and Southern Europe, which broke out as a result of the First World War. The commission facilitated extensive research on malaria, advised member governments and organised training of malariologists.[63]

Malaria posed the most serious epidemic problem in Siam. During the 1920s and 1930s, the disease claimed an average 40,000 lives annually in a population of 13 million (1937), a ratio not unusual in regional comparisons.[64] In late November 1930, Prince Sakol approached Dr. Raymond Gautier, Director of the League's Singapore Bureau, enquiring whether the League could assist Siam in the fight against malaria by sending an expert to survey the situation in the kingdom and provide advice to the government. Gautier proposed that Dr. Ludwik Anigstein, who was working at the Institute for Medical Research in Kuala Lumpur at the time, conduct the survey, and he received authorisation from the League's malaria commission by early December 1930.[65] It is notable that the initiative for this enquiry came from the administration in Bangkok as it shows that after a first decade of League membership Thai officials were well aware of the potential benefits the League could provide and well-versed in employing them to the benefit of Siam's development. At the same time, Prince Sakol's request was exactly the form of cooperation the League of Nations required to underline its authority outside Europe and the Western world.

Dr. Ludwik Anigstein, a Polish national and member of the malaria commission of the League's Health Organisation, arrived in Siam on 14 January 1931 and spent three and a half months working in the country, during which time he travelled extensively through the central,

61 Rajchman to Phraya Damrong and Rajchman to Prince Sakol, both 7 April 1931, LNA, R 5887/8A/13191/4621.

62 Prince Sakol to Burnet, 4 January 1932, LNA, R 5931/ 8A/30808/29090.

63 Bernhard Nocht, 'Report on the Activity of the Malaria Commission of the League of Nations and some Experiments on the Pathogenesis of Blackwater Fever', in Phya Damrong Baedyagun and Luang Suvejj Subhakich (eds), *Transactions of the Eighth Congress of the Far Eastern Association of Tropical Medicine held in Siam, December 1930*, Bangkok: Far Eastern Association of Tropical Medicine, 1931, vol. 2, pp. 329-247, here: p. 329. See also Boudreau, International Health Work, p. 201f.

64 On the malaria situation in, for example, Malaya see Lenore Manderson, *Sickness and the State*, p. 31 and 85ff. For an overview of malaria control in Vietnam see Andrew Hardy, 'One Hundred Years of Malaria Control in Vietnam: A regional Retrospective, Part I, 1900-1945', *Mekong Malaria Forum*, 5 (January 2000), pp. 91-101.

65 Various correspondence in LNA, R 5963/8C/24641/24641. Anigstein had been carrying out research in Malaya since 1929.

northern and southern regions of the kingdom, all the way from the border with Burma to the border with Malaya. Anigstein drew up a report later that year, entitled *Malaria and Anopheles in Siam*, which, although its findings were collected only through the dry season and not during the rainy season, was widely admired in Siam and internationally, and long served as a blueprint for what should ideally be done in Siam to combat malaria.[66] Anigstein's report examined the unequal spread of malaria in detail. It found that, while mosquitoes were prevalent, there were few cases of malaria in the central plains. On the contrary, malaria was widespread and severe in the kingdom's north and prevalent but not as severe in the southern coastal regions. The report left no doubt about the medical situation in northern Siam: 'the rural medical service is practically non-existent. The only places in the provinces provided with health and medical services are the administrative centres'.[67]

Anigstein recommended a malaria control scheme which took into account not only epidemiological factors but also the economic situation of the people in different regions. Improved and regionally specialised irrigation schemes played an important role in Anigstein's recommendations. His report drew a connection between economic development of the northern provinces of Siam and improvements in the health of the population. The report advocated the establishment of anti-malarial units to study the spread of malaria and to instruct local authorities in control and treatment. However, many of the recommendations made by Anigstein were too costly for the Thai government to implement in the light of the economic downturn of the early 1930s, a point which Anigstein himself acknowledged.[68] Nevertheless, the Department of Public Health organised a scheme under which quinine was sold to village headmen at cost price. The headmen were then encouraged to sell it with a small profit to persons infected with malaria. In addition, the poor could receive quinine tablets free of charge, as could all inhabitants of hyper-epidemic areas in northern and north-eastern Siam. In 1930, for example, the Thai government imported some 1.25 tons of quinine tablets from Java at a cost of close to 40,000 baht. However, without sufficient knowledge of the development of the disease both headmen and patients often did not administer quinine long enough to drive the parasites from the infected body. On the other hand, it was not practicable to make enough quinine available for all areas of the country, and where it was available, refusal to take it as a prophylaxis because of lack of education was also widespread.[69]

In 1937, the Thai government endorsed a malaria control scheme, which had been drawn up by Dr. Luang Bhayung Vejjasastra, Head of the Malaria Section in the Department of Public Health, and which was strongly inspired by Anigstein's enquiry. In fact, Dr. Luang Bhayung was the government's official liaison person with the League's malaria

66 For Anigstein's report and the relevant correspondence see LNA, R 5963/8C/24641/24641. The report was later published by the League of Nations as Ludwik Anigstein, 'Malaria and Anopheles in Siam', *Quarterly Bulletin of the Health Organisation*, 1, 2 (June 1932), pp. 233-308.

67 Ibid., p. 281.

68 See Thompson, *Thailand*, p. 702ff.; D.J.M. Tate, *The Making of Modern South-East Asia*, vol. 2: The Western Impact, Kuala Lumpur: Oxford University Press, 1979, p. 560.

69 Anigstein, Malaria and Anopheles in Siam, p. 282f.

Leading figures in public health development in Siam: Prince Rangsit (seated centre), Prince Sakol Voravarn (seated third from left), Prince Mahidol (seated second from right) in 1924 (Thai National Archives).

commission, and knew the commission's secretary, Dr. Emilio Pampana, personally from his visit to Siam as a member of the commission of enquiry on rural health in 1936.[70] Like Anigstein, Luang Bhayung also saw people suffering from chronic malaria as 'economic liabilities which are obstacles to progress in agriculture, industry and general national development.' It was because of this threat to progress that control and treatment had to be undertaken by the state.[71] The scheme was based on the creation of stationary and mobile malaria control units, which should successively cover the country, in order to allow rapid reaction to outbreaks and their containment. The scheme also included a component on anopheles research, similar to what Anigstein had undertaken, and, very importantly, an educational component designed 'to impart health knowledge to the local folks' through lectures, posters, pamphlets, motion pictures, radio talks, and school health education. The scheme further advocated continued free distribution of quinine in hyper-epidemic localities, while acknowledging shortages in quinine supply. Finally, the scheme explicitly advocated sending physicians to the League's Singapore Bureau for 'postgraduate malaria instruction', a training activity which will be detailed below.

70 See correspondence in LNA, R 6179/8C/28376/2290.

71 'Malaria Control Scheme', Enclosure in Luang Bhayung to Pampana, 15 January 1938, LNA, R 6177/8C/7258/1644.

In 1939, the League once again sent a questionnaire on the malaria situation to Bangkok and Phra Vaidaya Vidhikar, successor of Phraya Boriraksh Vejkar as Director-General of the Department of Public Health, submitted the reply to the League in August of that year.[72] By this time, the Department of Public Health had been able to implement a number of Anigstein's recommendations through the malaria control scheme. It already had two permanent malaria control units in place in Bangkok and Chiang Mai and operated one mobile unit as well as conducting research into the various indigenous species of anopheles.[73] But a regional conference on malaria sponsored by the League of Nations, which the Bandung Conference on Rural Hygiene of 1937 had proposed for 1939, did not materialise, and international coordination of malaria control efforts only picked up again in a WHO framework after the Second World War.

Commission of enquiry 4: rural hygiene, 1936

A fourth commission of enquiry on public health issues visited Siam in the year 1936. This commission had the task of gathering information pertaining to rural hygiene, identifying relevant issues through meetings with public health administrators and preparing an agenda for the international conference planned for the following year in Bandung on the island of Java in the Netherlands Indies. Rural hygiene was the modern approach in international public health in the 1930s and focused on the vast rural populations throughout the world, which had hitherto benefited little or none from international public health. Sunil Amrith summarises:

> Rural hygiene built upon new scientific knowledge, above all the knowledge of nutrition, and advances of vitamins and deficiency diseases. It brought together a set of techniques of public health, pioneered in locales across both Asia and Eastern Europe – health centres, experimental projects and institutes of medical research – in response to an overwhelming problem posed by the worldwide depression: the problem of agrarian decline (and the potential for political unrest in its wake).[74]

The commission was composed of three public health experts: Alwyn S. Haynes, former British colonial secretary in the Straits Settlements; Dutchman Professor C.D. de Langen, former dean of the medical faculty at Batavia; and Italian Dr. Emilio Pampana, secretary of the League of Nations malaria commission and later author of one of the basic textbooks on malaria eradication as well as the first WHO director of malaria eradication. Their itinerary included visits to British India, Ceylon, Malaya, Siam, French Indochina, Netherlands Indies, and the Philippines. They had been travelling since March when they arrived in Bangkok on a KLM flight on 10 May 1936. They were put up

72 Memorandum by Phra Vaidaya, 28 August 1939, in: LNA, R 6174/8C/34241/1561.

73 Department of Public Health, *Report for B.E. 2481 (1938-39)*, p. 66ff. See also TNA, *Bangkok Times*, 20 March 1936.

74 Sunil Amrith, *Decolonizing International Health: India and Southeast Asia, 1930-65*, Basingstoke: Palgrave, 2006, p. 21.

at the Oriental Hotel and Dr. Phra Charnvitivej of the Department of Public Health acted as their liaison person and guide during the visit. The commission met with several senior government officials, including the Minister of Interior and Prince Sakol, who was then adviser to the Ministry. The commission undertook field trips to Ayutthaya, Lopburi and Chiang Mai during their stay to study health conditions, sanitation and nutrition in rural Siam. They then continued onwards to French Indochina after having spent one short but very intensive week in Siam on 17 May.[75] After their five-month journey through Asia, the commission drew up a report on the situation concerning rural hygiene in the visited territories and circulated it among the conference participants as the basis for discussion at Bandung the following year.[76] It appears that the commission's visit strengthened the attention which public health authorities in Siam and surrounding colonies had been beginning to pay since the early 1930s to health issues, nutrition and health education for the rural populace, as opposed to the hitherto prevailing focus of attention on the urban centres.[77] The commission's visit fitted neatly into the policy of the Bangkok authorities, who had already commissioned two detailed studies on conditions in rural Siam, so-called rural economic surveys, by two Harvard scholars Carle C. Zimmerman in 1930 and James M. Andrews in 1934-35.[78]

Commission of enquiry 5: cholera, 1937

Cholera epidemics appeared in Siam 'at fairly regular intervals like a storm' since the disease spread from the Indian subcontinent in the early nineteenth century.[79] These cholera outbreaks were, until the mid-1920s, the local effects of six large cholera pandemics. Siam experienced its first cholera epidemic in 1820, which, according to the in-depth study by Terwiel, claimed some 30,000 lives.[80] Another cholera outbreak in 1886 led King Chulalongkorn to commence plans for the construction of a Western-style health care system in Siam during the following two decades. Bangkok's worst cholera outbreak during the interwar years occurred in 1919-21 with some 13,000 deaths. The 1925-26 epidemic with 8,000 victims was triggered by infected sailors who jumped ship in Bangkok in spite of quarantine measures. The 1929 epidemic claimed 1,600 lives in Bangkok, and cholera outbreaks remained a regularly recurring feature in Bangkok during the 1930s, chiefly because the brackish water in many of the *klongs* provided ideal conditions for the *Vibrio cholerae* bacterium.[81] The major cholera epidemic of 1935-37 led to 10,000 deaths in Siam, in spite of the free distribution of medicine and improvements in sanitation.

The fifth and final League of Nations commission of enquiry came to Siam in the person of Dr. Melville Douglas Mackenzie. Mackenzie was a British doctor of tropical medicine and hygiene who had previously worked for the League of Nations as special envoy to Liberia

75 On the visit of the commission of enquiry to Siam see Rajchman to Ministry of Foreign Affairs, 13 March 1936, TNA, KT 96.1.11/17; TNA, *Bangkok Times*, 11 May 1936.

76 'Intergovernmental Conference of Far Eastern Countries on Rural Hygiene: Report by the Preparatory Committee, 1937', LNA, document no. C.H.1234. Voluminous preparatory reports on Indochina, Burma, India, Malaya, Ceylon, Philippines, Siam, China, Japan, Hong Kong, North Borneo, Sarawak, Fiji, Gilbert and Ellice Islands, Salomon Islands and Netherlands Indies can be found in LNA, documents nos. C.H.1235(a) through C.H. 1235(j).

77 This point is made by Annik Guénel, 'The Conference on Rural Hygiene in Bandung of 1937: Towards a New Vision of Health Care?', Paper Presented at Conference on 'History of Medicine in Southeast Asia', Center for Khmer Studies, Siem Reap, Cambodia, 9-10 January 2006. An early mention of rural health in Siam can be found in the speech from the throne of 1930 in TNA, *Bangkok Times*, 3 March 1930.

78 Carle C. Zimmerman, *Siam Rural Economic Survey, 1930-31*, Bangkok: Bangkok Times Press, 1931; Andrews, *2nd Rural Economic Survey*. Both surveys, although focused on conditions of agricultural economy, also provided insight into general living conditions of the rural population, sanitation, nutrition, etc.

79 May, *Doctor in Siam*, p. 103.

80 Barend J. Terwiel, 'Asiatic Cholera in Siam: Its First Occurrence and the 1820 Epidemic', in Norman Owen (ed.), *Death and Disease in Southeast Asia: Explorations in Social, Medical, and Demographic History*, Singapore: Oxford University Press, 1987, pp. 142-160.

81 TNA, *Bangkok Times*, 11 February 1936; 11 January 1937. See also Thompson, *Thailand*, p. 705.

and who had acted as interim director of the Singapore Bureau in 1936. Mackenzie visited Siam in April 1937 not on the basis of a formal resolution by the League's Health Organisation, but rather under the authority of the Singapore Bureau to study the recent cholera outbreak in Siam and provide advice to the public health authorities.

According to the *Bangkok Times*, Mackenzie 'confirmed the belief that the health authorities in Siam are very actively engaged in applying every known measure to control the disease'.[82] During 1937, between 300 and 600 cholera deaths were recorded per week, according to Kenneth Landon. A law was passed making vaccination compulsory and everyone not complying was fined 50 baht. Although the enforcement of this law was a remarkable logistical achievement, the epidemic only receded with the arrival of the rainy season.[83] Mackenzie's visit to Siam coincided with the start of the rainy season, which was seen either as a good or a bad omen. Those who saw it positively argued that with the rain 'most of the cholera germs have taken to flight', while those who saw it as a bad omen worried 'that the doctor may contract cold'. In any event, the hope was expressed 'that the cholera germs will not enter Singapore by sticking on to the border of his coat'.[84]

A report by the Department of Public Health of 1942 shows that preventive measures against cholera had by then become rather sophisticated, and certainly so when compared to the early days of the League of Nations. Provincial health authorities ran awareness campaigns in schools, gave medical advice, handed out brochures, put up posters, screened educational films, and worked to improve wells and latrines. Importantly, anti-cholera inoculations were given annually and free of charge in densely populated districts of the kingdom.[85] In this context it is also interesting to note that already during the smallpox and cholera epidemics in 1921 airplanes were employed to bring medical officers and active vaccines to the provinces, underscoring also that Siam was at this time, according to the contemporary account by American automotive and aeronautical pioneer Charles J. Glidden 'leading most of the countries in the world in aeronautical development'.[86]

The 'epidemiological intelligence service' and the League's Far Eastern Bureau in Singapore

As we have mentioned above, the international dimension of epidemic diseases was forced on the agenda of the League of Nations as a result of the catastrophic hygiene conditions in large parts of Europe in the wake of the First World War. This resulted in the influenza and typhoid pandemics, which claimed millions of lives in the years before and immediately after 1920. The League set up a first 'epidemiological intelligence service' in Europe in 1921, in order to fight the typhoid pandemic in Poland and the Soviet Union.[87] During these first years of the League's existence, Japan in particular called for a constructive and permanent engagement of the League in the field of public health in

82 TNA, *Bangkok Times*, 12 May 1937. On measures taken by the government against cholera in the 1930s see also Rural Hygiene in Siam: National Monograph contributed by the Siamese Delegation to the Rural Hygiene Conference 1937, p. 22f., in TNA, KT 96.1.11/17.

83 Landon, *Siam in Transition*, p. 153f.

84 TNA, *Bangkok Times*, 5 May 1937.

85 Department of Public Health, *Report for B.E. 2481 (1938-39)*, p. 46.

86 TNA, *Bangkok Times*, 16 July 1921 on the cholera and smallpox epidemics and TNA, *Bangkok Times*, 12 August 1920 on the statement by Glidden.

87 See Martin A. Balinska, 'Assistance and not mere Relief: The Epidemic Commission of the League of Nations, 1920-1923', in Paul Weindling (ed.), *International Health Organisations and Movements*, Cambridge: Cambridge University Press, 1995, pp. 81-108.

Asia and argued that this 'would give a concrete proof that [the League's] work was not limited to European affairs, as unfortunately, the peoples of the Far East seemed more and more inclined to suspect'.[88] The Thai government was also strongly in favour of such an engagement, particularly after the first visit of a League of Nations commission of enquiry to Siam in late 1922. Only days after Dr. Norman White, who had studied sanitation and port health conditions in Bangkok, had left the kingdom, Prince Charoon informed the President of the League Council that his government recognised:

> ...the value and importance of the work of the Epidemic Commission, the work in Eastern Europe should be sustained by those countries which are more directly interested. Funds will be needed for the purpose of fighting the spread of contagious diseases in the Far East, a matter with regard to which the League of Nations has undertaken an investigation. In such a campaign His Majesty's Government could not fail to be most deeply interested and for which they desire, under present conditions, to preserve for such action as may appear to be desirable what funds they may have available for such purposes.[89]

The Council of the League of Nations, in response to these demands, decided on 11 March 1924 to establish a Far Eastern Bureau to carry out the work of the 'epidemiological intelligence service' of the League Health Section. The mandate of the bureau was to collect and transmit information on infectious diseases from all countries in the Far East, to collect statistical information as well as relevant laws and administrative measures in Far Eastern countries, to publish the gathered information and to make it available to the League and all Far Eastern countries and finally to respond to requests for assistance in health questions from individual governments in the region.[90]

At this point, the question of where the bureau was to be established was not yet decided. Three locations had been proposed by three respective governments: British Singapore, Batavia in the Netherlands Indies and Cap St. Jacques in French Indochina. Singapore was chosen by Council decision on 17 June 1924, and it also enjoyed the support of the Thai government. According to the Deputy Minister of Foreign Affairs, Prince Varn, the Department of Public Health in the Ministry of Interior favoured Singapore because of its strategic location and good communications facilities.[91] Indeed, Singapore seems to have been the most reasonable choice, although one may suspect that the Thai decision was also taken with an awareness of the fact that this choice would be positively received by the British government, with which negotiations for treaty revision were entering a decisive phase in mid-1924 before Francis Sayre embarked on his tour of European capitals in September.

88 Manderson, Wireless Wars, p. 110. No statement reflecting such sentiment on the side of Thai officials has been found at the Geneva or Bangkok archives.

89 Prince Charoon to da Gama, 26 December 1922, LNA, R 813/12B/6298/1719.

90 Attolico (Acting Secretary-General) to Thai Ministry of Foreign Affairs, 19 March 1924, LNA, R 925/12B/34860/ 34275. On Japan's role in international public health see Mahito H. Fukada, 'Public Health in Modern Japan: From Regimen to Hygiene', in Dorothy Porter (ed.), The History of Public Health and the Modern State, The Wellcome Institute Series in the History of Medicine, Amsterdam and Atlanta: Editions Rodopi, 1994, pp. 403-423.

91 Prince Charoon to Drummond, 14 May 1924; Prince Varn to Attolico, 11 May 1924; Drummond to Prince Varn, 21 June 1924; all LNA, R 925/12B/ 34860/ 34275. See also TNA, KT 96.1.11/8, 9 and 11. See on epidemiological intelligence service also League of Nations, Aims, Methods and Activity, p. 149f.

The bureau was formally established on 1 March 1925, after a founding conference had met in Singapore the previous month.[92] Siam was represented at this conference by Prince Sakol and he was joined by delegates from British India, British North Borneo, Ceylon, China, the Federated Malay States, French Indochina, Hong Kong, Japan, the Netherlands Indies, the Straits Settlements and, as an observer, the Philippines. Prince Sakol was carefully optimistic at this stage: 'I may state that Siam is prepared to co-operate and assist within the limitations imposed by the natural, administrative, medical, and other conditions of the country having similar significance.' In addition, Prince Sakol pointed to one of the central points in the future work of the new bureau when he asked for the development of unified statistical reporting from member states.[93]

The budget of the Singapore Bureau remained a contentious issue during the following years. Although its setup was covered to a large part by a generous grant from the Rockefeller Foundation, League members tended to haggle annually about their contribution.[94] The budget of the office was, for example, set at US$31,500 for 1925, US$35,400 for 1926, and US$46,700 for 1927. Siam contributed 2,000 Straits dollars or 2,500 baht annually to the budget of the bureau until the late 1930s. These funds were paid not from the budget of the Ministry of Foreign Affairs but from that of the Ministry of Interior.[95]

The Singapore Bureau was headed by the British Dr. Gilbert Brooke, a former port health officer in Singapore, from 1925 until 1927, then by Frenchman Dr. Raymond Gautier, before the Australian C. L. Park took over the post as director from 1932 until February 1942, when the bureau stopped functioning because of the Japanese invasion of Singapore.[96] It is interesting to note that the work of the bureau was considered to be of such benefit that even Japan continued to cooperate financially, personally and technically after having formally left the League over its invasion of Manchuria. Each League member with a stake in the bureau's work was represented on the bureau's advisory board, and Siam also sent representatives to the board's annual meetings.[97] Interestingly, Siam chose foreign medical experts to represent the kingdom at the board meetings during the first years of the Singapore Bureau, such as the American adviser to the Public Health Department, Dr. Ira Ayer. Gradually, foreigners were substituted by Thai experts from around 1930. This development can be interpreted as a sign of maturity and of an improvement in the skills and confidence necessary for Thai officials to participate in international technical meetings. In 1940, the Director-General of the Public Health Department, Phra Vaidaya Vidhikar, himself attended the board meeting and then travelled on to visit the modern leprosarium in Kuala Lumpur for ten days before returning to Siam.

92 The standard study of the Singapore bureau to date is Manderson, Wireless Wars.

93 Minutes of the conference to establish the Singapore Bureau, held in Singapore, 4-13 February 1925, LNA, R 925/12B/42212/34275 and TNA, KT 96.1.11/ 11. See also TNA, KT 96.1.11/9 and particularly Prince Sakol's report on the Singapore conference in TNA, KT 96.1.11/11.

94 The Rockefeller Foundation made US$50,000 available for the first year and US$125,000 for the following five years. See Avenol to Minister of Foreign Affairs, 26 September 1924, TNA, R7, M 7.2/1. On financial issues see also Memorandum by C. Hilton Young, 1926, Doc. 7 (W 10048/10048/98), BDFA, Part II, Series J, vol. 1, p. 14; Thai memorandum on the Advisory Council Meeting held in Singapore in January 1926, TNA, KT 96.1.11/9.

95 TNA, KT 96.1.11/20 contains the annual accounts of the Singapore Bureau and documentation of Siam's annual contribution. The file contains evidence of payments up to the year 1938.

96 Manderson, Wireless Wars.

97 TNA, SR 0201.17/6 contains detailed files on Siam's representation at the Advisory Council meetings.

147

The Singapore Bureau began its epidemiological intelligence service in March 1925 with the aim of monitoring and curbing the spread of epidemic diseases across borders by exchanging information on disease occurrences.[98] The bureau set up a system to broadcast once a week, normally every Friday, an epidemiological bulletin free of charge via the French wireless broadcasting station at Saigon. From Saigon the bulletin was relayed to Java, North Borneo and India. Some countries and territories, such as Siam, received the weekly bulletins via telegram during the early years of operation. The bulletins contained information on the epidemic diseases of plague, smallpox, cholera and meningitis[99], which were monitored from Singapore and which were reported directly by the national public health authorities. The bulletins were based mainly on the weekly reports submitted by Siam and the other cooperating countries and territories. However, at the outset there were also sceptical voices which questioned the benefits Siam could gain from the establishment of the Singapore bureau, as an editorial in the *Bangkok Times* on the occasion of the founding conference in 1925 shows:

> Siam will without a murmur pay her share of the cost of maintaining the international bureau which is being established at Singapore. At the same time one may venture to doubt if the administration here feels any real interest in epidemiology – horrid word!...Siam is going to pay out good money on this latest venture; and very soon all intelligent Siamese will be asking if the country is getting value for its money. In short they will be asking themselves, as the Straits Times put it the other day, if the careful collection of information about every form infectious disease does form a basis on which it may be possible to devise more effective means of checking the movements of infection than have existed in the past...Our faith is that the careful collection of information will point the way to better methods of prevention in regard to the health problem as a whole, and that Siam's contribution to this international activity will bring an appreciable return.[100]

But already in 1926 Prince Sakol and Dr. Ira Ayer evaluated the first year of the bureau's work as very positive:

> The Department [of Public Health] forwards epidemiological and pertinent information to the Health Organization of the League of Nations, of which Siam is a member, and exchanges similar information by telegraph and radio with the Eastern Bureau of the League in Singapore. The work of the Bureau in Singapore is regarded of great value, not only intending to standardize returns so that they are more easily comparable and in distributing information of practical value, but in bringing the different administrations into closer touch with one another and fostering a spirit of co-operation which should be of far reaching affect.[101]

98 League of Nations Health Organisation (ed.), *International Health Yearbook 1925*, Geneva 1926, p. 619, in LNA. See also Verma, *India and the League*, p. 207f.

99 The epidemiological reports transmitted from Bangkok to Singapore are collected in LNA, S 2344 through S 2357.

100 TNA, *Bangkok Times*, 28 February 1925.

101 Far Eastern Association of Tropical Medicine, *Siam*, p. 218. A similar evaluation is given in the memorandum on the Advisory Council Meeting held in Singapore in January 1926 of 15 February 1926, TNA, KT 96.1.11/9.

The necessity for such a form of international cooperation became readily apparent in Bangkok the same year when sailors jumped from the Norwegian steamer *Solriken*, which had been put under quarantine by the Bangkok port health authorities in November 1925, and triggered the serious cholera outbreak of 1925-26.[102] Fortunately, by this time the government had already adopted modern techniques for fighting diseases, and the death toll rose only to some 8,000, a low figure compared to earlier outbreaks which had claimed more than three times the number of victims. A contemporary account stated: 'Nothing in these circumstances can be regarded as in any way the fault of the Department of Public Health. But the Department, in close touch as it is with the epidemiological bureau of the League of Nations in Singapore, is fully alive to what happened in the case of the *Solriken*'.[103] In the following months, the *Solriken* incident led to accelerated preparations for an improved quarantine station at the Bangkok port. This had already been under consideration when the League's commission of enquiry had visited Bangkok in 1922, yet it took until 1930 for the grounds designated for the new facilities half-way between Paknam and Bangkok finally to be selected.[104] Only by the late 1930s was the new port quarantine station at Samut Prakan at last up and running. The Annual Report by the Department of Public Health for the year B.E. 2481 (1938-39) provides a number of examples which show how the station functioned, when authorities had been forewarned via Singapore of smallpox and cholera cases on inbound vessels. The case of the *Kwai Yang* of 1938 shows how the authorities were now much better able to cope with an infectious disease on an inbound vessel, as compared to the *Solriken* case of 1925-26:

> On the 5th August [1938] the S.S. 'Kwai Yang' arrived from Hongkong-Swatow with the report of one death from cholera among the deck passengers. The body had been disposed of into the sea on the 14th, before the arrival of the ship at Samut Prakan. It was understood that the infection took place at Swatow where cholera was then spreading. The ship had been detained at Samut Prakan for 5 days. The passengers and the crew numbering 466 were examined for carriers, of which 14 suspected cases were detected. These were taken to the Infectious Diseases Hospital for isolation and arrangement had been made with Samut Prakan Municipality to put up latrine pails on board the ship. There had been no new cases during the whole quarantine period.[105]

As the example illustrates, it was possible to warn port authorities of potential dangers from incoming ships and accordingly, the Bangkok port authority managed to decrease the number of passengers with infectious diseases entering the country through the port between 1926 and the late 1930s. Port health officials in Bangkok were able to examine passengers and crew of infected incoming ships more efficiently and

102 See, for example, TNA, *Bangkok Times*, 8 October and 6 November 1925; 18 May 1926.

103 Ibid.

104 TNA, *Bangkok Times*, 11 November and 9 December 1930.

105 Department of Public Health, *Report for B.E. 2481 (1938-39)*, p. 136.

disinfect the respective vessels. In addition to the public health benefits, the League's early warning system also had a beneficial impact on arrival procedures at the Bangkok port in general. According to Dr. Ira Ayer, adviser to the Thai Ministry of Interior, 'the [Singapore] Bureau is able to simplify the quarantine procedure and to speed up the measures and control to which shipping is subject, and…ships are no longer held up unnecessarily owing to out-of-date quarantine information'.[106]

By 1931, after six years of operation, the Singapore Bureau had established contacts with 135 ports in fifty states and territories in Asia, Africa and the Pacific region, up from sixty-six ports in 1926. In the year 1931, for example, the bureau reported a total of two cases of plague, nineteen cases of cholera, twenty-seven cases of smallpox and five cases of meningitis.[107] Later during the 1930s, the bureau reached 180 ports and transmitted its bulletins daily instead of weekly via nine radio stations throughout Asia. Via wireless telegraph the bureau was also able to inform ships en route of infected ports, so that the crew could take the necessary precautions, such as isolating passengers and disinfecting the ship. In 1932, for example, 188 ships were reported to the Singapore Bureau as having infectious diseases on board.

Siam, however, was not only at the receiving end of the epidemiological intelligence service. When a serious cholera epidemic broke out in Bangkok in 1935, the Singapore Bureau was informed by the Public Health Department and cabled the information to all 180 ports of its network. Because of this regional cooperation between Bangkok and Singapore it was possible to contain the epidemic to Siam, an aspect which was positively acknowledged by the press both in Bangkok and the Straits Settlements in early 1936.[108] In the late 1930s, such containment efforts also had to be expanded to air transport because of the prominent position of Bangkok on Asian air traffic routes. Commercial planes were disinfected and air passengers were inoculated before departure. The government even requested Bangkok residents to obtain inoculation certificates before being allowed to leave Bangkok on an international flight.[109] As a result, the Singapore Bureau began to expand its wireless epidemiological notifications to include airports.

In one instance, the epidemiological intelligence service, which was by then efficiently covering maritime Asia like a web, even affected King Ananda in 1939, when he left Bangkok for Lausanne after his celebrated first visit to Siam:

When H.M. the King was on his way back to Europe by the M.V. 'Selandia' which arrived at Ko Sichang from Saigon on 13th January, and when the M.V. 'Selandia' arrived at Singapore, it was found that one of the passengers boarded at Saigon was sick with smallpox. The vessel and all passengers were detained on board; no one was allowed to land, even His Majesty and his court.[110]

106 TNA, *Bangkok Times*, 18 January 1927.

107 League of Nations Health Organisation (ed.), *International Health Yearbook 1931*, Geneva 1932, p. 1092, in LNA.

108 See TNA, *Bangkok Times*, 18 February 1936; and *The Straits Echo*, Penang, 18 February 1936, TNA, KT 96.1.11/11.

109 Ironically, an official of KLM airlines himself became a victim of cholera shortly after visiting Bangkok in April 1937 in spite of holding a proper inoculation certificate issued by the Bangkok public health authorities. See TNA, *Bangkok Times*, 7 April 1937.

110 Department of Public Health, *Report for B.E. 2481 (1938-39)*, p. 136.

Further tasks of the Singapore Bureau: public health training and biological standardisation

After the setup years during the 1920s, the Singapore Bureau rapidly developing into a success story for the League of Nations. It gave the Geneva-based organisation a visible presence in Asia, and the bureau's work was considered to be relevant and beneficial to Asian states and territories. It is not surprising therefore, that the bureau soon began expanding its work. As Lord Cecil observed in 1929, 'Apart from its duties as Epidemiological Intelligence Centre, the Singapore Bureau acts more and more as the Health Organisation's general agency for the Far East'.[111] One expression of this expanding range of activities were the medical and public health training activities of the bureau.

The Singapore Bureau approached the new constitutional government in Bangkok in October 1932 with the offer to host a Thai doctor for training in methods of disease prevention. This suited the Ministry of Interior very well, as it was in the process of setting up the abovementioned modern quarantine station at the Bangkok port. The Department of Public Health decided to send Dr. Phra Charnvitivej to Singapore in 1933. The bureau agreed to his selection and suggested a specially-tailored training programme of fourteen weeks. During the programme, he visited public health facilities in Japan, the United States, China, Hong Kong, and Singapore, all at the League's expense. Phra Charnvitivej also proposed to the government to make the best use of the tour by extending his visits for two additional months, and to visit not only public health facilities but also sewage plants, tuberculosis control stations, prison hospitals, nurseries, and production facilities of insecticides, vaccines and sera. Prime Minister Manopakorn agreed with this proposal and authorised the additional expenses of 2,000 baht.[112] After this tour, Phra Charnvitivej went on to become one of the most knowledgeable public health managers in Siam. He also became a central figure in Siam's relations with the League of Nations in the field of public health. He repeatedly represented Siam on the Singapore Bureau's advisory board, acted as liaison officer for the League of Nations commission of enquiry on rural hygiene in Siam in 1936, and went on to represent Siam at the Bandung Conference on Rural Hygiene the following year.

Beginning in 1934, the Singapore Bureau organised an annual seminar on malaria diagnosis and treatment, to which practitioners from Siam and other Asian territories were sent by their respective governments. The bureau offered to fund one Thai participant to the two-month course on the condition that the government in Bangkok fund a second participant. As malaria remained top of the list of public health concerns in Siam throughout the 1930s, the government readily agreed to this scheme. The first two Thai doctors to participate in the League's malaria seminars in Singapore in April-May 1934 were Luang Ajurakith Khoson and Khun Chaloerm Atipat. Both doctors were staff of the Public Health

111 Cecil to Henderson, 25 September 1929, Doc. 22 (W 9934/374/94), BDFA, Part II, Series J, vol. 10, p. 78.

112 Correspondence related to this training can be found in TNA, SR 0201.17/3.

Department, and both had worked with Ludwik Anigstein and the League's malaria commission of enquiry in 1930. During the following two years, the seminar, to which Siam again sent two doctors each year, was expanded to include field work in Indochina and Java, which was also supported financially by the bureau. To the fourth malaria seminar in April 1937 Siam sent four public health officials, and it is interesting to note that they were no longer staff of the Department of Public Health in Bangkok, but came from Mae Hong Son, Chiang Mai, Pattani, and Singburi, again illustrating the widening perspective of public health administration during the 1930s to include rural Siam. In addition, the Ministry of Defence sent a fifth person from its medical staff to the 1937 seminar. By 1938, the Singapore Bureau was no longer able to fund participants from each member territory, but the government in Bangkok decided that the malaria training received by the doctors and public health officials from different provinces at the annual seminars was very valuable and, accordingly, sent two doctors, this time from Yala and Trang, to Singapore at its own expense. The 1938 seminar lasted seven weeks, including two weeks of fieldwork in Malaya. The last annual malaria seminar organised by the Singapore Bureau in April 1939 was also attended by two Thai officials, one from the Public Health Department in Bangkok and one from Singburi. The training in malaria prophylaxis and treatment offered by the League of Nations from 1934 to 1939 was an important contribution to human resource development in the Thai public health sector, not only on a central but also on a provincial level. That the government invested some 2,000 baht annually for the training shows that concerned officials were well aware of its value.[113]

Apart from its epidemiological intelligence service and these training activities, the Singapore Bureau also facilitated efforts for biological standardisation in the region. The international standardisation of medical substances was a fairly new field which became a pressing concern when modern means of transport and increased living standards led to a sharp increase in international travel during the interwar years.

> The importance of such standardization is illustrated by the case of a man with diabetes who is obliged to travel from country to country. Because of the League's work in this field he can be assured that the insulin he needs will be equally effective wherever he goes, and his doctors know that the dosage he is supposed to use will not differ from one country to another.[114]

Under the auspices of the League, a total of twenty-seven sera, vaccines, vitamins and other drugs were standardised. The files at the Bangkok archives show that the bureau's work and, in particular, the Intergovernmental Conference on Biological Standardisation, which was held by the League of Nations in October 1935 in Geneva, triggered

113 Comprehensive documentation on Siam's participation in the annual malaria seminars at Singapore in TNA, SR 0201.17/ 11. See also TNA, *Bangkok Times*, 29 June 1937.

114 Boudreau, International Health Work, p. 200.

activities on the part of the Thai public health authorities. These activities then led to the Royal Decree to Control Standardisation of Biological Substances, which was issued in 1940 and set new international standards for the production of sera and bacterial products, hormones, vitamins, etc. in Siam.[115]

Lenore Manderson concludes that the Far Eastern Bureau of the League of Nations Health Organisation managed 'to identify the primary public health concerns of the region, facilitate co-operation between individual researchers and research institutions, and develop public health expertise.'[116]

The Bandung Conference on Rural Hygiene of 1937

The League of Nations had organised a European conference on rural hygiene at Geneva in 1931, which had already attracted the interest of the Thai Public Health Department.[117] The department, accordingly, took a keen interest in the preparations for a regional Asian conference on rural hygiene, which was held in Bandung in August 1937. The *Bangkok Times* shared this interest and published lengthy editorials and articles on the conference in August and September, in which it highlighted its value in stimulating 'the interest of public-spirited citizens in the conditions under which the very poor live in their own land.'[118] The initiative for this conference came from the Indian and Chinese delegations to the League of Nations in 1932, but the conference was delayed for several years, during which the League's activities with regard to Asia were primarily absorbed with the intensifying Sino-Japanese conflict. By invitation of the government of the Netherlands Indies, the conference convened from 3 to 13 August 1937 in Bandung on the island of Java.[119] This first international conference in Asia on health and development focused on social factors influencing health, on questions of nutrition and the need for improved disease control of malaria, plague, tuberculosis, cholera, smallpox, leprosy and others, specifically through health education, improved living conditions, medical care in rural areas, and community participation.

The following governments sent delegations to Bandung: British Northern Borneo, Burma, Ceylon, China, Fiji and Australian Islands, Hong Kong, India, French Indochina, Japan, Federated Malay States, Netherlands Indies, the Philippines and Siam. As in the case of the Conference on Traffic in Women and Children, which was organised by the League of Nations at the same location six months earlier, in February 1937, a number of non-governmental organisations also took part in the conference as observers. They were the Red Cross, the Far Eastern Association for Tropical Medicine, the International Agricultural Institute in Rome, and the Rockefeller Foundation. The League of Nations was represented prominently by Dr. Rajchman and by the Director of the Singapore Bureau, Dr. Park. In total, over one

115 TNA, SR 0201.17/20. This file also contains the report of the Geneva Conference as well as the text of the Royal Decree of B.E. 2483 (1940). On the standardisation work of the Singapore bureau see also League of Nations, *Aims, Methods and Activity*, p. 151f.

116 Manderson, Wireless Wars, p. 109.

117 TNA, KT 96.1.11/16 contains documents relating to the European rural hygiene conference. The Department of Public Health expressed its interest towards the Ministry of Foreign Affairs in receiving the conference report, particularly with regard to issues pertaining to water supply, wells, and waste disposal. Siam had already sent a delegate to the International Sanitary Conference in Paris in May 1926, but did not see any benefit in signing the International Sanitary Convention of 1912; see TNA, R7, M 7.2/3.

118 TNA, *Bangkok Times*, 13 August and 23 September 1937.

119 Report of the Intergovernmental Conference of Far Eastern Countries on Rural Hygiene, held at Bandoeng (Java), serial document no. A.19.1937.III., LNA, League of Nations, *Official Journal*, no. 12, December 1937.

hundred delegates and observers were accredited to the conference. Topics of the meeting were medical services, rural reconstruction measures, sanitary improvements, improvements in nutrition and treatment of diseases in rural areas. Each of these topics was discussed in one of five separate commissions. The discussions revealed that a wide approach to the problems, which included improvements in the economic, educational and social situation in rural areas, was essential. It also became evident that, in spite of the voluminous documentation prepared by the participating territories for the conference, more information and statistical data was required on rural hygiene.

As Annik Guénel has pointed out, the Bandung conference was fundamentally different from previous international medical meetings in Asia, such as the aforementioned FEATM congresses, because it took place amidst a shift of colonial public health policies towards the indigenous populations from providing mere minimal prophylaxis and treatment to actually improving public health conditions for a majority of the population in the colonies.[120] The *Bangkok Times* commented in an editorial that the conference would help 'carry the torch of enlightenment into rural areas so that people will learn to value living in clean and sanitary surroundings'.[121] While improvements in nutrition and rural health were a means for colonial administrations to reaffirm their rule over indigenous Asian populations in their colonies, they allowed the Thai elite in Bangkok to reaffirm their rule over their fellow countrymen in rural Siam.

The government in Bangkok considered the conference to be 'very important for the progress of public health management in Siam', and the cabinet nominated two representatives to participate in the deliberations at Bandung, Phraya Prakit Kolasastra, Chief Engineer of the Public and Municipal Works Department in the Ministry of Interior, and Dr. Phra Charnvitivej, Chief of the Provincial Health Division in the same Ministry.[122] The Thai country report for the conference was prepared by the Department of Public Health and is a remarkably detailed and comprehensive document.[123] Particularly interesting is the very detailed information the report gives on the issue of nutrition. It provides data on the daily food intake of the population and on its nutritional value as well as on eating habits in rural Siam. The report concludes: 'the economic progress of the country depends upon a reform of the national diet. Nutrition is recognised as one of the most important items of preventive medicine'.[124]

The report and the Bandung Conference also highlighted the shift in Thai public health management from training only a small number of very good doctors in Western medicine to providing a large number of less well trained doctors for the benefit of the rural population.[125] Because of the acute shortage of qualified doctors versed in Western medicine, assistant doctors, also called medical officers, were trained and employed.

120 Guénel, Conference on Rural Hygiene.

121 TNA, *Bangkok Times*, 13 August 1937.

122 TNA, KT 96.1.11/17. See also Ministry of Foreign Affairs to Secretary-General of the League, 30 January 1937, LNA, R 6097/8A/26956/8855.

123 The report can be found with the title 'Rural Hygiene in Siam: National Monograph contributed by the Siamese Delegation to the Rural Hygiene Conference 1937' in TNA, KT 96.1.11/17, and with the title 'Intergovernmental Conference of Far-Eastern Countries on Rural Hygiene, Preparatory Papers: National Report of Siam, 1937' in LNA, C.H.1235(h). The former version is more complete but in a simple typed format, while the latter version is edited and includes a table of contents and a map of Siam.

124 National Report of Siam on Rural Hygiene, p. 39f.

125 This shift is also discussed one year prior to the conference by a senior Rockefeller Foundation official in TNA, *Bangkok Times*, 15 May 1936.

According to Siam's report, they were 'the primary units of health work in rural Siam'. These medical officers had studied traditional Thai medicine and received, in additional, a basic training in Western medicine, which enabled them to recognise some epidemic diseases, report them and, perhaps, provide the appropriate vaccinations and limited amounts of Western medicine for these diseases.[126] Under this scheme, which had already been proposed by Prince Sakol in the late 1920s and by Carle Zimmerman in his rural economic survey of Siam in 1931, medical officers were trained at four regional teaching hospitals in traditional Thai medicine and the basics of Western medicine, and medical services for the rural population were improved, despite the budgetary constraints at the Department of Public Health. This scheme also reduced the number of medical practitioners who did more harm than good. As Zimmerman put it, 'Siam needs *all* the good physicians it can secure. But the common mass of the population should be taken from the hands of quacks as quickly as possible'.[127] The government in Bangkok had already taken important steps in this regard in the wake of the Bandung conference, and the registration of all doctors practicing modern medicine became effective on 1 October 1937. This registration proved an important factor in eliminating unqualified practitioners.[128]

This policy was fully endorsed by the Bandung conference. It emphasised 'the importance of adequately training a large body of auxiliary personnel in order that the connecting link between the rural inhabitant and the medical men may be as efficient as possible'.[129]

After the conference, Thai public health officials judged the discussions held at Bandung to be very valuable for rural public health development in the country, but also, in an internal memorandum, pointed to shortages of funds and staff necessary to implement the resulting recommendations.[130] Some years later, at the time of the Japanese advance into Southeast Asia, the government was still able to provide only some five percent of the rural population with modern medical care. However, according to D.J.M. Tate, 'compared to what had gone before and in view of the chronic shortage of funds for the purpose at hand, what was achieved was considerable enough'.[131] But, by and large, the health and sanitary conditions of the rural population in Siam and Southeast Asia did not improve significantly before the Second World War. In addition to a much larger public health budget and a more efficient countrywide administration in Siam, it took, as Sunil Amrith points out, the technologies developed during the war, such as DDT and new vaccines, to achieve significant improvements after 1945.[132]

Conclusions

The late 1930s and early 1940s saw public health moving to the centre of a wide-reaching campaign, orchestrated by Luang Phibun, Luang Vichit

126 National Report of Siam on Rural Hygiene, p. 9ff.

127 Zimmerman, *Rural Economic Survey*, p. 238ff., quotation on p. 245.

128 See administrative details on the control of traditional healers in Department of Public Health, Report for B.E. 2481 (1938-39), p. 145ff. See also the later Act on the Control of the Practice in the Art of Healing B.E. 2483 (1940), TNA, KT 96.1.8.1/114.

129 Report of the Intergovernmental Conference of Far Eastern Countries on Rural Hygiene, held at Bandoeng (Java), serial document no. A.19.1937.III., LNA, League of Nations, *Official Journal*, no. 12, December 1937, p. 1311.

130 Memorandum of Ministry of Interior, n.d. (1938), TNA, KT 96.1.11/17.

131 Tate, *Making of Modern South-East Asia*, vol. 2, p. 561.

132 Amrith, *Decolonizing International Health*, p. 16.

and their followers, to turn Siam, or Thailand, as the country was called from 1939, into what they perceived as a progressive and civilised state. From 1938, a national nutrition programme was begun, funds for medical services and improvements in hygiene were increased and in 1942, this drive for public health improvements found a symbolic expression in the upgrading of the Department of Public Health under the Ministry of Interior to an independent Ministry of Public Health.[133] Although the League of Nations was fading into oblivion by 1940, the public health campaigns under the Phibun government clearly carried on the work, which had evolved through the cooperation between Siam and the League's Health Organisation during the preceding twenty years.

This chapter has shown that the elite-driven modernisation of Siam's public health sector during the 1920s and 1930s was closely connected with the League of Nations in a number of ways. Siam participated in many important innovations in medicine and public health which ultimately led to better health conditions for the population. Having acknowledged the wide range of cooperation between Siam and the League, it is important to keep in mind that Siam was not only on the receiving end of the League of Nations' international public health efforts. Siam contributed actively to meetings, conferences and the institutional setup of the Singapore Bureau, it contributed in form of numerous reports, questionnaires, statistical data, and epidemiological information. It contributed financially to the operational cost of the Singapore Bureau and, indirectly, to the operations of the League's Health Organisation in general. And Siam's contribution went even further: In 1921, Siam responded to a call by the League and donated £1,000 to the fight against typhoid fever in Poland.[134] Although the amount was not that large, the event as such remains remarkable. It is a significant example of how Siam's League membership led it to participate in solving a European problem, typhoid fever in Poland, despite at the time being far from regaining its complete fiscal and judicial sovereignty. In other words, a remote kingdom in Southeast Asia, which the politically interested public in Europe considered to be a British colony in all but the name, was helping fight typhoid in Europe.

However, Siam's willingness to contribute to the League's international public health activities also had its limits, particularly from the mid-1930s when the government in Bangkok increasingly tried to minimise the country's international financial contributions in the light of the general economic difficulties. During the League of Nations General Assembly of 1937, this financial policy became embroiled with public health matters and Siam's wider approach to international politics. During the Assembly, the committee in charge of health issues rallied member states to increase the League budget by two million Swiss francs, in order to assist China in its response to the outbreak of epidemics. Throughout the League's lifetime China was struck almost annually by

133 Baker and Pasuk, *History of Thailand*, p. 133. See on public health developments during the Phibun era, in particular the national nutrition programme, in detail also Davisakd, Medicalizing State, p. 334ff.

134 NA, KT 96.1.11/2 and 96.1.11/3 (Parts 1 and 2). The Thai government was well aware of the symbolism involved in making this donation. It is made even more remarkable by the fact that Siam was one of the few League members who actually lived up to their commitments and transferred the promised sums, while other European members committed funds but then did not pay. See also speech from the throne printed in TNA, *Bangkok Times*, 4 January 1921. On the typhoid epidemic and the League of Nations' response see Balinska, Assistance and not mere Relief.

natural disasters, floods, droughts, earthquakes and various epidemics, many of which rank among the worst disasters of the century. In addition, civil war raged between communist and nationalist troops, while in 1937 Japan expanded and intensified its invasion of the country, which had begun in 1931. Minister of Foreign Affairs Luang Pradist was adamant that Siam could not bear an increase in its contribution to the League. At the same time, however, he did not want Siam to stand out on the international stage yet again with an action that could be considered anti-Chinese or pro-Japanese, as had happened with the abstentions from condemning Japan the same year and earlier in 1933. He therefore instructed Foreign Affairs Adviser Prince Varn in July 1937 to 'rather pay and just consider it as merit-making', so that other League members would not 'become suspicious if we are really staying neutral or not'.[135] Later Luang Pradist specified this in a telegram to Phraya Rajawangsan, the Thai Permanent Representative at Geneva, instructing him to vote against an increase of the League budget if a vote was taken in the relative intimacy of the assembly's health committee, and to 'refrain from voting in the Assembly if the vote is taken by a show of hands, but you should vote against it if the vote is taken by ballot'.[136] In the end, no vote was taken, and the increase in the League's budget was accomplished without an increase of Siam's contribution; but the instructions from Bangkok show clearly that the appearance of neutrality on the international stage was the overriding priority of Siam's policy at Geneva. This episode also stands in marked contrast to the response to the disastrous floods which hit China in early 1932, when the Siamese Red Cross had set up a relief fund and collected, together with 11,000 baht donated by the king himself, some 100,000 baht in donations, with which rice was purchased and shipped to China.[137]

Altogether, the League's contacts with Siam in the promotion of public health over twenty years can be judged as progressive and relevant. While neither the League's influence nor Siam's responses to it were perfect, they reflected a sincere desire to improve living conditions for the Thai population. For Siam, for the League and for the world in general, the 1920s and 1930s were a period of many changes and innovations in public health, away from purely curative medicine and towards preventive medicine, sanitation and rural health. This chapter has also shown that public health was perhaps the one field of cooperation between Siam and the League, in which the superiority of Western knowledge and science among both Westerners and Thais was most overtly expressed. Western medicine and public health was, in the eyes of League officials and the experts appointed to travel to Asia, a means to lift backward Asian peoples out of their misery and allow them to benefit from the wonders of scientific progress; an attitude which could be seen as patronisingly colonial. The elite in Siam, as we have seen, readily took up this impetus for its own purposes; an impetus which

135 Confidential (handwritten) note by Luang Pradist for Prince Varn, 18 July B.E. 2480 (1937), TNA, KT 96.1.11/19.

136 Luang Pradist to Phraya Raja-wangsan, 4 October 1937, TNA, KT 96.1.11/19.

137 TNA, *Bangkok Times*, 22 February 1932.

was not created but rather amplified by the League of Nations and had already been a driving force for modernisation in Siam during the decades before 1920.

The activities of the League of Nations Health Organisation substantially increased the awareness of public health questions among Siam's elite, triggered legal change along Western lines in the public health sector, reduced the vulnerability of the Thai population to epidemic diseases, played an important role in expanding public health from urban centres to the rural hinterland in Siam as well as surrounding colonies, influenced the modernisation of institutions and procedures, provided training and expertise to Thai doctors in Western medicine and public health practices and facilitated greater regional cooperation between Siam and the colonial territories in Asia through information exchange, conferences and standardisation efforts. As in the case of opium control in the previous chapter, change in public health also came about during the 1920s and 1930s not through pressure groups or public opinion, but from the elite, royal and civilian, in their drive for modernisation of the country. And, again as in the case of opium control, it was because this elitist modernisation programme was strongly Western-oriented, that the League of Nations could play such a notable role in developments in Siam. This analysis is valid for pre-1932 and post-1932 royal, civilian and military administrations, as we have seen. In fact, the use of public health as a tool for modernising the country and consolidatiing the power of the elite peaked during the Phibun era when the League had already become nearly defunct.

The impact of the visits of five commissions of enquiry to Siam as well as international cooperation with the League at large on public health, sanitation and medical laws has become readily apparent. Perhaps less apparent is the fact that Siamese cooperation with the League in public health matters played a pivotal role in the establishment of a modern reporting system in public health. The Ministry of Interior was informed by Prince Devawongse as early as 1922 of the necessity to live up to the League's requirements by providing annual reports on the public health and epidemiological situation in the kingdom, and the Ministry duly replied that the Department of Public Health would act accordingly.[138] From then on, Siam submitted annual public health reports to the League throughout the 1920s and 1930s. By doing so, Siam not only modernised its national administrative procedures, but also contributed to the League's international reporting system, which was novel in itself. This public health reporting system relied heavily on statistical data. In the words of Lenore Manderson, 'the yardsticks of success were numerical',[139] to measure progress and to identify trends for future control.

The League's Singapore Bureau deserves mentioning once again, as, although not located in Siam, it had a rather profound impact on the

138 Minister of Interior to Minister of Foreign Affairs, 5 June B.E. 2465 (1922), TNA, KT 96.1.11/5.

139 Manderson, *Sickness and the State*, p. 234.

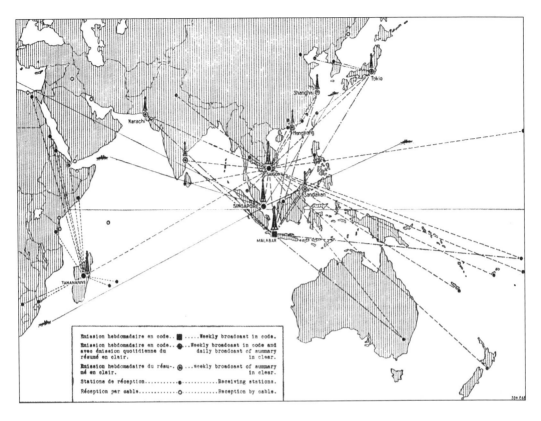

Émission hebdomadaire en code..■ .....Weekly broadcast in code.
Émission hebdomadaire en code.. ◆...Weekly broadcast in code and
avec émission quotidienne du   daily broadcast of summary
résumé en clair.   in clear.
Émission hebdomadaire du résu-. ◉ ...weekly broadcast of summary
mé en clair.   in clear.
Stations de réception...........● ....Receiving stations.
Réception par cable.............○ ....Reception by cable.

fight against epidemic diseases in Siam and the whole of Southeast Asia during the 1920s and 1930s. In addition, it represented the League of Nations' only institutionalised presence in Asia. In the light of recent experiences with epidemics in the region, such as SARS and Avian flu, and a general awareness of the importance of controlling the spread of such diseases across national borders, the epidemiological intelligence work pioneered by the League's Singapore Bureau can hardly be overrated. That Siam, as the only sovereign Southeast Asian state at the time, was actively involved in the establishment of this service some eighty years ago, that it contributed financially to the functioning of the service until the late 1930s, and that it took its epidemiological reporting obligations seriously, point to sound and farsighted policy. That Siam was actively involved in activities from training to fact-finding missions carried out by this first permanent office of an international organisation in Southeast Asia, underscores this positive evaluation.

In 1941, Virginia Thompson wrote in her outstanding book: 'At present Siam has the brightest record in the *League of Nations Far Eastern Health Bulletin*; and Bangkok, in spite of its past reputation for filth, is the envy of other Oriental cities of the same size or larger'.[140] We have seen that Siam's active involvement in the League's public health activities during the two preceding decades played a decisive role in achieving

Map showing the reach of the epidemiological intelligence service by the League of Nations' Far Eastern Bureau in Singapore (League of Nations Archives).

---

140 Thompson, *Thailand*, p. 725.

such a reputation by the early 1940s. Commissions of enquiry, international conferences, epidemiological surveillance, modern reporting standards, adaptation of modern Western medical methods and technologies, all contributed to the modernisation of public health in Siam within the framework of the League of Nations. In addition, Siam's international public health activities reaffirmed its sovereignty in relation to Western governments and their colonial administrations in Asia and formed part of a remarkable degree of regional cooperation in a largely colonial environment before the Second World War.

By the late 1930s, after nearly twenty years of League of Nations membership, the Department of Public Health employed 1,118 regular staff, half of which were based in the provinces, and an additional 382 extraordinary staff. Smallpox had been nearly eradicated and the mortality of other epidemic diseases was slowly decreasing, doctors, junior doctors and midwives were being trained in increasing numbers, and sanitary conditions were slowly improving.[141] By 1942, there were still only fifteen provincial hospitals and 343 health centres and in spite of the progress made during the interwar years, the rural public health situation was still in dire need of improvements by the year 1950. According to Wilfred Reeve, by then nearly every *changwat* had at least one hospital, 'but public health services in rural areas are inadequate and unsatisfactory', in particular with regard to a total number of between 1,500 and 2,000 fully qualified doctors in the kingdom, which Reeve describes as 'pitifully insufficient'.[142] In addition, infant mortality remained high, and cholera and malaria were far from being eradicated.

The work of the League's Health Organisation was cut short by the Second World War. But as early as 1943, the Western allies of the Second World War, fearing renewed post-war epidemics, drew up plans for public health activities under the new UNRRA (United Nations Relief and Rehabilitation Administration). The new World Health Organisation (WHO) was created at a conference on 22 July 1946 and began functioning after sufficient ratifications had been deposited on 7 April 1948. Fittingly, the WHO began its work in the Palais des Nations, the League of Nations' former headquarters on Lake Geneva. The WHO was able to begin its work very rapidly after the end of the war, primarily because it could build on the twenty years of pioneering work done in international public health by the League of Nations Health Organisation.

141 Department of Public Health, *Report for B.E. 2481 (1938-39)*, p. 3. On sanitary work see p. 31ff. This chapter provides detailed information on sanitary inspection, including markets, eateries, slaughterhouses, hotels, schools, cemeteries and crematories, etc.

142 Reeve, *Public Administration in Siam*, p. 54. A similarly bleak picture is painted by Tate, *Making of Modern South-East Asia*, vol. 2, p. 558.

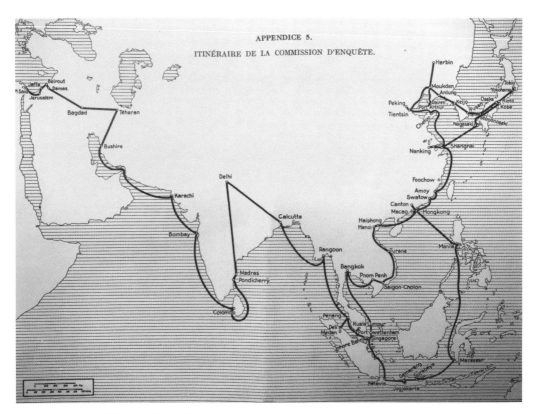

APPENDICE 5.

ITINÉRAIRE DE LA COMMISSION D'ENQUÊTE.

*Itinerary of League of Nations Commission
of Enquiry into Trafficking in Women and
Children 1930-1932 (League of Nations
Archives).*

5

Human Trafficking

Human trafficking as an issue before the League of Nations[1]

Trafficking of humans across borders is by definition an international issue, which cannot be tackled by one national administration alone. As a social and economic phenomenon, human trafficking requires a market in which there is a demand, and it involves both organised crime and illegal immigration. Today's standard definition of trafficking in human beings by the United Nations was laid down in 2000:

> 'Trafficking in persons' shall mean the recruitment, transportation, transfer, harbouring or receipt of persons, by means of the threat or use of force or other forms of coercion, of abduction, of fraud, of deception, of the abuse of power or of a position of vulnerability or of the giving or receiving of payments or benefits to achieve the consent of a person having control over another person, for the purpose of exploitation. Exploitation shall include, at a minimum, the exploitation of the prostitution of others or other forms of sexual exploitation, forced labour or services, slavery or practices similar to slavery, servitude or the removal of organs.[2]

The 'white slave traffic', as it was commonly called, became an issue of international concern when the phenomenon of globalisation in technology and communications led to increased mobility of people via railways and trans-ocean shipping during the late nineteenth century. New means of transport led not only to increased emigration but also to a virtual explosion of human trafficking. An International Bureau for the Suppression of Traffic in Women and Children was established in 1899. A first international agreement in 1904 and a first international convention in 1910, both concluded in Paris, aimed to define the problem and to agree on common aims in curbing human trafficking, mainly by improving immigration procedures.[3]

The League's founding fathers entrusted the organisation with the responsibility to take up the problem of international human trafficking on the basis of article XXIII(c) of the League of Nations Covenant. In pursuit of this mandate, the League of Nations set up two advisory committees under the Social Section of the Secretariat, which were formally created by the League Council. They were the Advisory Committee on the Traffic in Women and Children, created in 1922 to

1 The terms trafficking in women and children, traffic in persons, human trafficking, traffic in humans, and traffic in human beings are all used as synonyms in this chapter.

2 Article 3, paragraph (a) of the Protocol to Prevent, Suppress and Punish Trafficking in Persons, especially Women and Children of November 2000. See also Phil Williams, 'Trafficking in Women and Children: A Market Perspective', in Phil Williams (ed.), *Illegal Immigration and Commercial Sex: The New Slave Trade*, London and Portland (OR): Frank Cass, 1999, pp. 145-170.

3 The International Agreement was signed on 18 May 1904; the International Convention was signed on 4 May 1910. On early international efforts to combat human trafficking see H. Wilson Harris, *Human Merchandise: A Study of the International Traffic in Women*, London: Ernest Benn, 1928; Edward J. Bristow, *Prostitution and Prejudice: The Jewish Fight Against White Slavery, 1870-1939*, Oxford: Clarendon, 1982.

oversee the implementation of the international convention of the same year, and the Child Welfare Committee, which was created in 1924. In 1936, the two committees were combined to form the new Advisory Committee on Social Questions. The Secretariat's Social Section was headed by the charismatic Dame Rachel Crowdy until 1931 and then by Swedish diplomat Eric Ekstrand, who had previously been working in the field of opium control for the League and had repeatedly come into contact with Siam in this context.[4]

The 'white slave traffic' was a matter of concern for Western societies, as the term implies, because its victims were Western, or 'white' women. Asia came into the orbit of Western efforts to limit the trade mainly because of the increasing number of Russian and Jewish women from Eastern Europe, who, as a result of the Russian Revolution and the aftermath of the First World War, were brought to Asian brothels. One estimate puts the number of Jewish prostitutes in Asia at any one time during the first decades of the twentieth century at 700 to 800.[5] This globalisation of trafficking in women and children led to a clash between different standards of morality and different sexual conventions as well as gender roles. Western societies, in the words of Leslie Ann Jeffrey, 'were seeking to impose not a more equitable gender arrangement but, rather, a gender code that reflected a Western understanding of civilised gender roles'.[6]

Prostitution and human trafficking in Siam in the early twentieth century

Human trafficking happens predominantly for sexual exploitation and is, therefore, closely connected with prostitution, a particular society's attitude towards prostitution, and a state's policies regarding prostitution.[7] Throughout the period under review, prostitution in Siam was widespread, legal, profitable and, to a large extent, socially acceptable. Already during the Ayutthaya period, prostitution was being taxed by the government[8], and it remained fairly uncontroversial until King Chulalongkorn gradually abolished slavery between 1874 and 1905. This reform was a cornerstone of the king's modernisation programme, but it led to widespread social uprooting of uneducated women who lost their social status and the security provided by the traditional system of slavery.[9] This, in turn, led to an increase in the number of women who, lacking the option to sell themselves into socially accepted positions as second wives or mistresses, turned to prostitution. Complementing this social trend, prostitution became a lucrative investment for businessmen. In the words of Scot Barmé, it 'rapidly developed into a burgeoning industry [as] part of a broader regional phenomenon stimulated by the spread of imperialism and the concomitant growth of the international market economy'.[10] These socioeconomic changes, which were nothing other than local effects of the process of globalisation, prompted the need for control, and led the

4 For studies of the League's Social Section see Carol Miller, 'The Social Section and Advisory Committee on Social Questions of the League of Nations', in Paul Weindling (ed.), *International Health Organisations and Movements*, Cambridge: Cambridge University Press, 1995, pp. 154-157; Elsa Castendyck, 'Social Problems', in Harriet E. Davis (ed.), *Pioneers in World Order: An American Appraisal of the League of Nations*, 2nd ed., New York: Columbia University Press, 1945, pp. 229-239; see also League of Nations, *Aims, Methods and Activity*, p. 169ff. For the text of the Covenant of the League of Nations see LNA, League of Nations, *Official Journal*, February 1920, p. 3ff.

5 Bristow, *Prostitution and Prejudice*, p. 197.

6 Leslie Ann Jeffrey, *Sex and Borders: Gender, National Identity, and Prostitution Policy in Thailand*, Chiang Mai: Silkworm Books, 2002, p. 11.

7 Brown has emphasised the important distinction that human trafficking and sexual exploitation are closely connected but two separate issues. They are connected because victims of trafficking are highly likely to be forced into sexual slavery but some were rather forced into marriage to Chinese men in Siam. See Louise Brown, *Sex Slaves: The Trafficking of Women in Asia*, London: Virago, 2000, p. 21.

8 See Wathinee Boonchalaksi and Philip Guest, *Prostitution in Thailand*, Salaya (Nakhon Pathom): Institute for Population Research, Mahidol University, 1994, p. 2.

9 On the complex system of slavery see Barend J. Terwiel, 'Bondage and Slavery in Early Nineteenth Century Siam', in Anthony Reid (ed.), *Slavery, Bondage and Dependency in Southeast Asia*, St. Lucia, London and New York: University of Queensland Press, 1983, pp. 118-137.

10 Scot Barmé, *Woman, Man, Bangkok: Love, Sex and Popular Culture in Thailand*, Lanham (MD): Rowman and Littlefield, 2002, p. 5.

state to intervene by enacting the Prevention of Venereal Diseases Act in 1908. Indeed, it seems that during the first three decades of the twentieth century venereal diseases were rampant in Bangkok among Chinese and Thai prostitutes as well as among the male population as a whole. This act, which had originally been named Municipal Law on Prostitution in its draft stage in 1899 and which was, as Barmé explains, inspired by a Singaporean legal code, was issued because it became necessary to regulate prostitution for public health reasons. Underlying the act was the notion of the prostitute as the carrier of venereal diseases, which primarily made her, and not her male client, a public health risk which had to be controlled. Until it was expanded to the whole of Siam in 1913, the act applied only to Bangkok[11], where brothels and prostitutes accordingly had to register every three months and pay a registration fee. Brothels also had to meet certain minimal hygiene standards, prostitutes had to prove they were free of venereal diseases, and brothels had to be away from public view and marked by a green lantern. Importantly, prostitutes had to state that they were working of their own free will, and brothels had to ensure that they engaged only prostitutes who worked of their own free will and were at least fifteen years of age. And, finally, the act of 1908 also served as a tool for the state to tap this growing market by taxing brothels and prostitutes, thereby collecting some 40,000 baht during the first year of the new act's operation.[12]

One may be led to believe from this sketch that the position of women in Siam at the beginning of the twentieth century was generally bad, although this was not necessarily the case. While women, particularly in rural Siam, were disadvantaged by limited access to education, by polygamy and by limited social intercourse with men, already contemporary observers stated that 'women of all ranks enjoy greater liberty in Siam than is usually the case in Asia, and from all accounts they have always done so'.[13] An important factor contributing to the status of women in Siam was the general practice that land purchases and sales among married men always required the consent of their wives, while wives could conclude land deals without the consent of their husbands.[14] And women worked, as Baker and Pasuk describe, 'They dominated the street and canal markets to the extent that the government appointed women as market overseers. They planted rice and vegetables on the city outskirts. They laboured in the factories and public utilities'.[15] Scot Barmé has shown in his intriguing study of Bangkok in the 1920s and 1930s that a new urban middle class was emerging, among which the status of women was changing further in a positive direction, allowing them greater social participation, greater civil rights and better access to education, employment and even entertainment.[16]

Human trafficking and prostitution formed a social problem in Siam primarily in the context of the Chinese minority and Chinese

11 This important limitation was pointed out by Minister of Foreign Affairs Prince Traidos in a letter to Secretary-General Drummond of 4 November 1924, in LNA, R 674/12/40891/28438.

12 On the 1908 act see Barmé, *Woman, Man, Bangkok* , p. 78f.; Jeffrey, *Sex and Borders*, p. 12. The act contained a number of interesting provisions, such as section 5, which stipulated that only women could be brothel-keepers or sections 16 and 31 which stipulated that 'no prostitute shall behave in such a manner as to cause annoyance to people passing outside the brothel, for instance, pulling, dragging, or making jests at them.' Violations could be punished with imprisonment of up to one month and a fine of up to 20 baht. Ibid.; Wathinee and Guest, *Prostitution in Thailand*; Siriporn Skrobanek, Nataya Boonpakdee and Chutima Jantateero, *The Traffic in Women: Human Realities of the International Sex Trade*, London and New York: Zed Books, 1997; Bärbel Gräning, *Prostitutionstourismus in Thailand: Die sexuelle Verfügung über Frauen in ihrer historischen Entwicklung*, Bremen: Übersee-Museum und Geographische Gesellschaft Bremen, 1988; Lipi Ghosh, *Prostitution in Thailand: Myth and Reality*, New Delhi: Munshiram Manoharlal, 2002, p. 18ff. See also Tate, *Making of Modern Southeast Asia*, p. 561f.

13 Forty, *Bangkok: Its Life and Sport*, p. 24. In this sense see also Vella, *Chaiyo!*, p. 151ff.

14 TNA, *Bangkok Times*, 28 July 1931.

15 Baker and Pasuk, *History of Thailand*, p. 103.

16 Barmé, *Woman, Man, Bangkok*, p. 133ff. and 179f.

immigration. Whereas international trafficking in the sexual services trade is today both an inbound and an outbound problem for Thailand, it was mainly an inbound problem for Siam during the time of the League of Nations. Today Burmese women and girls are trafficked into Thailand and Thai women and girls are illegally brought to Japan, Taiwan or Europe, but before the Second World War the victims of human trafficking were mainly Chinese women and girls who were brought into Siam illegally. The demand for these women and girls came primarily from single Chinese men, who, as detailed in the previous chapter on opium control, immigrated to Siam in search of work in considerable numbers. These men desired Chinese women as brides and, more often, as prostitutes. As James Warren has shown in his study of prostitution in Singapore and Lenore Manderson has shown for British Malaya as a whole, this was by no means only a Thai problem. Rooted in the massive influx of male Chinese labourers into Southeast Asia, agrarian poverty in China and traditional Chinese social values, trafficking of Chinese women and girls was a phenomenon affecting the whole, largely colonised region.[17] Not only were the victims of trafficking predominantly Chinese, but so too were the traffickers and the 'clients'.

While Chinese immigrants during the nineteenth century were predominantly single men, authoritative studies by Skinner and Landon and the most recent study by Bao show that the number of women immigrating to Siam during the 1920s and 1930s increased dramatically, by a stunning 140 percent during the 1920s and again by nearly seventy percent between 1929 and 1937.[18] This changed immigration pattern had different reasons; according to Bao, social restrictions in Chinese villages eased as society as a whole changed after the end of empire, modern railways and shipping lines increased mobility, and Siam continued to stand for the promise of better material conditions than existed in impoverished Chinese villages.[19] This trend greatly improved the sex ratio among the Chinese minority in Siam and led to less assimilation, as it was now much easier for a Chinese man to marry a Chinese woman, and also because the children of a Chinese couple were considered Chinese, not Thai.

Cooperation between Siam and the League of Nations

We have seen that in the West the problem of the international traffic in women and children was put on the agenda of international politics at the end of the nineteenth century.[20] Following the first international agreement of 1904 and the international convention of 1910, the League was also entrusted with this matter after the First World War. The League of Nations in 1920 set out to cope with the task of suppressing human trafficking by first of all establishing a body of information and data, in order to assess the dimension of the problem. The immediate aim of this information gathering was to prepare for an

17 James Francis Warren, *Ah Ku and Karayuki-san, Prostitution in Singapore, 1870-1940*, Singapore: Oxford University Press, 1993, p. 29ff.; Manderson, *Sickness and the State*, p. 166ff. It is noteworthy that Warren makes extensive use of the report of the League of Nations Commission of Enquiry of 1933, which is discussed in detail in this chapter. On the social changes leading to an increase of prostitution and human trafficking in China during the early twentieth century see Sue Gronewold, *Beautiful Merchandise: Prostitution in China 1860-1936*, New York: Haworth, 1982, particularly p. 37ff.

18 George William Skinner, *Chinese Society in Thailand, An Analytical History*, Ithaca (NY): Cornell University Press, 1967, p. 172ff.; George William Skinner, *Leadership and Power in the Chinese Community of Thailand*, Ithaca (NY): Cornell University Press, 1958, p. 13ff.; Landon, *Chinese in Thailand*, p. 197ff., Jiemin Bao, *Marital Acts: Gender, Sexuality, and Identity among the Chinese Thai Diaspora*, Honolulu: Hawai'i University Press, 2005, p. 42. See also Barmé, *Woman, Man, Bangkok*, p. 83. Female immigrants from China to Siam during the nineteenth century were mostly prostitutes, but also wives or family members of Chinese merchants and workers.

19 Bao, *Marital Acts*, p. 27ff.

20 International Agreement for the Suppression of White Slave Traffic of 1904 and International Convention for the Suppression of White Slave Traffic of 1910. See Castendyck, *Social Problems*.

improved international agreement, which was to supersede the first basic agreement of 1904 and convention of 1910 and was to contain clear commitments for signatories.

The League first sent out questionnaires to member states enquiring about national legislation to combat human trafficking. The Thai government responded by submitting the relevant sections of the penal code (sections 243 to 246 and sections 273 to 277) and the Prevention of Venereal Diseases Act of 1908. The Thai Delegation to the League's General Assembly made it clear in their reply, which the League Secretariat circulated to all member states, that the modernisation of Siam's legislative system depended, first and foremost, on the willingness of the Western states to renounce their unequal treaties:

> With regard to the rest of the questionnaire, H.M.'s Government is contemplating new legislation on the subject; but, owing to the fact that at the present moment the treaties with foreign powers, with the exception of the United States of America, have not yet been revised, the putting into force of such legislation will be acquired with much difficulty.[21]

As we have seen in previous chapters on opium and public health, Thai policy makers again utilised the issue of human trafficking for their goal of regaining full sovereignty. The League of Nations Conference on Traffic in Women and Children opened on 30 June 1921 in Geneva with the objective to draw up a new and further reaching international convention on the issue. Minister of Foreign Affairs Prince Devawongse was unsure as to whether Siam should be represented. He decided that Siam should only participate if other Asian countries would do so. Indeed, both China and Japan asked to be represented at the conference, and Siam duly followed. While a sense of prostitution as a social phenomenon which required regulation was present among the Thai elite, a genuine sense of human trafficking as a problem can not be detected among Thai policy makers dealing with the League of Nations in 1920-21. The confinement of the problem largely to the Chinese minority in Siam was the main reason for this lack of interest. Prince Devawongse's careful approach to the question of participation in the forthcoming conference was also an expression of cautious Thai policies during these early days of multilateralism and international organisation. Thai foreign policy makers had only very limited experience on the international stage and conducted foreign policy mainly with an eye to Great Britain and France. As a result, stepping into the Geneva spotlight seemed more reasonable as one of several Asian states rather than doing so alone, in order to avoid the possible dangers of becoming involuntarily exposed over policy decisions, whose implications seemed fairly unclear, such as measures against human trafficking.[22]

While the quoted reply to the League did express the intention of drawing up national legislation to regulate immigration and check

21 Prince Charoon to Drummond, 29 June 1921, Serial Document C.45(s).M.22(s).1921.IV., LNA, S 178.

22 Prince Devawongse to Prince Charoon, 27 May 1921, TNA, KT 96.1.81/5. Interestingly, Prince Charoon did, however, vote against a British suggestion on a procedural question during the conference, which was aimed at accommodating France; see Prince Charoon to Prince Devawongse, 16 July 1921, TNA, KT 96.1.8.1/4.

human trafficking, Prince Charoon, Thai Minister in Paris and Siam's delegate to the conference, considered himself not exactly an expert on the matter, as he made clear in a telegram to Prince Devawongse, 'I know there are the cases in Siam of Chinese girls brought in from China but I am not aware of circumstances'.[23] Until 5 July the conference debated a draft convention, which was then presented to the League Council in the form of a draft resolution, and which was to be signed by League members during the General Assembly in the autumn of 1921 in Geneva. Prince Charoon advised that the Thai government 'should favourably consider the Resolution'.[24] The measures recommended by the convention were mainly aimed at improving immigration procedures. A major innovation was the introduction of a system of so-called central authorities in each country or territory, which were to be located in the respective ministry of interior or police headquarters and which should serve as domestic focal points for the international co-ordination of action against traffickers. Driven mainly by Western women's rights groups and social activists, the convention's ultimate goal was to prohibit prostitution altogether, a goal which Prince Charoon saw as impossible to achieve 'so long as human beings are'.[25]

At the conference the issue of the age of consent emerged as the main impediment for Prince Charoon's efforts to paint a picture of Siam as a progressive and civilised country. In 1921, the age of consent in Siam was twelve, to be raised to fourteen in the new penal code, which was being drafted. The conference proposed to set the age below which trafficking would be a criminal offence at twenty-one years of age, which should also serve as a universal age of majority. The Thai penal code, however, did not fix a legal age of majority or age of marriage, in addition to the age of consent. Siam was in the company of India and Japan, who faced a similar problem, with the age of consent in India being eleven and the age of majority in Japan at sixteen years. The Indian delegate expressed his concern in raising it being twenty-one and argued, interestingly, that one should acknowledge the 'much earlier age at which maturity was reached in the East'.[26] Prince Charoon agreed with the Indian delegate in calling on the conference to let each state decide on this issue individually, 'in accordance with the customs and climatic conditions [sic] of the land.' A Bangkok newspaper commented that 'it would be a lamentable thing if the Siamese delegate at Geneva has given out to the world that the penal code of thirteen years ago is Siam's last word on the subject' but, at the same time, advocated caution when considering whether to adopt Western legislation in regard to age of consent or not.[27] In a very pragmatic approach, Prince Devawongse did not regard this issue as problematic:

> Fixing the age of consent at 21 does not seem to present serious difficulties for Siam, because the age thus fixed is not to be considered the age of majority for other purposes but solely confined to the

23 Prince Charoon to Prince Deva-wongse, 11 June 1921, TNA, KT 96.1.81/5.

24 Prince Charoon to Prince Deva-wongse, 16 July 1921, TNA, KT 96.1.8.1/4.

25 Ibid.

26 Quoted in Verma, *India and the League*, p. 180.

27 TNA, *Bangkok Times*, 22 and 23 September 1921.

purpose of proposed agreement, namely Traffic in Women and Children. But, of course, if it could be agreed upon to leave each country free to fix its own age limit, all the better for us.[28]

In the end, article 5 of the resulting International Convention for the Suppression of the Traffic in Women and Children set the age of majority at twenty-one years. Accordingly, trafficking a woman or girl under this age was to be considered a criminal offence. The convention was signed by Prince Charoon on behalf of the Thai government on 30 September 1921 and ratified on 13 July 1922. At the same time, Siam also formally adhered to the agreement of 1904 and convention of 1910.[29] Siam adhered to the 1910 Convention with a reservation regarding the age of majority for Thai nationals in paragraph b, which set age of majority at twenty years, and signed the 1921 Convention with the same reservation regarding article 5.

King Vajiravudh was strongly in favour of Siam's new international commitments in this regard. Influenced by Western ideas of emancipation, he was interested in improving the position of women in society and in including women in his programmes to strengthen patriotic sentiments. The king, who expressed his belief that the status of women reflected a society's degree of civilisation, devoted a third of his entire annual speech from the throne in January 1923 to Siam's membership in the League of Nations and adherence to the convention:

> As you are all well aware, improvement in communications generally leads to an ever closer and more intimate intercourse between nations and such intercourse may, in turn, result in a community of thought and co-ordination of action, that is to say, it may, in short, cultivate and promote union among nations. It is the constant aim and purpose of my Government to keep abreast of the times in every direction, so as to be worthy of their status as member of the League of Nations. For the purpose, I have decided to sign and apply a number of international conventions and agreements. We have, for instance, signed the League of Nations Convention on the Traffic in Women and Children which covers the former international conventions for the Suppression of the White Slave Traffic and I have approved and confirmed the same by my ratification of the 11th April of this year.[30]

This move prompted a Bangkok newspaper to comment, 'Nobody seems to know quite clearly what Siam has committed herself to'; but the same commentary acknowledged that, 'Anyhow Siam is now one of the pioneers in this matter, having been the second power to ratify this new convention'.[31] In retrospect it appears that this assessment is accurate, and that the signature of the 1921 convention was indeed primarily intended for international rather than for domestic consumption. However, standing at the forefront of this progressive international

28 Prince Devawongse to Prince Charoon, 15 September 1921, TNA, KT 96.1.3/4.

29 LNA, R 643/12/13531/11024 and R 663/12/59796/21024; TNA, KT 96.1.8.1/6 and KT 96.1.8.1/7. The text of the International Convention for the Suppression of the Traffic in Women and Children of 30 September 1921 can be found in LNA, League of Nations Treaty Series, vol. IX, p. 416ff. and in TNA, KT 96.1.8.1/8. The convention came into force on 15 June 1922. The 1921 Convention declared ratification of the 1904 Agreement and the 1910 Convention prerequisites to signature in article 1.

30 TNA, Bangkok Times, 3 January 1923. This point on King Vajiravudh's interest in the role of women follows Vella, Chaiyo!, p. 151.

31 TNA, Bangkok Times, 18 July 1922. W.H. Mundie, editor of the Bangkok Times, sent a letter to Prince Devawongse on the same day asking 'to what definite action is the country committed thereby?', but he received only an evasive reply from the Minister of Foreign Affairs; see Mundie to Prince Devawongse, 18 July 1922 and Prince Devawongse to Mundie, 19 July 1922, TNA, KT 96.1.8.1/9.

initiative did also underscore the Thai elite's progressiveness and international standing domestically.

It took a number of years and a number of sessions of the League's Advisory Committee on the matter, however, until the national laws of Siam were adjusted to the convention, especially with regard to extending the authority of the Thai police towards traffickers.[32] Available official figures provided by the Thai government to the League regarding convictions related to trafficking in persons under the provisions of the 1908 penal code state that a total of fifty-six sentences were passed between 1921 and 1924, of which eight cases involved trafficking of minors under the age of twelve.[33]

In late 1924 a case of human trafficking stirred up media attention in the Thai capital. It involved two Chinese girls who had been lured to Siam to work as prostitutes under false pretences and put the spotlight on the ongoing trafficking of girls from Canton to Bangkok via Hong Kong. Under existing laws, Thai immigration authorities were unable to take Chinese girls, who were on average thirteen years of age, from their traffickers upon arrival in the kingdom, and the girls themselves were normally too frightened to accuse the traffickers. The *Bangkok Times* commented:

> Siam has shown an interest in the work along the same lines that is being done by the League of Nations; and there is no doubt she would readily respond to any practical suggestion of cooperation. But the first step is undoubtedly to institute a service at the port of Bangkok to deal with this shameful trade, a service as efficient as that maintained by the Straits Government in its ports.[34]

In this sense, one important institution lacking in Bangkok before the Second World War was a shelter for the victims, where they could be protected and where they would ultimately feel safe enough to disclose details of their ordeal and specifics concerning the trafficker. Such a place of safety already existed in the Federated Malay States by the mid-1920s, and the British colonial administrative even offered the Thai government technical assistance to set up such a shelter in Bangkok, but the offer seems not to have been taken up on the Thai side.[35]

According to official figures reported by the Thai government to the League, in 1924 Bangkok had 205 licensed brothels and 893 licensed prostitutes, with the vast majority of brothels (181) and prostitutes (796) being Chinese. They were complemented by Thai and a small number of Indochinese and Russian establishments and prostitutes. The report went on to explain that traffickers of Chinese women were normally Chinese, traffickers of Russian women Russians and that their business was going well, 'They live in a lavish style, but no estimate can be given of their earnings.' The 1924 report is remarkable also for its detailed description of how women and girls were lured into becoming prostitutes

32 TNA, *Bangkok Times*, 13 April 1925.

33 Report of the Fourth Session of the Advisory Committee on the Traffic in Women and Protection of Children of May 1925, Serial Document C.293.(1)1925.IV., LNA, R 674/12/44530/28438.

34 TNA, *Bangkok Times*, 7 January 1925.

35 Waterlow to Prince Traidos, 27 July 1926, TNA, KT 96.1.8.1/ 42.

in Bangkok. Chinese girls were 'deceived and persuaded that they will be given employment or assisted to find husbands', but were then forced to repay alleged debts to the traffickers by working as prostitutes; this scheme seemed to work as well eighty years ago as it does today. According to the report, Russian women were 'stranded in China' and 'were poor and accustomed to earning their livelihood by assisting in bars or places of entertainment.' The report further stated that there was no outbound trafficking of Thai women from Siam, but that some Thai prostitutes went to Malaya of their own will. In addition, the report conceded that Chinese women were trafficked from Siam into Malaya. It also gave reasons for why the victims fell prey to traffickers. In the case of Chinese girls, rural poverty and political turmoil in China were identified as the main reasons, while in case of Russian women the 'effect of the bolshevist regime' was cited to explain why they were homeless and adrift in China.[36]

Also in late 1924, Prince Traidos, Minister of Foreign Affairs, responded to an enquiry from the League's Advisory Committee on Traffic in Women and Children as to the state of affairs in Siam by once again transmitting the same sections of the penal code and the act of 1908. In addition, he explained procedures at the Bangkok port. When ships from China arrived, officials would board and question young women unaccompanied by relatives. If it was found that they were being brought to Siam against their will, they were entrusted to the care of the captain of a ship leaving for China 'with a letter to the Police Authorities in Hong Kong asking that they be sent to the Chinese Protectorate so that they may be returned to their respective homes by the Po Tieng Kok [Po Leung Kuk] Society.' Women who were, the Prince continued, willing to become prostitutes in Siam on the other hand, were granted licenses and were informed of their rights and duties.[37]

The League once again enquired into the age of consent in Siam in 1925. The judicial adviser to the government, Frenchman René Guyon, wrote a legal memorandum for the Ministry of Foreign Affairs, in which he laid down that the minimum age of marriage was governed in Siam by custom rather than by law, 'and it was generally admitted that puberty is the criterion.' Guyon's memorandum also reinforced the prevailing attitude that this was not an issue for the League as it was purely domestic, while the League was concerned only with international trafficking.[38]

As mentioned above, in the course of the 1920s, the number of Chinese women entering Siam legally or illegally increased sharply. Large numbers of these women married Chinese men who had already settled in Siam, and this led to gradual social change, as Chinese men no longer assimilated as easily as when they married Thai wives. Instead they remained increasingly isolated by founding Chinese families in Siam. It was clear to Thai immigration officials in the 1920s that the

36 Report to the League of Nations in Reply to the Questionnaire (C.L.61.1924.IV) concerning Traffic in Women and Children, sent on 30 April 1924, TNA, KT 96.1.8.1/24.

37 Prince Traidos to Drummond, 4 November 1924, LNA, R 674/12/40891/28438. Founded in 1878, the Po Leung Kuk is one of the most established charitable organisations in Hong Kong. According to Pauline Poon Pui-ting, its name translates as 'organization for the protection of the innocent', and it was created to care for the women and children who were kidnapped or trafficked for domestic servitude, adoption, marriage, or prostitution. Poon also gives rich details on how the Po Leung Kuk handled women and girls who had been placed in its hands; see Pauline Poon Pui-ting, 'Political Maneuverings in Early Twentieth Century Hong Kong: The Mui Tsai Issue', *E-Journal on Hong Kong Cultural and Social Studies*, 3 (June 2004), <http://www.hku.hk/hkcsp/ccex/ehkcss01/issue3_ar_pauline_poon.htm>.

38 Secretary-General to Thai Minister of Foreign Affairs, 8 July 1925 and Memorandum Guyon, n.d. (likely mid-1925), TNA, KT 96.1.8.1/37. René Guyon had been head of the drafting committee for the penal code and stayed on in Siam as adviser to the Ministry of Justice. He went on to publish a ten-volume opus entitled *Studies in Sexual Ethics* in the course of the 1930s and 1940s.

main route for trafficking in persons was by ship from Hong Kong to Bangkok, and that Hong Kong also served as a base for the major trafficking rings. The Thai Ministry of Interior would have liked to see the British governor of Hong Kong take effective action against this situation, especially in the light of the complaints the Ministry was receiving from British Malaya concerning illegal immigration from Siam, but it stepped short of officially approaching British authorities in this regard.[39] While cooperation with Hong Kong against human trafficking was limited, occasional cooperation between central authorities in Southeast Asia did begin in the mid-1920s. For example, in 1928 the central authorities of the Straits Settlements, the Federated Malay States and Siam conferred on how to improve control along their borders on the peninsula, particularly regarding the influx of Chinese women from Siam into the Malay Peninsula.[40]

By early 1926, the Thai government was ready to prepare for an immigration law in earnest. An inter-ministerial committee was set up under the chairmanship of Attorney-General Phraya Deb Vidul to draft the law, in which the Ministries of Justice, Foreign Affairs, and Commerce and Communications participated as well as representatives of the Railways Department and the Department of Legislative Redaction. Facilitated by Raymond Stevens, who was adviser to the Ministry of Foreign Affairs and a member of the drafting committee, the British Minister in Bangkok supplied the committee with the ordinances and regulations from the Straits Settlements and Federated Malay States on immigration in general and on the 'undesirable immigration...of Chinese prostitutes in particular'.[41] During the year, Stevens travelled to Kuala Lumpur to consult with British officials there, as well as the British Governor of Hong Kong, the port of embarkation for most Chinese immigrants into Siam. Then in September he provided the committee with a memorandum on Chinese emigration.[42] The new Immigration Act B.E. 2470 was promulgated on 11 July 1927 and was designed primarily to limit the influx of Chinese women. An additional aim of limiting Chinese immigration in general was, as expressed by the British Minister in Bangkok, to fend off communism, which was spreading in China.

The effectiveness of this new immigration act beyond the port of Bangkok was immediately questioned by international observers.[43] But the new act did serve the important purpose of meeting the country's international obligations in the fight against human trafficking under the League of Nations convention of 1921 and can, therefore, be attributed at least in part to the pressure created by Siam's League membership, a view shared already by contemporary observers.[44] By 1928, the first Thai law on human trafficking was enacted in compliance with the League of Nations international convention of 1921 and in response to international pressure from the League of

39 Minister of Interior to Minister of Foreign Affairs, 27 January B.E. 2470 (1928), TNA, KT 96.1.8.1/53.

40 'Extension of the Enquiry on Traffic in Women and Children to the East: Information Concerning Siam', p. 2, LNA, R 3045/11B/ 21823/ 5580.

41 Waterlow to Prince Traidos, 27 July 1926, TNA, KT 96.1.8.1/42.

42 Waterlow to Prince Traidos, 20 September 1926, TNA, KT 96.1.8.1/42.

43 Waterlow to Chamberlain, 12 August 1927, Doc. 253 (F 7775/ 7775/40), BDFA, Part II, Series E, vol. 49, p. 329f.

44 TNA, *Bangkok Times*, 13 May 1928.

Nations and from individual League members with colonies in Southeast Asia. The Traffic in Women and Girls Act B.E. 2471 came into force on 5 May 1928, although Raymond Stevens had already pressed unsuccessfully for it to be promulgated during the previous summer, so that Siam could demonstrate its compliance with the convention during the 1927 League of Nations General Assembly.[45] Under the new act, traffickers could be punished with up to seven years imprisonment and a fine of up to 1,000 baht. The act further gave authorities the right to detain the victim of trafficking for up to thirty days as a protective measure. Another provision, included in response to international pressure, was that if the woman freed from the trafficker was a foreign citizen, the act stipulated that she should be returned to her home country and the Thai government would bear the costs of repatriation up to the home country's border.[46] In the light of this progressive domestic legislation, it was fitting that Siam's new Permanent Representative to the League of Nations, Prince Varn, was elected rapporteur for the 1928 General Assembly's Fifth Committee of Traffic in Women and Children, and that his work received unanimous approval from his fellow delegates.[47]

The anti-trafficking legislation of 1928 was again aimed at Chinese women but seems to have had some effect on Western prostitutes in Siam, who, according to Leslie Ann Jeffrey, soon thereafter disappeared from brothels in Siam.[48] In the course of the 1930s the number of brothels decreased substantially, partially as a result of the much larger number of Chinese women available as potential partners for Chinese men in Siam, partially because the police began to enforce the laws of 1927 and 1928.[49] While in 1929 Bangkok officially counted 170 brothels, this figure had declined to ninety-three in 1936. The official number of registered prostitutes also decreased during this period by forty percent. The Thai government reported to the League that in 1937-38 there were seventy-six licensed brothels and ninety-two Thai and 249 Chinese prostitutes. This ridiculously small figure of 341 prostitutes in a country of fifteen million inhabitants shows that the system of licensing certainly did not work.[50] Consequently, during the same period, the number of unregistered brothels increased sharply, as did the number of prostitutes working clandestinely. Landon quotes a member of the Thai National Assembly, who, in 1939, apparently,

> …reported that, while there were only twenty-five brothels for Thai and thirty-seven for Chinese in the government register, during a three months' survey carried out by himself, he had discovered in Bangkok alone 274 brothels which were not registered in accordance with the law.[51]

A report by the Thai secret service of January 1928 listed thirteen Chinese women found to have been victims of trafficking and taken from

45 Stevens to Prince Traidos, 25 June 1927, TNA, KT 96.1.3/10.

46 The Traffic in Women and Girls Act was duly sent in Thai and English to the League of Nations where it can still be consulted today. It is important to note that this act applied only to international trafficking, not domestic trafficking. The provision on foreign nationals was highlighted as late as 1993 in a study by civil rights groups in: Asia Watch and The Women's Rights Project (eds.), *A Modern Form of Slavery: Trafficking of Burmese Women and Girls into Brothels in Thailand*, New York et. al: Human Rights Watch, 1993, p. 21. The act of 1928 is still considered today as an important landmark in the fight against human trafficking in Thailand; see, for example Pasuk Phongpaichit, Sungsidh Piriyarangsan and Nualnoi Treerat, *Guns, Girls, Gambling, Ganja: Thailand's Illegal Economy and Public Policy*, Chiang Mai: Silkworm Books, 1998, p. 211. See also Thompson, *Thailand*, p. 687ff.

47 These developments in Geneva again resonated in the Bangkok press: TNA, *Bangkok Times*, 28 October 1929.

48 Jeffrey, *Sex and Borders*, p. 14.

49 Landon, *Siam in Transition*, p. 155.

50 League of Nations Advisory Committee on Social Questions, Summary of Annual Reports for 1937/38, LNA, Serial Document C.68.M.30.1939.IV, p. 7.

51 Landon, *Chinese in Thailand*, p. 96.

ships arriving from Hong Kong between April and September 1927, most of whom were sent back to Hong Kong.[52] Also in January 1928, the Director of the Immigration Department reported to the Minister of Interior the case of two Chinese girls, aged seventeen and fourteen, who were picked up by the immigration authorities onboard an arriving ship. As they had no guardians in Siam and were unwilling to stay in the country, they were returned to Hong Kong in accordance with paragraph four of the Immigration Act. Arrangements were made by the authorities that the shipping company return the girls to Hong Kong and deliver them to the 'Tong Hua Ki Eu Hospital' there, which would arrange to return them to their families. The girls left Bangkok after seven days on 18 January, and the Immigration Department was awaiting a receipt from the hospital in Hong Kong confirming the arrival of the girls. The testimonies of the two girls from a village near Canton, who suddenly found themselves alone in an alien land, shed some light on the traumatic experiences these children had to endure as victims of trafficking some eighty years ago.[53]

The 1928 legislation had a significant impact on the number of convictions for trafficking in persons. The above-mentioned fifty-six convictions during the four years between 1921 and 1924 seem small in number compared to the twenty-seven offences involving Thai victims reported by the Thai government to the League of Nations for the year 1930 alone. The annual reports on human trafficking, which the Thai government submitted to the League, make for highly unpleasant reading, as they list, in very plain language, crimes involving boys and girls as young as five years of age. The reports show that offenders involved in human trafficking or running illegal brothels were mainly Chinese, followed by Thais; only occasionally do Western or other Asian nationals appear in the reports as traffickers. Sentences for traffickers in 1930, for example, ranged from three months to two years imprisonment.[54]

Already the international agreement of 1904 stipulated that each signatory country should nominate a central authority to deal with international trafficking of humans. But in 1922, Prince Devawongse had to admit to Secretary-General Drummond that no such central authority had yet been nominated in Siam, although it would likely be the Ministry of Interior.[55] In fact, it was only several years later, in 1928, that the Ministry of Interior formally designated the Director of its Immigration Department as the central authority in Siam to deal with international human trafficking, a designation which was later to be changed to the Director of the Police Department.[56] But in spite of the lack of a formally designated authority, the Ministry of Interior met its responsibility to furnish the League with annual reports on human trafficking and on related offences and convictions with admirable diligence from 1922 onwards.[57]

52 Secret Service Report of 12 January 1928, TNA, KT 96.1.8.1/53.

53 Enclosure in Minister of Interior to Minister of Foreign Affairs, 27 January B.E. 2470 (1928), TNA, KT 96.1.8.1/53. The hospital name most likely referred to the Tung Wah Hospital, which was associated with the aforementioned Po Leung Kuk.

54 Kingdom of Siam, Report on Traffic in Women and Children for the Year 1930, enclosure in Prince Damras to Drummond, 14 July 1931, LNA, R 3057/11B/29723/25849.

55 Prince Devawongse to Drummond, 20 October 1922, LNA, R 663/12/24998/21014 and TNA, KT 96.1.8.1/13. See on the lack of a formally appointed central authority by 1925 also TNA, KT 96.1.8.1/32.

56 Under Secretary of State in Ministry of Interior to Under Secretary of State in Ministry of Foreign Affairs, 29 October B.E. 2471 (1928), TNA, KT 96.1.8.1/15.

57 Annual Reports on Traffic in Women and Children, 1922 to 1930, TNA, KT 96.1.8.1/16.

To a much smaller extent than as a destination for inbound human trafficking, Siam was also a transit country for the trafficking of Chinese women overland from China to British Malaya. The reason for this lay in the fact that travelling by ship from China and then onwards to Malaya and the Straits Settlements by rail was cheaper than travelling directly by ship from China to Singapore. The British Minister in Bangkok, Richard Seymour, reported to the Thai government in April 1920 that, according to the British High Commissioner for the Malay States,

> …a considerable number of women and girls are brought into Perlis or Kedah by rail from Siam and are being dispersed through the Colony and the Federated Malay States. Between September and November of last year some 30 girls introduced in this way are believed to have been sold to an immoral life in the Colony.[58]

Seymour explained that authorities in Malaya were unable to check this trade properly because 'it seems that many Chinese women and girls leave the trains before leaving Kedah, and so avoid examination', and requested that the Thai government provide 'a more effective check on this immoral traffic' already when the ships from China arrive 'at the first port of call in Siam'. Prince Devawongse replied that he was aware of the seriousness of the matter and that improvements in immigration procedures were being considered.[59] A 1924 memorandum submitted to the British government painted a lively picture of trafficking in women and children by rail from Siam into British Malaya. The same study also criticised the lack of effective controls by immigration authorities at the Bangkok port.[60] The situation had not substantially changed the following year, when similar British complaints about human trafficking through Siam into Malaya appeared in the papers in Bangkok and Singapore.[61] But effective action against international human trafficking in Siam not only required better immigration procedures but also the full jurisdiction of the Thai authorities over all nationals within their border, an argument which the Thai government must have been pleased to read in a letter to the editor of the *Straits Echo*, which the *Bangkok Times* reprinted in April 1925:

> I do not think they signed [the International Convention of 1921] blindly although at the time, as still at this time, they have nothing of the machinery that exists in the Straits. It is doubtful if Siam is going to get a smack in the eye for not living up to the Convention. While Siam is to a certain extent a free country, I doubt if the Siamese are going to sit down and allow their country to become a breeding ground for young prostitutes…They cannot do just as they like unless the other and bigger nations will help them. It is a notorious fact that certain European nationals deliberately break the laws of the country and then take refuge behind their Consul.[62]

58 Seymour to Prince Devawongse, 9 April 1920, TNA, KT 96.1.8.1/3. See also Manderson, *Sickness and the State*, p. 166ff.

59 Prince Devawongse to Minister of Interior, 10 April 1920 and Prince Devawongse to Seymour, 29 April 1920, TNA, KT 96.1.8.1/3.

60 Memorandum by T.W.H. Kingston, 10 October 1924, PRO, FO 628/40 (-/-/-).

61 TNA, *Bangkok Times*, 23 March 1925.

62 TNA, *Bangkok Times*, 13 April 1925.

In 1927, newspaper reports in Bangkok suggested that human trafficking was on the rise in Bangkok itself, now involving more and more underage Chinese children being kidnapped or sold, 'a healthy child fetches 60 to 80 ticals', and then brought by rail or ship to Malaya.[63] Manderson has shown that the League of Nations had a strong influence on the policies of colonial authorities in Malaya towards prostitution during the 1920s, and consequently also on the protests they were sending to Bangkok.[64]

It is noteworthy in this context that the League's Child Welfare Committee, formally known as the Advisory Committee for the Protection and Welfare of Children and Young People, conducted a survey in 1927 on the position of illegitimate children in League member states. Out of the thirty-eight countries surveyed, Siam stood out as the single country in which the problem of illegitimate birth legally did not exist. Children in Siam had full rights of inheritance and succession, whether the parents' marriage was formal or not, and even if the father was unknown. It must have raised a number of eyebrows among the committee members when they learned that this remote Asian kingdom had the most progressive practice with regard to illegitimate births: 'It is impossible to include Siam in any of these legislative divisions, for in that country the marriage of the parents is not essential to ensure the legitimacy of the children.' The committee concluded, 'In Siam every child is legitimate.'[65] In a remarkable twist, when the League enquired once more in 1938, the promulgation of the Thai civil code in 1935 had darkened the bright picture of Siam with regard to illegitimate children. Now that polygamy was legally abolished, and marriages, under sections 1449 and 1451 of the civil code, had to be registered, children from unregistered marriages were illegitimate. In other words, Siam's progressiveness regarding legitimacy of child births, as expressed in its traditional customs towards the status of children, had been reversed because of Siam's progressiveness in introducing a Western codified legal system. Meanwhile in practice polygamy continued as before.[66]

The League of Nations commission of enquiry on trafficking in women and children, 1930

The League of Nations had conducted an enquiry into human trafficking in Europe as well as North and South America in the years 1924 to 1926, before setting its eyes on Asia. A commission of enquiry sent out by the League of Nations travelled extensively through East, Southeast and South Asia and the Middle East for eighteen months between October 1930 and March 1932. In Southeast Asia, the commission visited the Philippines, French Indochina, the Netherlands Indies, the Federated and Unfederated Malay States, the Straits Settlements, and Siam.[67] The commission was composed of Bascom

63 TNA, *Bangkok Times*, 19 February 1927.

64 Manderson, *Sickness and the State*, 166ff.

65 LNA, Serial Document C.P.E. 141(1). For the Thai side of this exchange and a memorandum by the Ministry of Justice see TNA, KT 96.1.8.1/82. The League undertook a second survey on illegitimate children in 1934/35, and again Siam received praise for its progressiveness. See the 1934/35 survey TNA, SR 0201.17/10. On the League's Child Welfare Committee and its pioneering work which cleared new paths in international law, see League of Nations, *Aims, Methods and Activity*, p. 173.

66 Memorandum by Judicial Adviser A.F. Thavenot, 18 August 1938, and various correspondence in TNA, KT 96.1.8.1/115. See also LNA, Serial Document C.70. M.24.1939.IV.

67 Apart from Southeast Asia, the commission visited Hong Kong, Macao, China, Japan, India, Pondicherry, Ceylon, Persia, Iraq, Syria, Lebanon, and Palestine. See LNA, R 3046/11B/23102/5580. On the first League enquiry on human trafficking in Europe and the Americas see Castendyck, Social Problems, p. 233. The report of the League of Nations' first enquiry, entitled Report of the Special Body of Experts on Traffic in Women and Children of 17 February 1927 can be found in LNA, Serial Documents C.52. M.52.1927.IV.

Johnson as chairman, Dr. Alma Sundquist and Carol Pinder as commission members, and Dr. Werner von Schmieden as secretary. They arrived in Bangkok on 6 November 1930 and spent that month in the kingdom. The Ministry of Interior appointed three people to assist the enquiry, Major-General P.I.E. Warming, the adviser to the ministry, who held the conferred noble title Phraya Bejra Indra, Phraya Adhikarana Prakas, Director-General of Police and Gendarmerie, and Phraya Vichai Prajabal, Director of the Immigration Department. The Thai government was, however, not willing to support the visit of the commission financially. As the government was, on the contrary, willing to cover expenses for other League commissions of enquiry in public health matters, this refusal shows once again the lower priority which human trafficking had for the government in comparison to other policy areas.[68]

The information provided by the Thai government to the League's commission provides an excellent summary of relevant developments during the first ten years of the League's existence.[69] The commission interviewed public health officials, immigration officials, police officers, judges, teachers, missionaries and many other official and non-official persons in order to assess the dimension and the specifics of human trafficking in Siam. Werner von Schmieden gave a brief account of the commission's stay in Siam after their arrival at their next stop in Saigon, in French Indochina:

> The Siamese authorities were particularly kind to the Travelling Commission. They had themselves appointed a Commission…to furnish us the information we required. In addition an officer of the police was put at our exclusive disposal. On our arrival we were given the written reply of the Government to our questionnaire, sent out from Geneva in September, and in this way the carrying out of our enquiry was greatly facilitated…We obtained valuable information…[70]

The commission compiled a report on their findings, which was 'the first comprehensive study ever made on the traffic in women and children in that area' and which 'aroused world-wide interest'.[71] According to this report, which was published in 1932, there was considerable traffic in women and young girls in Asia, the victims being mainly Chinese. The commission found the largest numbers in British Malaya, followed by Hong Kong, Macao and Siam.[72] The commission observed accurately:

> As a matter of fact, traffic in Chinese women appears to be intimately connected with the Chinese migratory movement and its aspects vary according to the different conditions of life and work and social standing of the Chinese immigrants to the different territories.[73]

68 The files relating to the League's commission of enquiry are in TNA, KT 96.1.8.1/69 through 73 and file 83. Large sections of these files are illegible because they have been destroyed by bookworm; see also TNA, *Bangkok Times*, 8 August and 27 October 1930.

69 'Extension of the Enquiry on Traffic in Women and Children to the East: Information Concerning Siam', in LNA, R 3045/ 11B/ 21823/5580.

70 Von Schmieden to Crowdy, 4 December 1930, LNA, R 3046/ 11B/23102/5580.

71 Report by the Commission of Inquiry into the Traffic in Women and Children in the East, LNA, serial document no. C.849.M. 393.1932.IV. Quotes from Castendyck, Social Problems, p. 233.

72 Report by the Commission of Enquiry into the Traffic in Women and Children in the East, LNA, serial document no. C.849. M.393.1932.IV., p. 13f. Interestingly, and in total contradiction to earlier official and unofficial statements, the British legation in Bangkok suddenly held the rather surprising and completely opposite view that 'traffic of foreign women and children… is non-existent in Siam'; see: Annual Report on Siam for 1930, PRO, FO 371/15532, F 1873/ 1873/40, p. 16.

73 Von Schmieden to Crowdy, 4 December 1930, LNA, R 3046/ 11B/23102/5580.

In Bangkok, the visit of this League commission did not attract the level of public attention given to the other commissions of enquiry on opium and public health, although it did spark a number of newspaper editorials and articles. Indeed, the *Bangkok Times* headline 'One More Inquiry' shortly before the commission's arrival points to a certain degree of saturation, as during the twelve preceding months Bangkok saw visits of no less than three League of Nations commissions of enquiry on opium smoking, leprosy, and malaria. The same *Bangkok Times* article also took a strong position against the 'theorists' at Geneva who refused to accept realities in Asia, i.e. polygamous societies, and lashed out at members of League commissions of enquiry as having 'two things in immeasurable strength – pre-conceived convictions and a superiority complex that can only regard any disagreement with their cut and dried views as an outcome of an ignorance that is pitiable'.[74] Only days before this article appeared in Bangkok, Prince Varn took the floor at Geneva for the first time ever in a plenary session of the League's General Assembly to praise League commissions of enquiry precisely for the fact that they contributed to acquiring first-hand knowledge of conditions 'in distant countries'.[75]

The most significant impact of the visit of the League of Nations commission of enquiry to Siam was that it led to the Penal Code Amendment Act of 1931. Eight years after ratifying the international convention of 1921, Siam still maintained its reservations with regard to the age of majority, which the convention set at twenty-one but which was still set at twelve years of age, the age of consent, in Siam. India had already amended its penal code in 1923 by inserting sections 366a and b, which made the procuring of girls younger than eighteen a punishable offence. Japan had followed suit in 1927 by accepting the age limit of twenty-one and had, accordingly, withdrawn its reservation to the International Convention of 1921.[76] Of a total of forty ratifications by the year 1927, this left only Siam with a significant reservation with regard to the age of majority. As Raymond Stevens pointed out in a frank letter to Prince Devawongse, Minister of Foreign Affairs, in late 1930, 'It will thus be noted that His Majesty's Government will have the lowest standard of all nations bound to the Convention'.[77] By the end of October 1930, just days before the arrival of the commission of enquiry in Bangkok, officials at the Ministry of Foreign Affairs became quite concerned about Siam's image in the light of the commission's visit, as a letter to the Ministry of Interior shows, with regard to the age of consent, 'His Majesty's Government would be subjected to criticism if these age limits are not increased', as the age limits of twelve years (age of consent) and fourteen years (maximum age of victim, the trafficking of which is considered a criminal offence) were considered as 'obviously too low'. After ratifying the 1921 convention, the Foreign Ministry had forwarded the relevant provisions in the draft new penal code to the

74 TNA, *Bangkok Times*, 29 October 1930.

75 TNA, *Bangkok Times*, 3 November 1930.

76 TNA, *Bangkok Times*, 14 February 1927.

77 Stevens to Prince Devawongse, 24 November 1930, TNA, KT 96.1.8.1/75.

League of Nations, according to which the age of consent was to be raised from twelve to fourteen years, but this draft was never enacted, a fact not communicated to the League. Minister of Foreign Affairs Prince Devawongse assumed that the whole plan of amending the penal code 'was laid aside and forgotten' when his father, the senior Prince Devawongse, became ill and passed away. Prince Devawongse worried that the League of Nations, therefore, 'considers the situation in Siam better than it is' and that the commission of enquiry's final report 'might not be beneficial to the standing of His Majesty's Government.' He concluded that the situation should be remedied before the commission submitted its final report and proposed to set up a drafting committee made up of the Ministries of Foreign Affairs, Interior, and Justice, in order to rapidly amend the penal code by raising the age limits.[78] This committee met within a matter of days and drew up amendments to the penal code, which were then presented to the cabinet council.[79] The cabinet council decided in early 1931 to set new age limits, with sections 241, 274 and 275 now stipulating that the trafficking and procurement of minors under eighteen (raised from twelve) years of age was a punishable offence with a maximum fine of 2,000 baht and up to five years of imprisonment. Although still three years below the limit stipulated by the International Convention of 1921, the limit of eighteen years of age went well beyond the fifteen years suggested by the inter-ministerial drafting committee, ostensibly to raise it at least as high as the Indian age limit. The minimum age of prostitution was also raised to eighteen in section 271 from the previous fifteen years of age, and sections 244, 245 and 246 finally marginally raised the age of consent from twelve to thirteen years of age.[80]

The League's enquiry was an important stepping stone on the path from the first League convention of 1921 to the second international conference on human trafficking and the resulting convention of October 1933. This second convention expanded the first by outlawing not only trafficking of underage girls, but of all women and girls regardless of their age. From the coming into force of this second international convention in August 1934, international trafficking of any woman or girl against her will, or even with her consent, was a punishable offence under international law. Siam, however, never signed or adhered to this convention of 1933, and only some twenty ratifications were deposited in total with the League before the outbreak of the Second World War.[81]

Only a few weeks after the commission of enquiry completed their extensive tour of Asia in March 1932, Siam witnessed profound political change with the overthrow of absolute monarchy in the coup d'état of June 1932. Among the manifold social and political changes this event brought about was a new approach to questions regarding the social position of women, which the civilian and military promoters of the

78 Draft Letter Minister of Foreign Affairs to Minister of Interior, 28 October 1930, TNA, KT 96.1.8.1/75. The miscommunication between Bangkok and Geneva and the abandoned amendment to the penal code is explained in detail in two lengthy memoranda by the Ministry of Foreign Affairs of 10 and 12 November 1930, both in TNA, KT 96.1.8.1/75.

79 Between 1925 and 1932, King Prajadhipok governed the country with the assistance of three councils, which had an advisory function: the supreme council of state, which was composed of five high-ranking princes, presided over by the king, and met weekly; the cabinet council, which was composed of all ministers and other high officials, including the members of the supreme council, presided over by the king, and met weekly; and the privy council, revived in 1927, which had been created in 1875 but had remained largely powerless; it was made up of members of the two above councils, plus some additional members appointed by the king. See a good overview of this system in Memorandum on Constitution in Siam, Enclosure in Dormer to Henderson, 23 January 1931, Doc. 23 and 24 (L 1271/89/ 405), BDFA, Part II, Series E, vol. 50, p. 17.

80 Note on meeting of cabinet council by Phraya Srivisarn (Deputy Minister of Foreign Affairs), 27 February 1931, TNA, KT 96.1.8.1/75.

81 League of Nations, Aims, Methods and Activity, p. 171. It is important to emphasise that the two League of Nations Conventions applied only to international trafficking of persons and did not regulate domestic trafficking, which has been a familiar phenomenon in Siam, where impoverished families in rural areas sold and continue to sell daughters to traffickers for the brothels in Bangkok and other urban centres. An estimate of 1991 put the number of children sold annually in Thailand at 60,000, see Gordon Thomas, Enslaved, New York: Pharos Books, 2nd ed., 1991, p. 258.

coup brought with them as they assumed power from the traditional royal elites. According to the new regime, women were to have equal voting rights as men, thereby preceding Japan by a decade and a half, female education was actively promoted and while it did not end the practice of men having minor wives or mistresses, polygamy was outlawed by the mid-1930s.[82]

In contrast to these liberalising tendencies, the 1930s also saw Siam's immigration legislation become increasingly restrictive towards Chinese immigrants in general and female immigrants in particular. Three years after the initial immigration act, the Immigration Act B.E. 2474 stipulated an immigration fee of 30 baht to be paid by every immigrant, in order to discourage the immigration of impoverished Chinese farmers. In addition, the act required all immigrants to be literate, thereby further discouraging immigration by uneducated Chinese peasants. The subsequent Immigration Act B.E. 2480 of 1937-38 increased the immigration fee to staggering 200 baht per person, making it nearly impossible for most potential Chinese immigrants to come to Siam. The Registration of Aliens Act B.E. 2479 (1936-37) already required all foreign nationals in the kingdom to register with the authorities and was applied not only to newly arriving immigrants but also retroactively to foreigners who were already living in Siam. In 1939 this act was amended and all foreigners from then on had to register annually with the Thai authorities. Together with other discriminatory measures enacted by the increasingly authoritarian administration, this led to an exodus of Chinese from Siam back to China by the late 1930s.[83]

As mentioned above, since the promulgation of the civil code in 1935, polygamy was illegal in Siam. This provision was a reaction to the increasing exposure of Siam's elite to Western morals, by the standards of which polygamy was judged to be uncivilised. Although polygamy did not end in practice with the promulgation of new legal codes, it did become less popular in Bangkok during the early 1930s, according to the *Bangkok Times*, and the paper cites mainly financial motives and changing attitudes – undoubtedly influenced by Western morals – among the young urban generation as the reasons behind this development.[84] When the League of Nations enquired yet again regarding the status of trafficking in humans in Siam in 1935, the government replied that women attain civil maturity at the age of twenty, while women from the age of fifteen were admitted to brothels as licensed prostitutes.[85]

The Bandung Conference on Trafficking in Women and Children, 1937

Immigration authorities, when acting alone, remained unable to effectively counter human trafficking in Asia. We have seen that isolated contacts, complaints or efforts to coordinate policies and procedures took place in the course of the 1920s and early 1930s between Siam, Hong

82 See also Barmé, *Woman, Man, Bangkok*, p. 232ff.

83 Landon, *Chinese in Thailand*, p. 204ff.

84 TNA, *Bangkok Times*, 3 February 1934. See also the chapter on polygamy in Barmé, *Woman, Man, Bangkok*, p. 157ff. and p. 233.

85 Circular Letter C.L.77(a).1935. IV of 14 June 1935 and Minister of Foreign Affairs to Secretary-General, 28 November 1935, LNA, R 4698/11B/21393/ 18248.

Kong, the Federated Malay States, and the Straits Settlements. But by the mid-1930s, the time was ripe for concerted action in the form of a regional conference of police and immigration authorities, the so-called central authorities. The facilitator and driving force behind this first Asian conference on trafficking in women and children was once again the League of Nations.

The plan to hold a conference on trafficking in women and children in Asia was brought forward during the 1933 General Assembly with a view to implementing the recommendations of the 1930-31 commission of enquiry. The conference was to be, in the opinion of a leading Thai official:

> ...the crowning result of several years of study and investigations conducted by [the] League Commission on the subject of the traffic in women and children in the Far East, and the methods of effectively combating the traffic and thereby promoting social security and welfare.[86]

Representatives of numerous League member states welcomed the plan. Among the advocates of a regional conference was also the Chinese delegation, which pointed particularly to the issue of female Russian refugees in Shanghai, an issue which Western governments cared about particularly in the context of human trafficking in Asia. The General Assembly of 1935 then took the formal decision to hold a regional Asian conference.[87] The Assembly first contemplated holding the conference in Singapore in conjunction with the annual meeting of the advisory council of the Singapore Bureau of the League of Nations Health Organisation, but then an invitation was received from the Netherlands government to host the event in Bandung on the island of Java.[88] The conference of the South, Southeast and East Asian central authorities met from 2 to 13 February 1937 with the following aims: to improve the exchange of information and the degree of cooperation between the central authorities of Asian countries and territories, to improve control of migration and to protect migrants from trafficking, to discuss the possibility of outlawing brothels in the region, to improve cooperation between officials and private organisations, to increase the number of female employees among law enforcement and immigration officials in the region, and finally, to enquire specifically into the situation of Russian women in the Far East who were in danger of becoming victims of trafficking.[89] These goals should be reached at the conference, albeit only through exchanges of information and discussions rather than by drawing up a formal agreement. This was one striking difference from the conference on trafficking in women and children held fifteen years earlier in Geneva, which drew up an international convention but lacked the authority the Bandung Conference had. While in 1921 diplomats had met at Geneva, at Bandung it was law enforcement and immigration

86 Speech of Prince Sakol to the Bangkok Rotary Club, *Siam Chronicle*, 13 March 1937, quoted in Landon, *Thailand in Transition*, p. 197.

87 See various correspondence covering the run-up to the conference in LNA, R 4695/11B/ 14852/14852 and TNA, KT 96.1.8.1/101 and 108; See also Cecil to Henderson, 27 September 1933, Doc. 114 (W 8702/43/ 98), BDFA, Part II, Series J, vol. 10.

88 Luang Pradist to Secretary-General, 16 March 1936 and Azcarate to Thai Ministry of Foreign Affairs, 14 April 1936, LNA R 4695/11B/14852/ 14852.

89 All relevant documents on the Conference of Central Authorities in Eastern Countries on Traffic in Women and Children in LNA, serial documents nos.C.228.M. 164.1937.IV.; C. 476.M.318.1937. IV.; C.516.M.357.1937.IV. The minutes of the conference can also be found in TNA, SR 0201.17/14 (Part 2 of 3) and in LNA, Serial Document C.476.M.318.1937.IV.

officials who sat around the conference table, people who had an intimate knowledge of the issues and who were directly in charge of implementing national polices to combat trafficking in persons. A further difference between the two conferences was that by 1937 a wealth of statistical, legal and empirical material had been collected in Asia and around the globe on human trafficking, giving the government representatives in Bandung a much clearer picture of the extent and the details of the problems.

Apart from the Netherlands Indies, the following governments sent representatives of their central authorities to Bandung: Siam, Great Britain (for the Straits Settlements, the Federated Malay States and Hong Kong), China, Japan, France (for Indochina), India, Portugal (for Macao) and finally, with the status of an observer, the United States (for the Philippines). A number of non-governmental organisations also took part in the conference as observers, such as the Salvation Army, the YMCA and YWCA, the International Missionary Council and the Pan-Pacific Women's Association. The conference proceedings were coordinated by Eric Ekstrand of the League Secretariat, who was elected secretary-general of the conference. The participation of Japan was remarkable because its resignation from the League of Nations in 1933 over its invasion of Manchuria had formally taken effect in 1935. This, therefore, highlights the importance and high hopes attached to the Bandung Conference among Asian administrations. As with earlier regional League of Nations conferences in Bangkok and Singapore, Siam, which had only recently regained its full judicial sovereignty from the colonial powers, participated in the Bandung deliberations on an equal footing with with representatives of Western colonial governments.

In preparation for the conference, a string of meetings took place in Bangkok at the Ministry of Interior and the Ministry of Foreign Affairs, as well as at cabinet level. The cabinet decided in December 1936 that Prince Sakol should represent Siam at Bandung in his capacity as adviser to the Ministry of Interior together with Colonel Phra Bicharn Nalakitch, Deputy Director-General of the Police Department under the same Ministry.[90] Because of the likelihood that this matter would come up at Bandung, the cabinet also took up an issue which had been discussed between the Ministries of Interior and Foreign Affairs for some time already, namely whether Siam should enact a law against procurers. While the Ministry of Foreign Affairs was in favour of such a law because it would underscore Siam's progressive image on the international stage, the Ministry of Interior maintained that since brothels in Siam were licensed and legal, procurement was also legal. On 11 November 1936, the cabinet followed the Ministry of Interior and decided against such a law but also decided to set up a committee to investigate the possible abolition of licensed brothels, thereby responding to a trend among international advocates of the fight against human trafficking and

90 Minutes of Cabinet Meeting, 11 November 1936; Minutes of Cabinet Meeting, 12 December B.E. 2479 (1936), TNA, SR 0201.17/14 (Part 1 of 3).

anticipating the discussions at Bandung.[91] At a meeting in the Ministry of Interior on the last day of 1936, the agenda for Bandung was prepared in detail. The issue of effective immigration control quickly emerged as the crucial element for any effective action against human trafficking. Participants at the meeting also agreed that Bandung was of particular interest for Siam with regard to the question of abolishing licensed brothels.[92] Following another cabinet meeting on the Bandung Conference on 6 January 1937, Minister of Foreign Affairs Luang Pradist met with Prince Sakol for a final briefing on the government's position. The main points of these instructions were an agreement for closer cooperation between the Bangkok immigration authorities and officials at the ports of origin of incoming vessels, a willingness to contact the few charitable associations in Siam for support in caring for the victims of trafficking, a committment to employ more female immigration officers, and the acceptance of abolishing brothels as a long-term goal. On this final point, however, Prince Sakol was to make it clear that such a policy could only serve as a long-term goal, because any immediate abolition of legal brothels would rob the government of its control over the brothels and the prostitutes, and would, therefore, likely lead to an increase in crime and venereal diseases.[93]

At the Bandung Conference during February 1937 the British delegates, while conceding that Singapore had become the regional hub for trafficking in persons, continued to demand stricter border controls from the Thai authorities. But in spite of the attention which trafficking across the Thai-Malay border was receiving by the British administration in Malaya, the number of persons involved was marginal compared to the large-scale influx of Chinese women into Siam as well as into the British territories on the Malay Peninsula. Prince Sakol explained that in Siam the sex ratio among the Chinese population had changed in recent years from three to one in favour of men to now two to one, due to both the increasing immigration of Chinese women and the decreasing immigration of men. Nevertheless, he continued, stricter immigration laws had very recently led to a decrease in female Chinese immigrants, and also of Chinese prostitutes in Siam.

The existence of licensed brothels was seen by the majority of conference participants as one of the main reasons for the trafficking of women and children. The abolition of licensed brothels and tolerated prostitution, as it was being enforced in Singapore since the late 1920s, was the ultimate goal of the conference. The Thai delegation submitted a draft resolution to the effect that the conference declared itself unanimously in favour of abolition of licensed brothels as a long-term goal, which was ultimately accepted by all delegates, in spite of reservations expressed by the delegates from Japan, India, China, and France. The conference participants were also aware that an eventual abolition had to 'be accompanied by administrative, medical and social

91 Minutes of Cabinet Meeting, 18 November B.E. 2479 (1936), TNA, SR 0201.17/14 (Part 1 of 3).

92 Report on Meeting at Ministry of Interior on 12 December B.E. 2479 (1936) on the Conference of Central Authorities at Bandung, 5 January B.E. 2479 (1937), TNA, SR 0201.17/14 (Part 1 of 3).

93 Minutes of the 68th Cabinet Meeting, 6 January B.E. 2479 (1937) and Memorandum by Ministry of Foreign Affairs, 12 January B.E. 2479 (1937), TNA, SR 0201.17/14 (Part 1 of 3).

measures in order to guarantee the permanence of its success'.[94] It appears that by setting the maximum goal of complete abolition, Siam's delegates had skilfully averted any more practical steps towards the abolition of brothels being adopted instead.

Anne Guthrie, who participated at the conference as an observer for the YWCA in Manila, gave the following account of Prince Sakol's role:

> Prince Sakol Varavarn, adviser to the Ministry of Interior of Siam, and one of the most active delegates at the Conference, spoke especially on this point [abolition of licensed brothels]. His oriental background combined with English education made him acutely aware of all the problems involved and the difficulty of finding solutions, yet at the same time he was one of the delegates most eager to work toward the creation of a better moral and social order...[95]

Prince Sakol and A.B. Jordan, delegate of the Straits Settlements and the Federated Malay States, were the main promoters of another idea, which was formulated as one of the final recommendations of the conference, namely to set up a Far Eastern bureau of the League to co-ordinate the fight against human trafficking. This bureau, which was intended to operate in a similar fashion to the Singapore Bureau of the League of Nations Health Organisation, should collect and distribute relevant information, so that every national central authority could identify traffickers who had been prosecuted or who were being searched for in another country. Although different League bodies discussed and further developed the proposal, the technical and financial details for such a bureau could not be solved before the outbreak of the war and, accordingly, the proposal did not materialise. The Bandung Conference further recommended improving controls on ships and in ports and involving ship owners in this process. It also suggested that all immigration authorities introduce the provision of photographs for the identification of female and minor emigrants, as practised in Hong Kong.[96]

Upon their return to Siam, Phra Bicharn and Prince Sakol submitted a very detailed report to the Minister of Interior and the cabinet, in which they rightly pointed out the positive Thai role during the Bandung deliberations.[97] At its outset, the report highlighted the role of the Thai delegates in the discussion on setting up a regional centre for better coordination of the national efforts against human trafficking. But the report conceded that Thai immigration authorities were not yet able to introduce compulsory photo identification papers for immigrants like British authorities in Hong Kong. The report also conceded that Bangkok was the only major port in Asia which did not have a shelter for the victims of trafficking and urged the government to take action in this regard. As far as the central discussion on the abolition of brothels was concerned, Phra Bicharn and Prince Sakol pointed out in their report

94 LNA, serial document no. C.476. M.318.1937.IV.

95 Anne Guthrie in TNA, *Bangkok Times*, 29 July 1937. On Siam's representation at the conference see TNA, SR 0201.17/14 (Parts 1-3); see also Phraya Rajawangsan to Ekstrand, 17 December 1936, LNA, R 4695/11B/14852/14852.

96 Annex 2 to the Minutes of the Bandung Conference entitled 'Creation of an Information Bureau in the East: Report of the Sub-committee', LNA, Serial Document C.476.M.318.1937. IV, p. 78.

97 Report on the Bandung Conference, dated 2 March B.E. 2479 (1937), submitted to Cabinet by Minister of Interior on 6 March B.E. 2479 (1937), TNA, SR 0201.17/14 (2 of 3).

that the adopted resolution corresponded exactly with the instructions they had received from the cabinet, i.e. to commit to abolition as the long-term goal without committing to any immediate steps. That the Thai delegates were invited by the conference chairman to a private dinner together with the delegates of Britain and Portugal on the day after the conference also featured in their report, as did a number of compliments they received for their active and constructive roles during the event.

The Bandung Conference clearly had an impact on public opinion in Bangkok. Shortly after the end of the conference, several Bangkok newspapers ran articles on the sale of Thai children by their parents, with the former then typically ending up in brothels. A *Bangkok Times* article commended the government for having set up the legal framework in the penal code to allow for the severe punishment of traffickers and went on to comment on the Bandung Conference:

> Siam also has membership in the League of Nations, one of whose Committees has recently been investigating, in Java, the question of the traffic in women and children, a Committee on which Siam was represented. The recommendations of that Committee are being awaited with some interest in the various countries concerned, but these recommendations must of necessity be international in conception and operation. In Bangkok, however, the problem is more in the nature of a domestic one...[98]

Nevertheless, the government did not manage to create awareness among the general public for combating the practice of selling girls from poor families in rural areas during the lifetime of the League, a practice which remains an issue of concern today.[99]

The Bandung Conference also had an impact on the perception of the League in Siam, where it was acknowledged that holding

> ...this Conference in the Far East is not only an indication that the work of the League in the social and humanitarian field is as actively pursued as ever, but also that the League does not restrict its efforts in this respect to any geographical area, and that it tries to deal with the problem wherever the need is most acute.[100]

With regard to human trafficking and prostitution, the view was expressed among the Bangkok elite in the late 1930s that 'the government hopes to better conditions in Thailand by co-operating in the plans for social advancement as laid down by the League of Nations Conference.' It is, of course, no coincidence that social advancement was also the main thrust of the public awareness and modernisation campaigns initiated in these years by Luang Phibun and Luang Vichit Vadhakarn, campaigns which were to dominate public discussion for much of the following years. One important aspect of this emphasis on

98 TNA, *Bangkok Times*, 3 March 1937.

99 It is quite interesting that this topic was a matter of public discussion in Siam as early as the 1930s; TNA, *Bangkok Times*, 16 April 1937. A case of selling a girl into prostitution which aroused public opinion immediately after the Bandung Conference is recalled in detail by Landon, *Siam in Transition*, p. 199f. Prince Sakol had expressed his admiration for such provisions for victimised children in Asian colonies and the desire that Siam could also claim to possess such provisions; see Minutes of the Bandung Conference, LNA, Serial Document C.476. M.318.1937.IV., p. 30.

100 TNA, *Bangkok Times*, 3 March 1937.

social advancement and 'Thai-ness' was an increasing anti-foreign sentiment, which was directed mainly against the Chinese minority in Siam. As a result, immigration procedures were tightened and, as mentioned earlier, the number of Chinese immigrants, male and female, dropped sharply by the late 1930s. While, according to Skinner, some 155,000 Chinese immigrated legally to Siam in 1927-28, this figure fell to only 25,000 in 1939-40.[101]

As in the field of public health, much of the impact of the League of Nations' activities on Siam's society during the 1920s and the 1930s was due to the activities of Prince Sakol, who rallied to deal with human trafficking, 'not, as he happily stated, from the point of view of equality and liberty, but from that of humanity.' After returning from Bandung, Prince Sakol gave lectures, wrote letters and used personal contacts to raise awareness of the issue in the Thai capital. As he outlined at a lecture to the Bangkok Rotary Club on 4 March and in an interview with the *Bangkok Times* the following days, his goal was to promote, as a result of the Bandung Conference, the 'four R's': re-education, not only of the prostitute but of the public, rescue, rehabilitation, and refuge. One initiative, for which Prince Sakol won the financial support of Prince (*Phra Ong Chao*) Aditya Dibabha, head of the Council of Regency, was to open a first mother-and-child home for prostitutes with newborn children. In order to counter the growing number of abandoned infants in Bangkok, mothers could find shelter at this house with their newborn children and receive training to enable them to later find employment as maids, cooks, etc. The home started with room for twenty-five mothers with newborn children and was headed by two female volunteers who had studied and been trained in social work in Europe. Prince Sakol urged widespread propaganda for the home and the whole issue of prostitution and human trafficking, in order to 'have a strong body of public opinion, seeking to eradicate an evil which all nations are desirous of abolishing'.[102]

The Bandung Conference also triggered action by the law enforcement agencies. The Thai government reported to the League that in 1937-38 eighteen people had been convicted for trafficking in women and children in Siam, of which seventeen had received prison sentences.[103] In the months after the conference, 'the Police Department of Siam have instituted a vigorous campaign against the nefarious practice obtaining in Siam of the sale of children, particularly females, ostensibly for domestic service, but to become, in time, probably inmates of brothels'.[104]

However, in spite of all the above-mentioned domestic, regional and international efforts, by the end of the 1930s, awareness for the plight of victims of human trafficking remained very limited and confined to parts of the urban, internationally-oriented elite. While for them the fight against human trafficking became important as a part of their efforts to

101 Skinner, *Chinese Society in Thailand*, p. 173.
102 TNA, *Bangkok Times*, 5 March 1937.
103 League of Nations Advisory Committee on Social Questions, Summary of Annual Reports for 1937/38, LNA, Serial Document C.68.M.30.1939.IV., p. 19.
104 TNA, *Bangkok Times*, 16 April 1937.

turn Siam into a Western-inspired modern and civilised country, it was of no particular concern to the general public. This assessment, which holds true to a certain extent today, and is not limited to Thailand, is reflected in a *Bangkok Times* editorial of 1937:

> [I]n Siam, so in the remainder of the East, the primary need is the awakening of the public conscience by propaganda and the establishment of voluntary organizations, whose special care will be these unfortunate and unwanted children who, unless effective measures are introduced, must face the prospect of drudgery till the end of their natural lives.[105]

The committee considering abolition of brothels, which had been set up by the cabinet, met again after the Bandung Conference under the chairmanship of Prince Sakol to examine the League of Nations draft international convention for suppressing the exploitation of prostitution of 1936. The committee judged that an application of this convention, which was aimed specifically at procurers and traffickers, would be impossible under the existing penal code in Siam and that it would require the immediate abolition of licensed brothels. The Bandung Conference had, however, endorsed the Thai approach of gradual abolition accompanied by public health and educational measures rather than an abrupt closure of brothels. Ultimately, the committee recommended that Siam not accept the draft international convention.[106]

In early 1940 the registration of brothels was suspended upon the recommendation of Prince Sakol's committee, and Siam followed the path of Singapore, which had closed licensed brothels already during the late 1920s in response to pressure from the League of Nations and women's rights groups in England, and had thereby deprived itself of the only means of control it possessed. As Warren has shown, '[closing] the brothels after 1927 was a fatal mistake. It left prostitutes to operate by and large clandestinely as individuals, while VD continued to wreck havoc upon the Chinese population right up to the eve of the fall of Singapore'.[107] Finally, by 1960, prostitution was declared illegal in Thailand, a decision which ironically served almost as a starting signal for prostitution to flourish like never before, fuelled by the arrival of large numbers of American servicemen. According to Jeffrey, there were an estimated 171,000 prostitutes in Thailand in 1964, compared to estimated 20,000 by the late 1930s.[108]

Conclusions

How Thailand is represented on the world stage is an issue of everyday discussion that plays out in national politics, particularly around the issue of prostitution. Within this context, prostitution policy becomes a forum for debates over national identity and foreign image over who Thais are and how the world perceives them.[109]

105 TNA, *Bangkok Times*, 16 April 1937.

106 Memorandum of the Committee Considering Abolition of Brothels by Prince Sakol, 16 March B.E. 2479 (1937), TNA, SR 0201.17/14 (Part 2 of 3).

107 Warren, *Ah Ku and Karayuki-san*, p. 177. See also Manderson, *Sickness and the State*, p. 199f.

108 Jeffrey, *Sex and Borders*, p. 37.

109 Ibid., p. ix.

This assessment was made by Leslie Ann Jeffrey in 2002 and as this chapter has shown, it could just as well have been made during the 1920s or 1930s. Policies on prostitution and against trafficking in persons, as well as policies relating to Chinese immigration were regarded by the political elite in Siam as highly important in portraying the image of Siam at the League of Nations and the Western world in general. We have seen that during the two interwar decades for a government to be progressive and civilised meant also to pursue modern policies on human trafficking and prostitution. In this context, the issues were largely forced on the Bangkok government by Geneva. Human trafficking was originally an issue which, if it concerned the Thai elite at all, was only a corollary of immigration policies regarding the Chinese minority. But policy makers in Bangkok, having rushed into signing the 1921 League of Nations convention perhaps without an extensive awareness of the implications of their actions, quickly took up human trafficking as a issue which needed to be addressed with the instruments of modern, Western law, in order to underscore Siam's sovereignty and demonstrate its modernity. The first national legislation to suppress human trafficking of 1928, promulgated amidst increasing League pressure, was a major milestone in this regard. During the 1930s a number of changes took place, beginning with a further improved legal framework for prosecuting traffickers and protecting their victims, and leading to an increased awareness of the necessity of protecting children from trafficking, and to serious reviews of government policies regarding prostitution.

The League of Nations did not immediately focus on trafficking of Asian women and children during the early 1920s, but rather evolved from Western concern for Western women who were the victims of human trafficking in Asia, to broader concern for non-Western victims of human trafficking. The League's landmark enquiry into human trafficking in Asia in 1930 marked a watershed in this respect. The enquiry was the first comprehensive assessment of the problem of subsequent human trafficking and government policies in Asia. The Conference of Central Authorities in Bandung in 1937 was the high point of regional cooperation to suppress human trafficking under the League's auspices before the Second World War. Through its large-scale enquiry in 1930 and the Bandung Conference in 1937, the League took up, as in to the case of opium smoking, a specific Asian problem of the times, namely the trafficking in Chinese women and children. And from 1920 the League stimulated, as a prerequisite to these actions, the collection of relevant data, information, and legislation from Siam and other Asian territories, while in parallel increasing a basic awareness among policy makers and parts of Asian societies of the problem of human trafficking and the other social effects of prostitution.

By encouraging unified law enforcement structures and immigration standards, the League facilitated, to a certain extent, an early form of regional cooperation within Southeast Asia. This regional cooperation took place between independent Asian governments and European colonial administrations, thereby highlighting both the League's remarkable role as a platform for cooperation during colonial times and the seriousness of the problem. It was the extent of human trafficking in Asia and the severity of the situation for independent and colonial administrations alike, which brought Siam and the surrounding colonies to search for regional strategies against human trafficking, inadequate immigration procedures, and unacceptable living conditions of prostitutes.

The League of Nations' work against international trafficking in humans, in the words of former British Prime Minister and Foreign Secretary Arthur Balfour in 1921, 'the most abominable stain upon civilisation which it is possible to conceive', paved the way for the much more elaborate and effective international control mechanisms, which were set up after 1945 and have, on a very simple human level, undoubtedly saved many an underage girl from a terrible fate.[110] The United Nations Convention for the Suppression of the Traffic in Persons and the Exploitation of the Prostitution of Others was concluded in 1949, came into force two years later and consolidated all previous international agreements and conventions of 1904, 1910, 1921, 1933 and the draft of 1936.[111] Nevertheless, until today neither the League of Nations nor the United Nations have managed to rally member states to stage an effort comparable to the fight against drug trafficking. A recent study conjectures that 'perhaps this comes about because the social costs fall on some of the world's poorer countries, unlike drugs which are largely a rich country problem'.[112]

Siam's involvement in the international cooperation of states to suppress human trafficking led to a League-induced change of laws and attitudes in Siam, as well to an improvement in the living conditions of some individuals. However, while acknowledging the progress made before the Second World War, this must be put into the context of the decades since the 1960s, when the American rest and recreation programmes during the unfolding Vietnam War led to a virtual explosion in the number of women entering prostitution in Thailand and an explosion of the problem of trafficking. In pre-war Siam the issues relating to prostitution and human trafficking were much more limited in scope and numbers; today human trafficking is both a major inbound and outbound problem in Thailand effecting unprecedented numbers of Thai, Cambodian, and Burmese adults and minors of both sexes. A main barrier to effective action against trafficking in humans remains the criminalisation of prostitution in Thailand, which was declared illegal in 1960 with the Prostitution Suppression Act under the Sarit regime, at the same time that opium smoking was also outlawed.

110 Lord Balfour's statement is quoted in Bristow, *Prostitution and Prejudice*, p. 297.

111 Ghosh, *Prostitution in Thailand*, p. 179f. and 194ff.

112 Pasuk, Sungsidh and Nualnoi, *Guns, Girls, Gambling, Ganja*, p. 190.

Siam's restrictive and oppressive policies towards male and female Chinese immigrants and the Chinese minority population during the late 1930s and early 1940s returned to haunt the post-war Thai administration in the context of the League of Nations, or, more precisely, of the League's successor, the United Nations, as Landon pointed out in 1972:

> The Chinese problem emerged sharply after World War II in January 1946 when Thailand was faced with the necessity of establishing relations with the Republic of China in order to become a member of the United Nations in which China was listed as one of the major powers with the privilege of veto. Thailand's long membership in the League of Nations made it unthinkable to the Thai leadership that Thailand would not be a member of the successor United Nations.[113]

The analysis of certain international aspects of human trafficking and prostitution policy in Siam before the Second World War in this chapter leads to the same assessment as that of Scot Barmé in his study of domestic socio-cultural developments, that 'Thailand's "modernity" is, in fact, far older than generally claimed, and is much more of an indigenous phenomenon, albeit one that evolved in response to European models, than the result of post-World War II political and cultural impositions from the West'.[114]

As we have seen, in 1921 the government of Siam signed the first international convention on human trafficking in order to be regarded as modern and civilised by the international community. Over eighty years later, on 5 April 2005, the Thai government established the National Human Trafficking Control Board, which, according to *The Nation*, 'signalled a major shift in the country's policy towards human trafficking'; the same paper also made it unmistakably clear that 'unless the government backs it [the Board] up with forceful action, Thailand's status as a civilised member of the international community will continue to be questioned'.[115] Attitudes and motivations today remain strikingly similar to those in 1921.

---

113 Landon, *Chinese in Thailand*, p. ii.

114 Barmé, *Woman, Man, Bangkok*, p. 257.

115 *The Nation*, 7 April 2005.

Prince Varnvaidya Voravarn, Permanent
Representative of Siam to the League of Nations,
1928-30 (Courtesy of Paisarn Piemmattawat).

APPEL NOMINAL

Question discutée *Assemblée extraordinaire*

Date *24 février* à *4 hm 25m*

Numéro de la séance

	PAYS	OUI	NON	ABSTENTION
1	Union Sud-Africaine.	/		
2	Albanie.	/		
C 3	Allemagne.	/		
4	République Argentine.			
5	Australie.	/		
6	Autriche.	/		
7	Belgique.	/		
8	Bolivie.			
C 9	Empire Britannique.	/		
10	Bulgarie.	/		
11	Canada.	/		
12	Chili.			
C 13	Chine.	oui		
14	Colombie.	/		
15	Cuba.			
16	Danemark.	/		
17	République Dominicaine.			
C 18	Espagne.	/		
19	Estonie.	/		
20	Éthiopie.			
21	Finlande.	/		
C 22	France.	/		
23	Grèce.	/		
C 24	Guatémala.	/		
25	Haïti.	/		
26	Honduras.			
27	Hongrie.	/		
28	Inde.	/		
29	Irak.			
C 30	État libre d'Irlande.	/		
C 31	Italie.	/		
C 32	Japon.		non	
33	Lettonie.	/		
34	Libéria.			
35	Lithuanie.	/		
36	Luxembourg.	/		
C 37	États-Unis du Mexique.	/		
38	Nicaragua.			
C 39	Norvège.	/		
40	Nouvelle-Zélande.	/		
C 41	Panama.			
42	Paraguay.			
43	Pays-Bas.	/		
44	Pérou.			
45	Perse.	/		
C 46	Pologne.	/		
47	Portugal.	/		
48	Roumanie.	/		
49	Salvador.			
50	Siam.			/
51	Suède.	/		
52	Suisse.	/		
C 53	Tchécoslovaquie.	/		
54	Turquie.	/		
55	Uruguay.	/		
56	Venezuela.	/		
57	Yougoslavie.	/		
	54 (+3)			
	40 (+14)			
	C = membres du Conseil = 14 Totaux	1 41	1	1

Signature *[signature] 24-II-33*

ont pris part au vote :
Membres du Conseil autres que les Parties au différend   12
autres membres de la Société, pour :   29
abstentions :   1
Parties au différend pour :   1
contre :   1
Total   44

Original list of votes in the Extraordinary General Assembly meeting on 24 February 1933, in which Siam was the sole country to abstain (League of Nations Archives).

6

Collective Security

Siam's independence and territorial integrity were no longer threatened by expansionist European powers at the time the League of Nations came into existence in 1920. As detailed in Chapter 2, Thai foreign policy makers were, therefore, able to concentrate on regaining full sovereignty, which was limited by the unequal treaties Siam had been compelled to conclude with Western states and Japan during the mid-nineteenth century. Commercial autonomy was restored during the mid-1920s, when Siam was increasingly integrating politically, primarily through the League of Nations, and economically into the Western-dominated international system. Thai foreign policy during the fifth, sixth, and seventh reigns meant predominantly balancing Western interests, namely those of Great Britain, France, the United States, and at times Germany, with a bias towards Great Britain, particularly in commercial and financial policies. The coup d'état of 1932 and the resulting changes in the ruling elite in Siam did not fundamentally change Thai foreign policy. It remained focused on juggling the various western interests and influences, albeit with Japan playing an increasingly important economic and political role for the Thai elite. Siam's foreign relations towards the most influential Western states have been described in detail above, therefore some remarks on relations with China and Japan will suffice to complete the picture, before turning to the League's collective security system.

Siam did not have formal diplomatic relations with China during the interwar period. It had stopped sending tributary missions to China from 1853 as a result of the decline in power of the last imperial dynasty. Since that time, a large number of Chinese immigrants had come to Siam in search of better living conditions. By the late 1930s an estimated 600,000 Chinese nationals and some 2.5 million Thais were ethnically and culturally Chinese.[1] Although rumours regarding the re-establishment of diplomatic relations surfaced occasionally during the 1920s and 1930s, Siam did not respond to Chinese invitations in this regard because of the large Chinese minority in the kingdom, which controlled a very large share of the commercial activities in Siam and which the government did not want to provide with an authoritative spokesperson.[2] On the other hand, during the period of the Mukden

1 E. Bruce Reynolds, 'International Orphans' – The Chinese in Thailand during World War II', *Journal of Southeast Asian Studies*, 2 (1997), pp. 365-388, here: p. 365, note 1.

2 Files of the British legation in Bangkok suggest that the fact that both Siam and China were members of the League of Nations created a degree of pressure on Thai policy makers to at least consider the possibility of re-establishing diplomatic relations with China during the 1920s and 1930s, and that this was one of the reasons for the recurring rumours. See, for example, Waterlow to Chamberlain, 21 July 1926, Doc. 222 (F 3499/3499/40), BDFA, Part II, Series E, vol. 49, p. 295ff.

Incident in the fall of 1931, Siam participated in the international relief effort for the victims of the disastrous flooding in China by sending 190 tons of rice and other goods.[3] In the course of the 1930s, Thai governments successively began curbing Chinese immigration and commercial activities, until by the end of the decade anti-Chinese policies became part of a chauvinistic nationalist programme, aiming at driving Chinese influence out of commercial activities in Siam and suppressing Chinese cultural activities. Intriguingly, while they did not maintain bilateral diplomatic relations, Thai and Chinese delegates worked together in a League of Nations framework on countless occasions during the 1920s and 1930s, thereby amounting to a de facto Thai recognition of China. After the Second World War, Siam finally agreed to formal relations, when China became a permanent member of the new United Nations Security Council and Siam required China's consent to become a United Nations member, Siam's paramount foreign policy goal. Thai-Chinese diplomatic relations were established with the Treaty of Amity signed in January 1946.[4]

Thai relations with Japan, on the contrary, were formalised in the first treaty of friendship and commerce in 1898, which was renewed along the lines of the treaty with the United States in 1924. Relations with Japan played a minor role for Siam during the 1920s in comparison with its relations with the West, but became economically important by the end of that decade. According to Virginia Thompson, between 1929 and 1932, some eighty-five percent of Japan's rice imports originated in Siam.[5] But it was mainly in the period following the economic depression, between 1932 and 1937, when Siam's purchasing power was low that, according to William Swan, low-priced Japanese goods became an attractive alternative to Western products.[6] Japan's self-confident foreign policy also found an increasing number of admirers among the Thai military elite during the 1930s, and when at the end of the decade Luang Phibun was in a position to take power from the more pro-Western civilian bureaucrats, Japan became the most important international reference point for Thai foreign policy. Twenty years earlier, in 1920, the world looked very different from 1940 and Siam joined the League of Nations not only with regard to social and technical policy areas, but also for the League's core task of providing collective security to Siam and all its other member states.

The League's collective security system

Collective Security is a system for the maintenance of international peace, in which states agree that any attack on one member states is considered an attack on all and will result in a collective response. The system aims at dissuading any member state or non-member state from launching an attack out of fear of a massive response by all. After the horrific experience of the First World War, the League of Nations was

3 Prince Sakol to Rajchman, 4 December 1931, LNA, R 5934/8A/32334/30816. Siam did not, however, follow a League request to furnish personnel for epidemic control in China after the floods.

4 See also Anuson Chinvanno, *Thailand's Policies towards China, 1949-54*, Basingstoke and London: Macmillan, 1992.

5 Thompson, Thailand, p. xxv and 102ff.

6 William L. Swan, 'Japanese Economic Relations with Siam: Aspects of Their Historical Development 1884 to 1942', Ph.D. Thesis, Australian National University, 1986, p. v; see also Edward Thadeus Flood, 'Japan's Relations with Thailand, 1928-1941', Ph.D. Thesis, University of Washington, 1967, vol. 1, p. 30ff.

established as the first such system, with articles X to XVII of the League covenant laying out how the collective security system was to function and by which means it was to deter any potential aggressor. Member states were obliged to protect each member's territorial integrity and political independence (article X), and the League was obliged to take up any armed conflict between states, or even the mere threat of war (article XI). Parties to a conflict were obliged to submit themselves to the League's arbitration and to refrain from resorting to war (articles XII, XIII and XV). Should a state nevertheless wage an aggressive act against another state, League members could apply collective sanctions (article XVI). The League did not, however, have any troops at its disposal to bring about or maintain international peace. Moreover, the sanctions mechanism was purposely kept vague, which made it a matter of interpretation as to whether sanction were to be applied against an aggressor or not.[7]

The League's collective security mechanism was reinforced in 1928 by the General Treaty for Renunciation of War as an Instrument of National Policy, more commonly known as the Non-Aggression Pact, the Briand-Kellogg Pact or Pact of Paris.[8] This Pact of Paris was particularly significant because it legally bound the United States to the collective security system of the League, despite the US, it will be recalled, having tragically not become a member after the First World War because of isolationist attitudes among American legislators at the time. Within the League's collective security system, the General Assembly was the highest decision-making body. However, the League Council played a very strong executive role in political and security issues from the outset, perhaps more than in any other field of the League's work. Similar to today's UN Security Council, it was largely the League Council which handled international conflict management on behalf of the organisation. On the Council, it was predominantly the permanent members Great Britain, France, Japan, Germany (from 1926) and Italy, complemented by a number of rotating smaller member states, who de facto had to make the collective security system work.

The implicit guarantee contained in the League's collective security system was to deter powerful states, which would be able to stage unilateral attacks, and to guard small states, which could fall victim to larger states without collective protection.[9] Siam was precisely one of those small states for which the collective security system was fundamentally designed, as it was potentially unable to withstand any of its immediate or regional neighbours in the event of an armed attack. But Siam in theory not only received protection from this system, but, as a member of the League of Nations, was also expected, in very practical terms, to contribute to the security of other League members. And while Siam's independence was never threatened between 1920 and the late 1930s, a number of other League of Nations member states endured various attacks on their

7 For the text of the Covenant of the League of Nations see LNA, League of Nations, *Official Journal*, February 1920, p. 3ff.

8 For the text of the Pact of Paris see Knipping, von Mangoldt and Rittberger, *System der Vereinten Nationen*, p. 1678ff. Siam adhered to the Pact of Paris on 16 January 1929.

9 Robert L. Rothstein, *Alliances and Small Powers*, New York and London: Columbia University Press, 1968, p. 221ff.; Walters, *League of Nations*; Northedge, *League of Nations*; Claude, *Swords to Ploughshares*; James T. Shotwell, 'Security', in Harriet E. Davis (ed.), *Pioneers in World Order: An American Appraisal of the League of Nations*, New York: Columbia University Press, 2nd ed., 1945, pp. 26-41; Egerton, Collective Security; Sally Marks, 'The Small States at Geneva', *World Affairs: Woodrow Wilson and the League of Nations*, Part One, 157, 4 (Spring 1995), pp. 191-196; Lorna Lloyd, 'The League of Nations and the Settlement of Disputes', *World Affairs: Woodrow Wilson and the League of Nations*, Part One, 157, 4 (Spring 1995), pp. 160-174.

independence and even succumbed to aggressors. During its lifetime, the League of Nations dealt with forty-four international conflicts.[10] It is the story of some of these tragic and violent international conflicts, and the role Siam played as one of the states obliged to uphold collective security, which make up this chapter.

Siam's involvement in political and security issues at Geneva falls into three distinct phases. Preoccupied with treaty revision and learning the ropes of multilateral diplomacy, Siam stayed completely out of any efforts to resolve the international conflicts on the League's agenda during the first decade of collective security (1920-31). An internationally more self-confident and rapidly modernising Siam then became involved more than it had intended in some of the dramatic international conflicts during the second decade (1932-39). Finally, the League become dormant, and Siam followed all other countries in turning away from the collective security system during the last phase (1940-46). Interestingly, these three phases also mirror important changes in Siam's domestic and international politics as well as providing a useful structure for the understanding of the genesis of the League's collective security system itself, from successful beginnings (1920s) through tragic failures (1930s) to, finally, irrelevance (1940s).

Conflicts before the League of Nations in the 1920s

The League of Nations' new system of collective security was put to the test virtually from the first day of the organisation's existence. A total of twenty-six international conflicts came before the League Council during its first decade, the large majority of which were European conflicts. Arguably the most significant of these conflicts were those between Sweden and Finland over the Aaland Islands (1920-21), the Tacna-Arica Dispute between Bolivia, Peru, and Chile (1920), the Corfu Conflict between Italy and Greece (1923), the Mosul Affair between Turkey and Iraq (1924-25), the Greco-Bulgarian Frontier Incident (1925), and the Gran Chaco Dispute between Bolivia and Paraguay, which began in 1928 but remained before the League until 1938.[11] The international conflicts of the 1920s were dealt with by the League Council, not by the League Assembly. As Siam was never a Council member, it was easy for its representatives to stay clear of any entanglement in these disputes, which did not touch on any interests vital to the Southeast Asian kingdom. However, it is also significant that Siam did not seek to become actively involved in solving any of these conflicts for the sake of supporting a collective security system from which it also benefited. Indeed, the files of the Foreign Ministry in Bangkok reveal a clear lack of interest in these conflicts.[12] We can, accordingly, ascribe a clear limit of the degree to which Siam was willing to acquire international recognition and prestige and this limit definitely lay below the threshold of becoming involved in international conflict management.

10 For a comprehensive list of all international conflicts before the League see Knipping, von Mangoldt and Rittberger, *System der Vereinten Nationen*, p. 1374ff.

11 James Barros, *The Aaland Islands Question: Its Settlement by the League of Nations*, New Haven (CT): Yale University Press, 1968; James Barros, *The Corfu Incident of 1923: Mussolini and the League of Nations*, Princeton (NJ): Princeton University Press, 1965; Vera Torunsky, 'Der Korfu-Konflikt von 1923', in Jost Dülffer, Hans-Otto Mühleisen and Vera Torunsky (eds), *Inseln als Brennpunkte internationaler Politik, Konfliktbewältigung im Wandel des internationalen Systems, 1890-1984: Kreta, Korfu, Zypern*, Köln: Verlag Wissenschaft und Politik, 1986, pp. 60-96; James Barros, *The League of Nations and the Great Powers: The Greek-Bulgarian Incident 1925*, Oxford: Clarendon, 1970; Christopher J. Bartlett, *The Global Conflict: The International Rivalry of the Great Powers, 1880-1970*, London and New York: Longman, 1984, p. 107ff. As a League member Siam was regularly informed of relevant developments in these conflicts. See, for example, on Siam and the Greco-Bulgarian Frontier Incident LNA, R 623/11/47271/47177.

12 For example, see on the conflict between Poland and Lithuania over Vilnius in 1920 TNA, KT 96.1.6/1 (Parts 1 and 2) and 2; on the border dispute between Albania and Yugoslavia of 1921-22 TNA, KT 96.1.3, and on the Greco-Bulgarian Frontier Incident of 1925 TNA, KT 96.1.4.

As we have seen in Chapter 3, the almost certain involvement in difficult international conflicts was the main reason why King Prajadhipok and Prince Traidos did not give in to Prince Charoon's wish to stand for election to the League Council in 1926. And when, two years later, the reluctance in Bangkok was seemingly overcome by Thai diplomats in Europe, and Siam could have stood for election, the bid for a Council seat was too half-hearted, and Siam, sure enough, lost out to rivals so early in the race that it ultimately did not even bother to put forward its candidature officially.

The lack of enthusiasm in Bangkok to seek involvement in the daunting task of settling the great international conflicts of the time was certainly understandable. Firstly, it showed a good sense of *realpolitik* to avoid becoming involved in conflicts between third states without necessity, particularly, as Thai foreign policy, during the 1920s, was still to a large extent focused on remaining as neutral as possible between British and French spheres of interest in Asia. In this respect, just the thought of a potential situation on the League Council, in which Siam would have had to decide in favour of one of the two against the other, must have sent shivers down the spines of foreign policy makers in Bangkok.

Second, it is highly questionable whether Siam could have brought to the Council any significant expertise, which would have enabled the body to better handle international conflicts. The administration in Bangkok and the Thai diplomats in Europe were, as we have seen in the preceding chapters, carefully treading the international paths during the 1920s, quietly working towards regaining sovereignty by abolishing old treaties, and learning the ropes of multilateral as well as bilateral diplomacy with the paramount objective of being treated equally and perceived as modern and civilised. It would have been highly unlikely that Thai diplomats could have, in this context, played an active role in settling an international dispute between, say, Turkey and Iraq, Bolivia and Peru, or even Germany and Poland.

Finally, the attitude among Western politicians and diplomats towards Siam, and, for that matter, Asia as a whole, during the 1920s, display a prevalent colonial superiority over Asians. It is fair to assume that Prince Charoon's or Prince Varn's colleagues on the League Council, should it hypothetically have become a member, would have regarded Siam with the same attitudes whether in 1926 or 1928. In such a setting, it is reasonably doubtful what contribution Siam would have even been allowed to make to any conflict settlement by the representatives of the powerful European states.

Conflicts before the League of Nations in the 1930s

The Kingdom of Siam was in many respects a different country in the 1930s than it was in the 1920s. The absolute monarchy and traditional rule by the king and royal princes was overthrown in the coup d'état of June 1932 by members of the elite civilian bureaucracy and the military. The coup led to a shift of power in Siam from the hands of a small group of royals to a larger group of relatively young, urban administrators and military officers. The coup did not, however, bring about profound change with regard to the project of modernising Siam. The old and the new elites rather shared a desire to turn Siam into a progressive and civilised state, in order to legitimise their rule over the country and to assert Siam's position internationally. In other words, the agents of modernisation changed, but adherence to the project remained. Equally, the League of Nations, the modern international experiment par excellence, did not lose its attractiveness for the new elite in 1932. Working with the League of Nations and utilising League membership for domestic modernisation were as important policy goals in 1925 as in 1935. Accordingly, the obligation to obey the rules set up by the League in international relations was incorporated as article 54 in the first Thai constitution of 10 December B.E. 2475 (1932). While the king retained the power to declare war and peace, paragraph 2 of the article implicitly acknowledged the League's collective security system and explicitly placed the authority of the League's Council and Assembly above the authority of the Thai king, 'A declaration of war will only be made when it is not contrary to the provisions of the Covenant of the League of Nations.'

It was only in the late 1930s, as we will see in the respective examples below, that the League's collective security system lost its appeal for the Thai elite, which was, at the same time, becoming less civilian-influenced and increasingly militaristic and chauvinistic in domestic and foreign policies.

While the League of Nations could claim some degree of success in managing international conflicts during the 1920s, the conflicts of the 1930s were a different matter, overwhelming not only the imperfect collective security system, but ultimately leading to the demise of the whole organisation. Throughout the 1930s, the collective security system was challenged by the aggressive and expansionist regimes of Italy, Germany and the Soviet Union in Europe, and Japan in Asia. Among the twenty-five international disputes and armed conflicts dealt with by the League of Nations between 1930 and 1940, were the severest aggressions since the First World War, which laid the foundation for the catastrophic outbreak of violence on a global scale in the Second World War.[13] In contrast to the conflicts before the League during the 1920s, those of the 1930s resonated in Bangkok, on two occasions even causing the eyes of the world to briefly look to the Southeast Asian kingdom. The main reason for Siam being drawn into these international conflicts was a change in the way the League of Nations tried to resolve them. While the Council was the League body which almost exclusively dealt

13 Peter J. Beck, 'The League of Nations and the Great Powers, 1936-1940', *World Affairs: Woodrow Wilson and the League of Nations, Part One*, 157, 4 (Spring 1995), pp. 175-189; Richard Schofield (ed.), *Reference of the Shatt al-'Arab Dispute to the League of Nations and Subsequent Bilateral Negotiations in Teheran and Geneva, 1934-1935*, The Iran-Iraq Border 1840-1958, vol. 8, Durham: Archive Editions, 1989; Richard Veatch, 'The League of Nations and the Spanish Civil War, 1936-9', *European History Quarterly*, 20 (April 1990), pp. 181-207; Marshall M. Lee, *Failure in Geneva: The German Foreign Ministry and the League of Nations, 1926-1933*, Ann Arbor: UMI, 1976.

with collective security issues during the first decade, now the gravity of the conflicts and the limits of the Council's authority led to the General Assembly becoming increasingly involved in crisis management. With this, Siam involuntarily became drawn in.

However, before analysing those events in detail, it seems appropriate to mention in passing two of the conflicts of the 1930s, in which Siam was able to continue its time-honoured policy of neutrality. The Chaco-Conflict between Bolivia and Paraguay, which had been troubling the League Council since 1928, came before the General Assembly in 1934. In preparation, Phraya Subharn Sompati, Siam's Permanent Representative to the League, suggested to the Ministry of Foreign Affairs in Bangkok that he attend the Assembly session in Geneva and that he 'vote with the majority because there should be no problem arising for us', as 'Siam does not have any close connection to those two parties in any way.' Foreign affairs adviser Stevens, in contrast, recommended not attending the session at all, and foreign affairs adviser Prince Varn, while first advocating the usual instructions, 'the delegate can abstain', eventually agreed and suggested to the cabinet that Phraya Subharn should not attend. The cabinet ultimately approved Prince Varn's recommendation and Phraya Subharn was instructed accordingly.[14] Equally, when German forces reoccupied the Rhineland in March 1936, Siam watched events unfolding at the League of Nations closely but managed to stay out of the proceedings in Geneva as well as remaining passive when the German Minister in Bangkok approached the Ministry of Foreign Affairs with the request for an official position.[15]

On two occasions Siam did stand in the bright international political spotlight at Geneva, ironically by not acting. On two of the League Assembly's most important decisions Siam abstained from voting.[16] In both cases, 1933 and 1937, Japan was the addressee of the votes. In 1933 the Assembly voted on officially accepting the famous Lytton Report at the end of the Manchurian Conflict, thereby explicitly condemning Japan for its aggressive actions in north-eastern China. In the second case, Japan, which was by this time no longer a member of the Geneva organisation, was again condemned by the international forum of states, this time for launching a full-scale intervention into the Chinese heartland. By abstaining from the votes, Siam twice, although in different political environments, put itself outside the mainstream of international politics.

Siam's abstention from voting to condemn Japan in 1933

'[T]hree events have made us better known to the world as a whole, namely, the change in our governmental system, our abstention from voting at Geneva on the Manchukuo question and the abdication of

14 Phraya Subharn to Ministry of Foreign Affairs, 23 October B.E. 2477 (1934); Memorandum Stevens and Note Prince Varn, 7 November 1934; Ministry of Foreign Affairs to Prime Minister, 11 November B.E. 2477 (1934); Secretary of Cabinet to Ministry of Foreign Affairs, 11 November B.E. 2477 (1934); all in TNA, KT 96.1.6/5. See also TNA, SR 0201.17/12.

15 TNA, KT 96.1.6/7.

16 The first abstention took place on 24 February 1933, See LNA, League of Nations, *Official Journal, Special Supplement no. 121: Records of the Special Session of the Assembly*, vol. IV, p. 22; the second abstention took place on 6 October 1937, see LNA, League of Nations, *Official Journal, Special Supplement no. 169: Records of the Eighteenth Ordinary Session of the Assembly*, Plenary Meetings, Texts of the Debates, p. 121.

King Prajadhipok'.[17] This statement by Minister of Foreign Affairs Luang Pradist in early 1936 encapsulates the fact that for contemporary observers Siam's single most important foreign policy decision in the interwar period was to instruct diplomat Luang Bhadravadi to raise his hand in the early afternoon of 24 February 1933 at Geneva and state 'Abstention!' on behalf of his government over the question of accepting the report of the so-called Committee of Nineteen, which brought to an end over a year of efforts to stop Japan's invasion of Manchuria.

After two decades of mounting Japanese economic activity and political influence in northeast China, the Japanese Kwantung Army decided in 1931 that time was ripe for the outright occupation of Manchuria. The army had been controlling Japanese-operated railway lines in Manchuria for many years already and had no difficulties in staging an incident on 18 September 1931 at Mukden, which served as a pretext for the invasion. Japanese troops met little resistance and quickly advanced throughout Manchuria.[18] The League's General Assembly was informed of the Mukden Incident on 19 September, and China invoked article XI of the covenant two days later. In dozens of meetings the League Council tried unsuccessfully to mediate in the conflict between September 1931 and February 1932, but failed because of Japan's determination and the Western powers' lack thereof. After passing three resolutions to no avail, the Council acceded to a Chinese request and passed on the dispute to an extraordinary General Assembly on 19 February 1932.[19] The Chinese request was based on article XV of the League Covenant and aimed at involving all League members. The Chinese government was hoping that a larger international public would have a greater influence on Japan. This very first extraordinary Assembly meeting dealing with an international conflict was convoked for 3 March 1932, and from this date the League's member state Siam was formally involved in dealing with one of the interwar period's most outright violations of the collective security system. By the time the extraordinary Assembly met, fighting in China had already spread to Shanghai and had for some weeks even threatened European possessions there. In Manchuria, which was by then fully occupied by Japanese troops, the Japanese vassal state Manchukuo was founded on 1 March 1932. Before transferring the Manchurian conflict to the extraordinary Assembly in the spring of 1932, the League Council had set up a commission of enquiry in December 1931, which became known as the Lytton Commission after its chairman Earl Lytton. The commission's mandate was to prepare a report on the situation in Manchuria, which would serve as a basis for a League verdict on the conflicting information it was receiving from the two parties. While at Geneva the conflict was being debated by the extraordinary Assembly, the Lytton Commission visited Japan and China from February to September 1932.

17 Translation of Interview given by Luang Pradist to *The Nation*, 28 January 1936, PRO, FO 371/20299, F 958/216/40.

18 Christopher Thorne, *The Limits of Foreign Policy: The West, the League and the Far Eastern Crisis of 1931-1933*, London: Hamish Hamilton, 1972; Ian Nish, *Japan's Struggle with Internationalism: Japan, China, and the League of Nations, 1931-33*, London and New York: Kegan Paul, 1993; Stefan Hell, *Der Mandschurei-Konflikt: Japan, China und der Völkerbund 1931 bis 1933*, Tübingen: Universitas, 1999, Dorothy Borg, *The United States and the Far Eastern Crisis of 1933-1938, From the Manchurian Incident through the Initial Stage of the Undeclared Sino-Japanese War*, Harvard East Asian Series, vol. 14, Cambridge (MA): Harvard University Press, 1964.

19 For the text of the Council resolution of 30 September 1931 see LNA, League of Nations, *Official Journal*, December 1931, p. 2307f.; for the text of the Council resolution of 24 October 1931 see p. 2340f.; for the text of the Council resolution of 10 December 1931 see p. 2374; for the text of the Council resolution of 19 February 1932, see LNA, League of Nations, *Official Journal, Special Supplement no. 101*, p. 10.

The government in Bangkok was well-informed on events in Manchuria even before the Mukden Incident. Phraya Subharn Sompati, at the time Thai Minister in Tokyo, informed Bangkok on 10 September 1931 that a conflict was likely to erupt 'any day', and his news of the Mukden Incident reached Bangkok immediately on 19 September.[20] Thai diplomats remained completely passive during the League Council's proceedings on the Sino-Japanese conflict in the autumn and winter of 1931-32. In fact, while in Geneva the Council was struggling to find a solution to the crisis, Siam's relations with the League reached its zenith when, in November 1931, the League of Nations' Conference on Opium Smoking convened in Bangkok, an event which was hailed by the Thai elite as the kingdom's greatest international success in years. Some three weeks after the Mukden Incident, Prince Varn, the former Permanent Representative of Siam to the League, gave a public lecture at Chulalongkorn University in Bangkok on the League of Nations, in which he was very optimistic that there was no serious cause for war between China and Japan and that the League would bring about reconciliation in due course.[21] Official Thai relations with China were, as we have seen, non-existent, and relations with Japan were as businesslike as ever, as seen in the the cordial welcome received by King Prajadhipok in Japan in April 1931, when he stopped over en route to the United States.

When the Sino-Japanese conflict was transferred to the extraordinary Assembly, King Prajadhipok and Prince Devawongse followed a very low-key approach by appointing Major-General Prince (*Mom Chao*) Pridi Debyabongse Devakul to represent Siam at the meeting, as he was already in Geneva as Thai delegate to the League of Nations Disarmament Conference. Prince Pridi was a son of the elder Prince Devawongse and half-brother of diplomat Prince Damras Damrong Devakul and Minister of Foreign Affairs Prince Traidos (Devawongse). Trained as an army officer in Germany, he was the last Thai Minister in Berlin before the closure of the legation in early 1932 for financial reasons. Prince Pridi was, therefore, conveniently available to represent Siam at the Geneva Disarmament Conference, which opened in February.[22] When the extraordinary Assembly opened on 3 March, Prince Pridi was given no specific instructions but was told to remain silent and observe the proceedings. Siam's participation in the extraordinary Assembly seems not to have been questioned at any point, as fifty of the League's fifty-five members participated, with only five Latin-American states absent. From Prince Pridi's detailed reports on the nine sessions of the extraordinary Assembly between 3 March and 30 April, it becomes clear that, as a novice at Geneva, he remained quite isolated and maintained a passive attitude towards approaches from other delegations.[23] When he was approached by the Chinese delegate some days before the Assembly opened with a request for Thai support for China's case, he avoided giving a clear answer to the positive or the

20 Phraya Subharn to Prince Deva-wongse, 10 and 19 September 1931, TNA, R7, T 20/14.

21 TNA, *Bangkok Times*, 16 October 1931.

22 On Prince Pridi's appointment see Prince Devawongse to Prince Pridi, 22 February 1932, TNA, KT 96.1.6.2./2; see also various reports and correspondence in TNA, R7, T 10/22. On the closure of the Berlin legation for financial reasons in 1932 see also Stoffers, *Im Lande des weißen Elefanten*, p. 181.

23 TNA, KT 96.1.6.2./2, 3 (Part 1 of 2 and 2 of 2), 4 (Part 1 of 2 and 2 of 2), 6, 7 (Part 1 of 2 and 2 of 2); LNA, League of Nations, *Official Journal, Special Supplement no. 101*.

24 Prince Pridi to Prince Devawongse, 29 February 1932, TNA,
KT 96.1.6.2./2.

25 Report on Meeting of Cabinet
Council on 22 February B.E.
2474 (1932), TNA, R7, T 10/22.

26 Prince Devawongse to Prince
Pridi, 4 March 1932, TNA,
KT 96.1.6.2/2. The identical
telegram including date of receipt
in Geneva can be found in TNA,
KT 96.1.6.2/3. Interestingly, the
instructions were received by
Prince Pridi just fifteen minutes
before the afternoon session of
the General Assembly opened at
4.30 p.m. For the text of the
General Assembly resolution of 4
March 1932 see LNA, League of
Nations, *Official Journal, Special
Supplement no. 101*, p. 43f.

27 Prince Damras to Ministry of
Foreign Affairs, 29 March 1932,
TNA, KT 96.1.6.2./4 (Part 1
of 2).

28 Prince Devawongse to Prince
Damras, 21 May 1932, TNA,
KT 96.1.6.2./6. On the same
day, Prince Devawongse asked
Prince Pridi to inform their
brother in London on events at
Geneva 'from time to time'; see
Prince Devawongse to Prince
Pridi, 21 May 1932, TNA, KT
96.1.6.2./6.

29 Siamese Delegation to the League
of Nations to Secretary-General,
7 July 1932, LNA, S 571/1/1923-
1937. See also LNA, R 3362/
15/35188/35186 and TNA, R7,
T 10/19. On Prince Pridi and the
Disarmament Conference see
LNA, R 2458/7B/34684/34684.
Another member of the Thai
delegation to the Disarmament
Conference was Admiral Phraya
Rajawangsan, who was himself
to become Permanent Represen-
tative of Siam at the League of
Nations in 1935; see LNA,
R 2446/7B/28820/26222. On
Prince Pridi's return to Siam see
Prince Pridi to Drummond, 13
July 1932, LNA, R 2446/7B/
28820/26222. Originally, Prince
Pridi had been appointed as
successor to Phraya Abhibal
Rajamaitri as Minister in Tokyo.
However, the coup d'état ruined
this plan.

negative.[24] In the opinion of Prince Pridi's brother, the Minister of Foreign Affairs, he was doing quite a good job, considering that he was new to the Geneva stage. The meeting report of the cabinet council on 22 February 1932, at which the king was present, reveals that Siam's paramount concern at this stage was that possible League sanctions against Tokyo could affect Siam's rice exports to Japan. But no strategy to counter this possibility was devised, and a passive policy at Geneva remained the order of the day.[25]

In Geneva, the immediate issue at hand for the extraordinary Assembly on 3 March was to bring the fighting in Shanghai to an end, as this threatened possessions and citizens in the city's Western concessions. Prince Pridi was instructed by Bangkok to vote in favour of the Assembly's resolution of 4 March which served as a basis for the multi-party negotiations that brought about an armistice in Shanghai on 5 May.[26] The plenary sessions of the Assembly during the following days, 4-8 March, were devoted to a general debate, which saw some of the most remarkable speeches of the League of Nations' twenty-six year history. Mainly delegates of small states took the floor, described Japan's aggression for what it was and demanded effective action from the great powers and the League as a whole. In contrast, the delegate of the one country in closest geographical proximity to the hostilities, Prince Pridi, remained silent throughout these debates.

As the Sino-Japanese conflict was rapidly becoming a major international issue during these months, Prince Damras in London was becoming increasingly anxious and felt bypassed, as he was instructed to watch the proceedings from the Thames rather than travel to Geneva. He even complained to Prince Devawongse in late March 1932, insisting that he was the kingdom's Permanent Representative to the League, not his half-brother. The fact that Prince Damras was, nevertheless, never instructed by Bangkok to participate in the extraordinary Assembly reflects his weak position in the diplomatic service in 1932 before his transfer to Washington the following year. And it underlines once again Siam's decidedly low-key approach to the conflict unfolding in Geneva.[27] Prince Devawongse replied to his half-brother Prince Damras in a harshly worded letter on 21 May 1932, that, as he, Prince Damras, had not found it necessary to attend the sessions of the Opium Advisory Committee in Geneva and had sent his London staff member Luang Bhadravadi in his place, the Minister of Foreign Affairs saw no sense in appointing him to the extraordinary Assembly now.[28] Following the coup in Bangkok four months later, Prince Pridi returned to Siam and substitute delegate Luang Bhadravadi took over representing Siam in the extraordinary Assembly. Prince Pridi retired from the diplomatic service but re-emerged after the end of the Second World War when he held the foreign affairs portfolio in 1948-49.[29]

Siam's policy of strict neutrality, practied in Geneva, also applied in bilateral contacts. An official request by the Ministry of Foreign Affairs of Manchukuo to the Ministry of Foreign Affairs in Bangkok requesting the establishment of formal diplomatic relations on 12 March 1932 remained unanswered, and persistent lobbying in this regard during the course of spring 1932 by the Japanese Minister in Bangkok was also to no avail. King Prajadhipok himself gave instructions by late May not to respond to the Japanese requests.[30] Meanwhile in Geneva, the flurry of activity during the winter and spring of 1932 quickly calmed down when it became clear that the League did not possess the legal instruments to check the Japanese action effectively, and that its major member states, Britain, France, Germany and Italy, possessed neither the means nor the determination to do so. In order to keep the matter alive, the Lytton Commission moved to the centre of attention. Consensus was quickly reached among the major players on the Council and in the extraordinary Assembly that, now that the threat of Western interests and citizens in Shanghai had been successfully averted, one could conveniently sit back and wait for Lytton. The hope was that the Lytton Commission's report would somehow show a way forward for the League, but the immediate effect was that from mid-March to late September 1932, the League did not move, or even attempt to move, one step closer to solving the Manchurian conflict.

Interestingly, in July 1932, while the League bodies were paralysed and waiting for the Lytton Report during this lost summer, Prince Varn wrote in the *Bangkok Times* that 'by its own peculiar method of common consultation, which is intended to clear the dark recesses of brooding temper by the light of publicity and reason' the League had 'averted war between Japan and China.' While this assessment sheds light on Prince Varn's strong conviction in the League ideals, it was to prove, unfortunately, both very premature and very inaccurate.[31]

The Lytton Commission completed its report in Beijing in September 1932. In ten chapters, the lengthy document gave a detailed and balanced account of the events in Manchuria and offered a solution to the conflict which not only respected Chinese territorial integrity but also legitimate Japanese interests in Manchuria.[32] However, by the time the report was made available to League members in October, Japan and its vassal Manchukuo had already moved far beyond any of the solutions suggested therein. Nevertheless, on 6 and 9 December 1932 the extraordinary Assembly met again to discuss the report. Unable to agree on any action against Japan, the Assembly entrusted a so-called Committee of Nineteen to draw up a final proposal for a settlement of the conflict based on the Lytton recommendations. The report by this Committee of Nineteen was completed on 14 February and put before the extraordinary Assembly on 21 February 1933.[33] A *Bangkok Times* editorial on 18 February 1933

30 All letters in this matter and King Prajadhipok's hand-written note of 28 May 1932, in TNA, R7, T 41/15.

31 TNA, *Bangkok Times*, 20 July 1932.

32 LNA, League of Nations (ed.), Appeal by the Chinese Government, Report by the Commission of Enquiry, Geneva 1932, serial document no. C.663.M.320.19 32.VII.

33 The report is published in LNA, League of Nations, *Official Journal, Special Supplement no. 112*, p. 56ff., serial document no. A (Extr.) 22.1933.VII.

34 TNA, *Bangkok Times*, 18 February 1933.

35 Pierre Fistié, *Sous-développement et utopie au Siam: le programme de réformes présenté en 1933 par Pridi Phanomyong*, Paris: Mouton, 1969, p. 102.

36 On Luang Bhadravadi's appointment see Prince Damras to Drummond, 18 February 1933, LNA, R 5215/15/2190/1121. He already represented Siam at the December 1932 session of the extraordinary General Assembly, see LNA, R 3362/15/35188/ 35186; see also Prince Damras to Phraya Srivisarn, 14 February 1933, TNA, KT 96.1.6.2/7 (Part 2 of 2); Prince Damras to Phraya Srivisarn and Phraya Srivisarn to Prince Damras, both 17 February 1933, TNA, KT 96.1.6.2/8.

37 Luang Bhadravadi, who was in London on that day, requested instructions from Bangkok by telegram on 21 February, see Luang Bhadravadi (London) to Phraya Srivisarn, 21 February 1933; his instructions were sent to London by telegram from Phraya Srivisarn to Prince Damras, 22 February 1933; both in TNA, KT 96.1.6.2/8. The story presented by Rong Syamananda of an *ad hoc* decision by the Prime Minister and Minister of Foreign Affairs during a lunch on 24 February is implausible. In this context, Rong Syamananda dates the Polish abstention to 1933, but, in fact, it took place four years later; see Rong Syamananda, *A History of Thailand*, Bangkok: Thai Watana Panich, 7th ed., 1990, p. 171.

38 Transocean News Service report, TNA, KT 96.1.6.2/9.

39 Verbatim Records of Extraordinary General Assembly sessions on 21 and 24 February 1933, in LNA, R 5215/15/2693/2125; see also LNA, League of Nations, *Official Journal, Special Supplement no. 112: Records of the Special Session of the Assembly convened in virtue of Article 15 of the Covenant at the Request of the Chinese Government*, vol. IV.

praised the Lytton Report for its balanced judgement, which did not simply demand a return to the *status quo ante* but took into account present-day realities; and the editorial also warned the League from adding fuel to the fire by publicly condemning Japan's actions.[34] But for the political elite in Bangkok the Lytton Report was of secondary importance, as it was focused on domestic developments during these turbulent first months of constitutional government. While the Committee of Nineteen presented its report to the extraordinary Assembly in Geneva, Luang Pradist was putting the final touches to his radical economic plan in Bangkok and presented it to the cabinet.[35]

With Prince Pridi Debyabongse having left Geneva in the summer, Siam was represented at the meetings of the extraordinary Assembly from 6 December by junior diplomat Luang Bhadravadi, Third Secretary at the London legation. Luang Bhadravadi also represented Siam at the sixteenth plenary meeting of the League's extraordinary Assembly, which convened in the afternoon of Tuesday, 21 February 1933 in Geneva and reconvened the following Friday, 24 February, at 10.30 a.m.[36] Prince Damras in London was instructed by the Minister of Foreign Affairs on 22 February as follows: 'His Majesty's Government does not want to take side on the Sino-Japanese issue. Therefore please instruct Bhadravadi (to) abstain from voting'.[37] On 24 February according to an eyewitness account, 'the large Assembly hall, as well as the diplomats', the public and the press galleries, were crowded to capacity, another message says thronged to suffocation'.[38] The delegates heard yet another lengthy statement by the Chinese and Japanese representatives, Yen and Matsuoka, followed by brief statements of the delegates of Venezuela, Canada and Lithuania, before proceeding to vote on accepting the report of the Committee of Nineteen. The vote was taken by roll-call. Of the forty-four delegations present, forty-two voted in favour of the report, Japan voted against, and Siam abstained. Matsuoka then rose to announce that Japan would, in effect, shortly submit its notification of withdrawal from the League. The records of the meeting do not indicate that Matsuoka referred to Siam's abstention in his final statement, and the accounts of what happened next differ.[39] Some report that Matsuoka rushed up to Luang Bhadravadi to congratulate him and confirm Japan's solidarity with Siam.[40] An eyewitness, however, gives a different account, which is corroborated by Luang Bhadravadi himself. Wunsz King, a member of the Chinese delegation, reports that Matsuoka gave his final statement and then:

> He strode defiantly down the centre aisle and summoned his some thirty colleagues and assistants who immediately rose and followed him out of the hall. Complete silence accentuated the pulsating tension of the moment...Everybody realized the gravity of the situation.[41]

The extraordinary Assembly adjourned at 1.50 p.m. on that Friday, and Siam had, for the first time ever, deviated from the mainstream of international politics and had unintentionally caused the biggest diplomatic incident of its history to date. Luang Bhadravadi himself left Geneva for London after the meeting and gave only a very prosaic account of the event in his telegram to Bangkok the following day: 'The report of the Committee of Nineteen has been adopted by [the] Special Assembly. Japan voted against [it]. I have abstained from voting'.[42] Three days after the abstention Prince Damras wrote to Secretary-General Drummond informing that he would be leaving his post as Minister in London and Permanent Representative to the League and would be substituted in both functions by Phraya Subharn Sompati. This change of personnel was, however, not directly related to the events at Geneva and was initiated well before the Thai abstention.[43]

Before analysing why Siam abstained from voting in favour or against the report of the Committee of Nineteen, we may review Siam's policy options in this, as Richard Sogn called it, 'first major foreign policy decision since the revolution'.[44] Three alternative paths of action were theoretically available for Siam's diplomacy. Siam could have voted in favour of accepting the report with China and the majority of states, against accepting the report with Japan, or it could have stayed away from the February Assembly session altogether. A favourable vote would have placed Siam right in the mainstream of global opinion and in the company of forty-two other states. But this option neglects the fact that senior officials in Bangkok were well aware of Japan's growing economic, political and military influence in the region, and particularly of Japan's importance as a key trading partner in the difficult period of economic depression. Thus voting with the majority would have gravely offended Japan and would have contradicted any sense of rational foreign policy in Asia in 1933.

Siding with Japan and voting against the report would have needlessly and dangerously isolated Siam from the major Western states and would have been contrary to the prevailingly Western orientation of Siam's foreign policy in 1933. It is undisputed among historians of Thailand that the foreign policy of post-1932 Siam became increasingly pro-Japanese. It would, however, be inaccurate to assume that such a major policy shift was accomplished within the few months between June 1932 and February 1933. Rather, such a policy shift took years and became relevant for policy formulation by the mid-1930, and certainly by the time of Siam's second abstention in Geneva in the context of the Chinese-Japanese conflict in 1937. Exposing itself to world criticism by voting as the only League member with Japan against accepting the report was neither a realistic option nor a reflection of majority sentiment among the political elite in

40 Flood, Japan's Relations with Thailand, vol. 1, p. 53; Flood gives as his source an interview with Direck Jayanama in 1966. See also Nuntana Kalipalakanchana, Phuangphet Suratanakawikun and Supatra Nilwatchala, *The Relationship between Japan and Thailand 1932-1945*, Bangkok: Institute of Asian Studies Chulalongkorn University, 1978, p. 56.

41 Wunsz King, *China and the League of Nations, The Sino-Japanese Controversy*, Asia in the Modern World, vol. 5, New York: St. John's University Press, 2nd ed.,1973, p. 57. See also Hell, *Mandschurei-Konflikt*, p. 180ff. Luang Bhadravadi's report on the meeting, dated 28 February 1933, can be found in TNA, KT 96.1.6.2 /9.

42 Luang Bhadravadi to Phraya Srivisarn, 25 February 1933, TNA, KT 96.1.6.2/8. Luang Bhadravadi's detailed report on the Assembly meetings in February 1933, dated 28 February 1933, can be found in TNA, KT 96.1.6.2/9.

43 Prince Damras to Drummond, 27 February 1933, LNA, R 5642/50/176/120. Phraya Subharn officially became the new Permanent Representative at the League of Nations on 26 April 1933, see Phraya Subharn to Drummond, 1 May 1933, LNA, R 5642/50/ 176/120; Minister of Foreign Affairs Phraya Srivisarn informed the British Minister in Bangkok Dormer already in early February, well before the Thai abstention at Geneva, that Prince Damras would be transferred to the Legation in Washington D.C. because of his inability to control the Thai students in England; see Dormer to Foreign Office, 2 February 1933, PRO, FO 371/17176, F 812/812/40, and Dormer to Foreign Office, 8 February 1933, PRO, FO 371/17177, F 1721/ 812/40. Prince Damras was informed of the American agreement to his appointment by Phraya Srivisarn on 18 February 1933; see Phraya Srivisarn to Prince Damras, 18 February 1933, TNA, SR 0201. 17/7 (Part 1 of 3).

44 Richard R. Sogn, 'Successful Journey: A History of United States-Thai Relations, 1932-1945', Ph.D. Thesis, University of Michigan, 1990, p. 98.

Bangkok.[45] Siding with Japan would have also likely led to a difficult domestic situation with regard to the significant Chinese population in Bangkok, which was closely following these international events, ready to protest or stage a boycott, if necessary to express their displeasure with the government's policy.

Finally, staying away from the Assembly session would not have been a realistic option either, as only Latin American League member states, a number of them entangled in their own international conflicts, did not take part in the meetings. All European and Asian states were present, and it can be considered highly unlikely that the absence of the only Far Eastern League member apart from the two conflicting parties would have gone unnoticed. On the contrary, it is reasonable to assume that a deliberate absence from the session would have been interpreted by many as a much more pro-Japanese act than the actual abstention. Staying away from the session on 24 February would have also signalled all to clearly an evasion of even a minimum of international obligation by a League member, particularly because, as we have seen above, Siam had had been interested in participating passively in the extraordinary Assembly for twelve months prior to the vote in order to stay informed on developments in the conflict. Siam's abstention, its fourth policy option, was therefore a reasonable policy choice, reflecting the desire neither to side with Japan nor China but to remain neutral.

The research on which this study is based did not unearth evidence to support the claim that Siam's abstention was intended as a pro-Japanese statement. That Siam's abstention was widely interpreted as a pro-Japanese act was largely due to the events which followed. The abstention itself, a perhaps clumsy but sincere expression of a position of neutrality, was tainted by massive Japanese propaganda during the months and even years that followed. Already in the days before and after the abstention, rumours surfaced in London that Siam was purchasing arms from British firms as a front for Japan. The rumours were picked up by numerous European and Asian newspapers and even found their way onto the floor of parliament in London in late February. Indeed, the Thai military had ordered thirty-six tanks and artillery from Vickers-Armstrongs in England, which were scheduled for delivery late that month, but they were not intended for Japan. Rather, Minister of Defence Phraya Rajawangsan lamented that even with these additional armaments Siam was still short of weapons.[46] In fact, as it turned out in late March, the rumours were planted purposely by the London *Daily Express* in order to drive up shares of Vickers-Armstrongs. The Thai Foreign Ministry issued an official communiqué denying the allegations, and 'the bubble was pricked'.[47]

Press coverage of the event in the wake of 24 February in Bangkok and the world over was extensive.[48] On the day after the abstention the

45 Reynolds reports a statement made in 1936 by the Japanese Minister in Bangkok, Yatabe Yasukuchi, who claimed that Thai officials signalled to him that they had wished to vote with Japan but were blocked from doing so because of the Chinese minority in Siam. While there might well have been an official who thought accordingly in early 1933 or at least made such a statement to Yatabe in the following years, I share Reynolds' scepticism as to the value of this statement for explaining Siam's motivation in abstaining. See E. Bruce Reynolds, *Thailand and Japan's Southern Advance, 1940-1945*, Basingstoke: Macmillan, 1994, p. 242, notes 31 and 32.

46 Phraya Rajawangsan (Minister of Defence) to Phraya Srivisarn, 17 February B.E. 2475 (1933); Prince Damras to Phraya Srivisarn, 24 and 27 February 1933; both on TNA, KT 96.1.6.2/8. In this file a large number of international press clippings on the supposed Thai-Japanese arms deal can also be found.

47 Clipping from the *Bangkok Times*, 28 March 1933, TNA, KT 96.1.6.2/9.

48 A large collection of press clippings from around the globe can be found in TNA, KT 96.1.6.2/9.

Bangkok Daily Mail featured an editorial which was so rich in analysis that it deserves to be quoted here at length:

> It was the only course open to the League of Nations...the action of Siam's delegate at Geneva is extremely interesting. The vote of Siam was necessarily to be significant and important in the eyes of the world because Siam is the only Asiatic member of the League not directly concerned in the Sino-Japanese affair. From Siam's point of view the question before her was an extremely delicate one.

Approval of Japan could have caused unrest among the Chinese in Siam and 'would probably in the long run represent a blow to our prestige in the eyes of every nation in the world except Japan.' Voting for the report would also excite the Chinese in Siam and 'strain somewhat the friendly relations between this country and Japan.' A 'material point of view' suggests that a small country like Siam should always go with the weak against the strong.

> It was undoubtedly a delicate question. What Siam did was to abstain from voting. This may have been extremely wise or it may have been extremely unwise. Siam's action is open to a thousand different interpretations, all of them more or less unfavourable as far as we can see. What Siam would like to do, of course, is to maintain a purely neutral policy toward the Sino-Japanese affair. Yet it is a question whether the whole idea of the League, of which Siam is a member, is not that nations of the world can no longer remain neutral; that no nation can say that a charge of Military Aggression does not concern it; that all nations must be concerned in such a situation. We may admit this in theory, since it is quite true, but in practice we may also ask whether the small nations in Europe and America have as much at stake as Siam in this particular situation. Would the small nations of Europe, in other words, be so vociferous if the affair were Franco-Italian instead of Sino-Japanese? All in all, and admitting that sooner or later Siam will have to adopt a definite policy in Asia, the occasion at Geneva was perhaps not the ideal moment for an unequivocal expression on Siam's part.[49]

An equally lengthy editorial appeared in the *Bangkok Times* on 27 February, which agreed that Siam had 'acted wisely' at Geneva in the face of its two powerful neighbours China and Japan, and also that the League had acted justly towards both conflicting parties, before asking plainly, 'And Now? Well nobody quite knows'.[50]

Besides media coverage, the abstention triggered something of a communication frenzy in which the Thai government went out of its way to declare its policy of neutrality and refute any suggestion of the abstention being a pro-Japanese act, while the Japanese government launched a fully-fledged campaign exploiting the Thai abstention to its benefit and hailing the new pan-Asian unity, and the rest of the world

49 TNL, *Bangkok Daily Mail*, 25 February 1933.

50 TNA, *Bangkok Times*, 27 February 1933. The paper reaffirmed its standpoint that Siam had 'acted wisely' in another editorial on 5 April in response to Chinese newspaper reports condemning Siam's action as pro-Japanese. But the *Bangkok Times* was by no means one-sided in this issue, as could be seen when a letter to the editor was published on 4 May, including a poem praising Matsuoka Yosuke, the Japanese delegate at the League of Nations; see TNA, *Bangkok Times*, 4 May 1933.

was scratching its head uncertain what to believe. Let us look at all three aspects of the aftermath of Luang Bhadravadi's abstention.

The Ministry of Foreign Affairs in Bangkok immediately instructed its legations in Paris, Washington and Tokyo to assure their respective host governments of Siam's neutrality as opposed to any pro-Japanese stance.[51] Under the pressure of Japanese propaganda and countless newspaper articles and wire reports in the wake of 24 February, the Ministry issued an official communiqué on 2 March, which was sent to newspapers in Siam and abroad. The communiqué read:

> It is the policy of His Majesty's Government to be neutral in the controversy between China and Japan regarding Manchuria. For this reason its representative at Geneva abstained from voting when the question came before the Assembly. Rumours appearing in the foreign press that His Majesty's Government is acting as an agent for Japan in the purchase of arms or in any way aiding Japan are entirely without foundation.[52]

The communiqué appeared, for example, in the *Bangkok Times* and the *Bangkok Daily Mail* on 2 March and in a number of Chinese papers in Hong Kong as well as on Reuters wire reports and in the London *Times*. It mainly served to refute speculations about a secret understanding between Siam and Japan, which had appeared in a number of Chinese papers.[53]

In the Japanese media, propaganda, and even public sentiment, the events were presented quite differently. The Japanese daily *Tokyo Nichi Nichi* published a report by its correspondent in Bangkok on 27 February 1933, to the effect that Siam had clearly acted in a pro-Japanese manner. With this action, Siam had defied its traditional relations with Great Britain and had disregarded the considerable economic influence of ethnic Chinese in the kingdom. The correspondent went so far as to identify this Chinese economic influence as the 'cancer' of the country and explained that Siam had now 'recognized her future and the prospects of the oriental nations'.[54] Matsuoka Yosuke, who had represented Japan before the League during most of the Manchurian Conflict, gave a widely publicised interview in Geneva on the evening of 24 February to a journalist of the British *Daily Herald*, in which he stated that Japan would rush to Siam's side and 'fight for her' if Europeans would try to 'crush Siam'. Obscure as this statement was, it served its purpose of arousing the interest of the Western media and governments for the supposed new Japanese-Thai alliance.[55] Reference to the Thai abstention was also made in the Japanese Diet a day after the Geneva vote. Siam's action was seen by one deputy as a clear sign of improved relations and as a signal for intensified trade prospects between Siam and Japan, as well as for trade between Japan and other 'coloured races'.[56] The Thai legation in Tokyo received a large number of

51 These letters are filed in TNA, KT 96.1.6.2/8.

52 The communiqué in its final form and as a handwritten draft can be found in TNA, KT 96.1.6.2/8.

53 TNA, *Bangkok Times*, 2 and 8 March 1933; J.T. Bagram (Consul-General of Siam in Hong Kong) to Ministry of Foreign Affairs, 4 March 1933, TNA, KT 96.1.6.2/9.

54 An English translation of the article of 27 February as well as an article in the same paper of 25 February can be found in TNA, KT 96.1.6.2/8. The article is also referred to prominently in Lindley (British Ambassador in Tokyo) to Simon, 7 March 1933, PRO, FO 371/17166, F 2302/1652/23.

55 *The Times*, 3 March 1933; *Daily Herald*, 25 February 1933, TNA, KT 96.1.6.2/8.

56 Lindley to Simon, 7 March 1933, PRO, FO 371/17166, F 2302/1652/23. The Foreign Office in London, nevertheless, remained indecisive as to whether Siam's action indeed reflected a clear shift of policy towards Japan. One official remarked: 'Siam's abstention is still unexplained'; PRO, FO 371/17166, F 2302/1652/23.

congratulatory telegrams, and the Foreign Ministry in Bangkok also received a considerable number of letters to the same effect from individuals and organisations in Japan. The widespread Japanese propaganda on the perceived new chapter in Japanese-Thai relations opened by the abstention was a matter of considerable embarrassment to the Foreign Ministry in Bangkok.[57] Minister of Foreign Affairs Phraya Srivisarn rushed to ensure the British Minister that he 'resented' the Japanese propaganda and that Siam had refused the Japanese advances to recognise Manchukuo on the grounds of the adverse effect this would have on the large Chinese population in the kingdom. Minister Cecil Dormer did not doubt the sincerity of these statements. By late March 1933, the Foreign Office in London shared Dormer's assessment that Siam's abstention was the result of its traditional policy of strict neutrality, calling this 'the explanation of Siam's attitude, and doubtless the true one'.[58]

This interpretation was further reinforced in early April, when the Foreign Office received information from the British Ambassador in Tokyo, Sir F.O. Lindley, that the Thai abstention 'at Geneva seems to have made some impression in certain quarters' and that it was being interpreted in Japan as an expression of Siam having 'achieved the knowledge of where her future lay and of what the path of all eastern peoples was.' Lindley's report triggered one Foreign Office official to remark that 'the gratitude to Siam [and] the interpretation put upon her action is another example of the Japanese tendency to believe what they want to believe', while a colleague remarked accurately that 'the Siamese will not altogether appreciate these eulogies'.[59]

Thai officials did not sound out the attitudes of Britain and France before 24 February, as one would have expected, if the abstention was seen in Bangkok as a major policy statement. Rather, circumstances suggest that policy makers in Bangkok were truly unaware of the impact the abstention would have. After all, an abstention is, in principle, the most uncontroversial action that can be taken. A further element in support of this interpretation is that fact that it was a junior diplomat rather than the properly accredited Permanent Representative to the League of Nations, who, highly unusually, attended the meetings. This underscores the low profile Siam was seeking in contrast to the almost certain international attention it could have expected, had the abstention been designed as a pro-Japanese statement. A junior diplomat abstaining from voting was meant to be seen as a simple and uncontroversial act by the Thai government. That it became a major diplomatic incident for Siam was unintended.

After February 1933, Japanese officials went out of their way to stress the new friendship between the two Asian neighbours, a development that in turn made Thai officials so anxious that they continuously reassured Western diplomats of their neutrality in spite of the visible

57 Various telegrams and letters as well as reports on the congratulatory correspondence can be found in TNA, KT 96.1.6.2/8 and 10. See also TNA, *Bangkok Times*, 1 March 1933.

58 Dormer to Foreign Office, 30 March 1933, PRO, FO 371/17079, F 2084/33/10; Dormer to Simon, 30 March 1933, PRO, FO 371/17080, F 3121/33/10. See also the Annual Report on Siam for 1933 in PRO, FO 371/18210, F 1991/1991/40.

59 Hand-written notes on file PRO, FO 371/17166, F 2302/1652/23.

rapprochement with Japan.[60] A good example of the embarrassment felt by Thai officials in the face of Japanese actions originated in the American capital Washington D.C., where the Japanese Ambassador met his Thai colleague at a dinner on 28 February and thanked him for Siam's abstention. Phraya Subharn reported this to Bangkok and Minister of Foreign Affairs Phraya Srivisarn replied by repeating the official communiqué and added 'that if in the future any Japanese should call or write to express his thanks for our attitude at Geneva, it would be well not to reply, otherwise it may give rise to a misunderstanding'.[61]

Similarly, when the Japanese Minister in Bangkok, Yatabe Yasukichi, toured Japan in autumn 1933 giving lectures on the perceived new friendship between Japan and Siam since the abstention in February and their common front against 'foreign aggression', this caused some discomfort to Phraya Abhibal Rajamaitri, the Permanent Secretary for Foreign Affairs in Bangkok. The British Minister Dormer, in a discussion on the Yatabe lectures, however, supported the view that Siam's abstention was intended to mark its neutrality rather than signifying a pro-Japanese sentiment.[62]

The same Yatabe Yasukichi had, in Bangkok, lobbied Minister of Foreign Affairs Phraya Srivisarn in the days before the vote to side with Japan, but was unable to change the position of strict neutrality.[63] In parallel, the Japanese consul, Kase Shunichi, paid a visit to Phraya Abhibal Rajamaitri, on 18 February, also with the aim of convincing him to side with Japan. Their discussion is of particular interest as to the meaning of the abstention. Phraya Abhibal made it very clear that Siam did not wish to take sides and that Luang Bhadravadi would certainly request instructions in the event of an important decision. Kase pointed out that it was likely that many states would abstain from voting and many would vote for adopting the report. He hoped that Siam would neither vote with the majority nor abstain. Phraya Abhibal remained non-committal and reiterated the position of neutrality.[64] Two points are important when interpreting Siam's abstention. Firstly, Kase's remarks make it clear that he did not see an abstention as a pro-Japanese vote, this was rather what Japanese propaganda turned the abstention into afterwards. Secondly, the discussion reveals an expectation that several states would abstain from voting. Had this actually been the case on 24 February, Siam's abstention would have likely been rendered largely insignificant and incapable of exploitation by Japan.

Two interpretations of Siam's abstention have emerged during the past seventy-five years. One group of historians sees the abstention as primarily an expression of Siam's traditional policy of international neutrality vis-à-vis her two large neighbours China and Japan, which had a secondary, unintended and, in the view of some historians, undesired pro-Japanese effect.[65] A second group of scholars interprets Siam's abstention as a pro-Japanese policy statement at an event when

60 A document which reflects both of these aspects is the memorandum by Cecil Dormer of 6 February 1934, PRO, FO 371/18210, F 1691/1691/40.

61 Phraya Subharn to Phraya Srivisarn, 3 March 1933; Phraya Srivisarn to Phraya Subharn, 13 April 1933; TNA, KT 96.1.6.2/ 8.

62 Dormer to Simon, 10 November 1933, PRO, FO 371/17176, F 7922/42/40. See also Nicholas Tarling, 'King Prajadhipok and the Apple Cart: British Attitudes towards the 1932 Revolution', *Journal of the Siam Society*, 64, 2 (1976), pp. 1-38, here: p. 9.

63 The discussion between Yatabe and Phraya Srivisarn is recorded by Flood, Japan's Relations with Thailand, vol. 1, p. 53f., who cites Japanese sources.

64 Memorandum Phraya Abhibal, 21 February B.E. 2475 (1933), TNA, KT 96.1.6.2/8. This conversation is mentioned by Ian Nish, 'Research Notelet: Thailand, Japan and the League, 1933', in Suntory and Toyota International Centre for Economics and Related Disciplines (STICERD), London School of Economics (ed.), *Japan-Thailand Relations*, International Studies Discussion Paper no. IS/91/228, London: STICERD, September 1991, pp. 77-80, here: p. 78.

65 Flood, Japan's Relations with Thailand, vol. 1, p. 53ff. and vol. 2, p. 743; Reynolds, *Thailand and Japan*, p. 11; Crosby, *Crossroads*, p. 63; Charivat, *Thai Foreign Policy*, p. 114; Aldrich, *Key to the South*, p. 125; Stowe, *Siam becomes Thailand*, p. 38; Nuntana, Phuangphet and Supatra, *Japan and Thailand*, p. 56f.

forty-two other states stood up against Japan.[66] It is undisputed that affinity or admiration can be detected in 1933 Siam, particularly in military circles, for Japan as an independent Asian state managing its own domestic and international affairs on a par with Western countries.[67] But this affinity was not the motivation behind Siam's abstention. Rather, Siam abstained in 1933 because it wanted to demonstrate its neutrality in Asia and in the Western world, not least because of the scepticism prevailing in London and Paris as to the foreign policy orientation of the new constitutional government, which had taken power only months before the abstention. As Sir Josiah Crosby put it in 1945, Siam did well,

> ...to take up an impartial position upon so highly contentious an issue. She was not siding *with* the Japanese; on the other hand, by declining to take sides *against* them she was indicating her realisation of the fact that Japan had become, in addition to Britain and France, one of those countries which she could not afford to antagonise.[68]

As mentioned above, the end of the absolute monarchy in 1932 did not immediately affect Siam's policy in Geneva. As Kobkua Suwannathat-Pian points out, the basic rationale of Siam's pro-Western foreign policy was not fundamentally affected by the end of the absolute monarchy at all.[69] After having reconstructed the actual policy decision, the views which describe Siam's abstention in February 1933 as the result of a pro-Japanese policy are not convincing. They are also not convincing when put into the larger foreign policy context of early 1933. The traditional policy of neutrality in international conflicts led to the abstention, although the abstention afterwards backfired on Thai policy makers through extensive Japanese propaganda, and although the abstention was afterwards increasingly seen as marking a shift in the kingdom's traditionally pro-Western foreign policy.[70] Furthermore, the bias in Siam's foreign relations for Japan and against war-torn China, which had been detectable since the rise of Japan as a regional power in the early twentieth century, was seen by contemporary Western observers as an obvious choice, as positive, and in the words of the eminent Arnold J. Toynbee in 1929 even as 'a matter of congratulation, not only to Siam herself but to Mankind!'[71]

Reactions to Siam's abstention in China were much less vocal than those in Japan. And they did not resonate internationally, unlike the Japanese reactions, although scattered Chinese newspaper articles did find their way into the international and the Bangkok press. Moreover, the Thai government did not have to bother with official repercussions because it did not maintain formal diplomatic relations with China. However, in Bangkok the Manchurian Conflict did resonate in a different, much more serious manner, as it led to anti-Japanese boycotts among the Chinese population, which began immediately after the Mukden Incident.[72] Chinese boycotts of Japanese goods were a recurring phenomenon in Siam and other Asian territories, which had turned

66 Terwiel, *Political History*, p. 269 and Terwiel, *History of Modern Thailand*, p. 339; Terwiel also points to Siam's pro-Japanese abstention in 1933 as an early expression of later irredentist policies for which Japan provided an example in Manchuria, see Barend J. Terwiel, 'Thai Nationalism and Identity: Popular Themes of the 1930s', in Craig J. Reynolds (ed.), *National Identity and Its Defenders, Thailand, 1939-1989*, Monash Papers on Southeast Asia, no. 25, Clayton (Victoria): Centre of Southeast Asian Studies, Monash University, 1991, pp. 133-154, here: p. 142. Other scholars who adhere to the view that the abstention was a clear pro-Japanese policy statement are Batson, *End of Absolute Monarchy*, p. 179; Helmut Fessen and Hans-Dieter Kubitscheck, *Geschichte Thailands*, Bremer Asien-Pazifik Studien, vol. 7, Münster and Hamburg: Lit, 1994, p. 117 (although the authors confuse the Polish abstention of 1937 with the vote of 1933); Ian Nish also follows this interpretation, albeit carefully, as he bases his view only on Japanese sources.; see Nish, *Japan's Struggle*, p. 218, and Nish, Research Notelet.

67 In this sense also Terwiel, *Political History*, p. 269.

68 Crosby, *Crossroads*, p. 63 (emphasis in original).

69 Kobkua Suwannathat-Pian, *Thailand's Durable Premier: Phibun through Three Decades, 1932-1957*, Kuala Lumpur: Oxford University Press, 1995, p. 243.

70 See Memorandum Dormer, 6 February 1934, PRO, FO 371/18210, F 1691/1691/40.

72 Prince Devawongse to Royal Secretariat, 29 September 1931, TNA, R7, T 20/14; Dormer to Marquess of Reading, 31 October 1931, PRO, FO 371/15503, F 7190/1391/10; see also Swan, *Japanese Economic Relations*, p. 38ff.

violent in Bangkok in 1928 after the assassination of Chang Tso-lin by Japanese agents. The non-violent boycott of late 1931 continued into 1932, and when Chinese troops managed to halt the Japanese advance in Shanghai in March, Chinese victory celebrations and a demonstration in Bangkok led Thai authorities to arrest 166 persons overnight. By autumn of that year police in Bangkok again arrested participants in Chinese rallies for the boycott of Japanese goods.[73] Further afield, Siam's abstention even triggered a limited boycott of Thai goods in Canton in March 1933.[74]

Crippled by Japan's departure from Geneva, all the League could do was to ensure effective non-recognition of Manchukuo by its members. Siam assured the League that it would not recognise Manchukuo in any way, but made arrangements for issuing *laissez-passers* to individuals entering Siam with identity documents from Manchukuo.[75] Siam's adherence to the League's non-recognition policy was seen by the Ministry of Foreign Affairs as very important because it underlined the kingdom's position of neutrality towards both conflict parties.

The Manchurian Conflict was the most serious blow the League of Nations had suffered in over a decade of existence. In addition, it also developed into the most serious challenge to Siam's policy of neutrality in foreign affairs. Officials must have been equally relieved in Bangkok and in Geneva when the troublesome affair began to fade from the attention of the world in the course of 1933. But only some two years later both Siam and the League of Nations would find themselves embroiled in a new international conflict which posed a similarly grave challenge.

Siam's sanctions against Italy over its invasion of Ethiopia in 1935

In a bid to expand its colonial empire in Africa and exploit the region's natural resources, the fascist Italian regime under Benito Mussolini attacked Ethiopia, or Abyssinia, as the country was then called, on 3 October 1935 from the neighbouring Italian colonial possessions of Eritrea and Somaliland. This outright invasion marked the culmination of nearly a year of tensions and skirmishes since the so-called Wal-Wal Incident, a battle between Ethiopian and Italian forces which had left 200 troops dead in December 1934. Since January 1935 the League of Nations had been trying to mediate on the basis of article XI of the covenant between Italy and the African country, which had been a League member since 1923. Mediation efforts were still in progress when Mussolini decided to act and invade Ethiopia with over 100,000 Italian troops. On 7 October 1935 the League of Nations judged that Italy was waging outright war and was in breach of article XII of the covenant. The General Assembly therefore decided to apply sanctions against the aggressor on 19 October 1935 under article XVI of the covenant.[76]

73 Johns to Simon, 9 March 1932, PRO, FO 371/16163, F 33324/1/10; TNA, *Bangkok Times*, 10 October 1932; see on the boycott also Flood, Japan's Relations with Thailand, vol. 1, p. 31ff.; for Chinese boycotts in response to the Manchurian Conflict in the Philippines see Antonio S. Tan, 'The Philippine Chinese Response to the Sino-Japanese Conflict, 1931-1941', *Journal of Southeast Asian Studies*, 12, 1 (1981), pp. 207-223.

74 Memorandum by Phraya Abhibal, 1 March 1933, TNA, KT 96.1.6.2/8.

75 Drummond to Ministry of Foreign Affairs, 14 June 1933 and Phraya Abhibal to Drummond, 27 September 1933, LNA, R 3607/1/3603/207. On passport questions see Minister of Foreign Affairs to Prime Minister, 4 September B.E. 2476 (1933), TNA, SR 0201.17/5. On the connection between non-recognition and neutrality see Under Secretary of State for Foreign Affairs to Prime Minister, n.d. [August 1933], TNA, KT 96.1.6.2/11.

76 Albert E. Highley, 'The Actions of the States Members of the League of Nations in the Application of Sanctions against Italy, 1935/1936', Ph.D. Thesis, University of Geneva, 1938; George W. Baer, *The Coming of the Italian-Ethiopian War*, Cambridge (MA): Harvard University Press, 1967; George W. Baer, *Test Case: Italy, Ethiopia, and the League of Nations*, Stanford (CA): Hoover Institution Press, 1976; Northedge, *League of Nations*, p. 221ff.

During the following months, no less than twenty-nine League of Nations committees and sub-committees were created to devise, enforce and coordinate the first multilateral sanctions ever imposed by an international organisation.[77] Significantly, major European powers did not wish to offend Italy too strongly, sanctions were imposed on arms and an array of commercial goods and raw materials, but not on oil. Italy could, therefore, continue to fuel its military operations in East Africa. The Italian invasion, which ended in May 1936 with Emperor Haile Selassi's flight into exile and the formal annexation of Ethiopia by Italy, was particularly brutal. Italian troops widely employed the new instrument of aerial bombardments, as well as firebombs, and made substantial use of mustard gas, even though Italy was a signatory to the Geneva Protocol of 1925 banning use of chemical weapons.[78] Because of the League's condemnation of Italy's actions and because of the sanctions, Italy ultimately followed the precedents set by its future war allies Japan and Nazi-Germany in 1933 and declared its withdrawal from the League in December 1937.

Siam's policies during the Ethiopian Crisis and the attitudes among the Bangkok elite reflect the growing divisions among the civilian and military factions during the 1930s. Luang Pradist, at the time Minister of Interior and the most visible and verbal representative of the civilian group among the ruling elite, yet again proved a supporter of the League of Nations' ideals during the Ethiopian Crisis. During his tour of Europe, he actually attended the deliberations of the League of Nations on 20 September 1935 together with Phraya Rajawangsan and Phra Riem Virajapak, Ministers in London and Paris respectively.[79] Ironically, Luang Pradist was received by Benito Mussolini in Rome on 5 October 1935 and informed personally by the *Duce* of the Italian attack on Ethiopia two days earlier.[80] Also in favour of sanctions were the two foreign affairs advisers Prince Varn and Frederick Dolbeare, as well as Minister of Foreign Affairs Phraya Srisena Sompatsiri (Ha Sompatsiri).[81] On the other side stood the Ministry of Defence under Luang Phibun, who had by 1935 already discarded the League of Nations as the guardian of Siam's security and maintained close relations with Italy in military training and arms contracts. The Italian Minister in Bangkok, Count Vittorio Negri, was very active in lobbying the Thai government during the second half of 1935 not to join in the sanctions against his country. To this end, he entered into a lengthy exchange of letters and memoranda with Phraya Srisena.[82] Count Negri found a supporter in Luang Phibun who sent an urgent and confidential memorandum to the Minister of Foreign Affairs advising that Siam should not be part of sanctions, but if joining was unavoidable, the Minister should at least assure Count Negri of the friendship of the Thai government.[83] A secret report by Sir Josiah Crosby in June 1936 also reflected this divide between the civilian and military factions:

77 See very detailed Highley, Actions of the States, p. 94ff.

78 Siam signed the 'Protocol for the Prohibition of the Use in War of Asphyxiating, Poisonous or Other Gases and Bacteriological Methods of Warfare' at Geneva on 27 June 1925. The protocol entered into force on 8 February 1928; Siam ratified the protocol on 6 June 1931. See for the text and parties to the protocol Knipping, von Mangoldt and Rittberger, *System der Vereinten Nationen*, p. 1614ff.

79 TNA, *Bangkok Times*, 3 October 1935.

80 Minister of Foreign Affairs to Prime Minister, 7 October B.E. 2478 (1935), TNA, KT 96.1.6.1/ 9; TNA, *Bangkok Times*, 8 October 1935.

81 See the memoranda by Dolbeare and Prince Varn, both 18 October 1935, TNA, KT 96.1.6.1/8.

82 See correspondence between Count Negri and the Ministry of Foreign Affairs in TNA, KT 96.1.6.1/4 and 5.

83 Minister of Defence to Minister of Foreign Affairs (Urgent and Confidential), 19 October B.E. 2478 (1935), TNA, KT 96.1.6.1/ 8.

It was, I suppose, inevitable that the unhappy Ethiopian business should have its repercussions even in distant Siam, and efforts to exploit the situation created by it were promptly made with some success by Count Negri, my Italian colleague, in concert with Captain Alberto Gehe, the naval attaché of Italy at Tokyo, whose presence in Siam a week or two ago has already been reported to you. It is true that Siam figures among the sanctionist countries and that Luang Pradist, the State Councillor for Foreign Affairs, has publicly announced the fidelity of his Government to the League of Nations and to the principle of collective security, but Luang Pradist, who is by conviction a Radical, in no way reflects the views Luang Phibul, the State Councillor for Defence, or of Luang Sindhu, the Chief of the Naval General Staff, both of whom are of a quite different political complexion. Moreover, the volume of trade between Siam and Italy has always been so exiguous that the former's participation in the scheme of sanctions represents little more than a gesture on her part, with which it seems that the naval and military authorities are in practice not concerning themselves.[84]

Indeed, relations between the Thai and Italian military were developing well; Thai air force and naval officers had been sent to Italy for training earlier in 1935, among them a son of Luang Phibun. The divisions between the Ministries of Foreign Affairs and Defence over the question of sanctions were so apparent that rumours of Siam being opposed to sanctions even surfaced in the United States and found their way into a *New York Times* article.[85] But eventually, the pro-sanctions group in the Ministry of Foreign Affairs prevailed over Luang Phibun, and Siam voted in favour of imposing economic, financial and arms sanctions against Italy at the General Assembly on 19 October 1935. The motivation was clearly spelled out by Dolbeare, 'inaction in this matter incurs the risk of serious and possibly public criticism in Geneva and serious embarrassment for the Siamese Delegate and anyone sharing responsibility in the present situation'.[86] Some two years after the fiasco created by the abstention over Manchuria, senior officials in Bangkok were certainly not willing to be dragged into the international limelight in such a way once again. To make matters worse, in 1935 Siam was already under fire in the League's Advisory Committee on Opium in Geneva for the opium smuggling scandal exposed by financial adviser James Baxter and could not afford yet more negative publicity by abstaining from imposing sanctions against Italy. A third motivation leading Siam to cooperate with League actions in late 1935 was probably its immediate goal of concluding new treaties with Western states and thereby reclaim full sovereignty by ending the last remnants of extraterritorial jurisdiction, an aim which was eventually achieved in late 1937. Clearly, Thai demands that Western states respect it as an independent and responsible member of the international community

84 Crosby to Eden, 2 June 1936, Secret, Doc. 200 (F 3502/216/40), BDFA, Part II, Series E, vol. 50, p. 244. Luang Pradist changed his portfolio from interior to that of foreign affairs in 1936, after returning from his European trip.

85 The article appeared in the 13 October issue of the *New York Times*; see Phraya Abhibal (Minister in Washington) to Phraya Srisena, 13 October 1935, TNA, KT 96.1.6.1/8.

86 Memorandum Dolbeare, 21 October 1935, TNA, KT 96.1.6.1/8.

during the mid-1930s would have been undermined if Siam would have avoided its responsibilities on the Geneva stage. It was in this sense, that Sir Josiah Crosby judged the matter almost ten years later, 'And I might mention, as further proof of adherence to democratic principles, the fact that the Siamese Government of the time signified its approval of the sanctions declared by the League against Italy on the occasion of her attack upon Abyssinia'.[87] Richard Sogn, when studying relations with the United States, later also confirmed the connection between Ethiopia and Thai sovereignty and judged that Siam's 'international cooperation seemed to be confirmed by Thailand's full cooperation with the League of Nations in its efforts to impose economic sanctions against Italy in the Ethiopian War'.[88] Before looking at the sanctions themselves, we must also acknowledge that the entire political drama was played out at a domestically uncertain time when, in an unprecedented act, King Prajadhipok, residing in England, stepped down from the throne in March 1935 out of deep frustration, leaving ten-year-old Ananda Mahidol, who was living a stone's throw from Geneva at Lausanne, to be declared king.

Thai sanctions against Italy were imposed by four royal decrees, the first of which was issued on 28 October 1935 with regard to the arms embargo. The sentence for offences was up to five years imprisonment and up to a 10,000 baht fine.[89] The following three royal decrees, which imposed economic and financial sanctions, were issued on 17 November 1935.[90] As these sanctions were primarily economic in nature and Siam's trade with Italy was quite limited, there was not much at stake for this demonstration of international solidarity.[91] Thai trade figures for the year B.E. 2477 (1934-35) show imports from Italy valued at 250,000 baht, while exports to Italy totalled 342,000 baht. This trade with Italy therefore made up only a quarter of one percent of Siam's total foreign trade. While Siam exported mainly teak wood and small quantities of rice and hides, it imported small quantities of a wide array of goods, the highest value items being marble, embroideries, lace and various other textiles. And, as one would expect, Italian noodles and wines also featured prominently on the list of imports, likely consumed by the Western expatriates in Bangkok.[92] While Italian-Thai trade was limited, it was seen as having potential for future expansion, and for this reason an Italian commercial delegation visited Bangkok in spring 1934 to explore business opportunities.[93]

The Thai government duly set up an inter-ministerial sanctions committee to coordinate national action. It transmitted monthly statistics on Siam's trade with Italy from November 1934 to June 1936 to the League of Nations Sanctions Coordination Committee. According to these statistics, trade between Italy and Siam came to a virtual halt during the first half of 1936, with Thai exports to Italy of between 0 and 18,000 baht per month consisting of wood and small quantities of

87 Crosby, *Crossroads*, p. 82.

88 Sogn, Successful Journey, p. 134.

89 TNA, *Bangkok Times*, 28 and 31 October 1935.

90 The royal decrees can be found in TNA, KT 96.1.6.1/10 (Part 1 of 2) and 11 (Part 2 of 2). The cabinet discussed how to comply with the League sanctions and the wording of the decrees on 23 and 28 October and on 8 and 15 November; minutes of the cabinet meetings can be found in TNA, SR 0201.17/18. See also TNA, *Bangkok Times*, 19 November 1935; and see Pierre Fistié, *L'évolution de la Thaïlande contemporaine*, Paris: Armand Colin, 1967, p. 174. All four decrees can also be found in LNA, R 3677/1/20585/20406.

91 Memorandum Dolbeare on Agenda of the 1936 League of Nations General Assembly, 10 August 1938, TNA, KT 96.1.3/20; statistics of trade between Siam and Italy in LNA, R 3686/1/23583/22448 and identical in TNA, KT 96.1.6.1/6.

92 Note by Director of Statistical Office, 21 October 1935, TNA, KT 96.1.6.1/7.

93 TNA, *Bangkok Times*, 9 May 1934.

rice and Thai imports from Italy ranging from 280 and 7,000 baht per month, made up mainly of marble and textiles.[94]

Once Siam had voted for imposing sanctions, Luang Phibun changed his strategy from trying to prevent the sanctions outright to aiming to exempt the warships being built in Italy for the Thai navy. As part of the military expansion programme of the post-absolutist regimes, Siam had ordered seven torpedo boats and two mine-layers from the firm Cantieri Riuniti dell'Adriatico at Monfalcone near Trieste in 1934-35. The vessels were scheduled for delivery between late 1935 and 1937, while some ten additional ships were at the same time being built in Japan and were scheduled for delivery in 1938.[95] Buying warships fell under the League sanctions, and the government in Bangkok, therefore, had a serious problem at hand. Instead of cancelling the orders in the spirit of the League sanctions, however, Thai officials tried to have the ships exempted. It seems an interesting coincidence that it was Phraya Rajawangsan, the newly appointed Minister in London and Thai Permanent Representative, who represented Siam at the League of Nations, together with the experienced but junior Luang Bhadravadi, during the period of sanctions against Italy. While he received his instructions from the Ministry of Foreign Affairs, he was an admiral in the Royal Thai Navy and a former Minister of Defence himself, and had a strong interest in exempting the war ships.[96] Moreover, Luang Sindhu, Phraya Rajawangsan's brother and a close ally of Luang Phibun, was still serving as Navy Chief of Staff. In concert with Luang Phibun and the Ministry of Defence, the Ministry of Foreign Affairs instructed Phraya Rajawangsan and Luang Bhadravadi to lobby the British and French delegations in Geneva for their support for this exemption.[97] The issue seemed particularly delicate because no other League members asked for exemptions, as Mani Sanasen of the League Secretariat informed Phraya Rajawangsan confidentially in October 1935. The Committee of Eighteen, as the executive organ of the Sanctions Coordination Committee was called, decided on 31 October that, basically, all contracts for which total payment had not been made before 19 October, the date of the Assembly decision, fell under the sanctions. But during the last days of that month the Committee of Eighteen received three further requests for exemption by the delegations of Poland, the Soviet Union, and Norway, concerning contracts which were partially paid for, and it therefore decided to re-examine those three cases together with the Thai case. Between 4 and 11 November, the so-called Economic Committee under the Sanctions Coordination Committee considered the requests in secret sessions. Holding secret sessions was deemed necessary because the question of exempting of arms contracts was, rightly, considered dangerous for the unity of states in the application of sanctions. On 11 November, the Committee

94 Monthly Trade Statistics Siam-Italy, November 1934 to June 1936, LNA, R 3686/1/23583/22448. The Bangkok Customs House duly reported to the League that in June 1936 one pistol, valued at 20 baht, was imported from Italy.

95 Landon, *Thailand in Transition*, p. 66; see also TNA, *Bangkok Times*, 4 May 1934 and 18 November 1935.

96 Phraya Rajawangsan to de Vasconcellos, 15 October 1935, LNA, R 3670/1/20371/20347.

97 Minister of Foreign Affairs to Minister of Defence, 4 November B.E. 2478 (1935), Phraya Srisena to Luang Bhadravadi, 30 October 1935; all in TNA, KT 96.1.6.1/7. See also the urgent and confidential letter by Luang Phibun to the Prime Minister, 11 October B.E. 2478 (1935), TNA, SR 0201.17/18.

decided to exempt from sanctions the contracts for all ships being built in Italy for the Thai navy under proposal number 3, paragraph 3 of the decision of 19 October.[98] One week later the first of the torpedo boats was launched at Monfalcone in the presence of Luang Pradist and the Thai Minister to Italy, 'marked by the greatest cordiality between Siamese and Italian authorities'.[99] On the same day, the *H.M.S. Chao Phraya* set sail from Bangkok to Monfalcone to escort the first two torpedo boats back to Siam, where they arrived on 14 March 1936 amidst great fanfare and cheering crowds. Fittingly, the Minister of Foreign Affairs was again on hand to greet the new ships after his office had successfully prevented League sanctions from being imposed against them.[100] By mid-1937, Siam took delivery of seven more torpedo boats and two minelayers from Italy, while two sloops, three patrol boats and two submarines were delivered from Japan.[101]

Thai diplomats in Europe and officials in Bangkok did what their colleagues from France, Great Britain and other countries also did, they stressed towards Italian officials whenever they could that the sanctions were simply an unfortunate necessity, which should not affect the cordial relationship between their governments. Following protest notes by Count Negri to the Thai government in November 1935 and January 1936, Luang Pradist pointed out to the count in February 1936 that Siam felt 'genuine friendship for Italy' and that if Siam had 'to apply economic and financial sanctions…it is only because we are bound to do so by the provisions of the Covenant'.[102] Indeed, the files in Bangkok reveal no statements, confidential or official, which suggest that the Thai government genuinely felt that the sanctions were necessary and just. In addition to the navy contracts, another factor contributed to the pro-Italian sentiments among parts of the Thai elite and to undermining effective concerted action at Geneva. By the mid-1930s, Benito Mussolini and his Fascist movement possessed a considerable degree of attraction for Luang Phibun and the military faction in the government.[103] Accordingly, it does not come as a surprise that Siam reopened its legations in Rome and Berlin during this period.[104] Just as the appeal of authoritarian rule and sense of necessity for increasing arms expenditure grew in the course of the 1930s, so did the attraction of the League as guardian of collective security decline for Thai policymakers and the ineffectiveness of the League's sanctions against Italy had a strong impact on this change of attitudes.[105] Fittingly, an article in the Thai Navy Magazine expressed the attitude of the military faction very clearly. Referring to the Italian-Ethiopian Conflict, the author asked rhetorically:

> What has the League of Nations succeeded in doing? In the event, Abyssinia has had to depend on herself alone, and when her own strength was ruined, she was ruined…It is all very well to develop our agriculture, our education, our commerce and so forth, but the

98 Phraya Rajawangsan to Phraya Srisena, 23 October 1935, TNA, KT 96.1.6.1/8; Luang Bhadravadi to Phraya Srisena, 31 October and 11 November 1935, TNA, KT 96.1.6.1/7. See also various correspondence on the exemption in TNA, KT 96.1.6.1/11 (Parts 1 of 2 and 2 of 2). A detailed list of all contracts placed for the nine vessels by the Thai navy in Italy, including total prices, payment instalments and outstanding payments was submitted by Phraya Rajawangsan to the Sanctions Coordination Committee of the League of Nations on 4 and 8 November 1935; see LNA, R 3677/1/20585/20406. The relevant proceedings of the Coordination Committee and its sub-committees are documented in LNA, League of Nations, *Official Journal, Special Supplement*, nos. 145, 146, 147, 148, 149, 150, 151, and 164. See also Highley, Actions of States, p. 175ff. After Siam's request, that of Poland was also approved. The verdict on the Soviet and Norwegian requests could not be determined by the author.

99 TNA, *Bangkok Times*, 28 October 1935.

100 TNA, *Bangkok Times*, 18 November 1935 and 16 March 1936.

101 Annual Report for 1937, PRO, FO 371/22215, F 2080/2080/40, p. 15. See also TNA, *Bangkok Times*, 6 September 1937. On Siam's armaments purchases between 1933 and 1938 see also Terwiel, *Political History*, p. 268.

102 See for all mentioned correspondence TNA, KT 96.1.6.1/1.

103 In this sense see French and British observations in Ray to Flandin, 27 May 1936, Ministère des Affaires Étrangères, Commission de Publication des Documents relatifs aux Origines de la Guerre 1939-1945 (ed.), *Documents Diplomatiques Français 1932-1939*, 2° Serie (1936-1939), Paris: Imprimerie Nationale, 1964, Tome II, p. 398ff.; Annual Report for 1936, PRO, FO 371/21053, F 1067/1067/40, p. 11.

104 Aldrich, *Key to the South*, p. 174.

105 See also Annual Report for 1936, PRO, FO 371/21053, F 1067/1067/40, p. 14.

world is in a troubled state, and our independence is sustained by nothing beyond our own strength.[106]

Concerted economic sanctions were new for all countries and Siam was no exception. On 4 January 1936, Count Negri enquired officially to Minister of Foreign Affairs Phraya Srisena whether an Italian national, who was driving up the Malay Peninsula in a Fiat automobile, would be allowed to enter the kingdom or whether this would constitute an illegal import of an Italian product under the sanctions. The matter caused some confusion at the Ministry of Foreign Affairs, the Ministry of Finance was consulted, foreign affairs adviser Dolbeare wrote a one-page memorandum on the issue, and nearly two weeks later Phraya Srisena was able to reply to Count Negri that, yes, the adventurous motorist was allowed to cross into Siam because private possessions, such as a Fiat car, were exempted from the sanctions under section 6 of the royal decree.[107] Another instance causing some confusion was when, on 11 March 1936 the Bangkok customs department decided to withhold a consignment of two Emmenthal cheeses imported from Switzerland via the Italian port of Genoa by the trading company Diethelm & Co. on the grounds that the cheeses were subject to the sanctions. This matter prompted the Swiss consul in Bangkok to intervene, pointing out that the cheese was of Swiss origin and due to its 'perishable nature' the owners were 'very anxious to take delivery of the goods quickest possible.' The customs department, however, maintained that the cheese was consigned from Italy and therefore was indeed subject to sanctions. Diethelm representatives and the Swiss consulate did what they could during the following weeks to convince customs and Foreign Ministry officials that the consignment was never Italian-owned but simply had had to be transported to a port from landlocked Switzerland. A two-page memorandum jointly drawn up by foreign affairs adviser Prince Varn and judicial adviser René Guyon of 30 March then decided the matter in favour of Diethelm & Co., and official notice of the decision regarding 'the detention by His Majesty's Customs of a shipment of Swiss cheese' was sent by the Minister of Foreign Affairs to the Swiss consulate on 9 April. As a result, customs officials 'released the cheese in question', now aged a further month.[108] Further controversial cases concerned the import of a consignment of dried flowers and of automobile parts.[109] But these were all isolated cases and overall, according to an assessment by the Ministry of Foreign Affairs, the Thai sanctions against Italy, which formally lasted some eight months, only had a negligible impact as trade between Italy and Thailand was almost insignificant anyhow. Such an assessment is accurate when one omits, as the ministry did, the abovementioned navy contracts, which were far from insignificant.[110]

With the important navy contracts exempted and sanctions limited largely to these economically rather unimportant cases, Siam was able to pursue a 'middle position, that is, scrupulously to fulfil all obligations

106 'The Siamese Must Take Thought', by Commander Ananda Natr Bojana in *Navy Magazine*, PRO, FO 371/20300, F 5070/216/40.

107 The matter is documented in TNA, KT 96.1.6.1/2.

108 The whole matter is documented in TNA, KT 96.1.6.1/14.

109 See details in TNA, KT 96.1.6.1/16 and 26.

110 The Thai Ministry of Foreign Affairs gave this assessment to the League of Nations Secretary-General on 23 September 1936, TNA, KT 96.1.6.1/25 and LNA, R 3680/1/24979/20406.

vis-à-vis the League and at the same time make every effort to retain Italian goodwill', as outlined by Dolbeare.[111] But it was not all smooth sailing. According to a British report, 'discourtesy' by Italian navy officers towards a visiting Thai delegation at Trieste led to an incident in Bangkok in 1936 'when strong words were used between the Italian Minister in Bangkok and the Minister for Foreign Affairs', the blame for which the British observer put on the 'tactlessness' of Count Negri. In addition, Count Negri took his aggressive lobbying in Bangkok one step too far when he issued strongly-worded press communiqués without informing the Ministry of Foreign Affairs in February 1936. While the ministry did not contest the right of the Italian legation to issue press communiqués, it did summon Count Negri for a discussion with Prince Varn, during which the Count gave in and explained that he was convinced that no need for another communiqué to the press regarding sanctions would arise. The matter was laid to rest for the time being but Count Negri was eventually recalled to Italy a few months later.[112]

Eventually, the League sanctions against Italy proved ineffective, largely because League members applied them only half-heartedly. However, it was mainly the Hoare-Laval Pact between Great Britain and France of December 1935 accepting Italy's action, which undermined the League's multilateral efforts, and rendered the sanctions virtually useless. Italy went on to annex Ethiopia on 9 May 1936 and later left the League Assembly, following the example set by the other two Axis powers-to-be, Japan and Germany. Stunned and paralysed, the League of Nations General Assembly decided in July 1936 to lift the sanctions. As the historian of the Ethiopian Conflict, George Baer, put it, 'the League of Nations had not kept the peace, had not protected one of its members, had not deterred or punished an aggressor, and by its failures…the League as a political institution was humiliated and doomed.[113] Siam again abstained from voting, this time from the decision to lift the sanctions, because, as Phraya Rajawangsan explained, Siam was also a small country which could one day face an invasion. In such an event, he went on, Siam might need to appeal to the League and a vote in favour of lifting the sanctions against Italy should not come back to haunt Siam in such a situation.[114] After the sanctions were lifted, the prestige of the League in the field of collective security diminished further in Siam as it did all over the world. The 'unhappy Ethiopian business', to borrow Sir Josiah Crosby's expression cited above, encouraged the Thai elite to turn away from their traditional allies in Europe and towards Japan even more, as reflected by a Bangkok commentary in April 1936: 'In view of the League's failure to save Ethiopia, observers prophesy that a regional security system will replace the Geneva idea, and that a League of Asiatic nations will be eventually organized for guaranteeing peace in East Asia'.[115] And, in a sense, this prophecy actually turned into reality some years later.

111 Memorandum Dolbeare, 14 May 1936, TNA, KT 96.1.6.1/ 20.

112 TNA, KT 96.1.6.1/15; Annual Report for 1936, PRO, FO 371/ 21053, F 1067/1067/40, p. 11.

113 Baer, *Coming of the Italian-Ethiopian War*, p. 375.

114 Phraya Rajawangsan gives a very lively report of the dramatic atmosphere at the plenary session and details on the vote in Phraya Rajawangsan to Ministry of Foreign Affairs, 6 July B.E. 2479 (1936) and 15 September 1936, TNA, KT 96.1.6.1/21. A royal decree lifting the sanctions on a national level was put into force on 15 July 1936; see TNA, KT 96.1.6.1/27.

115 TNA, *Bangkok Times*, 23 April 1936.

When the General Assembly convened a few months after the sanctions disaster for its annual meeting in Geneva, Phraya Rajawangsan reported that the mood among delegates was extremely sober because of the Ethiopian Crisis, the Spanish Civil War and the German rearmament of the Rhineland, and he went on to point out that it had been the Western powers themselves, and in the first place France, which had discredited the collective security system of the League. In the opinion of Phraya Rajawangsan, it was only a question of time before the League would cease to exist.[116] In fact, when at the outset of this General Assembly the final episode of the Italian-Ethiopian Conflict unfolded over the question of the validity of the credentials of the Ethiopian delegation, Phraya Rajawangsan once again abstained from voting, an act which was once again favourably received by the Italians.[117] But in 1936 it was still too early to write off the League's role in collective security completely, as two final acts were still to play out in Geneva with Thai involvement.

Siam's second abstention from voting to condemn Japan's actions in China in 1937

In July 1937 the so-called Marco Polo Bridge Incident provided the pretext for Japan's large-scale southward military advance into China and marked the starting point for the second Sino-Japanese War, which lasted until 1941, when, after the attack on Pearl Harbor, it merged with the greater conflict of the Second World War for another four years. China once again appealed to the League of Nations for help, but all the League Assembly could do in October 1937 was to condemn the actions of Japan yet again. This condemnation had no effect on Japan whatsoever, because the political and military leadership in Tokyo was by this time determined to occupy China. Japan was not even present in Geneva, as the country had formally left the League of Nations in the wake of the Manchurian Conflict.[118] Siam abstained from voting to condemn Japan's actions.

Siam's relations with Japan had changed substantially since Luang Bhadravadi abstained from voting at Geneva for the first time in early 1933, just as the world around Siam had also changed significantly during those years. While Japan was becoming increasingly influential in Asia, the Western colonial powers in the region, the United States, Britain, France and the Netherlands were increasingly unwilling and unable to counter this Japanese dominance. Siam's ever closer economic and political relations with Japan were primarily a result of these developments, while they were also driven by domestic changes within Siam, where the military increasingly dominated politics and the government was moving towards authoritarian rule with an ideological affinity for Japan. This shift in Thai foreign policy was not sudden but rather a gradual process. While Minister of Foreign Affairs Luang Pradist still defended Siam's neutral and pro-Western policies in 1937,

116 Report on the General Assembly of 1936, dated 29 October B.E. 2479 (1936), TNA, KT 96.1.3/20. Francis Walters recalls: 'No Assembly had ever come together in such a mood of ill humour, discouragement, and anxiety as that which gathered at Geneva [in] 1936.' See Walters, *League of Nations*, p. 684.

117 Annual Report for 1936, PRO, FO 371/21053, F 1067/1067/40, p. 14. Also see Walters, League of Nations, p. 688ff.

118 Japan officially declared its withdrawal from League on 27 March 1933; according to the League's procedures, the withdrawal formally took effect two years thereafter, on 27 March 1935. Since declaring its withdrawal, Japan merely maintained a small liaison office in Geneva to continue cooperation in selected social and technical fields of the League's work, before ending its cooperation with the organisation completely in 1938.

Defence Minister Luang Phibun and his military colleagues in the government openly favoured close ties with Japan, large-scale armament programmes, and a reorientation of foreign policy away from collective security and towards aggressively expansionistic states such as Germany and Italy.[119] The League of Nations' inability to settle the disputes over Manchuria, the Rhineland, and Ethiopia was a key element in this change of perspective among the Thai elite from West to East.[120] As Robert Rothstein has pointed out:

> No period was as unattractive for Small Powers as the one which existed in the 1930s…Small Powers found themselves without a single viable policy choice. Nonalignment, bloc alignment, and Small Power alignment were all disastrous. It seemed likely that the best of the bad options still involved choosing the winning side.[121]

Rothstein's analysis focused on Europe, but equally holds true for Siam. By the mid-1930s the Thai political and military leadership was increasingly inclined to also choose the 'winning side', which, in Asia, was undoubtedly ever more influential Japan. Sir Josiah Crosby accurately observed this growing pro-Japanese sentiment among parts of the Thai elite as early as 1934.[122] It was in that year that Japan sent military and trade missions to Siam, airline connections between Bangkok and Tokyo were expanded and Japan permanently stationed a military attaché in its legation in Bangkok. In 1935, press reports of a Thai 'goodwill mission' studying economic and political conditions in Japan and Manchukuo suggested that recognition of the young state was imminent.[123] In September 1935 a 'Japanese-Siamese Cultural Association' was founded in Japan aimed at promoting a pan-Asian ideology.[124] This was followed in November by the founding of a 'Siam-Japan-Association' in Bangkok, for the purpose of establishing a Japanese-language school.[125] In the same year, Siam opened consulates in Kobe and Nagoya.

The American Minister in Bangkok reported on a dinner hosted by the Prime Minister, in his capacity as acting Minister of Defence, in honour of visiting Japanese naval officers in March 1935. In his table speech the visiting Japanese admiral referred to the events in Geneva in February 1933:

> It is still fresh in the memory of the Japanese people that the delegate of your country was courageous enough to call out in a loud voice 'Abstention', to the embarrassed surprise of the delegates of other countries. I feel bound to express a sense of gratitude for this gesture, which I take as a symbol of reasonable understanding and deep sympathy with my country. Japan's withdrawal from the League of Nations is to take effect in a few days.[126]

In April of that year the *Bangkok Times* commented on an article in *The Nation* which pointed out 'that ever since Siam refused to vote against

119 TNA, *Bangkok Times*, 3 April 1937; see also Reynolds, Thailand and Japan, p. 16; Stoffers, *Im Lande des weißen Elefanten*, p. 187.

120 One of the few studies to acknowledge the League of Nations dimension in this reorientation of Thai policies is Nicholas Tarling, *Britain, Southeast Asia and the Onset of the Pacific War*, p. 19 and 51.

121 Rothstein, *Alliances and Small Powers*, p. 234.

122 Crosby to Simon, 25 September 1934, Doc. 131 (F 6575/30 35/40), BDFA, Part II, Series E, vol. 50, p. 153ff.

123 TNA, *Bangkok Times*, 4 September 1935.

124 TNA, *Bangkok Times*, 11 September 1935.

125 TNA, *Bangkok Times*, 15 November 1935.

126 Political Report for March 1935, TKRI, United States Department of State, Consular Reports Siam, 890.00 P.R./72, p. 2. See also TNA, *Bangkok Times*, 22 March 1935.

Japan over the dispute about Manchuria in the League of Nations, Japan always bears that friendly act in mind when Siam is mentioned.' The *Bangkok Times* went on to state that 'the *Nation* does make it plain that the relations between the two countries are friendly and are based simply on business dealings'.[127] But already later that year a long article in the *North China Daily News* detailed the rapprochement between Bangkok and Tokyo in economic, political and military relations, which was to become even closer by 1937.[128]

All the while Luang Pradist continued to reaffirm his 'adherence to the League of Nations and to the principle of collective security', particularly during his time as Minister of Foreign Affairs, when rumours surfaced that Siam would enter into a Japan-led 'Asiatic League' in early 1936. The Minister explained:

> Firstly, that Siam is a member of the League of Nations, and has been since the beginning. Moreover, Siam has always met all the obligations which that membership has entailed. I might mention, added the Minister, that even in the matter of contribution, we have regularly paid ours before some other countries. Then, secondly, Siam is an independent country. The first and foremost thing that Siam desires is peace. Siam's first aim is not to alienate her friends or endanger her independence. Personally, I think the suggestion of an Asiatic League is a dream. The League of Nations, it is true, does not embrace every nation on its roll of members; some nations have even resigned from it. It does not always succeed in its policies, but even if it not always successful it has achieved something towards bringing about international co-operation.[129]

The rumours of an 'Asiatic League' led by Japan with Thai participation were also fuelled during 1936 by the League's failure over Ethiopia, which, according to the *Bangkok Times*, would likely lead to regional collective security arrangements replacing the global system of the League.[130] In 1937, in spite of continuing propaganda from Japan hailing Siam's 1933 abstention as a pro-Japanese policy, Luang Pradist constantly stressed a policy of strict neutrality. Already contemporary accounts pointed out that in Siam 'those in authority fear the military strength of Japan' and that the 'Siamese can hardly be blamed for taking up a position of strict neutrality'.[131] Luang Pradist was credited by Western observers for his genuine policy of neutrality, in the words of Sir Josiah Crosby even to the extent of being almost anti-Japanese.[132]

As we have seen in the context of immigration and human trafficking in the previous chapter, Siam's policies towards the Chinese minority also changed during the years between the first and the second Geneva abstention. In the wake of the economic crisis of the early 1930s, the government began suppressing the Chinese dominance of commercial activities by issuing discriminatory laws against Chinese businesses.

127 TNA, *Bangkok Times*, 18 April 1935.

128 TNA, *Bangkok Times*, 2 October 1935.

129 'Siam's Policy Towards Foreign Nations', enclosure in Crosby to Eden, 10 March 1936, Doc. 189 (F 1525/100/40), BDFA, Part II, Series E, vol. 50, p. 230; TNA, *Bangkok Times*, 10 March 1936; see on the rumours of Siam joining an 'Asiatic League' also a comment in the *Straits Times*, which was reprinted in the *Bangkok Times*: TNA, *Bangkok Times*, 17 March 1936. The comment of the newspaper on this policy statement read: '...the categorical denial of any co-operation in an Asiatic League should silence the reports that have emanated in some cases from Japan itself. Apart from her membership in the League of Nations, Siam is not likely to do anything which would endanger her independence.'

130 TNA, *Bangkok Times*, 23 April 1936.

131 Annual Report for 1937, PRO, FO 371/22215, F 2080/2080/40, p. 15. For an example of Japanese propaganda in 1936 see a reprinted article from the *Japan Advertiser* in TNA, *Bangkok Times*, 22 August 1936.

132 Crosby to Halifax, 27 October 1938, PRO, FO 371/22214, F 11680/1321/40.

Although openly aggressive anti-Chinese policies became popular only by the late 1930s, policies to drastically curb Chinese immigration as well as the closure of Chinese schools and newspapers were already pursued years earlier.[133] But the dominant domestic issue in 1937 was neither anti-Chinese nor pro-Japanese policy, but rather the crown land scandal, in which a number of senior members of the government were embroiled. The scandal led the government and the privy council to resign in July and to general elections in late December.[134] In the realm of foreign policy, the recovery of complete sovereignty and the end of consular jurisdiction was the dominant issue. New treaties with Western states and Japan to this end were concluded by November and December.[135]

China brought Japan's large-scale military operation before the League of Nations on 12 September 1937 by invoking articles X, XI and XVII of the covenant.[136] Ten days later, Phraya Rajawangsan wrote from London to the ministry in Bangkok that 'everyone, including China, knows that nothing will be accomplished because the League no longer possesses the necessary power'.[137] The conflict was brought before the League Assembly in late September and was then transferred to the Far Eastern Advisory Committee, which had been set up by the extraordinary Assembly on the very day, 24 February 1933, on which Siam had first abstained from condemning Japan for its actions in China. The Advisory Committee, which had nominally existed ever since 1933, met and drew up a report which once again condemned Japan's renewed invasion of China. It presented the report to the General Assembly on 5 October 1937. Four delegates raised objections in that meeting, stating that they had been unable to consult with their governments and receive instructions, namely the delegates of South Africa, Poland, Norway, and Siam. Phraya Rajawangsan had remained silent and later even absented himself from the first meeting on the conflict on 28 September, which was also the very first assembly meeting in the new hall of the Palais des Nations, the League's grand new palace overlooking Lake Geneva. At the plenary meeting on 5 October the Thai representative made the following statement:

> As a sister nation of China and Japan, to both of whom my country is bound by close ties of traditional friendship, Siam deeply deplores the present conflict and ardently desires the restoration of peace with the least possible delay. My Government would therefore be happy to welcome any action that would bring about the blessing of peace desired by us all. In order to secure peace, the various contributing factors must be determined as effectively to lead to the common end desired. As it has not been possible for me to put my Government in a position to study the draft resolution with all the elements required for taking a decision, I shall abstain from voting.[138]

133 See Thompson, *Thailand*, p. xvi; Reynolds, International Orphans; Lin Yu, 'Twin Loyalties in Siam', *Pacific Affairs*, 2, 9 (June 1936), pp. 191-200.

134 Thompson, *Thailand*, p. 97ff.

135 Charivat, *Thai Foreign Policy*, p. 134ff.

136 LNA, Serial Document C.377. M.254.1937.VII. See also TNA, KT 96.1.6.2/12.

137 Phraya Rajawangsan to Ministry of Foreign Affairs, 21 September B.E. 2480 (1937), TNA, KT 96.1.6.2/12.

138 LNA, League of Nations, *Official Journal, Special Supplement no. 169: Records of the Eighteenth Ordinary Session of the Assembly*, Plenary Meetings, Text of the Debates, p. 121. On Phraya Rajawangsan's actions in the meeting of 28 September, see Phraya Rajawangsan to Minister of Foreign Affairs, 28 September 1933, TNA, KT 96.1.6.2/12.

As a result of these objections, the session was adjourned to late afternoon of the following day, in order to give these representatives time to consult with their respective governments. On 6 October, South Africa and Norway then dropped their objections in support of the report, but both Poland and Siam maintained their abstentions. In accordance with League procedures, this meant that the report of the Advisory Committee was unanimously adopted by the Assembly on 6 October, with the abstentions by Poland and Siam.

On 29 September, one day after the League Assembly's first meeting on the conflict, Luang Siddhi Sayamkarn (Tien Hook Hoontrakul), head of the League of Nations Section in the Foreign Ministry, sent an urgent handwritten note to the two advisers, Dolbeare and Prince Varn, requesting their opinions on whether any instructions should be sent to Phraya Rajawangsan for the forthcoming Assembly meetings. While Dolbeare advised in one sentence not to send any instructions, Prince Varn submitted a lengthy three-page memorandum in reply.[139] In essence, Prince Varn advised that Phraya Rajawangsan should make a statement condemning air bombardments if there were a roll-call, but to otherwise abstain from voting. The prince's memorandum also stated that, irrespective of this advice, it would be even more preferable to instruct Phraya Rajawangsan not to attend the Assembly meeting at all. But after discussion with Minister of Foreign Affairs Luang Pradist, Phraya Rajawangsan was, on the same day, instructed to make a statement condemning air bombardments and to abstaining from voting in the forthcoming meeting on 5 October.[140] On 1 October, the Minister of Foreign Affairs informed the Prime Minister that the League was about to publicly condemn the Japanese bombings of Chinese cities, which were causing high civilian casualties. Luang Pradist, with the support of Prince Varn, explained that if the Thai delegate would stay silent during a vote at Geneva, this would likely be interpreted by other delegates as an implicit approval of the aerial bombardments and of Japan's military action in general. Prime Minister Phraya Phahon agreed that Phraya Rajawangsan should make the said statement and the Minister of Foreign Affairs once again confirmed his instructions to Geneva on 4 October.[141]

As we have seen, Phraya Rajawangsan's statement at Geneva was made on 5 October and he maintained the Thai abstention on 6 October, when the resolution condemning Japan was formally passed. Intriguingly, Phra Mitrakarm Raksha, Thai Minister in Tokyo, sent a telegram to Bangkok also on 6 October, but too late to influence proceedings at Geneva. In this telegram, which sheds light on Thai-Japanese relations in the second half of the 1930s, he reported on a luncheon hosted in his honour by the Japanese Minister of Foreign Affairs that day. At the luncheon his host 'request[ed] that Siam oppose [the] League resolution' and went on to say that this action

139 Note Luang Siddhi with reply Dolbeare, and Memorandum by Prince Varn, all 29 September 1933, TNA, KT 96.1.6.2/12.

140 Luang Pradist to Phraya Rajawangsan, 29 September 1933, TNA, KT 96.1.6.2/12.

141 Minister of Foreign Affairs to Prime Minister, 1 October B.E. 2480 (1937), TNA, SR 0201.17/5; the identical letter can also be found in TNA, KT 96.1.6.2/12; Cabinet Secretary to Minister of Foreign Affairs, 3 October B.E. 2480 (1937), TNA, KT 96.1.6.1/12; Luang Pradist to Phraya Rajawangsan, 4 October 1937, TNA, SR 0201.17/5; Memorandum by Prince Varn, 4 October 1937, TNA, KT 96.1.6.2/12.

on the part of Siam would mark a turning point in the history of Asia. Phra Mitrakarm informed in his telegram that he replied vaguely to the Japanese Minister of Foreign Affairs that he could not guarantee such an action, also because 'during [the] Manchurian Incident Japan replied to Siam's abstention by putting [a] ban on Siamese rice.' His host 'replied that he felt the wrong done to Siam, but he assured me implicitly that all pending questions with regard to treaty and rice will be settled'.[142]

Another intriguing aspect of the Thai abstention of 1937 is revealed in the correspondence between Geneva and Bangkok. As we have seen, on 5 October Phraya Rajawangsan stated in the Assembly that he had not been able to fully inform his government on the details of the conflict and the resolution. Indeed, in his telegram to Bangkok the following day he reported that the documents for consideration were too long to send by telegram and he was therefore sending them by airmail. However, in his confidential letter to the Minister of Foreign Affairs of the same day he explained that he had written this sentence in the telegram only so that his public statement would hold firm even if it was read by a third party.[143] The inability to consult with Bangkok was obviously a pretext and abstention was always the intended course of action.

The pro-Japanese sentiment underlying the abstention in 1937 was understandable as by then Thai diplomats were already on better terms with the Japanese than with the League, which was seen more and more, in the words of Charnvit Kasetsiri, as 'an organization dominated by Europeans and their interests'.[144] Although Sir Josiah Crosby judged that Siam was still acting in a strictly neutral fashion and was simply 'sitting upon the fence', the abstention in 1937 was, to a much larger degree than that of 1933, taken by the international political public as a vote in favour of Japan.[145] On 26 September 1937, only days before the League's vote, festivities commemorating the fiftieth anniversary of the Thai-Japanese treaty of 1887 took place in Tokyo and Bangkok.[146] It was clear to observers in Siam and abroad that by 1937 political relations between Siam and Japan had become cordial and were accompanied by increasingly close economic and military relations. Siam's 1933 abstention had been used as proof of close relations time and again. But it was also clear to many observers that Japan was the driving force behind this rapprochement and that the 1933 abstention was being exploited by Japan to a degree which clearly exceeded whatever intention might have laid behind the act itself.[147]

On the other hand, the situation in Siam and in Asia in 1937 was such that a vote in Japan's favour by Siam would have been, in the light of the above, a much more realistic policy option than it had been in 1933. That the Thai government, and Minister of Foreign Affairs Luang Pradist in particular, nevertheless chose to abstain in the League Assembly, can therefore also be interpreted as a vote with a bias against Japan. In other words, while abstaining in 1933 meant deviating from a

142 Phra Mitrakarm to Minister of Foreign Affairs, 6 October 1937, TNA, KT 96.1.6.2/12. Phra Mitrakarm repeated the report in a letter to the Foreign Ministry on the same day, which can be found in the same file.

143 Telegram and letter Phraya Rajawangsan to Minister of Foreign Affairs, both dated 6 October 1937, TNA, KT 96.1.6.2/12.

144 Charnvit Kasetsiri, 'The First Phibun Government and Its Involvement in World War II', *Journal of the Siam Society*, 62, 2 (1974), p. 25-88, here p. 58. See also Annual Report for 1937, PRO, FO 371/22215, F 2080/2080/40, p. 15; TNA, SR 0201.17/5. A similar judgement of the events is found in Flood, Japan's Relations with Thailand, vol. 1, p. 183.

145 Crosby to Eden, 29 October 1937, PRO, FO 371/21017, F 9818/6799/10. Interestingly, Prince Varn, who was as adviser to the ministry something of a '*de facto*' Minister of Foreign Affairs, explained to Crosby as early as 1935 that, in his view, the two pivotal points of Siam's foreign policy had shifted from Britain and France to Britain and Japan; see Crosby to Simon, 19 November 1935, PRO, FO 371/19374, F 22/22/40.

146 A number of official telegrams marking the occasion are reprinted in TNA, *Bangkok Times*, 27 September 1937. See also Supaporn Jarunpattana, *Siam-Japan Relations 1920-1940*, Visiting Research Fellow Monograph Series, no. 159, Tokyo: Institute of Developing Economies, 1989, p. 35, note 57.

147 See, for example, Baker to Secretary of State, 18 May 1935, FRUS, 1935, vol. III: The Far Eastern Crisis, p. 170ff. This very detailed memorandum by the American Minister in Bangkok goes to great lengths in examining Thai-Japanese relations in the 1930s from political and economic perspectives and quotes a number of Japanese media reports which appeared during the very first days after the abstention on 24 February 1933.

seemingly broad international consensus, abstaining in 1937 meant taking a position against an otherwise ever closer Thai-Japanese rapprochement and decreasing influence of traditional Western powers on Thai policies.[148]

The statement read by Phraya Rajawangsan at the General Assembly was also the text of an official communiqué issued by the Bangkok government to explain its renewed abstention to the world. The statement was printed in the *Bangkok Times* on 6 October 1937 with the additional remark that the abstention merely reflected Siam's traditional policy of neutrality.[149] As if history was repeating itself, the abstention and the government's subsequent communiqué again prompted a series of newspaper commentaries in Siam and abroad. But the world was now much clearer as to Siam's motivation than it had been in 1933. Among the commentaries was a particularly accurate analysis of Siam's policy in the *Singapore Free Press* on 13 October, which explained the dilemma of Siam's foreign policy between the two poles, China and Japan, coupled with a strong Western orientation and domestic instability. Siam evidently felt, the article explained, 'that further to endanger Sino-Siam relations, which have been none too cordial in recent years was better than to risk offending Japan who has so often claimed to be her best friend.' While the commentator showed understanding for Siam's motives in abstaining, it concluded with a warning and with a reference to the conflict over Ethiopia:

> Siam must realize, however, that she will not always benefit by claiming neutrality in all world disputes. The time is fast approaching when the democracies must join hands against those who cannot observe the decencies of international law. Self-interest as well as her people's belief in modern democracy will then persuade Siam to make common cause with Britain, France and other European democracies as she did, to her great credit, when she voted against Italy when the Abyssinian question was before the League.[150]

Japan's renewed attack on China sparked further boycotts of Japanese goods among the Chinese population in Bangkok in autumn 1937, which this time turned violent. The government had established a decidedly anti-Chinese policy in order to reduce Chinese economic dominance of Siam, and now it forcefully cracked down on the boycott.[151] On 8 December 1937, Siam and Japan put their relations on a new legal basis by concluding a new treaty which no longer gave Japan the right of consular jurisdiction in Siam.[152]

In the course of the 1930s, the international political situation, particularly vis-à-vis Japan, the League's failure to settle the international conflicts involving the future war allies Japan, Germany and Italy, and the domestic changes in government in Siam inevitably led to a change in the attitudes of many Thai foreign policy makers towards the League.

148 In this sense, Brailey characterised the 1937 abstention as a 'blunt assertion of Bangkok's total neutrality'; see Brailey, *Thailand and the Fall of Singapore*, p. 89.

149 TNA, *Bangkok Times*, 7 October 1937.

150 Reprinted in TNA, *Bangkok Times*, 18 October 1937.

151 TNA, *Bangkok Times*, 6 November 1937. According to Bruce Reynolds, the government crackdown was motivated by the desire to avoid creating any tensions with Japan; see Reynolds, *International Orphans*, p. 365. See on the 1937 boycott also Swan, *Japanese Economic Relations*, p. 80ff.

152 See Nuntana, Phuangphet and Supatra, *Japan and Thailand*, p. 43.

Phraya Rajawangsan in 1938 stated unequivocally that the League no longer possessed the authority to prevent war and that League member states must seek salvation in their own military strength or in regional security arrangements.[153] In late 1938, a number of the military officers in the Thai cabinet advocated a withdrawal of Siam from the League, as the organisation had suffered a great loss of prestige since the 'affair of Ethiopia'. This demand was motivated mainly by financial concerns, as a withdrawal would have meant saving the annual contributions to the League's budget. The civilians in the cabinet, however, eventually prevailed over the military officers, and Siam remained a League member. Minister of Foreign Affairs Chao Phraya Sridharmadhibes explained to the British Minister in Bangkok, Sir Josiah Crosby, in March 1939 that he and the other advocates of League membership in the cabinet acknowledged the League's continuing importance as an international clearing house and for its work in the fight against drugs and human trafficking, 'despite its regrettable failure to settle serious international disputes or to intervene as an effective protector of the rights of small nations'. The cabinet did, however, decide to push for a reduction in Siam's annual contribution to the League's budget. A letter to this effect was sent to the Secretary-General of the League on 9 September 1938, British support for the proposal was sought by the Minister of Foreign Affairs, and it was understood in Bangkok that a reduction was a condition for continuing League membership.[154] Sir Josiah realised the political significance of this financial issue:

> So long as Siam retains her membership of the League it will be apparent to all that she has not cast in her lot with the totalitarian States. If, on the other hand, she resigns from it, I have no doubt that the fact would be exploited by those States and by the Japanese to our detriment, and Siam would then be assumed to have taken a step which led her away from the democratic countries and brought her proportionately nearer to their opponents.[155]

British support on the League Council for the Thai proposal was eventually secured and Siam was granted a reduction of its annual contributions to the League and remained a League member. But by the end of the decade the League as guardian of collective security had, nevertheless, lost much of its credibility in Siam, as it had around the globe:

> The long-continued flouting of the League's authority by Japan in the East and the totalitarian States in the West has gradually destroyed all Siamese belief in the efficacy of that institution as an instrument for the preservation of peace or for the protection of weak countries against an aggressor. Tribute is still paid to the ideals of the League by such genuine believers in international peace and friendship as Luang Pradist, but it may be taken as certain that the seizure of Austria, the treatment of Czecho-Slovakia and the

153 Report on the League of Nations General Assembly of 1937, dated 13 August B.E. 2481 (1938), TNA, KT 96.1.3/21.

154 See the comprehensive memorandum by Crosby to Halifax, 22 March 1939, PRO, FO 371/23596, F 3219/3219/40.

155 Memorandum Crosby to Halifax, 22 March 1939, PRO, FO 371/23596, F 3219/3219/40.

ever-lessening distance between Siam and the present scene of warfare in China have combined to make all Siamese believe that, if their country is involved in a war or in an 'incident', she will have to depend on her own efforts rather than on any resolutions of sympathy passed at Geneva.[156]

Minister of Foreign Affairs Luang Pradist, as ever reiterating the mantra of Siam's policy of neutrality, stated in an interview in January 1938 that in abstaining Siam had merely followed the example of Poland and sincerely wished to be neutral between Japan, with which it had close economic ties, and China because of the large Chinese minority in the kingdom. In this interview he also made it clear that not even evidence of 'acts of war out of all proportion of the original incident' or 'air bombardments, useless and murderous' could lead Siam to take sides in this conflict involving its two neighbours.[157] Richard Sogn, who studied the American role in Siam's foreign policy during these events, summarised contemporary Western assessments of Thai policy as follows: 'To Western observers Thailand…seemed to be evolving into a Switzerland of the East, using its neutrality, balanced diplomacy, and amicable relations with all nations to ensure the favourable conditions for its continued economic success'.[158]

But as the decade drew to a close the League of Nations had not lost all of its importance in the realm of international conflicts for the government in Bangkok just yet. When outright war erupted in Europe with Germany's invasion of Poland in September 1939, Britain and France declared war on Germany. On 25 September, Phraya Rajawangsan telegraphed his ministry that 'many countries have informed the League of Nations about their proclamations of neutrality during the war' and asked, 'Do you wish me to do the same?'[159] Frederick Dolbeare advised to 'leave the whole matter alone', in order not to be drawn into League sanctions, however unlikely. Prince Varn, on the other hand, advocated to informing the League officially as to Siam's neutrality in 'this conflict', in order to underline the kingdom's 'strict and impartial neutrality in accordance with international law'. Direck Jayanama and Luang Phibun sided with Prince Varn, and the Royal Proclamation for the Observance of Neutrality B.E. 2482, signed by Regent Prince Aditya and President of the Council of Ministers Luang Phibun, was sent to the League on 16 October 1939.[160]

Expulsion of the Soviet Union from the League of Nations in 1939

During the dying days of the League of Nations in late 1939, the General Assembly managed to make a last public statement by expelling the Soviet Union from the world organisation. By December 1939, Germany, Japan and Italy had all formally resigned League membership, and the Second World War had begun in Europe. The Soviet Union

156 Annual Report on Siam for 1938, 25 January 1939, PRO, FO 371/23596, F 2390/2390/40.

157 TNA, *Bangkok Times*, 7 January 1938.

158 Sogn, *Successful Journey*, p. 170.

159 Phraya Rajawangsan to Minister of Foreign Affairs, 25 September 1939, TNA, KT 96.1.6/8.

160 See respective memoranda by Dolbeare and Prince Varn, as well as internal notes and correspondence with Phraya Rajawangsan and the League of Nations in TNA, KT 96.1.6/8. The declaration of neutrality is also available as serial document no. C.345.M.260.1939.VII. in LNA, R 3692/1/39194/38989.

attacked neighbouring Finland on 30 November, after Finland had refused to give in to Soviet territorial demands. On 3 December, Finland appealed to the League of Nations in a desperate gesture on the grounds of articles XI and XV of the covenant. The League Council took up the matter on 9 December and transferred it to the General Assembly where, as a result, Siam became involved.[161]

The era of amicable relations between Siam and Russia, marked by cordial visits of the Tsarevitch, later Tsar Nicholas II, to Bangkok in 1893 or of King Chulalongkorn to the Russian imperial family in 1897, had long passed. Siam had closed its legation in St. Petersburg in 1917 in response to the revolution and had not maintained diplomatic relations with the Soviet Union since. When the Soviet Union successfully applied for membership to the League of Nations in 1934, Minister of Foreign Affairs Phraya Abhibal had instructed Phraya Subharn not to attend the meeting of the General Assembly which was to vote on the admission, and Siam did not sign the invitation letter to the Soviet Union.[162]

Siam's Permanent Representative to the League in 1939, Phraya Rajawangsan, was instructed to attend the General Assembly meeting on 6 December, after a cabinet meeting had discussed the matter in Bangkok. In that cabinet meeting, Prince Varn and Luang Pradist advocated that Phraya Rajawangsan attend because they could see no danger resulting for Siam from whatever decision the League would take. But it was Prime Minister Luang Phibun who impressed the meeting by stating that this was an excellent opportunity for Siam to contribute to boosting world morale. He suggested that Siam not only be represented at the Assembly but also vote in favour of eventual sanctions against the Soviet Union, in an effort to impress Great Britain and France. Luang Phibun also pointed to the positive effect that such a symbolic statement would have for the forthcoming border negotiations with France.[163] In stark contrast to the abstentions in 1933 and 1937, the instructions of Deputy Minister of Foreign Affairs Direck Jayanama to Phraya Rajawangsan, spelled out specifically that he was to 'go even as far as the adoption of sanctions against Russia' in the support of 'the attitude of the various Powers in favour of the upholding of international law and morality.' Strikingly, Phraya Rajawangsan was explicitly instructed 'not to abstain from voting'.[164]

When the General Assembly convened for one of its last meetings on 11 December 1939, Phraya Rajawangsan was not only elected to the nine-member Credentials Committee, but also nominated for the so-called Special Committee, which the General Assembly created for the purpose of dealing with the Finnish appeal and which consisted of twelve delegates.[165] Already before the Assembly opened, plainly worded protest letters from several Latin American states had been received in Geneva demanding the expulsion of the Soviet Union; Argentina and

161 Peter J. Beck, 'The Winter War in the International Context: Britain and the League of Nations in the Russo-Finnish Dispute 1939-1940', *Journal of Baltic Studies*, 12 (1981), pp. 58-73; Walters, *League of Nations*, p. 804ff.

162 Phraya Abhibal to Phraya Subharn, 10 September 1934, TNA, KT 96.1.3/18: 'you should absent yourself from the meeting on the day of voting on the question of admission of the Soviet Union.' In this context, Phraya Subharn reported on a dinner hosted by the Aga Khan, at which he was approached by the Soviet Minister of Foreign Affairs Maxim Litvinov. Litvinov's first words were, according to Phraya Subharn, 'isn't Siam a close friend of Japan?' See Phraya Subharn to Phraya Abhibal, 11 October B.E. 2477 (1934) and Minister of Foreign Affairs to Prime Minister, 12 November B.E. 2477 (1934), TNA, SR 0201.17/4. See also Doc. 225 (N 5443/2/38), BDFA, Part II, Series J, vol. 2.

163 Minutes of 69th Cabinet Meeting on 6 December B.E. 2482 (1939), TNA, SR 0201.17/23.

164 Direck to Phraya Rajawangsan, 6 December 1939, TNA, SR 0201.17/23.

165 For the proceedings see LNA, League of Nations, Records of the Twentieth Ordinary Session of the Assembly, Geneva, 1940. See also Phraya Rajawangsan to Minister of Foreign Affairs, 12 December 1939, TNA, SR 0201.17/23.

Uruguay announced their resignation from the League if the Soviet Union were not expelled.[166] The cabinet in Bangkok considered the Geneva proceedings once more on 13 December in the light of Phraya Rajawangsan's role in the Assembly. Prime Minister Luang Phibun asked whether a vote to expel the Soviet Union would have any consequences for Siam's relations with Germany but was reassured that this would not be the case, and the cabinet reaffirmed its original policy.[167] Consequently, on 13 December, the Special Committee and the following day the General Assembly and the League Council adopted resolutions respectively, which condemned the Soviet Union's aggression as an act of war and, for the first time in the League's history, expelled a member from the organisation in accordance with the provisions of article XVI of the covenant. In the Assembly vote Sweden, Norway, Denmark, Lithuania, Latvia, Estonia, Bulgaria, China, and Switzerland abstained, while Siam voted in favour of the resolution.[168]

The League of Nations had, with the vote of Siam, stood firmly behind Finland and now urged its members to support that country and 'refrain from any action which might weaken Finland's power of resistance.' Phraya Rajawangsan assured the Secretary-General that Siam, although it was unable to provide material assistance due to the great geographical distance, was fully supportive of the Finnish cause.[169] Finland, although it put up staunch resistance against the superior invader, ultimately had to negotiate a peace settlement with the Soviet Union in March 1940. For Siam the Geneva vote in favour of the expulsion of the Soviet Union had unexpected consequences, as Sir Josiah Crosby was informed by Direck Jayanama in December 1940, a full year later. When the war in Europe forced a considerable number of Thai students to abandon their studies and return to Siam, the Soviet government refused to issue transit visas for them on the basis of Siam's anti-Soviet action at the League of Nations.[170]

The expulsion of the Soviet Union was the last significant act of the League of Nations. From 1940 onwards, the League drifted off into oblivion while Europe and the world were engulfed by the horrors of the Second World War. Siam abandoned the last remains of its policy of neutrality and rendered all the talk following the abstentions in 1933 and 1937 meaningless when it chose to side with Japan and against the West. On 5 August 1941, Siam finally recognised Manchukuo.[171] Had the League possessed any significant influence in international affairs during the war years, it appears very likely in retrospect that Japan would have urged Luang Phibun's government to follow Tokyo's example and formally leave the League. That Siam never renounced its membership in the League during the war, therefore, says more about the League's irrelevance than about any conviction among government circles in Bangkok. On the tenth anniversary of Luang Bhadravadi's abstention at Geneva, an editorial of the pro-Japanese and pro-Phibun daily *Bangkok Chronicle*

166 See Phraya Rajawangsan to Minister of Foreign Affairs, 6 and 9 December 1939, and Direck to Prime Minister, 12 December B.E. 2482 (1939), both in TNA, SR 0201.17/23.

167 Minutes of 70th Cabinet Meeting on 13 December B.E. 2482 (1939), TNA, SR 0201.17/23.

168 The Council and General Assembly resolutions of 14 December 1939 can be found in LNA, League of Nations, *Official Journal*, November/December 1939, p. 506ff. and 540ff. See also Phraya Rajawangsan to Minister of Foreign Affairs, 13 and 14 December 1939, TNA, SR 0201.17/23.

169 Circular letter C.L.181 of 18 December 1939 and Phraya Rajawangsan to Secretary-General, 19 January 1940, both in LNA, R 3697/1/39555/39392.

170 Sir Josiah reported this conversation with Direck by telegram to the Foreign Office; see Crosby to Foreign Office, 12 December 1940, PRO, FO 371/24747, F 4669/3268/40.

171 TNA, SR 0201.37/49. The cabinet decided on recognition of Manchukuo on 30 July 1941, and a public announcement was made on 5 August. See also Grant to Secretary of State, 2 and 8 August 1941, in FRUS, 1941, vol. V: The Far East, p. 250 and 260; Crosby to Foreign Office, 26 January 1941, PRO, FO 371/28135, F 438/438/40.

declared in 1943: 'The League of Nations today is as dead as the Dodo'.[172] True as this was, the League was reborn as the United Nations only two years later, and after the end of its pro-Japanese and expansionist interlude it became the top priority of Siam's foreign policy to become a member of the world body once again.

Conclusions

The events reconstructed in this chapter lead to the conclusion that Siam, irrespective of the many benefits it reaped from its League membership in other policy areas, was not willing to support the collective security system of the League of Nations. During the 1920s, Siam could elegantly stay out of mediation efforts in international conflicts because it was not a member on the League Council and the disputes at hand did not concern it directly. In the 1930s, Siam was involuntarily drawn into the international search for solutions to some of the major global conflicts but was not willing to take a stand for collective security and international law because of bilateral and regional policy concerns.

Siam abstained from condemning Japanese aggression in the 1933 extraordinary General Assembly because of an over-accentuated neutrality policy, which, while acknowledging Japan's growing economic and political role in Asia, was aimed primarily at Western countries. The abstention was intended as a low-key statement of neutrality in a highly charged international political situation in February 1933 but it then backfired when Japan skilfully exploited the abstention as a pro-Japanese statement, and when Western policy makers were initially unable to provide a differing explanation. In spite of this, the abstention was ultimately not overstated in Western capitals, and the negative political fallout for Siam was limited. As we have seen, it remains questionable whether a different course of action on behalf of the young constitutional government in Bangkok in spring 1933 would have been more advantageous or even realistically possible in the complex international situation Siam was facing between the Western states on the one hand and Japan and China on the other. Nevertheless the event has remained in the collective memory as a stain on Siam's record of multilateralism.

Siam voted in favour of imposing League of Nations sanctions against Italy for invading Ethiopia in 1935, and it did so because of Italy's limited economic and political importance, but also in reaction to the unexpected fallout from the 1933 deviation from the international political mainstream. Siam gained its first experiences in 1935-36 of transforming international sanctions into national law and of enforcing them in practice. But Siam also gained dubious prominence for being one of only four out of some fifty states to have armament contracts with Italy exempted from the otherwise, as far as Thai-Italian trade was concerned, largely symbolic

172 TNL, *Bangkok Chronicle*, 25 February 1943.

sanctions. Siam's policy in this episode was very much in line with that of the main actors on the multilateral stage, in that sanctions and the League were outwardly supported strongly, but privately Italy was assured at every possible opportunity that this did not affect cordial relations in any way. The later history of multilateral economic sanctions since 1935 has shown this to be generally the case with governments, keeping a pragmatic eye on future political and commercial benefits even while publicly condemning another party's actions.

Siam abstained from condemning Japan again in 1937, this time in recognition of the changing patterns of power in Asia and a strong pro-Japanese sentiment among large parts of the government. This abstention was much less an expression of a policy of neutrality than a vote in support of Japan. By 1937, as we have seen, a vote against Japan on the League stage was no longer a viable policy option, as Japan's dominance in Asia was readily apparent and the military faction in Siam's government, which harboured decidedly pro-Japanese sentiments, had already strongly marginalised pro-Western and liberal voices. At the same time, the League's prestige had by 1937 already suffered so greatly that it seemed futile to put any hopes into the collective security system.

Siam's vote in favour of expelling the Soviet Union from the League of Nations in late 1939 came at a time when League resolutions were about to become all but meaningless. In any event, Siam's military-led government had nothing at stake in this matter and could, therefore, easily make this symbolic gesture.

Besides these four examples, the League dealt with another sixteen international conflicts in Europe, Latin America, the Middle East and East Asia during the 1930s, a number of which were just as serious as the four mentioned above, but in the resolution of which Siam, as a proud and sovereign member of the League of Nations, was not involved at all. Nevertheless, Siam's policy at Geneva with regard to collective security was, by and large, a reasonable one. As in other fields of cooperation with the world body, the remote Southeast Asian kingdom, some ten thousand kilometres away from Geneva, managed to maximise its domestic gains and minimise its international commitments while avoiding offending any League members with whom it maintained important economic or political relations. In this sense, Siam serves as a prime example of a small state which was happy to stand in the shadow of the big powers on the diplomatic stage, was aware of the limits of its foreign policy, and skilfully used the system to its benefit whenever possible. It appears utterly unrealistic, in the light of Siam's abilities in foreign policy and of international political and economic realities, to imagine Siam forcefully and visibly taking the stage in Geneva against Japan in 1933 or 1937 or cancelling arms contracts with Italian firms during the Ethiopian Conflict. One may criticise Siam's policies at

Geneva regarding Japan, Italy and the Soviet Union as opportunistic or unprincipled, but they were nevertheless reasonable and reflected Siam's international position and possibilities.

This chapter has painted the picture of a small state in international relations, which tended its bilateral relations with important states carefully while at the same time treading the uncharted paths of an evolving collective security system. That Siam managed not to be involuntarily drawn further into collective security issues during the 1930s may even be seen as an achievement, given that Siam's foreign policy was not built on a wealth of experience comparable to those of European League members, and given that Thai foreign policy in the interwar period was conducted during times of profound social, political and economic upheaval and change in Bangkok. Surrounded throughout the interwar decades by European colonies, independent Siam managed to conduct a reasonable, independent foreign policy regarding multilateral conflict resolution, not long after a time when its own territorial integrity and independence was still under threat from those Western states with which it was now sitting at the General Assembly.

After the Second World War, Thailand was again part of the efforts to re-establish an improved collective security system, and concerned persons in Bangkok were well aware of the difficult legacy the League had left them in this regard, as a 1947 article in the English-language *Thai Newsmagazine* shows:

> The very fact that the League of Nations failed to prevent World War II from occurring within the short period of twenty years from the first one shows that there must have been some serious defects somewhere in the constitution of the League.[173]

The League of Nations appears in this chapter as an organisation incapable of upholding the collective security system during the 1930s, although it had largley managed to do so during the 1920s. The reasons for this inability are complex and can only partially be ascribed to the League itself.[174] First and foremost, the major League members, in particular Great Britain and France, were unwilling and to some extent also unable to support the collective security system and the League to the degree which would have been necessary to counter effectively such aggressive acts as Japan's invasion of China, Italy's invasion of Ethiopia or the Soviet Union's invasion of Finland. While the League could rely on the necessary support of the major powers in the largely European conflicts during the 1920s, economic and political changes led to a situation where the League could no longer count on Britain, France, Germany or Italy during the following decade. The joint British-French sabotage of League sanctions against Italy in 1935 was certainly an inglorious low point in this development. Without determined powers throwing their weight and might behind League decisions, an aggressor

173 TNL, *Thai Newsmagazine*, 16 March 1947.

174 For a detailed analysis of factors determining the League's inability to uphold collective security during the Manchurian Conflict see Hell, *Mandschurei-Konflikt*, p. 203ff.

was free to pursue his course of action, a feature of international organisations which has remained unchanged since the League's days. But, to make things worse, unlike today's United Nations, the League did not have peacekeeping forces at its disposal, which made it perhaps even more dependent on its powerful member states than the United Nations. Although Scandinavian and other states did repeatedly stand up to voice outrage and demand action, in the end small states like Siam were unable to influence events through their League membership.

Secondly, although it may seem trivial, the League of Nations failed to mediate the major conflicts of the 1930s because the violators of the international system were determined to stay their course irrespective of international opinion, protest, resolutions, or even sanctions. All the aggressors mentioned in this chapter, Japan, Italy and the Soviet Union, were willing to pay the price for their actions in the form of leaving the League or being expelled from the organisation. Once they stood outside the League system, the League was virtually powerless in trying to check their actions. Such determination the by aggressor states also rendered public opinion, once the League's most powerful instrument, completely useless. None of the conflicts described in this chapter led to massive protests in Western countries, who saw the issues as involving either a remote conflict between two Asian states or the enlargement of a European colonial empire in distant Africa. However, even if the conflicts had engendered large-scale protests, it seems unlikely that they would have influenced the actions of Japan or Italy.

Thirdly, the League, although entrusted with the task of guaranteeing collective security, was not equipped with the legal instruments necessary to force its member states to take decisive action against violators of the collective security system. The basic deficiency was the sanctions mechanism in the covenant, which was purposely not designed to lead inevitably to the imposition of sanctions if the covenant was violated. This left room for interpretation and negotiation, which undermined the sanctions mechanism from acting as a deterrent. In the language of the covenant, it was possible to deal with an international conflict on the basis of articles X to XV, without necessarily invoking the 'sanctions article' XVI. And the only time article XVI was actually invoked, as we have seen, its effectiveness was again undermined by League members.

It was the combination of these factors, which led to the League's decline as the guardian of collective security during the 1930s, and which together with the above mentioned particular factors influencing Siam's foreign policy, led to the League losing its appeal for Siam. Once the axis states unleashed the horrors of the Second World War, the League became insignificant, and Siam sided with Japan and against the West. Nevertheless, half a decade later, when a new collective security system was being established, Siam hurried to be part of the international order once more.

Prince Damras Damrong Devakul, Permanent Delegate of Siam to the League of Nations, 1931–1933 (Thai National Archives).

0.70 metre
๐.๗๐ เมตร

1.40 metres
๑.๔๐ เมตร

ด้านข้าง
side view

Sketch of the book cabinet presented by Siam to the League of Nations in 1934 for its new building in Geneva (League of Nations Archives).

7

Conclusions

T
he broadest conclusion one can draw from this study is that the foreign policy and domestic modernisation of the Kingdom of Siam during the 1920s and 1930s had a distinct multilateral dimension as a result of Siam's membership in the League of Nations.

Among the wide spectrum of political questions dealt with by the League of Nations, this study has examined four areas: opium control, public health, the fight against human trafficking and collective security. The first three were key activities of the League and essential to the organisation's relevance. They were also areas of the League's work which possessed particular relevance to Siam. The fourth example examined here, collective security, was at the very heart of the League of Nations raison d'être, and Siam, as we have seen, was involuntarily drawn into this area of the League's work. While Siam's elite actively employed opportunities offered by the League of Nations to modernise the country in the first three areas, foreign policy makers were forced by the country's League membership to take a stand in matters of collective security on a number of occasions during the 1930s. Interestingly, Siam thereby became much more involved in the great international conflicts of the decade than is generally acknowledged. In other words, globalisation with its political and economic interdependencies put significant pressures on Siam in this regard before the Second World War.

The League of Nations was, as the previous chapters have shown, the epitome of modernity and progress in international relations for Thai foreign policy makers during the 1920s and large parts of the 1930s. The League embodied the core ideals which Thai foreign policy was striving to realise during this period namely, independence, sovereignty, neutrality, and respect as an equal member of the family of nations. At the same time, the Thai elite, implicitly and explicitly, accepted the leadership of European culture and Western technological achievements in the new international order for two reasons. In a pragmatic approach to its foreign relations, the Thai elite genuinely believed in Western superiority to a considerable degree but, at the same time, used the country's development along Western lines to break away from the Western Powers during the 1920s, ultimately forcing them to renounce their unequal treaties and grant Siam full sovereignty. In the realm of domestic politics, the assertion of the Thai elite, whether royal or non-royal, as being modern and civilised through its import of Western laws, administrative and cultural practices, and technology reinforced its claim to leadership of the country. The League of Nations as the embodiment of the new and egalitarian West was, therefore, a focal point and a key instrument for the Thai elite in the modernisation of Siam during the 1920s and 1930s.

Sally Marks wrote in 1995 that small states primarily sought collective security when joining the League of Nations.[1] As we have seen, this was indeed a motivation for Siam's League membership. But even more important was the League of Nations' role in Siam's modernisation and regaining of full sovereignty. To this end, Siam worked with the League primarily in the fields of opium control, public health development, and efforts against human trafficking. Siam thus provides an excellent case for regarding the League not simply as a collective security instrument, a realm in which it failed dramatically, but rather as an instrument for a much broader range of international political issues. We should remember that Francis Walters devoted only some thirty pages to the social, technical and humanitarian activities in his standard 800-page history of the League of Nations. This illustrates once again the image problem which the League has had among historians. Although much has changed since the Walters era, the general assessment remains not that the League failed as a collective security system, but that it failed in its entirety. In fact, to the contrary, the picture of the League of Nations, which has emerged from the preceding chapters, is of an organisation, which, although flawed in many ways, nevertheless achieved remarkable successes, particularly outside the realm of international conflicts. As Frederick Northedge stated regarding the social and technical aspect of League activities:

> The League nevertheless managed to acquire, through its network of committees to discuss what to do in these various fields, the rudiments of machinery for world co-operation with a writ as broad as that of any government, though far less cumbrous and elephantine as that of its UN successor. Later, as the League's life drew to a close, many thought that this work in the economic and social fields was the best it ever did.[2]

For the League, Siam was an important member. Not primarily for its impact on the League's policy, for although its contributions were notable in some areas, they can, of course, not be compared to those of France or Great Britain, Japan or Germany, but mainly because it was the only member in the Southeast Asian region and, apart from Japan until 1933 and China, the only member state in the whole Far East. Siam thereby provided support to the essentially European League of Nations' claim to global authority. It was in this sense, that a Bangkok daily commented on the Bandung Conference in 1937: 'The holding of this Conference in the Far East is…an indication… that the League does not restrict its efforts in this respect to any

1 Marks, Small States, p. 191.

2 Northedge, *League of Nations*, p. 66.

geographical area, and that it tries to deal with the problem wherever the need is most acute'.[3]

Geography also played a role in limiting Siam's involvement, along with other Asian and South American states. Occasions when the League held meetings in Asia were few and far between as the centre of activity was undoubtedly always Geneva. This made it impracticable for Siam to send a government minister, let alone the prime minister, to attend a League meeting, while European governments could do so with relative ease. But geographical distance did not keep Thai officials from working closely with the League. A remarkable symbolic expression of Thai concern for European problems was King Vajiravudh's donation of funds for the League's fight against typhoid fever in Poland in 1920, at a time when Europe was slowly recovering from the devastating war and Siam was seen largely as a backward and distant feudal state in the eyes of Europeans.

Rong Syamananda has stated that Siam 'did not play a really active role in the League of Nations until the Manchurian Incident broke out in 1931'.[4] As the preceding chapters have shown, this statement is inaccurate. On the contrary, Siam played a very active role in the League in an array of areas, and it was precisely the Manchurian Conflict and the following international conflicts, in which Siam remained as inactive as circumstances allowed. Rong's statement may also be taken as the prevailing view of many historians and general readers alike, whereby Siam and the League had merely a single point in time when they came into notable contact, namely the abstention on 24 February 1933. I have argued that this abstention has been substantially overrated, due in part to the ensuing propaganda by Japan, which used it for its own political purposes. In fact, the abstention had only minor political implications at the time. But Siam's cooperation with the League of Nations in improving public health, preventing epidemic diseases, or protecting women and children from trafficking and forced prostitution, did have very concrete implications for policies in Siam. The same can also be said for cooperation in the area of opium control. While in all these examples a greater degree of success would have been desirable in retrospect, cooperation did take place and led to tangible results. Naturally, membership of the League of Nations did not solve all Siam's problems. As I have shown, membership did, however, significantly contribute to the development of strategies to address a number of the issues faced by Siam and the Southeast Asian region. At the same time, it must be acknowledged that, while Thai governments during the 1920s and 1930s often skilfully maximised the benefits of League membership and kept their international commitments to a minimum, Siam did not make as much use of the League's opportunities as they could have done. While the Bangkok Opium Conference and other initiatives stand out as examples to the contrary, Thai diplomats and government officials would

3 TNA, *Bangkok Times*, 3 March 1937.

4 Rong, *History of Thailand*, p. 153.

have had numerous other opportunities when they could have acted more proactively in League activities to the benefit of social development in Siam. We have also seen that in some instances Siam, like every other League member state, fulfilled its international obligations only to the degree it had to in order to remain a respected member of the international community.

If we step back from the different policy areas analysed in this study, we can identify ten interlinked and overlapping systematic aspects, which characterise the twenty years of Siam's active membership in the League of Nations from 1920 to 1940.

Firstly, as we have seen throughout this study, the League of Nations was a tool used by Siam's policy makers to put pressure on Western powers to regain its sovereignty, particularly during the first half of the 1920s. This aspect was dominant during the Paris Peace Conference and the formative first years of the League, and it was reiterated subtly more often than not when Thai officials dealt with representatives of Western states on social or humanitarian issues under a League umbrella until the mid-1920s. In this context, we have also seen how central the goal of obtaining League membership was for Thai policy makers before and during the Paris Peace Conference.

During the 1920s and later in the mid-1930s, Siam did not formally transfer treaty revision from a bilateral to a multilateral level, in recognition of the unwillingness of European states to discuss treaty revision at Geneva, and the reluctance of the young League of Nations itself to become involved in this question, which was charged with strong national interests in London and Paris. This strategy served the country well, as it managed to revise the unequal treaties in a remarkably smooth and overall non-confrontational fashion. As we have seen, however, Thai policy makers readily used League membership and the League's ideals as leverage to influence bilateral treaty negotiations. In other words, the League of Nations symbolised a new ideal of international relations based on the equality of states, which, although it largely remained an ideal, formed an important prerequisite for the willingness of Great Britain, France and other states to relinquish their unequal treaties with Siam by the mid-1920s. In addition, by cooperating actively with the League of Nations, the Thai government of the early 1920s demonstrated a degree of constructive cooperation and sincere adherence to the League's ideals, which ultimately made the continuation of unequal treaties anachronistic.

Secondly, the League of Nations was a shield, the existence of which contributed to protecting Siam's independence through its system of collective security and peaceful conflict resolution. Although no concrete threat of invasion or armed conflict existed for Siam between the early years of the twentieth century, when Great Britain and France still posed very real potential threats, and the early 1940s, when Siam actually gave in to the very real Japanese threat, Siam nevertheless did benefit from the protective umbrella which the collective security system provided. As mentioned above, in this regard Siam was a typical 'small state' in an international organisation, which counted on the collective security guarantee as did dozens of others in Europe, Africa, America and the Middle East.

Thirdly, the League of Nations was a means for the Thai elite to demonstrate its modernity and its degree of civilisation to the international community, both by participating in this progressive enterprise and by demonstrating its own worthiness and sophistication. Thai governments were often very quick in adapting international conventions into national law, as the example of the 1921 International Convention for the Suppression of the Traffic in Women and Children has shown. Thai governments were also generally supportive of most Southeast Asia-wide or Asia-wide League initiatives, such as the creation of the Singapore Bureau in 1925 or the two Bandung conferences of 1937. We have seen in the previous chapters how important the creation of a progressive, modern, and civilised image was for Thai officials with regard to League activities, and how positively remarks from League officials were received in Bangkok, when they lauded the government's achievements in a particular social sector or the role of an individual official involved in League activities. And the League, indeed, proved a very useful tool for the Thai image campaign, as reactions from League officials and representatives of Western governments were often quite positive and contributed to a change of perception regarding Siam during the interwar decades.

Fourthly, the League of Nations was a unique platform, in some respects even a stage, on which Thai diplomats could interact as equals with representatives of other countries and gain international respect Indeed, the importance of Siam's formal equality in this regard cannot be overstated. Although inequalities between Siam and Western states were manifold in practice, they were formally, or legally, equal. When voting in the General Assembly, Siam's vote counted as much as that of the representative from Britain or France. The platform provided by the League of Nations not only endured in Geneva for twenty years, but on occasion also moved to Singapore or Bandung for multilateral conferences, and was once even set up in Bangkok for the landmark opium conference of 1931. Employing different terminology, the League could be described, particularly in the 1920s, as providing a unique inroad for Thai diplomats to their Western counterparts, allowing countless opportunities for contact and exchange, most of which would certainly not have existed without the League.

Fifthly, and central to the argument of this study, the League of Nations had a distinct modernising impact on Thai society in a wide range of areas by providing expertise and technical assistance, and thereby serving as a means for the elite to modernise the country. Thai governments during the two decades under review sometimes did not use this tool as extensively as they could have done and sometimes only half-heartedly, but it was often employed for the benefit of administrative, legal or social change in Siam in certain policy areas. By utilising League expertise, which was available via countless reports, expert meetings and the impressive number of commissions of enquiry visiting Siam, the administration of public health, opium control, and policies against human trafficking could be effectively improved over time. We have seen that these improvements, because of the global nature of the League's work, were mostly in international policy areas, such as opium import procedures, international epidemiological intelligence, or immigration procedures. But the impact was also visible on a domestic level. The reform of Siam's legal system was, for example, in some instances a direct result of cooperation with the League, while in other cases it was at least influenced by the League. This statement also holds true for Siam's first constitution, which expressly referred to the authority of the League of Nations in limiting the right of the Thai king to declare war. With regards to managing the opium monopoly, a number of the changes implemented during the interwar period were in response to League influences. A range of public health improvements were developed in close cooperation with League experts, notably malaria control schemes and the training of Thai doctors in malariology, as well as raising awareness of issues such as human trafficking as a result of information provided by League representatives.

Sixthly, the League of Nations also had a distinctly modernising impact on Thai society by creating international pressure for domestic modernisation, which was not necessarily intended by the elite or even ran counter to its intentions. This aspect, although it concerns the same general phenomenon as the previous point, differs in the much stronger reactive and much less proactive manner in which change was brought about in Siam. The League, in other words, imposed normative rules, which had to be respected if one desired a place in the modern international system, irrespective of differing domestic policies or conditions. The area of opium policy with its very important financial aspects is a good example in support of this assessment. Thus, it is difficult to imagine that Thai governments, particularly during the 1920s, would have developed such progressive opium control policies without the activities and pressure of the League. Interestingly, opium control also serves as the prime example for showing two opposing, but modernising effects. On the one hand, revenue from the opium monopoly was important for generating the public expenditure necessary for modernisation, while, on the other hand, limiting opium revenue was part of a modern opium control policy. The pragmatic, middle-of-the-road approach chosen by Thai governments during the 1920s and 1930s demonstrated the desire to have the best of both worlds and achieved some success in painting a progressive picture of Siam internationally, in which the country modernised opium policy, but did not blindly follow international trends. While the Thai government was repeatedly blamed for not instituting a registration and rationing scheme for opium smoking, we can see with hindsight that such a scheme would have most certainly failed, as it would have driven smokers to purchase readily available and cheap contraband opium. Another example illustrating this sixth aspect was the suppression of human trafficking. We have seen that creating awareness of human trafficking as a problem requiring regulation via laws and procedures was clearly triggered from outside Siam, primarily by the League of Nations.

Seventhly, the League of Nations provided unique training opportunities for Thai diplomats and other officials to acquire the etiquette and behaviour suited for the international diplomatic scene of the twentieth century, when imperialism was giving way to new ideals of political participation and international equality. This holds true for successive generations of Thai diplomats as well as for officials representing both the pre-1932 system of absolute monarchy and the post-1932 system of civilian and military rule. We have seen that numerous prominent Thai diplomats and officials came into contact with the League in one way or another. The Thai delegations to the General Assemblies during the 1920s, in particular, read like a who's who of Thai diplomacy. It was the 'old guard', which led Siam to Geneva, mainly Princes Charoon and Devawongse, of whom the former was certainly influenced strongly by the new League of Nations. Representatives of the next generation of royal diplomats, most notably Prince Varnvaidya, who proved to be a staunch believer in the benefits of international organisation, took over from the late 1920s. As for commoners, the long list of those who benefited from the League's 'training' included Phraya Srivisarn Vacha, Luang Bhadravadi, and Luang Vichit Vadhakarn, the latter of whom described his training at the League 'as akin to attending the most prestigious university in the world'.[5] Of course, none of the aforementioned could rival the expertise of Mani Sanasen after fifteen years in the League Secretariat, the only Thai ever having worked for the League of Nations.

The preceding chapters have demonstrated that Thai diplomats were learning the rules of multilateral international politics on a stage, which was built by diplomats and officials from around the globe, who themselves were all learning and, at the same time, defining the new rules of multilateral diplomacy under the bright spotlight of an emerging international public opinion. It is likely that the learning process was more intense for Thai diplomats than for the European League members, as Siam had only a very young diplomatic tradition. In addition, its diplomats, particularly up into the 1920s, often had to cope

5 Cited by Barmé, *Luang Wichit Wathakan*, p. 42.

with a sense of inferiority in dealings with their Western colleagues, whom they perceived as more civilised or progressive, and who themselves were often still in a colonial mindset with its innate Western superiority.

Eighthly, Siam's membership in the League of Nations meant that its diplomats were actively involved in shaping the world's first international organisation, perhaps the most revolutionary and ambitious experiment in global politics of the twentieth century. This often put Thai diplomats and other officials at the forefront of the development of international law and, more importantly, added a whole new multilateral dimension to a hitherto almost exclusively bilateral Thai foreign policy. From today's perspective, it is useful to emphasise this aspect, as multilateral foreign relations under the umbrella of a standing international organisation are an essential feature of our world. This study has shown how unusual, innovative, and idealistic, but also necessarily deficient and incomplete multilateral foreign relations were in the early 1920s, when they were first tried out in the world's very first international organisation. In this regard, League membership gave Siam, to quote Michael Kennedy's evaluation of Ireland's League membership, a new 'inter-national identity, purpose and sense of place'.[6] Siam's support for the League, its work and its ideals, was also expressed in its willingness to pay its membership dues regularly, an aspect in which Siam compared very favourably to many other League members.

Ninthly, Siam's membership in the League of Nations assisted the governing elite in Bangkok, both before and after 1932, in consolidating its power domestically by legitimising its rule and making its progressiveness apparent to the rest of society. Not only was being a member of the League of Nations modern in itself, but the League helped the policies of the elites in numerous ways with regard to developing Siam. We have seen numerous official statements, both from the throne and, after 1932, from the civilian governments, which emphasized the administration's modernity and that the country was in the forefront of international progress. Being part of the progressive League of Nations and cooperating in forward-looking public policies, such as opium control or public health, legitimised elite rule, because it implied that they would transmit the benefits of such policies to society as a whole. Siam's activities in a League context were, therefore, often also intended for public consumption in Bangkok.

The authoritarian regime of Luang Phibun in the years immediately preceding and during the Second World War could no longer utilise the League of Nations for its programmes of modernising and 'civilising' Siam, as the League was already discredited by the failures over Manchukuo, Ethiopia and Germany. Instead, as with governments the world over, Siam put her hopes on bilateral agreements and rearmament in the face of looming aggression. Nevertheless, we may

6 Kennedy, *Ireland and the League*, p. 257.

speculate that, if in 1940 the League had retained the prestige it had ten years earlier, the Phibun regime would most likely have found a number of contact points, which it could have utilised for its social and cultural campaigns.

We have also seen in this context that members of the traditional elite, royals and royalists, were actively involved in legitimising elite rule through progressive policies well beyond the political watershed of 1932, as the new civilian and military governments continued to rely on their technical or diplomatic expertise and their international experience.[7]

Tenthly, and finally, the existence of the League of Nations, particularly during the 1930s, forced Siam's governments to take a stand in international conflicts and had an impact on the country's traditional foreign policy making. Siam emerges from this study as a country strongly involved in the League's social and technical activities, but only reluctantly taking responsibility for the League's primary aim of providing collective security around the globe. In this regard, the earlier chapters on drugs, public health and human trafficking stand in stark contrast to the final chapter on collective security. In the former cases, Siam's governments were often open, willing, constructive and committed to working with the League of Nations for the betterment of certain social conditions in Siam. In the case of collective security, Siam understandably avoided involvement as far as possible. This approach worked well until the early 1930s, although the picture undoubtedly would have looked somewhat different if Siam's half-hearted bids for non-permanent Council membership in the 1920s had been successful.

It took over ten years, during which Siam stood in the shadows of the collective security system, before it unwillingly stirred up a hornet's nest with its abstention in 1933. This public relations fiasco led Siam to strengthen its policy of non-involvement even further during the following years. Siam's sanctions against Italy over the invasion of Ethiopia were, as we have seen, little more than lip service, as commercial interests between Bangkok and Rome were marginal, and the only important contracts with Italy for the construction of navy vessels, were exempted from the sanctions. Nevertheless, the fact remains that in 1935 Siam was part of the very first multilateral economic sanctions ever imposed by an international organisation. Siam's second abstention from voting to condemn Japan's actions in China in 1937 was, as I have shown, the expression of the political realties in Asia, with Siam increasingly caught in the middle, between its traditional Western allies and the emerging economic and military powerhouse, Japan. Finally, the vote to expel the Soviet Union in 1939, although on paper only, was perhaps the clearest example of Siam taking a stand against an aggressor, albeit a symbolic gesture by the Phibun government, which it could make at no cost whatsoever.

7   I am grateful to Han ten Brummel-huis for pointing me to this particular aspect of continuity, which one might even extend through the periods of Phibun rule to the second half of the twentieth century.

Siam's League membership was a cornerstone of its foreign policy for the better part of two decades. It played a crucial role in creating an international environment which allowed the country to regain its sovereignty by abolishing unequal treaties during the 1920s, and again during the 1930s. A significant number of Thai laws and administrative reforms during the sixth, seventh, and eighth reigns were issued in response to League pressure or in order to comply with League demands. Furthermore, a remarkably large part of the broad modernisation drive in Thai society during the 1920s and 1930s was a reaction to stimuli from the League.

Siam played a significantly more active role in early multilateral relations among states than has hitherto been acknowledged. In fact, during the late colonial period, Siam was the sole Southeast Asian state able to act independently on the international stage at Geneva, making genuine contributions to improving that international system.

Siam went on to become a member of the United Nations after the Second World War and has continued its tradition of successful multilateral diplomacy for the past sixty years. Bangkok today houses the headquarters and regional offices of a number of UN organisations. The role of Thai individuals on the multilateral diplomatic stage has also greatly evolved from the days of Prince Charoon and Mani Sanasen. In 1956 Prince Varn was able to crown his long diplomatic career when he was elected President of the eleventh United Nations General Assembly and more recently in 2002, Supachai Panitchpakdi became the first Director-General of the World Trade Organisation from a developing country and, since 2005, head of the United Nations Conference on Trade and Development (UNCTAD) as its Secretary-General. The bid by former Minister of Foreign Affairs Surakiart Sathirathai to succeed Kofi Annan in 2006, although controversial and ultimately unsuccessful, also stands in this long tradition of international civil servants from Thailand, which began with Mani Sanasen.

When Thai diplomats today proudly point to their country's eighty year-old tradition of cooperation with international organisations, they do so justifiably. Although we have seen that Siam's League membership was not always cooperative and productive, the balance sheet for Siam is clearly positive, as is the balance sheet for the League of Nations. Future studies may examine further policy areas in which the League and Siam came into contact, and their findings can test this assertion further. Undoubtedly, an understanding of Siam's policies with regard to the League of Nations and its manifold activities is important for an understanding of the country's foreign relations during the 1920s and the 1930s and of the major international influences on the elite-led modernisation of Siam's society during those two decades.

The problems addressed in this study, drug policies, human trafficking, collective security, and public health, were far from solved

when the League of Nations ceased to exist in 1946. On the contrary, they remain at least as pressing today as they were during the 1920s and 1930s. And some of them, namely drug trafficking and human trafficking, remain of particular concern in present-day Thailand. However, this does not diminish the importance of the earliest multi-lateral efforts to deal with these problems under the League of Nations, and Siam's readiness to actively take part in these first steps.

The League of Nations is history, but the problems the League dealt with will remain. The League's headquarters, the Palais des Nations overlooking Lake Geneva, still stands and serves as the European headquarters of the United Nations. The building's foundation stone still contains the Thai baht coins, which were provided by Siam's delegates to the League of Nations in 1929.[8]

Aerial photograph of League of Nations building in Geneva, taken by King Bhumibol 'with a red filter over the lens of the camera, thus elimi-nating the light mist that was floating over Geneva at the time'. *Printed in* The Standard, *7 December 1946 (Thai National Library).*

8 See TNA, R7, T 10/12 and TNA, KT 96.1/37.

Appendices

1 Chronology of Events

1855	Bowring Treaty
1878	Universal Postal Union
1896	Anglo-French Declaration
1899	First Hague Peace Conference
1904	International Agreement for the Suppression of White Slave Traffic
	Entente Cordiale between Great Britain and France
1905	Slavery abolished
1908	Government Opium Monopoly established
	Prevention of Venereal Diseases Act
	Thai Penal Code promulgated
1909	Shanghai Opium Commission
1910	Death of King Chulalongkorn and first Coronation of King Vajiravudh
	International Convention for the Suppression of White Slave Traffic
	Agricultural Exhibition in Bangkok
1911	King Vajiravudh's second Coronation
	International Opium Conference at The Hague (until 1912)
	Siam accedes to International Telegraph Convention
1913	International Opium Conference at The Hague (since 1911) and Opium Convention
	Law for the Prevention of Infectious Diseases promulgated
1914	Vaccination Law promulgated
1917	Siam declares War on Germany and Austria-Hungary
1918	Woodrow Wilson's Fourteen Points
	Thai Troops in France and Germany
	Department of Public Health created under Ministry of Interior
1919	Paris Peace Conference
	Siam signs Peace Treaties of Versailles, Neuilly, and Trianon
	International Convention for Aerial Navigation
1920	League of Nations founded
	Treaty of Friendship and Commerce between Siam and United States
1921	Opium Law
	Barcelona Transit Conference and Convention
	Siam signs International Convention on Trafficking in Women and Children
1922	Bangkok Public Health Exhibition
	League of Red Cross Societies meets in Bangkok
	League Commission of Enquiry on Port Health and Epidemic Diseases visits Siam

1923	Harmful Habit Forming Drugs Law B.E. 2465
	Siam implements international Import Certificate System for Raw Opium
	Medical Law B.E. 2465
	International Convention for the Suppression of the Circulation of and Traffic in Obscene Publications
1924	Geneva Opium Conferences (until 1925)
1925	Geneva Opium Conferences (since 1924)
	Promulgation of Thai Civil and Commercial Codes
	New Treaties of Friendship and Commerce concluded between Siam and European States
	Creation of the Far Eastern Bureau of the League of Nations Health Organisation in Singapore
	Death of King Vajiravudh and Coronation of King Prajadhipok
1926	Penal Code Amendment Act B.E. 2468
	Admission of Germany to the League
1927	Immigration Act B.E. 2470
	First International Economic Conference at Geneva
	Penal Code Amendment Act B.E. 2470
1928	Siam campaigns unsuccessfully for Non-permanent League Council Seat
	Traffic in Women and Girls Act B.E. 2471
	Act for the Suppression of the Circulation of, and Traffic in, Obscene Articles B.E. 2471
1929	Opium Act B.E. 2472
	League Commission of Enquiry on Opium Smoking visits Siam
1930	Eighth Congress of the Far Eastern Association of Tropical Medicine in Bangkok
	League Leprosy Commission visits Siam
	League Commission of Enquiry on Trafficking in Women and Children visits Siam
1931	League Commission of Enquiry on Malaria visits Siam
	League of Nations holds Bangkok Conference on Opium Smoking in the Far East
	Penal Code Amendment Act B.E. 2474
	Immigration Amendment Act B.E. 2474
	Mukden Incident and Japanese Occupation of Manchuria
1932	Geneva Disarmament Conference
	Extraordinary League Assembly on Sino-Japanese Conflict

Bloodless Coup changes Siam's Political System from Absolute to Constitutional Monarchy

Penal Code Amendment Act B.E. 2475

First Constitution of Siam

1933   Immigration Amendment Act B.E. 2475

Siam abstains in Extraordinary League Assembly Vote to condemn Japan's Occupation of Manchuria; Japan gives Notice of Withdrawal from the League

International Monetary and Economic Conference at London

Germany gives Notice of Withdrawal from the League League of Nations Expert Nijhoff surveys Bangkok Port

Penal Code Amendment Act B.E. 2476

1934   Opium Act B.E. 2472

Amendment Act B.E. 2476

Malaria Training Courses begin at Singapore Bureau of League Health Organisation

Admission of Soviet Union to the League

1935   Promulgation of remaining Thai Legal Codes

Opium Smuggling Scandal implicates Government and draws international Attention; Resignation of Financial Adviser Baxter

Intergovernmental Conference on Biological Standardisation at Geneva

King Prajadhipok abdicates; Ananda Mahidol proclaimed King

Public Health Act and Communicable Diseases Act

Siam imposes Sanctions on Italy for Invasion of Ethiopia (Abyssinia)

1936   League Commission of Enquiry on Rural Hygiene visits Siam

1937   League Commission of Enquiry on Cholera visits Siam

League of Nations holds Bandung Conference of Central Authorities on Trafficking in Women and Children

League of Nations holds Bandung Conference on Rural Hygiene

Siam abstains in League Assembly Vote condemning Japanese Invasion of China

Italy gives Notice of Withdrawal from the League

1938   Government of Siam officially authorises Opium Production to counter Smuggling

1939   German Invasion of Poland and Outbreak of Second World War in Europe

Siam votes in favour of Expulsion of Soviet Union from the League of Nations

1940   Decree to Control Standardisation of Biological Substances

1941   Siam recognises Manchukuo

Japanese Attack on Pearl Harbour and Outbreak of Second World War in Asia and the Pacific

1942   Creation of Ministry of Public Health

1943   Greater East Asia Co-prosperity Sphere Conference in Tokyo

1945   End of Second World War

Founding of the United Nations

1946   Death of King Ananda; Bhumibol ascends the Throne

League of Nations dissolves itself in Final General Assembly Meeting and hands over Assets and Responsibilities to United Nations

Siam admitted as 55th Member to the United Nations

World Health Organisation created

1949   United Nations Convention for the Suppression of the Traffic in Persons and the Exploitation of the Prostitution of Others

1959   Thailand outlaws Opium Consumption

1960   Thailand outlaws Prostitution

1961   United Nations Single Convention on Narcotic Drugs

2 Permanent Delegates of Siam to the League of Nations, 1920-1939

Prince Charoonsakdi Kritakara (1875-1928)	1920-1928
Phraya Prabha Karawongse *(ad interim during Prince Charoon's absence)* (1877-1954)	*1925-1926*
Prince Varnvaidya Voravarn (1891-1976)	1928-1930
Prince Damras Damrong Devakul (1886-1944)	1931-1933
Phraya Subharn Sompati (1882-1971)	1933-1935
Phraya Rajawangsan (1886-1940)	1935-1940
Prince Chula Chakrabongse (1908-1963)	1940-1946

3 Thai Delegations to the General Assemblies of the League of Nations

I. General Assembly (November/December 1920)

Prince Charoon (Minister in Paris & Permanent Representative to the League of Nations)	Delegate
Phraya Buri Navarasth (Minister in London)	Delegate
Phraya Bibadh Kosha (Minister in Rome)	Delegate
Chuen Charuvastra (Paris Legation)	Secretary
Chuen Jotikasthira (——)	Secretary
Sidh Saukathia (——)	Secretary
Ms. Bibadh Kosha (Rome Legation)	Secretary

II. General Assembly (September/October 1921)

Prince Charoon (Minister in Paris & Permanent Representative to the League of Nations)	Delegate
Phraya Bibadh Kosha (Minister in Rome)	Delegate
Chuen Charuvastra (Paris Legation)	Substitute Delegate
Tienliang Hoontrakul (Paris Legation)	Substitute Delegate
Kimleang Vathanaprida (Paris Legation)	Attaché
Ms. S. Bibadh Kosha (Rome Legation)	Secretary
Ms. J. Bibadh Kosha (Rome Legation)	Secretary
Ms. C. Bibadh Kosha (Rome Legation)	Secretary

III. General Assembly (September 1922)

Prince Charoon (Minister in Paris & Permanent Representative to the League of Nations)	Delegate
Phraya Bibadh Kosha (Minister in Rome)	Delegate
Navy Capt. Phraya Rajawangsan (Paris Legation)	Delegate
Chuen Charuvastra (Paris Legation)	Substitute Delegate
Tienliang Hoontrakul (Paris Legation)	Substitute Delegate
Kimleang Vathanaprida (Paris Legation)	Attaché
Ms. L. Bibadh Kosha (Rome Legation)	Secretary

IV. General Assembly (September 1923)

Prince Charoon (Minister in Paris & Permanent Representative to the League of Nations)	Delegate
Phraya Sanpakitch Preecha (Minister in Rome)	Delegate
Prince Damras Damrong (Chargé d'Affaires in The Hague)	Delegate
Tienliang Hoontrakul (Paris Legation)	Substitute Delegate
Khun Biraj Bisdara (Paris Legation)	Substitute Delegate
Kimleang Vathanaprida (Paris Legation)	Secretary
Luang Bahidda Nukara (Rome Legation)	Secretary
Phra Sarasasna (London Legation)	Secretary

V. General Assembly (September/October 1924)

Prince Charoon (Minister in Paris & Permanent Representative to the League of Nations)	Delegate
Phraya Sanpakitch Preecha (Minister in Rome)	Delegate
Khun Biraj Bisdara (Paris Legation)	Secretary
Kimleang Vathanaprida (Paris Legation)	Secretary
Luang Bahidda Nukara (Rome Legation)	Secretary
Chin Jumajoti (Paris Legation)	Secretary

VI. General Assembly (September 1925)

Phraya Prabha Karawongse (Minister in London & Permanent Representative to the League of Nations *ad interim*)	Delegate
Prince Vipulya Svastiwongse (Minister in Copenhagen)	Delegate
David Mason (London Legation)	Attaché
Luang Srivisarn Vacha (Paris Legation)	Secretary
Luang Vichit Vadhakarn (Paris Legation)	Secretary
Boon Leur Tiran (Copenhagen Legation)	Secretary

Extraordinary General Assembly (March 1926)

Phraya Sanpakitch Preecha (Minister in Rome)	Delegate

VII. General Assembly (September 1926)

Prince Charoon (Minister in Paris & Permanent Representative to the League of Nations)	Delegate
Prince Vipulya Svastiwongse (Minister in Copenhagen)	Delegate
M.R. Smaksman Kritakara (Paris Legation)	Delegate
Thawin Arthayukti (Paris Legation)	Delegate
Khun Prasert Maitri (London Legation)	Secretary ad interim

VIII. General Assembly (September 1927)

Prince Charoon (Minister in Paris & Permanent Representative to the League of Nations)	Delegate
Prince Vipulya Svastiwongse (Minister in Copenhagen)	Delegate
Prince Varnvaidya (Minister in London)	Delegate
Luang Biraj Bisdara (Paris Legation)	Secretary
Khun Prasert Maitri (London Legation)	Secretary
Thawin Arthayukti (Paris Legation)	Secretary
Prince Thongtor Thongthaem (London Legation)	Secretary
M.R. Smaksman Kritakara (Paris Legation)	Secretary

IX. General Assembly (September 1928)

Prince Charoon (Minister in Paris & Permanent Representative to the League of Nations)	Delegate
Prince Vipulya Svastiwongse (Minister in Berlin)	Delegate
Prince Varnvaidya (Minister in London)	Delegate
M.R. Smaksman Kritakara (Paris Legation)	Attaché
Luang Chara (Paris Legation)	Secretary
Prince Thongtor Thongthaem (London Legation)	Secretary
Khun Prasert Maitri (Paris Legation)	Secretary
Thawin Arthayukti (Paris Legation)	Secretary

X. General Assembly (September 1929)

Prince Varnvaidya (Minister in London & Permanent Representative to the League of Nations)	Delegate
Phraya Vichitvongse Vudhikrai (Minister in Paris)	Delegate
Dr. jur. Subhavarn Varasiri (London Legation)	Attaché
Luang Jamni Kolakarn (London Legation)	Secretary
Prince Thongtor Thongthaem (London Legation)	Secretary
M.R. Pantip Devakul (Paris Legation)	Secretary

XI. General Assembly (September/October 1930)

Prince Varnvaidya (Minister in London & Permanent Representative to the League of Nations)	Delegate
Phraya Abhibal Rajamaitri (Minister in Rome)	Delegate
Dr. jur. Subhavarn Varasiri (London Legation)	Attaché
Luang Siri Rajamaitri (Rome Legation)	Secretary
Prince Thongtor Thongthaem (London Legation)	Secretary

XII. General Assembly (September 1931)

Prince Damras Damrong (Minister in London & Permanent Representative to the League of Nations)	Delegate
Phraya Abhibal Rajamaitri (Minister in Rome)	Delegate

Luang Visutra Virajdes (Paris Legation)   Secretary
Luang Siri Rajamaitri (Rome Legation)   Secretary
Luang Ladakavad (Rome Legation)   Secretary
Dr. jur. Subhavarn Varasiri (London Legation) Secretary

Extraordinary General Assembly (March/April, July, December 1932; February 1933)

Major-General Prince Pridi Debyabongse
Devakul (Minister in Berlin & Delegate to
Disarmament Conference)   Delegate
Luang Bhadravadi (London Legation)   Secretary/
                        Substitute Delegate/Delegate

XIII. General Assembly (September/October 1932)

Prince Damras Damrong (Minister in London
& Permanent Representative to the League
of Nations)   Delegate
Phra Bahidda Nukara (London Legation)   Secretary
Luang Bhadravadi (London Legation)   Assistant
                                               Secretary

XIV. General Assembly (September/October 1933)

Phraya Subharn Sompati (Minister in London
& Permanent Representative to the League of
Nations)   Delegate
Luang Bhadravadi (London Legation)   Substitute
                                               Delegate

XV. General Assembly (September 1934)

Phraya Subharn Sompati (Minister in London
& Permanent Representative to the League
of Nations)   Delegate
Luang Bhadravadi (London Legation)   Substitute
                                               Delegate
Khun Prakob Santisuk (London Legation)   Secretary
René C. Guyon (Ministry of Justice, Bangkok)   Technical
                                               Adviser

Extraordinary General Assembly (May 1935)

Phraya Rajawangsan (Minister in London
& Permanent Representative to the League
of Nations)   Delegate
Luang Bhadravadi (London Legation)   Secretary

XVI. General Assembly (September/October 1935; June/July 1936)

Phraya Rajawangsan (Minister in London
& Permanent Representative to the League
of Nations)   Delegate
Luang Bhadravadi (London Legation)   Substitute
                                               Delegate

XVII. General Assembly (September/October 1936)

Phraya Rajawangsan (Minister in London
& Permanent Representative to the
League of Nations)   Delegate
Luang Bhadravadi (London Legation)   Substitute
                                               Delegate
Khun Bibidh Viraijakar (London Legation)   Secretary

Extraordinary General Assembly (May 1937)

Phraya Rajawangsan (Minister in London
& Permanent Representative to the League
of Nations)   Delegate
Luang Bhadravadi (London Legation)   Substitute
                                               Delegate

XVIII. General Assembly (September/October 1937)

Phraya Rajawangsan (Minister in London
& Permanent Representative to the League
of Nations)   Delegate
Luang Bhadravadi (London Legation)   Substitute
                                               Delegate

XIX. General Assembly (September 1938)

Phraya Rajawangsan (Minister in London
& Permanent Representative to the League
of Nations)   Delegate
Luang Bhadravadi (London Legation)   Substitute
                                               Delegate
Somboon Palasthira (London Legation)   Secretary

XX. General Assembly (December 1939)

Phraya Rajawangsan (Minister in London
& Permanent Representative to the League
of Nations)   Delegate
Chalee Yongsundara (London Legation)   Secretary
Somboon Palasthira (London Legation)   Secretary

No Assembly took place in 1940-1945. Siam was not represented at the Final Assembly in 1946.

4 Siam's Financial Contribution to the League of Nations

Year	Units	Gold Francs[a]	Paid in actual currency		
			Swiss Francs	US Dollars	Pounds Sterling
1919-20	3	35,232	---	---	1,948
1920	3	62,760	---	12,110	---
1921	3	125,000	---	24,119	---
1922	3	121,360	---	23,417	---
1923	10	271,965	---	52,477	---
1924[b]	10	249,288	---	48,101	---
1925	10	242,333	---	46,759	---
1926	9	220,252	---	42,498	---
1927	9	204,085	---	39,379	---
1928	9	210,034	---	40,527	---
1929	9	230,103	---	44,399	---
1930	9	247,088	---	47,677	---
1931	9	274,883	---	53,040	---
1932	9	295,580	---	57,033	---
1933	9	297,148	---	57,336	---
1934	9	273,890	273,890	---	---
1935	6	181,768	181,768	---	---
1936	6	172,662	172,662	---	---
1937	6	138,363	195,619	---	---
1938	6	133,734	189,075	---	---
1939	6	133,595	188,878	---	---
1940[c]	5	92,805	65,604	---	---
1941[c]	5	72,142	50,998	---	---
1942[c]	5	72,141	50,997	---	---
1943[c]	5	93,025	65,760	---	---
1944[c]	5	84,898	60,015	---	---
1945[c]	5	124,899	176,584	---	---
1946[c]	5	135,723	191,887	---	---

For a compilation of Siam's annual contributions to the League of Nations see TNA, KT 96.1.1/19.

[a] Gold francs were the accounting currency used by the League of Nations. Until September 1936, one gold franc corresponded to one Swiss franc. 5 gold francs corresponded roughly to one US dollar and 20 gold francs roughly to one pound sterling.

[b] An additional US$17,545.86 for the year 1924 were paid in 1925.

[c] As the League became defunct during the war years, Siam did not pay its annual contributions during 1940-44. Based on an agreement with the League's Treasury in 1946, Siam then paid 50% of its contribution for 1940-44 and 100% of its contribution for 1945-46. After deduction of Siam's share of the League's capital reserve fund, this amount of 661,845.84 Swiss francs was further reduced to 604,095.39 Swiss francs.

5 Conventions and Agreements within the League of Nations' Framework, signed by, acceded to and ratified by Siam

[S: place & date] Signed by Siam, [A: date] Acceded to by Siam, [R: date] Ratified by Siam

1919   Treaty of Versailles with Covenant of the League of Nations [S: Paris, 28 June 1919; R: 10 January 1920]

1920   Protocol of Signature of the Permanent Court of International Justice [S: Geneva, 16 December 1920; R: 27 February 1922]

Optional Clause Recognising the Court's Jurisdiction, as described in Article 36 of the Statute [S: Geneva, 16 December 1920; R: 7 May 1930 and Renewal 9 May 1940]

1921   Convention and Statute on Freedom of Transit (Barcelona Convention) [A: 29 November 1922]

Convention, Statute and Additional Protocol on the Regime of Navigable Waterways of International Concern [A: 29 November 1922]

Declaration Recognising the Right to a Flag of States Having no sea-coast [A: 29 November 1922]

International Convention for the Suppression of the Traffic in Women and Children [S: Geneva, 30 September 1921; R: 13 July 1922]

Protocol of an Amendment to Article 16 of the Covenant of the League of Nations [S: Geneva, 5 October 1921; R: 12 September 1922]

Protocol of an Amendment to Article 26 of the Covenant of the League of Nations [S: Geneva, 5 October 1921; R: 12 September 1922] *(Not in force)*

1923   International Convention for the Suppression of the Circulation of and Traffic in Obscene Publications [S: Geneva, 12 September 1923; R: 28 July 1924]

Protocol on Arbitration Clauses in Commercial Matters [S: Geneva, 24 September 1923; R: 30 September 1930]

International Convention Relating to the Simplification of Customs Formalities, and Protocol [S: Geneva, 30 November 1923; R: 19 May 1925]

Convention and Statute on the International Regime of Railways, and Protocol of Signature [S: Geneva, 9 December 1923; R: 9 January 1925]

Convention and Statute on the International Regime of Maritime Ports, and Protocol of Signature [S: Geneva, 9 December 1923; R: 9 January 1925]

Convention Relating to the Development of Hydraulic Power Affecting More than One State, and Protocol of Signature [S: Geneva, 9 December 1923; R: 9 January 1925]

1924   Protocol of an Amendment to Article 16 of the Covenant of the League of Nations [S: Geneva, 27 September 1924; R: 30 September 1925] *(Not in force)*

1925   Agreement on the Application in the Far East of Chapter II of the International Opium Convention of 1912, with Protocol and Final Act (First Geneva Opium Conference) [S: 11 February 1925; R: 6 May 1927]

Agreement Concerning the Suppression of the Manufacture of, Internal Trade in, and Use of, Prepared Opium, with Protocol and Final Act (First Geneva Opium Conference) [S: Geneva, 11 February 1925; R: 6 May 1927]

International Convention Relating to Dangerous Drugs, with Protocol and Final Act (Second Geneva Opium Conference) [S: 19 February 1925; R: 11 October 1929]

Convention for the Supervision of the International Trade in Arms and Ammunition and in Implements of War [S: Geneva, 17 June 1925] *(Not ratified)*

Protocol for the Prohibition of the Use in War of Asphyxiating, Poisonous and Other Gases and of Bacteriological Methods of Warfare [S: Geneva, 17 June 1925; R: 6 June 1931]

Protocol of an Amendment to Article 16 of the Covenant of the League of Nations [S: Geneva, 21 September 1925] *(Not in force, not ratified)*

1927   Convention on the Execution of Foreign Arbitral Awards [S: Geneva, 26 September 1927; R: 7 July 1931]

International Convention, Agreement and Protocol for the Abolishment of Import and Export Restrictions [S: Geneva, 8 November 1927] *(Not ratified)*

1929   Protocol Relating to the Accession of the United States of America to the Protocol of Signature of the Statute of the Permanent Court of International Justice [S: Geneva, 14 September 1929; R: 2 June 1930]

1931   Convention for Limiting the Manufacture and Regulating Distribution of Narcotic Drugs and Protocol of Signature (Geneva Limitation Convention) [S: Geneva, 13 July 1931; R: 22 February 1934]

General Convention to Improve the Means of Preventing War [S: Geneva, 26 September 1931] *(Not ratified)*

Agreement on the Suppression of Opium-Smoking (Bangkok Agreement) [S: Bangkok, 27 November 1931; R: 19 November 1934]

1936   Procès-Verbal to Alter the Latest Date of Issue of the Annual Statement of the Estimated World Requirements of Dangerous Drugs, drawn up by the Supervisory Body, as provided for by the International Convention of 13 July 1931, for Limiting the Manufacture and Regulating Distribution of Narcotic Drugs [S: Geneva, 26 June 1936] *(Not ratified, not in force)*

Compilation based on LNA, Serial Documents A.6(a).1937.Annex I.V. and C.25.M.25.1943.V. Annex; and on 'Liste des Conventions et Accords don't le Siam est Partie', TNA, KT 96.1.13/14. Siam did not sign any of the numerous labour conventions concluded under the auspices of the International Labour Organisation.

6 Thai Kings of the Chakri Dynasty in the Twentieth Century

Chulalongkorn (Rama V) (1853-1910)	1868-1910
Vajiravudh (Rama VI) (1881-1925)	1910-1925
Prajadhipok (Rama VII) (1893-1941)[a]	1925-1935
Ananda Mahidol (Rama VIII) (1925-1946)	1935-1946
Bhumibol Adulyadej (Rama IX) (b. 1927)	Since 1946

[a] *Abdicated.*

7 Thai Prime Ministers, 1932-1946

Phraya Manopakorn Nitthithada (1884-1948)	1932-1933
Phraya Phahon Phonphayuhasena (1887-1947)	1933-1938
Luang Phibun Songkhram (1897-1964)	1938-1944
Khuang Aphaiwongse (1903-1968)	1944-1945
Thawee Bunyaket (1904-1971)	1945
Mom Rajawongse Seni Pramoj (1905-1997)	1945-1946
Khuang Aphaiwongse [second term]	1946
Pridi Phanomyong (1900-1983)	1946
Thawan Thamrongnawasawat (1901-1988)	1946-1947

8 Thai Ministers of Foreign Affairs, 1885-1946

Prince Devawongse Varopakarn (1858-1923)	1885-1923
Prince Traidos Prabandh (1883-1943) [acting]	1923-1924
Prince Traidos Prabandh [1929 Prince Devawongse Varothai]	1924-1932
Phraya Srivisarn Vacha (1893-1968)	1932-1933
Phraya Abhibal Rajamaitri (1885-1961)	1933-1934
Phraya Phahon Phonphayuhasena (1887-1947)	1934-1935
Phraya Srisena Sompatsiri (1889-1982)	1935-1936
Luang Pradist Manudharm (1900-1983)	1936-1938
Chao Phraya Sridharmadhibes (1885-1976)	1938-1939
Luang Phibun Songkhram (1897-1964)	1940-1941
Direck Jayanama (1905-1967)	1941
Luang Phibun Songkhram [second term]	1941-1942
Luang Vichit Vadhakarn (1898-1962)	1942-1943
Direck Jayanama [second term]	1943-1944
Phraya Srisena Sompatsiri [second term]	1944-1946
Mom Rajawongse Seni Pramoj (1905-1997)	1946
Direck Jayanama [third term]	1946-1947

9 Selected Foreign Advisers to the Thai Government

British Financial Advisers, 1904-1951

Sir Walter James Franklin Williamson	1904-1925
Sir Edward Cook	1925-1930
Sir Edmund Leo Hall-Patch	1930-1932
James Baxter	1932-1935
William A.M. Doll	1936-1942 & 1946-51

American General and Foreign Affairs Advisers, 1902-1940

Prof. Edward H. Strobel	1902-1907
Prof. Jens I. Westengard	1907-1915
Prof. Wolcott H. Pitkin	1915-1917
Prof. Eldon R. James	1917-1923
Prof. Francis B. Sayre[a]	1923-1925
Courtney Crocker[a]	1924-1925
Raymond B. Stevens	1926-1935
Frederick R. Dolbeare	1935-1940

[a] *The terms of Sayre and Crocker overlapped due to Sayre's extended travel in Europe.*

10 Name Glossary

Individuals mentioned in the text and appendices are listed; individuals mentioned only in references are not listed. The given names of Thai individuals or their princely rank respectively are given in parenthesis behind the name by which they were known during the period of this study.

Abhibal Rajamaitri, Phraya (Tom Bunnag) (1885-1961)
Thai diplomat, younger brother of Phraya Subharn Sompati. Chief of Protocol in Ministry of Foreign Affairs 1927-30; Minister in Rome 1930-31, also accredited to Spain and Portugal; appointed Minister in Tokyo 1931, but did not take up post; Permanent Secretary for Foreign Affairs 1931-33; Minister of Foreign Affairs 1933-34; Minister in Washington D.C. 1935-40. Thai delegate to League of Nations General Assemblies in 1930 and 1931.

Adhikarana Prakas, Phraya (Louis Chatikavanij) (1876-1955)
Director-General of Police & Gendarmerie. Member of the commission appointed by the Ministry of Interior to assist the League of Nations commission of enquiry on trafficking in women and children 1930.

Aditya Dibabha, Prince (Phra Ong Chao) (1904-1946)
Grandson of King Chulalongkorn. Regent for King Ananda 1935-44.

Ajurakith Khoson, Luang
Medical doctor; staff of Department of Public Health. Assigned to work with Dr. Anigstein on malaria survey in 1931. Participated in malaria seminar in 1934 at the Far Eastern Bureau of the League of Nations in Singapore.

Ames, Sir Herbert Brown (1863-1954)
Canadian politician and social reformer. Head of Treasury Section of League of Nations Secretariat 1919-26. Responsible for hiring of Mani Sanasen as League Secretariat staff in 1925.

Amoradat Kritakara, Prince (Mom Chao) (1886-1952)
Thai diplomat. Son of Prince Nares Vorarit and grandson of King Mongkut, brother of Prince Charoon and Prince Bovoradej. Minister in Washington D.C. 1928-31; Minister in Paris 1932-34, also accredited to the Netherlands, Belgium, Italy, Spain, and Portugal. His wife Mom Proisubin divorced him to marry Prince Varn in 1930.

Ananda Mahidol, King Rama VIII (1925-1946)
Grandson of King Chulalongkorn, son of Prince Mahidol. Reigned 1935-46. Resided in Lausanne, Switzerland until 1945. Briefly visited Bangkok in 1938-39. Died from gunshot wound in 1946.

Andrews, James M.
American anthropologist at Harvard University. Author of second rural economic survey of Siam 1934-35, commissioned by Thai government.

Anigstein, Dr. Ludwik (1891-1975)
Polish parasitologist. Worked for the State Institute of Hygiene in Warsaw 1919-39; served as consultant in several African and Asian countries; member of the Malaria Commission at the League of Nations in Geneva; drew up innovative malaria control scheme for Siam based on extensive field studies in 1931. In 1939 fled from the Nazis and immigrated to the United States.

Annan, Kofi (b. 1938)
Ghanaian national. Seventh United Nations Secretary-General 1997-2006.

Avenol, Joseph Louis Anne (1879-1952)
French diplomat. Second Secretary-General of the League of Nations 1933-40.

Ayer, Dr. Ira
American medical doctor. Adviser to the Thai Department of Public Health. Represented Siam at early meetings of the advisory board of the Singapore Bureau during mid-1920s.

Bahidda Nukara, Phra (Suan Navarasth)
Thai diplomat. Staff at Thai legation in Rome during 1920s; Minister in Paris and Vichy 1937-41, also accredited to the Netherlands (until 1938), Brussels, Italy (until 1938), Spain and Portugal. Minister in Rome 1942; Ambassador in London 1950-53. Member of Thai delegation to League of Nations General Assembly 1923 and 1924.

Balfour, Arthur James, Earl of (1848-1930)
British politician. Prime Minister 1902-05 and Foreign Secretary 1916-19.

Baxter, James (b. 1896)
British Financial Adviser to the Thai government 1932-35. Resigned over opium smuggling scandal.

Bhadravadi, Dr. jur. Luang (Subhavarn Varasiri) (b. 1904)
Thai diplomat. Studied law in Poitiers and obtained a doctorate. In charge of League of Nations matters at London legation 1929-42 and 1946. Thai delegate to the League of Nations on numerous occasions, often *de facto* delegate. Abstained from voting to condemn Japan in 1933. Applied unsuccessfully for position at League Secretariat 1936.

Bhayung Vejjasastra, Dr. Luang
Head of Malaria Section in Department of Public Health. Thai government liaison person for Dr. Anigstein during 1931 malaria enquiry. Drew up the 1937 malaria control scheme.

Bhumibol Adulyadej, King Rama IX (b. 1927)
Grandson of King Chulalongkorn, son of Prince Mahidol, younger brother of King Ananda. Grew up in Lausanne, Switzerland until 1945. Succeeded his brother on the throne in 1946. Thailand's longest-reigning monarch.

Bicharn Nalakitch, Phra
Deputy Director-General of the Police Department in the Ministry of Interior. Thai delegate to the 1937 League of Nations Conference of Central Authorities on Trafficking in Women and Children in Bandung.

Bibadh Kosha, Phraya (Celestino Xavier) (1864-1922)
Thai diplomat of Portuguese-Thai descent. Minister in Rome 1914-22, also accredited to Spain and Portugal; delegate to the Paris Peace Conference; delegate to League of Nations General Assembly 1920-22.

Bibadh Kosha, Ms. S, Ms. J., Ms. C., Ms. L.
Daughters of Phraya Bibadh Kosha; members of Thai delegation to League of Nations General Assembly 1920-22.

Bibadhanakorn, Phraya (Chim Besayanu)
Director-General of Opium Department in Ministry of Finance. Member of inter-ministerial opium commission; interviewee of the League of Nations commission of enquiry on opium smoking 1929; member of Thai delegation to League of Nations Bangkok Opium Conference 1931.

Bijai Janriddhi, Major-General Phraya (later Lieutenant-General Phraya Devahastin) (1877-1951)
Commander of the Thai expeditionary force in Europe during the First World War.

Birabongse Bhanudej, Prince (Mom Chao, *1927* Phra Ong Chao) *(1914-1985)*
Grandson of King Mongkut and cousin of Prince Chula. Renowned racing car driver, who participated in European Grand Prix races before and after the Second World War.

Biraj Bisdara, Khun (1927 Luang)
Thai diplomat in Paris. Member of Thai delegation to League of Nations General Assembly 1923, 1924 and 1927.

Boon Leur Tiran
Thai diplomat in Copenhagen. Member of Thai delegation to League of Nations General Assembly 1925.

Boriraksh Vejkar, Phraya (d. 1968)
Director-General of Department of Public Health in Ministry of Interior in 1930s. Member of Cabinet 1948-52.

Bovoradej Kritakara, Prince (Mom Chao, *1929* Phra Ong Chao) *(1877-1953)*
Son of Prince Nares Vorarit and grandson of King Mongkut, brother of Prince Amoradat and Prince Charoon. Educated in England. Minister in Paris 1909-12, also accredited to Italy, Spain, and Portugal; Viceroy of Chiang Mai from 1916; Minister of War 1925-31. Leader of reactionary counter coup attempt 1933.

Brent, Bishop Charles Henry (1862-1929)
Episcopal missionary bishop of the Philippines 1902-18. American anti-opium activist.

Brooke, Dr. Gilbert Edward (1873-1936)
British medical official; formerly port health official in Singapore; first Director of the Far Eastern Bureau of the League of Nations Health Organisation in Singapore 1925-1927.

Buri Navarasth, Phraya (Chuan Singhaseni)
Thai diplomat. Minister in London 1919-22, also accredited to Belgium and the Netherlands; Minister in Washington D.C. 1923-25. Delegate to League of Nations General Assembly 1920.

Burnet, Dr. Etienne (1873-1960)
French microbiologist, worked for the Pasteur Institutes in Paris and Tunis. Secretary of the League's leprosy commission; participated in the Bangkok meeting of the commission 1930.

Cecil, Lord Robert (1923 Viscount Cecil of Chelwood) (1864-1958)
British politician and diplomat. One of the most influential individuals in the history of the League of Nations. Nobel Peace Prize laureate 1937.

Chai Unipan
Thai student in Europe, considered by Ministry of Education as possible candidate for a position in the Information Section of the League of Nations Secretariat 1931.

Chalee Yongsundara
Member of Thai delegation to League of Nations General Assembly 1939.

Chaloerm Atipat, Khun
Medical doctor; staff of Department of Public Health. Assigned to work with Dr. Anigstein on malaria survey in 1931; participated in malaria seminar in 1934 at the Far Eastern Bureau of the League of Nations in Singapore.

Chang Tso-lin, Marshal (Zhang Zuolin) (1873-1928)
Chinese warlord in Manchuria. Assassinated by Japanese agents 1928.

Chara, Luang
Thai diplomat in Paris. Member of Thai delegation to League of Nations General Assembly 1928.

Charnvitivej, Dr. Phra
Medical doctor; staff of the Department of Public Health in the Ministry of Interior. Underwent extensive training in disease prevention at the Far Eastern Bureau of the League of Nations Health Organisation; Thai liaison person for the League of Nations commission of enquiry on rural hygiene 1936; delegate to the League of Nations Conference on Rural Hygiene in Bandung 1937.

Charoonsakdi Kritakara, Prince (Phra Ong Chao) *(1875-1928)*
Son of Prince Nares Vorarit and grandson of King Mongkut, brother of Prince Amoradat and Prince Bovoradej. Educated in England. Assistant to the General Adviser's Office; provincial official under Ministry of Interior; Minister in Paris 1906-09, also accredited to Italy, Spain, and Portugal; Deputy Minister of Justice 1909; Minister of Justice 1910-12; followed his brother Prince Bovoradej as Minister in Paris 1912-28, also accredited to Italy, Spain, and Portugal 1912-14. Delegate of Siam at the Paris Peace Conference and Permanent Representative of Siam to the League of Nations 1920-28. Since 1912 married to Mom Juam, sister of coup promoter Luang Kowit Aphaiwongse.

Chin Jumajoti
Member of Thai delegation to League of Nations General Assembly 1924.

Chuen Jotikasthira, see Sanpaktich Preecha, Phraya

Chuen Charuvastra, see Sarasasna Prabandhu, Phra

Chula Chakrabongse, Prince (Phra Ong Chao) *(1908-1963)*
Grandson of King Chulalongkorn and son of Prince Chakrabongse. Educated in England and resided there. Visited Bangkok 1931, 1937 and 1938. Manager of motor-racing team of his cousin Prince Birabongse. Married Mom Elisabeth Hunter 1938. Last Permanent Representative of Siam to the League of Nations, 1940-46. Joined the Home Guard in England during the Second World War.

Chulalongkorn, King Rama V (1853-1910)
Son of King Mongkut. Reigned 1868-1910 and implemented far-reaching reforms.

Clemenceau, Georges (1841-1929)
French Prime Minister, who represented France at the Paris Peace Conference.

Coode, A.T.
British engineer. Consultant to League of Nations Communications and Transit Organisation; member of League of Nations commission of experts to study the improved access to the port of Bangkok 1933.

Cook, Sir Edward (b. 1881)
British Financial Adviser to the Thai government 1925-30.

Crocker, Courtney
Harvard law graduate. American Foreign Affairs Adviser to the Thai government 1924-25.

Crosby, Sir Josiah (1880-1958)
British diplomat who spent 35 years in Siam between 1904 and 1941. Staff at British legation in Bangkok 1904-19; Consul General in Bangkok from 1921; Minister in Bangkok from 1934. Interned by Japanese 1941, repatriated in exchange of diplomatic personnel 1942. Author of *Siam: The Crossroads* (1945).

Crowdy, Dame Rachel Eleanor (1884-1964)
British social reformer. League of Nations official. Head of Opium Traffic and Social Questions Section in League of Nations Secretariat 1919-31.

Damras Damrong Devakul, Prince (Mom Chao) *(1886-1944)*
Son of Prince Devawongse, younger brother of Prince Traidos, older half-brother of Prince Pridi Debyabongse. Diplomat. Minister in The Hague 1924; Minister in Berlin 1925-28; Minister in Copenhagen 1929-30; Minister in London 1930-33, also accredited to Berlin and Denmark 1932-33; Minister in Washington D.C. 1933-35. Member of Thai delegation to the League of Nations General Assembly 1923; Permanent Representative of Siam to the League of Nations 1931-33,

Damrong Baedyagun, Major-General Phraya (1881-1953)
Director of Chulalongkorn Hospital. One of the central figures on the Thai side for the meeting of the League of Nations leprosy commission and the Congress of the Far Eastern Association of Tropical Medicine, both in Bangkok 1930.

Damrong Rajanubhab, Prince (Phra Ong Chao) *(1862-1943)*
Son of King Mongkut and brother of King Chulalongkorn. Instrumental in major administrative reforms of Siam as Minister of Interior 1892-1915. Eminent historian. Visited the headquarters of the League of Nations in Geneva 1930; attended the opening of the League of Nations Bangkok Opium Conference 1931.

Deb Vidul, Phraya
Attorney-General of Siam. Chairman of inter-ministerial committee to draft immigration law 1926.

Delevingne, Sir Malcolm (1868-1950)
British politician and diplomat. Deputy Permanent Under-Secretary in Home Office 1913-32. One of the leading anti-opium activists of his time and a prime architect of the League's international opium control system.

Participated in all major League of Nations opium bodies and conferences, including the Bangkok Opium Conference of 1931.

Devawongse Varopakarn, Prince (Phra Ong Chao) *(1858-1923)*
Son of King Mongkut and younger half-brother of King Chulalongkorn. Father of Princes Traidos Prabandh, Damras Damrong, and Pridi Debyabongse. Minister of Foreign Affairs for thirty-eight years from 1885 to 1923.

Devawongse Varothai, Prince, see Traidos Prabandh, Prince

Direck Jayanama (1905-1967)
Thai politician and diplomat. Member of the coup group 1932. Cabinet Secretary 1935-40; Deputy Minister of Foreign Affairs 1940-41; several stints as Minister of Foreign Affairs 1941, 1943-44, 1946-47; Ambassador in Tokyo 1942-43, after Second World War Ambassador to Great Britain and Germany. Member of Free Thai leadership during the Second World War.

Dolbeare, Frederick R.
Yale law graduate; State Department official. American Foreign Affairs Adviser to the Thai government 1935-40.

Doll, William A.M. (b. 1895)
British Financial Adviser to the Thai government 1936-42 and 1946-51.

Dormer, Cecil
British Minister in Bangkok 1930-34.

Drummond, Sir James Eric, Earl of Perth (1876-1951)
British diplomat and first Secretary-General of the League of Nations 1919-33. British Ambassador to Rome 1933-39.

Ekstrand, Eric Einar (1880-1958)
Swedish diplomat and international civil servant. Head of Opium Trafficking and Social Questions Section in League of Nations Secretariat 1931-39; visited Bangkok with League commission of enquiry on opium smoking in 1929 and again for Bangkok Opium Conference 1931. Continued his career with United Nations after Second World War.

Gautier, Dr. Raymond (1886-1957)
Swiss national. Director of the Far Eastern Bureau of the League of Nations Health Organisation in Singapore 1927-31. Acting Director of the League's Health Organisation 1939-42.

Gehe, Captain Alberto
Naval Attaché at Italian Embassy in Tokyo. Visited Siam in 1936.

Guthrie, Anne (1890-1979)
American social reformer. Participated in the 1937 League of Nations Conference of Central Authorities on Trafficking in Women and Children in Bandung as an observer for the YWCA Manila.

Guyon, René C. (1876-1963)
French lawyer. Judicial Adviser to the Thai government and Supreme Court judge. Technical Adviser to delegation of Siam to League of Nations General Assembly 1934. Well-known for his writings on sexual ethics.

Haile Selassi I, Emperor of Ethiopia (Abyssinia) (1892-1975)
Reigned 1930-74; in exile 1936-41. Appealed to the League of Nations after Italian invasion of Ethiopia.

Haynes, Alwyn Sidney (1878-1963)
British colonial official in the Straits Settlements and Malaya. Member of the League of Nations commission of enquiry on rural hygiene, which visited Siam in 1936.

Heide, Homan van der (1865-1945)
Dutch engineer. Adviser to the government of Siam 1902-09; founding director of the Thai Royal Irrigation Development.

Heiser, Dr. Victor George (1873-1972)
American doctor and Rockefeller Foundation official.

James, Eldon R. (1875-1949)
Harvard law professor. American Foreign Affairs Adviser to the Thai government 1918-23.

Jamni Kolakarn, Luang
Staff at the Thai legation in London. Member of Thai delegation to League of Nations General Assembly 1929.

Johns, John Francis
British diplomat, long-time resident in Siam. Held various diplomatic posts, among them Vice Consul in Phuket 1914-15; Consul in Songkhla 1924-25; staff at British legation in Bangkok 1924-32.

Johnson, Bascom (b. 1883)
American chairman of the League of Nations commission of enquiry on trafficking in women and children, which visited Siam in 1930.

Jordan, A.B.
British colonial official. Delegate of the Straits Settlements and the Federated Malay States at League of Nations Conference of Central Authorities on Traffic in Women and Children in Bandung 1937.

Kase Shunichi
Japanese Consul in Bangkok 1933.

Kimleang Vathanaprida, see Vichit Vadhakarn, Luang

Kitiyakara Voralaksana, Prince of Chandaburi (Phra Ong Chao) *(1874-1931)* Son of King Chulalongkorn. Minister of Finance 1908-23; Minister of Commerce 1923-26; chairman of inter-ministerial opium commission from 1925; Minister of Commerce and Communications 1926-31.

Komarakul Montri, Phraya (Chuen Komarakul na Nagara)
Minister of Finance 1929; Minister of Economy 1933-34.

Koo, V. K. Wellington (Ku Wei-chun) (1888-1985)
Chinese diplomat and politician. Represented China at League of Nations for nearly two decades. Continued his career after Second World War as representative of China, later Republic of China (Taiwan), at United Nations until 1956. Judge at International Court of Justice.

Kowit Aphaiwongse, Luang (Khuang Aphaiwongse) (1903-1968)
Studied in France, had contact to coup promoters. Member of the coup group 1932. Held various cabinet positions and had several stints as Prime Minister during 1940s. Brother-in-law of Prince Charoon.

Ladakavad, Luang
Thai diplomat in Rome. Member of Thai delegation to League of Nations General Assembly 1931.

Langen, Prof. C.D.
Dutch doctor. Former Dean of Medical Faculty at Batavia. Member of the League of Nations commission of enquiry on rural hygiene, which visited Siam in 1936.

Lester, Sean (1888-1959)
Irish politician. Third and last Secretary-General of the League of Nations 1940-46.

Lie, Trygve(1896-1968)
Norwegian politician. First Secretary-General of the United Nations 1946-52.

Lindley, Sir Francis Oswald (b. 1874)
British Ambassador in Tokyo 1931-34.

Lloyd George, David (1863-1945)
British politician. Prime Minister 1916-22; represented Britain at the Paris Peace Conference.

Lytton, Victor Alexander George Robert Edward Robert Bulwer, Earl of (1871-1947)
British colonial official and diplomat. Chairman of League of Nations commission of enquiry in the Manchurian Conflict ('Lytton Commission') 1932-33.

Mackenzie, Dr. Melville Douglas (1889-1972)
British doctor of tropical medicine and hygiene. Conducted enquiry for the League of Nations in Liberia 1931-32; director *ad interim* of the Far Eastern Bureau of the League of Nations Health Organisation in Singapore 1936; visited Siam in 1937 for enquiry on cholera.

Mahidol Adulyadej, Prince (Chao Fa) **(1892-1929)**
Son of King Chulalongkorn, father of Kings Ananda and Bhumibol. Heir-presumptive to the throne from 1925 until his death. Studied public health and medicine at Harvard University; worked in Siam as Director-General of the University Department in the Ministry of Education and, from 1928, as medical practitioner in Chiang Mai.

Malcolm, Alec
British chairman of Bangkok International Chamber of Commerce 1929.

Mani Sanasen (1898-1978)
Son of Thai diplomat Phraya Visut Kosha. Grew up in England, studied at Oxford. Worked for the Treasury Section of the League of Nations Secretariat 1925-40; only Thai staff at the League Secretariat. Attached to Thai legation in Washington D.C. 1941; then joined Free Thai movement in England 1942-44. Worked for United Nations Secretariat after the Second World War until his retirement and continued to live in Geneva until his death.

Manich Jumsai, Mom Luang (1908-2009)
Thai historian. Student in Europe, considered by Ministry of Education as possible candidate for a position in the Information Section of the League of Nations Secretariat 1931.

Manjuvadi, Phra
Head of League of Nations Section in Thai Ministry of Foreign Affairs 1931.

Manopakorn Nitthithada, Phraya (Kon Hutasinha) (1884-1948)
British-educated lawyer, Supreme Court judge and Minister of Justice. First Prime Minister of Siam 1932-33. Exiled to Penang in 1933.

Manuwej Waitayavitmonat, Phra (Pian Sumawong)
Thai Minister in London 1940-41, also accredited to Denmark. Member of cabinet under Prime Minister Luang Phibun 1948.

Mason, David
Attaché to Thai legation in London; member of Thai delegation to League of Nations General Assembly 1925.

Matsuoka Yosuke (1880-1946)
Japanese politician and diplomat. Permanent Representative of Japan to the League of Nations during the Manchurian Conflict in early 1930s. Minister of Foreign Affairs in early 1940s. Tried as war criminal by the International Military Tribunal for the Far East after the end of the war, but died before he could be convicted.

Maugham, William Somerset (1874-1965)
Popular English playwright and novelist. Visited Bangkok in 1922.

May, Jacques M. (1896-1975)
French surgeon, who practiced in Bangkok 1932-36. Professor of tropical medicine at Hanoi University, French Indochina 1936-40. Author of *A Doctor in Siam* (1951).

Mitrakarm Raksha, Phra (Nattha Buranasiri)
Thai diplomat. Minister in Tokyo 1934-37.

Mongkut, King Rama IV (1804-1868)
Father of King Chulalongkorn, reigned 1851-68.

Mundie, William H.
British resident in Bangkok since 1896. Sub-editor and editor of the *Bangkok Times* newspaper until 1942. Interviewee of League of Nations commission of enquiry on opium smoking 1929.

Mussolini, Benito (1883-1945)
Fascist Italian Prime Minister and dictator 1922-43. Received Luang Pradist 1935.

Nangklao, King Rama III (1788-1851)
Reigned 1824-51.

Naradhip Prabandhabongse, Prince (Phra Ong Chao) (1861-1931)
Son of King Mongkut and father of Princes Varn and Sakol.

Nares Vorarit, Prince (Phra Ong Chao) (1855-1925)
Son of King Mongkut and father of Princes Charoon, Amoradat and Bovoradej. Minister in London 1883-87, also accredited to the United States.

Narubesr Manit, Luang (Sa-nguan Chudatemiya)
Director-General of Excise Department in Ministry of Finance and minister without portfolio 1933-35. At the centre of the opium smuggling scandal of 1935, which led to the resignation of J. Baxter, British Financial Adviser to the Thai government. Minister without portfolio 1937-39; Deputy Minister of Finance 1939-42; Minister of Industry 1946.

Negri, Count Vittorio Marcello
Italian diplomat. Minister in Asuncion 1928-33; Minister in Bangkok 1933-1936.

Nijhoff, G.P. (1877-1956)
Dutch engineer. Consultant to the League of Nations Communications and Transit Organisation; member of League of Nations commission of experts to study the improved access to and expansion of the port of Bangkok 1933.

Nocht, Dr. Bernhard (1857-1945)
German naval physician. Director of Hamburg Institute for Maritime and Tropical Diseases 1900-30 (in 1942 renamed after him). Worked at League of Nations Leprosy

Research Centre at Rio de Janeiro; chairman of the Bangkok meeting of the leprosy commission of the League of Nations 1930.

Orlando, Vittorio Emmanuele (1860-1952)
Italian diplomat and politician. Prime Minister 1917-19. Represented Italy at the Paris Peace Conference.

Pampana, Dr. Emilio
Italian medical scientist. Secretary of the League of Nations malaria commission; member of the League of Nations commission of enquiry on rural hygiene, which visited Siam in 1936; first WHO director of malaria eradication after the Second World War. Author of a standard textbook on malaria eradication.

Pantip Devakul, Mom Rajawongse (1909-1987)
Daughter of Minister of Foreign Affairs Prince Traidos. Member of Thai delegation to League of Nations General Assembly 1929. Since 1930 married to Prince Chumbhotbongse Paribatra of Nakorn Savarn

Park, Dr. Charles Leslie (b. 1886?)
Australian medical doctor. Staff of the League's Health Organisation; Director of the Far Eastern Bureau of the League of Nations Health Organisation in Singapore 1932-42; participated in League of Nations Conference on Rural Hygiene in Bandung 1937.

Patch, Sir Edmund Leo Hall- (1896-1975)
British Financial Adviser to the Thai government 1930-32.

Phahon Phonphayuhasena, Phraya (Phot Phahonyothin) (1887-1947)
Army Colonel, trained in Germany and Denmark. Leader of the coup group in 1932. Prime Minister of Siam 1933-38; Minister of Foreign Affairs 1934-35.

Phibun Songkhram, Field Marshal Luang (Plaek Khittasangkha) (1897-1964)
One of the senior leaders of the 1932 coup group. Of Sino-Thai origin. Trained in France 1920-27, where he joined coup promoters. Cabinet Minister 1932-34; Minister of Defence 1934-41; Prime Minister 1938-44 and 1948-57; Minister of Interior 1938-41; Minister of Foreign Affairs 1940-41, 1941-42 and 1949; Supreme Military Commander 1939-44; Convicted as war criminal and imprisoned 1945-46. Died in exile in Japan.

Pin Malakul, Mom Luang (1903-1995)
Student in Oxford 1921-31. Considered by Ministry of Education as possible candidate for a position in the Information Section of the League of Nations Secretariat 1931. Permanent Secretary in Ministry of Education 1946-57; Minister of Education 1957-68.

Pinder, Carol
Member of the League of Nations commission of enquiry on trafficking in women and children, which visited Siam in 1930.

Pitkin, Wolcott Homer (b. 1881)
Harvard law professor. American Foreign Affairs Adviser to the Thai government 1915-17.

Prabha Karawongse, Phraya (Wong Bunnag) (1877-1954)
Thai diplomat. Minister in Washington D.C. 1913-22; Minister in London 1923-26, also accredited to Belgium; Permanent Representative of Siam to the League of Nations and Minister in Paris *ad interim* during absence of Prince Charoon 1925-26.

Pradist Manudharm, Dr. jur. Luang (Pridi Phanomyong) (1900-1983)
Of Sino-Thai origin. Studied law in Paris 1920-27; came into conflict with Prince Charoon; staff of Ministry of Justice 1927-32; prominent civilian member of 1932 coup group; member of cabinet 1932-34; exiled over economic plan 1933; Minister of Interior 1934-36; Minister of Foreign Affairs 1936-38; Minister of Finance 1938-41; Regent 1941-45; leader of Free Thai movement in Bangkok during Second World War; Prime Minister 1946. Exiled 1947 to China and France. Founder and Rector of Thammasat University.

Prajadhipok, King Rama VII (1893-1941)
Youngest son of King Chulalongkorn, brother of King Vajiravudh. Reigned 1925-35. First constitutional monarch 1932-35. Only king of Chakri dynasty to abdicate. Left Siam in 1934 and lived in self-imposed exile in England until his death 1941.

Prakit Kolasastra, Phraya
Chief engineer of the Public and Municipal Works Department in the Ministry of Interior. Thai delegate to the League of Nations Conference on Rural Hygiene in Bandung 1937; Minister of Communications 1947.

Prakob Santisuk, Khun
Staff at Thai legation in London; member of delegation of Siam to League of Nations General Assembly 1934.

Prasert Maitri, Khun
Thai diplomat in London and Paris during the 1920s; member of Thai delegation to League of Nations General Assembly 1926-28.

Pridi Debyabongse Devakul, Major-General Prince (Mom Chao) (1893-1970)
Son of Prince Devawongse, younger half-brother of Princes Traidos and Damras Damrong. Military Attaché at London Legation 1921-23; Minister in Berlin 1930-32, also accredited to Denmark; delegate of Siam to World Disarmament Conference and to Extraordinary League of Nations General Assembly on Sino-Japanese conflict until June 1932. Minister of Foreign Affairs 1948-49.

Pridi Phanomyong, see Pradist Manudharm, Luang

Prisdang Jumsai, Prince (Mom Chao, 1883 Phra Ong Chao) (1852-1935)
Grandson of King Nangklao (Rama III). Thai Ambassador-at-large to Europe and America, based in London 1882-83 and Paris 1883-87. Accredited to France, United Kingdom, United States, Germany, Denmark, Netherlands, Belgium, Austria-Hungary, Italy, Spain, and Portugal.

Proisubin Bunnag (Mom) (1893-1982)
Wife of Prince Amoradat until 1930, remarried to Prince Varn. Elder sister of Mom Pien, wife of Minister of Foreign Affairs Prince Traidos.

Rangsit Prayurasakdi, Prince of Jainad (Phra Ong Chao) (1885-1951)
Son of King Chulalongkorn. Director-General of Dept. of Public Health 1918-26; member of Privy Council to King Vajiravudh 1910-25 and to King Prajadhipok 1925-32. Imprisoned 1939-44. Later chairman of Council of Regency 1946-49, Regent 1949-51. Married to German Elisabeth Sharnberger.

Rajawangsan, Admiral Phraya (Sri Kamolnawin) (1886-1940)
Elder brother of Luang Sindhu. Member of Thai delegation to League of Nations General Assembly 1922; Navy Chief-of-Staff; Minister of Defence 1932-33; Minister in Paris 1934-35, also accredited to Italy, Spain, Portugal, Belgium, and the Netherlands; Minister in London 1935-40, also accredited to Germany (until 1937) and Denmark; Permanent Representative of Siam to the League of Nations 1935-40.

Rajchman, Dr. Ludvik J. (1881-1965)
Polish bacteriologist. Headed the League's Health Organisation 1921-39. One of the most influential individuals in modern international public health; driving force behind League's technical assistance programme to China in the 1930s; one of the founding fathers of UNESCO 1946.

Reeve, Wilfred D. (b. 1895)
British adviser to the Excise Department in the Thai Ministry of Finance 1932. Author of *Public Administration in Siam* (1951).

Renborg, Bertil Arne (1892-1980)
Swedish diplomat. Staff of League Secretariat since 1929; member of the League of Nations commission of enquiry on opium 1929; participated for the League Secretariat in the 1931 Bangkok Opium Conference; head of Opium Section in League of Nations Secretariat 1939-46. Later head of the United Nations Postal Service.

Riem Virajapak, Colonel Phra (Riem Tanthanon) (b.1891)
Thai diplomat. Minister in Paris 1935-37, also accredited to Italy, Spain, Portugal, Belgium, and the Netherlands. Editor of a French-Thai dictionary published in Bangkok 1924.

Sakol Varnakorn Voravarn, Prince (Mom Chao) (1888-1953)
Grandson of King Mongkut, son of Prince Naradhip Prabandhabongse, older half-brother of Prince Varn. Educated in England. Director-General of Department of Public Health in Ministry of Interior 1926-32; after the coup briefly Deputy Minister of Agriculture and Commerce, then Advisor to Ministry of Interior from 1932. Supported Pridi's economic reform plan. Married to German Johanna Weber since 1914. Strongly involved in League of Nations public health and human trafficking activities in Siam and Asia. Visited League of Nations headquarters 1928. Delegate of Siam to the League of Nations Conference of Central Authorities on Trafficking in Women and Children in Bandung 1937.

Sanoh Tanboonyuen
Leader of Free Thai movement during Second World War in England together with Mani Sanasen.

Sanpakitch Preecha, Phraya (Chuen Jotikasthira)
Thai diplomat during 1920s; Counsellor at Thai Legation in Washington D.C. 1921; Minister in Rome 1922-28, also accredited to Spain and Portugal; member of Thai delegation to League of Nations General Assembly 1920, 1923-24; Thai delegate to extraordinary League of Nations General Assembly 1926.

Sarasasna Balakhand, Phra (Long Sunthanonda) (1889-1966)
Diplomat posted in Europe in 1920s; assistant to Minister in The Hague; Thai Consul in Calcutta, where he won the Calcutta sweepstake in 1927. Retired from government service in 1928 and became nationalist propagandist. Minister of Economy 1934; fled to Japan in 1935 and bought property in Manchukuo. Convicted as war criminal after Second World War.

Sarasasna Prabandhu, Phra (Chuen Charuvastra)
Diplomat in Paris in early 1920s. Obtained Law doctorate in Paris in 1921. Member of Thai delegation to League of Nations General Assembly 1920-23; from 1923 staff in Ministry of Justice in Bangkok; Deputy Minister of Education with the rank of a cabinet member 1933-34; Minister of Education 1935; Minister of Agriculture 1935-36; Minister without portfolio 1937-38.

Sarit Thanarat, Field Marshal (1908-1963)
Military strongman and Thai Prime Minister 1958-63.

Sayre, Francis B. (Phraya Kalayana Maitri) (1885-1972)
Harvard law professor; son-in-law of President Woodrow Wilson. American Foreign Affairs Adviser to the Thai government 1923-25. Was instrumental in revising unequal treaties with European states in 1925. Siam's representative at Permanent Court of International Justice in The Hague until early 1930s; Assistant Secretary of State 1935; American High Commissioner in the Philippines 1939-42.

Schmieden, Dr. Werner von (b. 1892?)
League Secretariat staff. Secretary of the League of Nations commission of enquiry on trafficking in women and children, which visited Siam in 1930.

Seni Pramoj, Mom Rajawongse (1905-1997)
Thai diplomat and politician. British-trained lawyer. Minister in Washington D.C. 1940-45; Prime Minister 1945-46, 1975 and 1976; Minister of Foreign Affairs 1946. One of the leaders of Free Thai movement during Second World War.

Seymour, Richard
British Minister in Bangkok 1919-21.

Siddhi Sayamkarn, Luang (Tien Hook Hoontrakul) (d. 1963)
Thai government official. Head of League of Nations Section in Ministry of Foreign Affairs 1937; later Deputy Minister of Foreign Affairs.

Sidh Saukathia
Member of Thai delegation to League of Nations General Assembly 1920.

Sindhu Songkhramchai, Luang (Sin Kamolnawin) (1902-1975)
Younger brother of Phraya Rajawangsan. Met coup promoters in Paris in 1920s and played important role in coup. Held various cabinet positions 1932-45, among them Minister of Education (1937-42), Commerce (1942), and Agriculture (1942-45); Navy Chief-of-Staff 1933-51. Visited Japan and Italy in 1935-36.

Siri Rajamaitri, Luang (Charoon Singhaseni)
Thai Diplomat at Paris, London and Rome legations. Member of the promoters' group in Paris in the mid-1920s. Member of Thai delegation to League of Nations General Assembly 1930-31; Minister without portfolio 1933; Minister in Rome 1939-42.

Smaksman Kritakara, Mom Rajawongse
Staff at Paris legation. Member of Thai delegation to League of Nations General Assembly 1926-28.

Somboon Palasthira
Thai diplomat in London. Member of Thai delegation to League of Nations General Assembly 1938-39; Ambassador in Rome 1967.

Sridharmadhibes, Chao Phraya (Jit na Songkhla; Phraya Chinda) (1885-1976)
Thai government official and politician. Minister of Justice 1928-32. Elevated to Phraya Sridharmadhibes 1931. Minister of Finance 1933-34; then speaker of the Assembly; Minister of Justice 1937-38; Minister of Foreign Affairs 1938-39; Minister of Justice 1944-45 and, concurrently, Minister of Public Health; Minister of Justice 1946.

Srisena Sompatsiri, Phraya (Ha Sompatsiri) (1889-1982)
Thai diplomat and government official. Minister of Foreign Affairs 1935-36 and 1944-45; Minister/Ambassador in Tokyo 1938-41; Minister of Interior 1946.

Srivisarn Vacha, Phraya (Tienliang Hoontrakul, 1925 Luang Srivisarn Vacha) (1893-1968)
Thai diplomat and politician. Staff at Thai legation in Paris in early 1920s; member of Thai delegation to the League of Nations General Assembly 1921-23 and 1925; Deputy Minister of Foreign Affairs 1928; President of League of Nations Bangkok Opium Conference 1931; Minister of Foreign Affairs 1932-33 and 1947-48; Minister of Finance 1946.

Stevens, Raymond Bartlett (1874-1942)
Harvard law graduate; politician and member of Congress. American Foreign Affairs Adviser to the Thai government 1926-35.

Strobel, Edward Henry (1855-1907)
Diplomat and Harvard law professor. American Minister to Ecuador and Chile in the 1890s; American General Adviser to the Thai government 1902-07.

Subharn Sompati, Phraya (Tin Bunnag)(1882-1971)
Thai civil servant and diplomat. Elder brother of Phraya Abhibal Rajamaitri. Educated at King's College, Cambridge. Director-General of Customs, Minister in Tokyo 1928-31; Minister in Washington D.C. 1931-33; Minister in London 1933-35, also accredited to Germany and Denmark; Thai Permanent Representative to the League of Nations 1933-35.

Subhavarn Varasiri, Dr. jur., see Bhadravadi, Luang

Sundquist, Dr. Alma
Member of the League of Nations commission of enquiry on trafficking in women and children, which visited Siam in 1930.

Supachai Panitchpakdi (b. 1946)
Thai politician and international civil servant. Deputy Prime Minister 1992-95 and 1997-99; Director-General of the World Trade Organisation (WTO) 2002-05; Secretary-General of the UN Conference on Trade and Development (UNCTAD) since 2005.

Surakiart Sathirathai (b. 1958)
Thai politician. Law professor at Chulalongkorn University, Bangkok. Minister of Finance 1995-96; Minister of Foreign Affairs 2001-05; Deputy Prime Minister 2005-06. Campaigned unsuccessfully to succeed Kofi Annan as UN Secretary-General in 2006.

Svasti Sophon Vatanavisishtha, Prince (Phra Ong Chao) (1865-1935)
Son of King Mongkut, half-brother of King Chulalongkorn, father-in-law of King Prajadhipok. Minister of Justice 1912.

Thawan Thamrongnawasawat, Admiral (Luang Thamrong Nawasawat) (1901-1988)
Member of coup group 1932. Cabinet Minister 1933-44; Prime Minister 1946-47; Minister of Foreign Affairs 1947.

Thawee Bunyaket (1904-1971)
Cabinet Secretary 1939-43; held various ministerial positions during 1940s; Prime Minister 1945.

Thawin Artayukti
Staff at Paris legation; member of Thai delegation to the League of Nations General Assembly 1926-1928.

Thongtor Thongthaem, Prince (Mom Chao) (1893-1958)
Grandson of King Mongkut. Thai diplomat at London legation; member of Thai delegation to the League of Nations General Assembly 1927-30.

Tienliang Hoontrakul, see Srivisarn Vacha, Phraya

Toynbee, Arnold J. (1889-1975)
British historian. Director of Studies at the Royal Institute of International Affairs in Chatham House 1925-55.

Traidos Prabandh Devakul, Prince (Mom Chao, 1922 Phra Ong Chao, 1929 Krom Muen Devawongse Varothai) (1883-1943)
Grandson of King Mongkut, son of Prince Devawongse, older brother of Prince Damras Damrong and older half-brother of Prince Pridi Debyabongse. Educated in England and France. Minister in Washington D.C. 1911-12; Minister in Berlin 1913-17, also accredited to Denmark and Austria-Hungary; Thai delegate at Paris Peace Conference 1918; Deputy Minister of Foreign Affairs 1918-24; Minister of Foreign Affairs 1924-32 (acting 1923-24).

Vaidaya Vidhikar, Phra
Director-General of the Department of Public Health in Ministry of Interior 1939-1940. Represented Siam at advisory board meeting of League of Nations Health Organisation Far Eastern Bureau in Singapore 1940.

Vajiravudh, King Rama VI (1881-1925)
Son of King Chulalongkorn, elder brother of King Prajadhipok. Reigned 1910-25.

Varnvaidya Voravarn, Prince (Mom Chao, 1939 Phra Ong Chao, 1952 Krom Muen Naradhip Bongseprabandh) (1891-1976)
Diplomat and politician. Grandson of King Mongkut, son of Prince Naradhip Prabandhabongse, younger half-brother of Prince Sakol. Educated in England and France. Married to Mom Proisubin Bunnag, previously wife of Prince Amoradat, 1930. Staff at London and Paris legations 1917-19; staff at Ministry of Foreign Affairs 1919-24; Deputy Minister of Foreign Affairs 1924-26; Minister in London 1926-30, also accredited to the Netherlands 1927-28 and Belgium 1926-28; Permanent Representative of Siam to the League of Nations 1928-30; Thai Foreign Affairs Adviser 1933-45; Thai representative to Greater East Asia Conference in Tokyo 1943; Ambassador in Washington D.C. 1947-52; Minister of Foreign Affairs 1952-1959; concurrent with the previous two assignments Permanent Thai Representative to the United Nations 1947-60; Thai representative to SEATO Council and Bandung Conference 1955; President of United Nations General Assembly 1956-57; Deputy Prime Minister 1959-69; professor at Chulalongkorn University; Rector of Thammasat University 1965-70; President of National Assembly.

Vichai Prajabal, Phraya
Director of Immigration Department in Ministry of Interior. Member of the commission appointed by the Ministry of Interior to assist the League of Nations commission of enquiry on trafficking in women and children 1930.

Vichit Vadhakarn, Luang (Kimleang Vathanaprida) (1898-1962)
Thai politician and diplomat, of Chinese origin. Entered Foreign Ministry in 1918; staff at Paris legation from 1921; member of Thai delegation to the League of Nations General Assembly 1921-25; transfer to legation in London after dispute with Prince Charoon over handling of Thai students in Paris in 1926; returned to Ministry of Foreign Affairs in Bangkok 1927; resigned from Foreign Ministry 1932; Minister of Foreign Affairs 1942-43; Ambassador in Tokyo 1943-45. Detained as war criminal after Second World War; Ambassador in Berne 1954-59. Close collaborator of Luang Phibun and influential nationalist and pan-Thai propagandist.

Vichitwongse Vudhikrai, Lieutenant-General Phraya (Mom Rajawongse Siddhi Sudasna) (1877-1954)
Military officer, diplomat and government official. Military commander of Korat 1911-13; Governor of Phuket 1913-20; military commander of Bangkok 1920-26; Minister in Washington D.C. 1926-28; Minister in Paris 1928-31, also accredited to Belgium and the Netherlands. Delegate of Siam to the League of Nations General Assembly 1929.

Vipulya Svastiwongse Svastikul, Prince (Mom Chao) *(1885-1940)*
Grandson of King Mongkut. Minister in Copenhagen 1924-29, also accredited to Sweden and Norway. Delegate of Siam to the League of Nations General Assembly 1925-28.

Visut Kosha, Phraya (Phak Sanasen)
Thai diplomat. Father of Mani Sanasen. Minister in London 1902-03 and 1906-10, during second term also accredited to Belgium and Netherlands; Minister in Berlin 1903-06.

Visutra Virajdes, Luang
Thai diplomat in Paris. Member of Thai delegation to the League of Nations General Assembly 1931.

Viwatchai Chayant, Prince (Mom Chao, *1950* Phra Ong Chao) *(1899-1960)*
Grandson of King Mongkut. Educated in England. Deputy Minister of Finance 1929; Director-General of Opium Department in Ministry of Finance 1931; first Governor of Bank of Thailand 1942; member of Cabinet 1947-48. Interviewee of the League of Nations commission of enquiry on opium smoking 1929. Participated in a number of League of Nations and, after the Second World War, United Nations economic and financial conferences.

Walters, Francis Paul (b. 1888)
British citizen. Official in League of Nations Secretariat; from 1939 Deputy Secretary-General. Author of *A History of the League of Nations* (1952).

Ward, Sir Thomas
British irrigation expert. Commissioned by government of Siam to draw up irrigation scheme 1914.

Warming, P.I.E. (Phraya Bejra Indra)
Danish Adviser to the Thai Ministry of Interior. Member of the commission appointed by the Ministry of Interior

to assist the League of Nations commission of enquiry on trafficking in women and children 1930.

Waterlow, Sir Sydney Philip (1878-1944)
British diplomat. Minister in Bangkok 1926-29.

Watier, P.H.
French engineer. Consultant to the League of Nations Communications and Transit Organisation. Member of League of Nations commission of experts to study the improved access to the port of Bangkok 1933.

Westengard, Jens Iverson (1871-1918)
Harvard law professor. American General Adviser to the Thai government 1907-15.

Wettum, W.G. van
Head of the opium monopoly in Netherlands Indies. Dutch representative at Hague Opium Conference, on Opium Advisory Committee and other League of Nations opium conferences. Chairman of First Geneva Opium Conference 1924 and vice chairman of Bangkok Conference on Opium Smoking 1931.

White, Dr. Norman
Former British official of the Indian Medical Service. Deputy Director of the League of Nations Secretariat Health Section and Chief Epidemic Commissioner 1920-23; conducted enquiry on port health and epidemic diseases in Siam and Asia 1922-23; first Director of the Greek School of Public Health in Athens 1929.

Williamson, Sir Walter James Franklin (b. 1867)
British Financial Adviser to the Thai government 1904-25.

Wilson, Woodrow (1856-1924)
28th President of the United States. Founding father of the League of Nations.

Wood, W.A.R. (1878-1970)
Long-time British resident in Siam. British Consul in Chiang Mai.

Wright, Elizabeth Washburn (1876-1952)
Wife of Dr. Hamilton Wright. American observer on the League of Nations Opium Advisory Committee during early 1920s; American delegate to the Second Geneva Opium Conference 1924-25; first American woman to be granted plenipotentiary powers.

Wright, Dr. William Hamilton (1867-1917)
American physician and anti-opium activist. Delegate to Shanghai Opium Commission 1909 and Hague Opium Conference 1911-12.

Yada Chonosuke
Japanese diplomat with postings in China, Mexico, United States, Canada; Minister in Bangkok 1922-26.

Yatabe Yasukichi
Japanese Minister in Bangkok 1928-36.

Yen, Weiching Williams (Yan Huiqing) (1877-1950)
Chinese politician and diplomat. Five-time Prime Minister until mid-1920s. Chinese delegate at the League of Nations during the Manchurian Conflict.

Zimmerman, Dr. Carle Clark (b. 1897)
Professor of Sociology at Harvard University. Commissioned by the government of Siam to conduct a rural economic survey 1930-31.

Bibliography

A. Bibliographies and Guides

Allison, Gordon H. and Auratai Smarnond (eds), *Thailand's Government (including all Ministries, Agencies, and Dictionary Locator)*, Bangkok: Siam Security Brokers, 1972.

Aufricht, Hans (ed.), *Guide to League of Nations Publications, A Bibliographical Survey of the Work of the League, 1920-1947*, New York: Columbia University Press, 1951.

Baer, George W. (ed.), *International Organizations 1918-1945: A Guide to Research and Research Materials*, Guides to European Diplomatic History, Research and Research Materials, vol. 4, Wilmington: Scholarly Resources, 1981.

Batson, Benjamin A., 'Sources in Thai History: The Papers of Prince Damrong', *Journal of the Siam Society*, 63, 2 (1975), pp. 334-342.

Bibliography of Thailand, A Selected List of Books and Articles with Annotations by the Staff of the Cornell Thailand Research Project, Data Paper no. 20, Ithaca (NY), 1957.

Carroll, Marie J. (ed.), *Key to League of Nations Documents Placed on Public Sale 1920-1929*, Boston: World Peace Foundation, n.d.

Chulalongkorn University, Central Library (ed.), *Bibliography of Material about Thailand in Western Languages*, Bangkok: Chulalongkorn University Press, 1960.

Dalby, Andrew (ed.), *South-East Asia, A Guide to Reference Material*, Regional Reference Guides, vol. 2, London et al.: Zell, 1993.

Gall, Lothar (ed.), *Historische Zeitschrift, Sonderheft 12: Südostasien, Literaturbericht über neue Veröffentlichungen von 1959-1979*, Bearbeitet von Michael Sarkisyanz, München: Oldenbourg, 1983.

Ghebali, Victor Y. (ed.), *Bibliographical Handbook of the League of Nations*, Provisional Edition, United Nations Library Publications Series C, no. 3, 3 vols, Geneva: United Nations Library, 1980.

———— and Catherine Ghebali (eds), *A Repertoire of League of Nations Serial Documents, 1919-1947*, Carnegie Endowment for International Peace, 3 vols, Dobbs Ferry (NY): Oceana, 1973.

Gunzenhäuser, Max (ed.), *Der Genfer Völkerbund 1920-1946*, Reprint from: Jahresbibliographie der Bibliothek für Zeitgeschichte Stuttgart 1969, Frankfurt a.M., 1971.

Hay, Stephen N. and Margaret H. Case (eds), *Southeast Asian History: Bibliographic Guide*, New York: Praeger, 1962.

Hill, Martin, *The Economic and Financial Organization of the League of Nations: A Survey of Twenty-five Years' Experience*, Studies in the Administration of International Law and Organization, vol. 6, Washington D.C.: Carnegie Endowment for International Peace, 1946.

Johnson, Donald Clay (ed.), *Index to Southeast Asian Journals, A Guide to Articles, Book Reviews, and Composite Works*, vol. 1: 1960-1974, vol. 2: 1975-1979, Boston: Hall & Co., 1977 and 1982.

Jones, Robert B., *Thai Titles and Ranks, Including a Translation of Traditions of Royal Lineage in Siam by King Chulalongkorn*, Data Paper no. 81, Ithaca (NY): Cornell University Southeast Asia Program, 1971.

Leifer, Michael, *Dictionary of the Modern Politics of South-East Asia*, London and New York: Routledge, 1995.

National Library Bangkok (ed.), *Periodicals and Newspapers Printed in Thailand between 1844 and 1934: A Bibliography*, Bangkok: Chulalongkorn University Press, 1970.

Office of His Majesty's Principal Private Secretary (ed.), *Compilation of Publications in English on the Chakri Dynasty*, Bangkok: Office of His Majesty's Principal Private Secretary, 1983.

Ottlick, Georges (ed.), *Annuaire de la Société des Nations*, 1920-1939, Geneva: Editions de l'Annuaire de la Société des Nations, 1920-1939.

Pearson, James D. (ed.), *A Guide to Manuscripts and Documents in the British Isles Relating to South and Southeast Asia*, 2 vols, London and New York: Mansell, 1989 and 1990.

Pérotin, Yves, 'The League of Nations', in: Daniel H. Thomas and Lynn M. Case (eds), *New Guide to Diplomatic Archives of Western Europe*, Philadelphia: University of Pennsylvania Press, 1975, pp. 383-389.

Ruser, Ursula-Maria, 'Das Archiv der Vereinten Nationen in New York und des Völkerbundes in Genf', in: Verein Deutscher Archivare, Fachgruppe 6 (ed.), *Archivare an Archiven der Parlamente, der politischen Parteien, Stiftungen und Verbände*, no. 19, Stuttgart, 1993, pp. 7-33.

Simon, Werner, 'Das Historische Archiv der Bibliothek der Vereinten Nationen in Genf', *Vereinte Nationen*, 4 (1981), pp. 122-126.

Thomas, Daniel H. and Lynn M. Case (eds), *New Guide to Diplomatic Archives of Western Europe*, Philadelphia: University of Pennsylvania Press, 1975.

Tillmann, Wigbert (ed.), *Bibliography of Bibliographical Materials Relating to Thailand*, Düsseldorf: Tillmann, 1978.

Truhart, Peter (ed.), *International Directory of Foreign Ministers, 1589-1989*, München et al.: Saur, 1989.

———— (ed.), *International Dictionary of States: States, State-like Communities from their Origins to Present*, München et al.: Saur, 1989.

UNESCO (ed.), *Guide to the Archives of International Organizations, Part I: The United Nations System*, UNESCO Series, Documentation, Libraries and Archives: Bibliographies & Reference Works, Paris, 1984.

United Nations Library, Geneva (ed.), *Guide to the Archives of the League of Nations*, Publication Series E: Guides & Studies, no. 2, Geneva, 1978.

Wagner, Alfred, 'Das Archiv des Völkerbundes in Genf, Ein Beitrag zu seiner Benutzung und Erschließung', *Der Archivar*, 2 (1972), pp. 171-176.

Watts, Michael (ed.), *Thailand*, World Bibliographical Series, vol. 65, Oxford, Santa Barbara and Denver: Clio Press, 1986.

Wenk, Klaus and Prachum Phongsawadan, 'Ein Beitrag zur Bibliographie der thailändischen historischen Quellen', *Oriens Extremus*, 2 (1962), pp. 232-257.

Wilson, Constance M. (ed.), *Thailand: A Handbook of Historical Statistics*, Reference Publication in International Historical Statistics, Boston: Hall, 1983.

Win, May Kyi and Harold E. Smith (eds), *Historical Dictionary of Thailand*, Asian Historical Dictionaries, vol. 18, Lanham (MD) and London: Scarecrow Press, 1995.

Wyatt, David K. and Constance M. Wilson (eds), 'Historical Materials in Bangkok', *Journal of Asian Studies*, 25, 1 (1965), pp. 105-118.

B. Unpublished Sources

B.1 League of Nations Archives, United Nations at Geneva, Switzerland [LNA]

Boxed Files:

Registry Files:

1919-1927: Boxes R 39, R 283, R 373, R 381, R 471, R 472, R 475, R 476, R 481, R 536, R 537, R 573, R 583, R 617, R 618, R 623, R 643, R 663, R 673-679, R 692, R 693, R 710-724, R 734, R 736-741, R 744, R 755, R 762, R 775-783, R 787-791, R 812-814, R 843-844, R 925, R 1014, R 1015, R 1053, R 1054, R 1063, R 1064, R 1097, R 1112-1116, R 1198, R 1199, R 1201, R 1210-1212, R 1243, R 1244, R 1259, R 1280, R 1301, R 1339, R 1389, R 1441, R 1442, R 1475, R 1478-1479, R 1491, R 1594, R 1597, R 1604, R 1728, R 1729, R 1767.

1928-1932: Boxes R 1961, R 1962, R 1979, R 1980, R 1987, R 1988, R 1990-1994, R 2069, R 2070, R 2075, R 2350, R 2351, R 2398, R 2427, R 2446, R 2458, R 2523, R 2563, R 2773, R 2790, R 2977, R 2998, R 3001, R 3030-3032, R 3045, R 3046, R 3057, R 3058, R 3159-3161, R 3168, R 3169, R 3195, R 3196 R 3201-3204, R 3219, R 3238, R 3239, R 3246, R 3248, R 3311, R 3312, R 3318, R 3327, R 3331, R 3339, R 3340, R 3362, R 3363, R 3396, R 3405, R 3406, R 3562, R 3567, R 3568, R 3594, R 5887, R 5892, R 5929-5934, R 5963, R 5977, R 5985.

1933-1946: Boxes R 3607, R 3608, R 3624, R 3657, R 3670, R 3677, R 3680, R 3686, R 3689, R 3692, R 3697, R 3815, R 3816, R 3818-3820, R 3864, R 3865, R 3880, R 3883, R 4040, R 4041, R 4212, R 4213, R 4256, R 4257, R 4269, R 4629, R 4630, R 4675, R 4695-4698, R 4821, R 4873, R 4875, R 4900, R 4901, R 4919, R 4939, R 4942, R 4975-4981, R 5006, R 5017, R 5018, R 5106, R 5212, R 5213, R 5215,
R 5231, R 5232, R 5236, R 5237, R 5241, R 5242, R 5245, R 5246, R 5250, R 5255-5259, R 5286, R 5287, R 5399, R 5642, R 5739, R 5759, R 5772, R 5773, R 5793, R 5794, R 5803, R 5812, R 5813, R 6097, R 6173-6179.

Section Files:

Boxes S 178, S 188, S 194, S 209, S 571, S 874, S 2344-57.

Collection Files:

Boxes COL 115, COL 167, COL 173, COL 197, COL 307, COL 320, COL 325, COL 332, COL 346.

Serial (Circulated) Documents:

C.77.M.39.1921.XI.

A.73.1922 (C.652.1922.II).

A.91.1922(C.657.1922.II).

C.416.M.254.1922.XI.

C.155.M.75.1923.XI.

C.184.M.184.1923.XI.

C.66.M.24.1924.II.

C.397.M.146.1924.XI.

C.684.M.244.1924.XI.

C.760.M.260.1924.XI.

C.82.M.41.1925.XI.

C.602.M.192.1925.XI.

A.10(b).1926.VI.C.393.

M.136.1926.XI.

C.52.M.52.1927.IV.

C.86.M.35.1927.XI.

C.557.M.199.1927.XI.

C.P.E.141(1).(1929).

C.514.M.173.1929.V.

C.360.M.151.1930.II.

C.635.M.254.1930.XI.

Conf.O.F.B. 16 (1931).

C.C.T./T.P.O.N./54 (1931).

C.C.T./T.P.O.N./54(a) (1931).

C.161.M.57.1931.XI.

C.577.M.284.1932.XI.

C.T.F.E.606.(1934).

C.258.M.130.1935.XI.C.341.

M.216.1936.XI.

C.511.M.323.1936.XI.

C.H.1235(h) (1937).

C.476.M.318.1937.IV.

C.516.M.357.1937.IV.

C.L.178.1939.X.

C.68.M.30.1939.IV.

C.70.M.24.1939.IV.

C.25.M.25.1943.V.Annex.

B.2 National Archives of Thailand, Bangkok [TNA]

Files of the Ministry of Foreign Affairs,
United Nations Section:

KT 75	General: Files 1-20.

Files of the Ministry of Foreign Affairs,
League of Nations Section:

KT 96.1	General: Files 1-87.
KT 96.1.1	Financial Contribution: Files 1-19.
KT 96.1.2	Covenant: Files 1-20.
KT 96.1.3	General Assembly: Files 1-23.
KT 96.1.4	Codification of International Law: Files 1-11.
KT 96.1.5	Disarmament: Files 1-35.
KT 96.1.6	International Conflicts General: Files 1-8.
KT 96.1.6.1	Italian-Abyssinian Conflict: Files 1-28.
KT 96.1.6.2	Chinese-Japanese Conflict: Files 1-13.
KT 96.1.7	Permanent Court of International Justice: Files 1-83.
KT 96.1.8	Social and Humanitarian Questions General: Files 1-66.
KT 96.1.8.1	Women and Children: Files 1-118.
KT 96.1.8.2	Slavery: Files 1-10.
KT 96.1.8.3	International Relief Union: Files 1-8.
KT 96.1.8.4	Labour: Files 1-179.
KT 96.1.9	International Treaties: Files 1-40.
KT 96.1.10	International Finance General: Files 1-69.
KT 96.1.10.1	Cheques and Balances: Files 1-6.
KT 96.1.10.2	Counterfeit Currency: Files 1-10.
KT 96.1.11	Public Health: Files 1-20.
KT 96.1.12	Mandates: Files 1-14.
KT 96.1.13	Refugees: Files 1-17.
KT 96.1.14	Minorities: Files 1-16.
KT 96.2	Drugs General: Files 1-47.
KT 96.2.1	Laws and Regulations: Files 1-46.
KT 96.2.2	Import and Export: Files 1-45.
KT 96.2.3	Drug Control: Files 1-40.
KT 96.2.4	International Meetings: Files 1-12.
KT 96.2.4.1	Bangkok Agreement on Opium-Smoking: Files 1-13.
KT 96.2.4.2	Limitation Conference and Annual Estimates: Files 1-61.
KT 96.2.4.3	Suppression of Illicit Trade: Files 1-9.
KT 96.2.5	Advisory Committee on Traffic in Opium and Other Dangerous Drugs: Files: Files 1-94.

KT 96.2.6	Commission of Enquiry into the Control of Opium Smoking in the Far East: Files 1-5.
KT 96.2.7	Annual Reports: Files 1-11.
KT 96.2.8	Health Committee: Files 1-23.
KT 96.3	Communication and Transit General: Files 1-37.

Files of the Ministry of Finance, Office of the
Financial Adviser:

KKh 0301.1.6	Opium: Files 1-50.

Files of the Office of the Prime Minister, Secretariat
of the Cabinet:

SR 0201.17	League of Nations: Files 1-23.

Files of the Royal Secretariat:

SR 0201.29	International Treaties: Files 1-26.

Files of the Royal Secretariat (until 1932)/Office of
the Prime Minister, Secretariat of the Cabinet
(from 1932):

SR 0201.37	Files 49 and 56.

Files of the Office of the Prime Minister, Secretariat
of the Cabinet:

(3) SR 0201.7.2.1	United Nations: Files 1-5.

Files of the Royal Secretariat, Sixth Reign, Ministry
of Foreign Affairs:

R6, T 13	Files 1-3.
R6, T 15	Files 2-3.

Files of the Royal Secretariat, Sixth and Seventh
Reign, Ministry of Foreign Affairs:

R6-7, T 10	Files 1-5.

Files of the Royal Secretariat, Seventh Reign,
Ministry of Foreign Affairs:

R7, T 1	File 25.
R7, T 10	Files 6-24.
R7, T 20	File 14.
R7, T 41	File 15.

Files of the Royal Secretariat, Seventh Reign,
Ministry of Interior:

R7, M 7.2	Files 1-3.

*B.3 Thai Kadi Research Institute at Thammasat University,
Bangkok, Thailand [TKRI]*

United States of America, Records of the
Department of State, Consular Reports Siam
(Microfilm Collection).

B.4 Public Record Office, Kew, Great Britain [PRO]

Files FO 371, FO 415, FO 628.

C. Periodicals

Bangkok Chronicle, Bangkok Daily (National Library of
Thailand).

Bangkok Daily Mail, Bangkok Daily (National Library of
Thailand).

Bangkok Post, Bangkok Daily.

Bangkok Times, Bangkok Daily (National Archives of
Thailand).

Bangkok Times, Bangkok Weekly (National Library of
Thailand).

Daily News, London Daily (British Library Online Newspaper Archive: www.uk.olivesoftware.com).

Siam Observer, Bangkok Daily (National Library of Thailand).

The Nation, Bangkok Daily.

The Standard, Bangkok Daily (National Library of Thailand).

Thai Newsmagazine, Bangkok Weekly (National Library of Thailand).

The Times, London Daily (Times Online: archive.timesonline.co.uk/tol/archive).

D. Published Sources, Contemporary Secondary Works, and Memoirs

Ahmad, H. Manzooruddin, *Thailand, Land der Freien*, Leipzig: Goldmann, 1943.

American Missionary Association (ed.), *Bangkok Calendar for the Year of the Lord 1864*, Bangkok, 1863.

Anigstein, Ludwik, 'Malaria and Anopheles in Siam', *Quarterly Bulletin of the Health Organisation*, 1, 2 (June 1932), pp. 233-308.

Anti-Opium Information Bureau (ed.), *Special Document no. 4: The Opium and Narcotic Drug Situation in China before the XXIInd Session of the League of Nations Opium Advisory Committee, Statement by Stuart J. Fuller, American Representative*, Geneva: Anti-Opium Information Bureau, 1937.

Andrews, James M., *Siam: 2nd Rural Economic Survey, 1934-1935*, Bangkok: The Bangkok Times Press, 1935.

Auswärtiges Amt (ed.), *Akten zur deutschen auswärtigen Politik 1918-1945*, Göttingen: Vandenhoek & Ruprecht and Bonn: Hermes.

Serie A:	1918-1925, vol. XI (5. August bis Dezember 1924), Göttingen, 1993.
Serie B:	1925-1933, vol. V (17. März bis 30. Juni 1927), Göttingen, 1972.
	1925-1933, vol. XX (1. März bis 15. August 1932), Göttingen, 1983.
Serie D:	1937-1945, vol. XI, 1 (1. September bis 13. November 1940), Bonn, 1964.
	1937-1945, vol. XI, 2 (13. November 1940 bis 31. January 1941), Bonn, 1964.
	1937-1941, vol. XII, 1 (1. Februar bis 5. April 1941), Göttingen, 1969.
	1937-1941, vol. XIII, 1 (23. Juni bis 14. September 1941), Göttingen, 1970.
	1937-1941, vol. XIII, 2 (15. September bis 11. Dezember 1941), Göttingen, 1970.
Serie E:	1941-1945, vol. I (12. Dezember 1941 bis 28 Februar 1942), Göttingen, 1969.
	1941-1945, vol. II (1. März bis 15. Juni 1942), Göttingen, 1972.
	1941-1945, vol. II (16. Juni bis 30. September 1942), Göttingen, 1974.

Bailey, Stanley H., *The Anti-Drug Campaign: An Experiment in International Control*, London: P.S. King, 1936.

Bangkok Daily Mail (ed.), *The Coronation of His Majesty Prajadhipok, King of Siam, B.E. 2468*, Bangkok, 1926.

Batson, Benjamin A. (ed.), *Siam's Political Future: Documents from the End of the Absolute Monarchy*, Cornell University Data Paper no. 96, Ithaca (NY), 1974.

Berdahl, Clarence A., *The Policy of the United States with Respect to the League of Nations*, Publications of the Graduate Institute of International Studies, no. 4, Geneva: Kundig, 1932.

Berjoan, A., *Le Siam et les accords Franco-Siamois*, Thèse Faculté de Droit, Université de Paris, Paris: Les Presses Modernes, 1927.

Bourne, Kenneth et al. (eds), *British Documents on Foreign Affairs: Reports and Papers from the Foreign Office Confidential Print, Part II: From the First to the Second World War*, Frederick (MD): University Publications of America. [BDFA]

Series E: Asia, 1914-1939:

Vol. 49: Siam and South-East Asia, 1914-1929, ed. by. Ann Trotter, 1997.

Vol. 50: Siam and South-East Asia, 1930-1939, ed. by Ann Trotter, 1997.

Series J: The League of Nations, 1918-1941:

Vol. 1: Britain and the League of Nations, 1918-1941: Attitudes and Policy, ed. by Peter J. Beck, 1992.

Vol. 2: The League of Nations and Its Members, 1924-1939, ed. by Peter J. Beck, 1992.

Vol. 9: Legal and Administrative Questions, 1924-1939, ed. by Peter J. Beck, 1995.

Vol. 10: Mandates, Minorities and Economic and Social Questions at the League, 1925-1940, ed. by Peter J. Beck, 1995.

Buell, Raymond L. (ed.), *The International Opium Conferences with Relevant Documents*, World Peace Foundation Pamphlet, vol. VIII, nos 2-3, Boston: World Peace Foundation, 1925.

Butler, Sir Geoffrey, *A Handbook of the League of Nations*, London: Longmans, Green & Co., 1925.

Butler, Rohan et al. (eds), *Documents on British Foreign Policy, 1919-1939*, Second Series, London: His Majesty's Stationery Office. Vols XI, XIV, XX, XXI.

Campbell, William K.H., *Technical Collaboration with China: Co-operation for Economically Underdeveloped Countries*, Geneva: League of Nations, 1938.

Chula Chakrabongse, *The Twain Have Met, or An Eastern Prince Came West*, 2nd ed., London: G.T. Foulis, 1957.

Committee on Traffic in Opium of the Foreign Policy Association (ed.), *International Control of the Traffic in Opium: Summary of the Opium Conferences held at Geneva, November 1924 to February 1925, with Appendices Containing Complete Texts of Final Agreements and the Hague Convention of 1912*, Pamphlet no. 33, New York: Foreign Policy Association, 1925 (Reprint in: Gerald N. Grob (ed.), *Narcotic Addiction and American Foreign Policy, Seven Studies, 1924-1938*, New York: Arno Press, 1981.)

Credner, Wilhelm, *Siam, das Land der Thai, Eine Landeskunde auf Grund eigener Reisen und Forschungen*, Stuttgart: Engelhorns, 1935.

Crosby, Sir Josiah, *Siam: The Crossroads*, London: Hollis & Carter, 1945 (Reprint New York: AMS Press, 1973).

Damrong Baedyagun, Phya and Luang Suvejj Subhakich (eds), *Transactions of the Eighth Congress of the Far Eastern Association of Tropical Medicine held in Siam, December 1930*, 2 vols, Bangkok: Far Eastern Association of Tropical Medicine, 1931.

Das, Taraknath, *Foreign Policy in the Far East*, New York and Toronto: Longmans, Green & Co., 1936.

Deignan, Herbert G., *Siam – Land of Free Men*, War Background Studies, vol. 8, Washington D.C.: Smithsonian Institution Press, 1943.

Department of Public Health (ed.), *Report of the Department of Public Health, Including the Report of the Office of the Medical Officer of Health, Bangkok*, Bangkok: Department of Public Health, B.E. 2465 (1922).

————— (ed.), *Report for B.E. 2481 (1938-39)*, Bangkok: Department of Public Health, B.E. 2485 (1942).

Department of State (ed.), *Foreign Relations of the United States, Diplomatic Papers*, Washington D.C.: Government Printing Office. [FRUS]

1917, Supplement I: The World War.

1919, vols I, II, III, V, XI, XIII: Paris Peace Conference.

1921, vol. II.

1922, vol. II.

1928, vol. I.

1933, vol. III: The Far East.

1934, vol. III: The Far East.

1935, vol. III: The Far East.

1936, vol. IV: The Far East.

1937, vol. IV: The Far East.

1939, vol. III: The Far East.

1940, vol. IV: The Far East.

1941, vols I: General, V: The Far East.

1942, vol. I: General, The British Commonwealth, The Far East.

1943, vol. III: The British Commonwealth, Eastern Europe, The Far East.

1944, vol. V: The Near East, Southeast Asia, Africa, The Far East.

1946, vols I: General, The United Nations, VIII: The Far East.

Direck Jayanama, *Thailand im Zweiten Weltkrieg, Vom Kriegsausbruch in Europa bis zu Hiroshima, Ein Dokument zur Zeitgeschichte Asiens*, Tübingen and Basel: Erdmann, 1970.

Directory for Bangkok and Siam, 1922, A Handy and Perfectly Reliable Book of Reference for all Classes, Bangkok: Bangkok Times Press, 1922.

Directory for Bangkok and Siam, 1930, Bangkok: Bangkok Times Press, 1930.

Far Eastern Association of Tropical Medicine, Executive Committee of the 8th Congress (ed.), *Siam: General and Medical Features*, Bangkok: Bangkok Times Press, 1930.

Forty, C.H., *Bangkok: Its Life and Sport*, London: H.F. & G. Witherby, 1929.

Göppert, Otto, *Der Völkerbund, Völkerrecht und Internationales Staatensystem*, vol. 4, ed. by A. Walz, Stuttgart: Kohlhammer, 1938.

Graham, Walter Armstrong, *Siam*, 2 vols, 3rd ed., London: Moring, 1924.

Great Britain, Foreign Office (ed.), *The Opium Trade 1910-1941*, 6 vols, Wilmington/London: Scholarly Resources, 1974.

Greaves, Harold R.G., *The League Committees and World Order*, London: Oxford University Press, 1931.

Grob, Gerald N. (ed.), *Narcotic Addiction and American Foreign Policy, Seven Studies, 1924-1938*, New York: Arno Press, 1981.

Hagenbeck, John and Victor Ottmann, *Südasiatische Fahrten und Abenteuer: Erlebnisse in Britisch- und Holländisch-Indien, im Himalaya und in Siam*, Dresden: Verlag Deutscher Buchwerkstätten, 1924.

Harris, H. Wilson, *Human Merchandise: A Study of the International Traffic in Women*, London: Ernest Benn, 1928.

Hurst, Michael (ed.), *Key Treaties for the Great Powers*, 2 vols, London: David & Charles, 1972.

Hyde, Charles C., 'The Relinquishment of Extraterritorial Jurisdiction in Siam', *American Journal of International Law*, 15 (July 1921), pp. 428-430.

James, Eldon R., 'Jurisdiction Over Foreigners in Siam', *American Journal of International Law*, 16 (October 1922), pp. 585-603.

—————, 'Siam in the Modern World', *Foreign Affairs*, IX, 4 (1931), pp. 657-664.

Knipping, Franz, Hans von Mangoldt and Volker Rittberger (eds), *Das System der Vereinten Nationen und seine Vorläufer, vol. II: 19. Jahrhundert und Völkerbundszeit*, ed. by Franz Knipping, München: C.H. Beck and Berne: Stämpfli & Cie, 1996.

Kontsri Subamonkala, *La Thaïlande et ses Relations avec la France*, Paris: Pedone, 1940.

Landon, Kenneth P., *The Chinese in Thailand*, 2nd ed., New York: Russell & Russell, 1975 (Revised Issue of New York: Institute of Pacific Relations and Oxford University Press, 1941).

—————, *Siam in Transition, A Brief Survey of Cultural Trends in the Five Years since the Revolution of 1932*, Chicago: University of Chicago Press, 1939.

League of Nations (ed.), *Chronique de l'Organisation d'Hygiène*, Geneva, 1939.

————— (ed.), *Official Journal*, Geneva, 1920-1940. Vols. VIII (1923), X (1928), I (1929), V (1930), VI (1930), VII (1930), II (1931), VII (1931), III: Parts 1 and 2 (1932), VII (1932), XII (1937).

————— (ed.), *Official Journal, Special Supplements*, Geneva, 1920-1946. Vols. 13-18, 23, 28, 38, 39, 48, 49, 58-60, 64, 68, 69, 75-81, 84-90, 93-99, 101, 102, 104-109, 111, 112, 115-120, 125-130, 138-151, 155-162, 164, 167, 169-175, 183, 184, 187, 188, 190, 193.

————— (ed.), *Quarterly Bulletin of the Health Organisation*, 1, 2 (June 1932), Geneva, 1932.

————— (ed.), *Records of the First Assembly, Plenary and Committee Meetings*, 3 vols, Geneva, 1920.

————— (ed.), *Records of the Second Assembly, Plenary and Committee Meetings*, 3 vols, Geneva, 1921.

————— (ed.), *Records of the Third Assembly, Plenary and Committee Meetings*, 7 vols, Geneva, 1922.

————— (ed.), *Records of the Twentieth Assembly, Plenary Meetings*, Geneva, 1940.

————— (ed.), *Ten Years of World Co-operation*, Geneva, 1930.

————— (ed.), *The Aims, Methods and Activity of the League of Nations*, Geneva, 1935.

————— (ed.), *Treaty Series*, Geneva, 1920-1946. Vols. 185, 186, 188-193, 197, 200, 203.

—————, Information Section (ed.), *Essential Facts about the League of Nations*, 9th ed., Geneva, 1938.

Lin Yu, 'Twin Loyalties in Siam', *Pacific Affairs*, 2, 9 (June 1936), pp. 191-200.

Llewellyn-Jones, Frederick, *The League of Nations and the International Control of Dangerous Drugs*, Cambridge: W. Heffer & Sons, 1931.

MacCallum, Elisabeth P., *Twenty Years of Persian Opium (1908-1928)*, New York: Opium Research Committee of the Foreign Policy Association, 1928. (Reprint in: Gerald N. Grob (ed.), *Narcotic Addiction and American Foreign Policy, Seven Studies, 1924-1938*, New York: Arno Press, 1981.)

Manich Jumsai, M.L. (ed.), *Foreign Records of the Bangkok Period up to A.D. 1932*, Bangkok: Office of the Prime Minister, 1982.

Matsushita, Masatoshi, *Japan in the League of Nations*, New York: Columbia University Press, 1929.

May, Herbert L., *Survey of Smoking Opium Conditions in the Far East: A Report to the Executive Board of the Foreign Policy Association*, New York: The Opium Research Committee of the Foreign Policy Association, 1927. (Reprint in: Gerald N. Grob (ed.), *Narcotic Addiction and American Foreign Policy, Seven Studies, 1924-1938*, New York: Arno Press, 1981.)

May, Jacques M., *A Doctor in Siam*, London: Cape, 1951.

Ministère des Affaires Étrangères, Commission de Publication des Documents relatifs aux Origines de la Guerre 1939-1945 (ed.), *Documents Diplomatiques Français 1932-1939*, 2° Serie (1936-1939), Paris: Imprimerie Nationale, 1964.

Tome II (11 Avril-18 Juillet 1936).

Tome VII (19 Septembre 1937-16 Janvier 1938).

Ministry of Commerce and Communications of Siam (ed.), *The Record: The Organ of the Board of Commercial Development*, Bangkok: Ministry of Commerce and Communications, 1925-1931.

————— (ed.), *Siam: Nature and Industry*, Bangkok: Ministry of Commerce and Communications, 1930.

Ministry of Foreign Affairs of Thailand (ed.), *Statements by Chairmen of the Delegations of Thailand at the 2nd-40th Sessions of the United Nations General Assembly (1947-1985)*, Bangkok: Ministry of Foreign Affairs, B.E. 2529 (1986).

Nathabanja, Luang, *Extra-Territoriality in Siam*, Bangkok: Bangkok Daily Mail, 1924.

Nocht, Bernhard, 'Report on the Activity of the Malaria Commission of the League of Nations and some Experiments on the Pathogenesis of Blackwater Fever', in: Phya Damrong Baedyagun and Luang Suvejj Subhakich (eds), *Transactions of the Eighth Congress of the Far Eastern Association of Tropical Medicine held in Siam, December 1930*, Bangkok: Far Eastern Association of Tropical Medicine, 1931, vol. 2, pp. 329-247.

Opium Research Committee of the Foreign Policy Association (ed.), *The Opium Situation in India: Recent Developments*, Pamphlet no. 39, New York: Foreign Policy Association, 1926. (Reprint in: Gerald N. Grob (ed.), *Narcotic Addiction and American Foreign Policy, Seven Studies, 1924-1938*, New York: Arno Press, 1981.)

Pitkin, Wolcott Homer, *Siam's Case for Revision of Obsolete Treaty Obligations Admittedly Inapplicable to Present Conditions*, with Supplement, New York, 1919.

Pollock, Frederick, *The League of Nations*, 2nd ed., London: Stevens & Sons, 1922.

Pracherd Aksorluksna, Luang, *La Constitution Siamoise de 1932*, Thèse pour le Doctorat Sciences Politiques et Economiques, Paris: Editions Domat-Montchrestien, 1933.

Pridi Phanomyong (Luang Pradist Manudharm), *Le Siam pacifiste et la politique étrangère du gouvernement Siamois*, Bangkok: Assumption Press, 1937.

Ranshofen-Wertheimer, Egon Ferdinand, *The International Secretariat: A Great Experiment in International Administration*, Studies in the Administration of International Law and Organization, vol. 3, Washington D.C.: Carnegie Endowment for International Peace, 1945.

Rappard, William E., 'Small States in the League of Nations', *Political Science Quarterly*, 4 (1934), pp. 544-575.

Renborg, Bertil A., *International Drug Control, A Study of International Administration By and Through the League of Nations*, Washington D.C.: Carnegie Endowment for International Peace, 1947.

Report of the Financial Adviser in connection with the Budget of the Kingdom of Siam for the Year B.E. 2480 (1937-1938), Bangkok: The Bangkok Times Press, 1937.

Robertson, C.J., 'The Rice Export from Burma, Siam and French Indo-China', *Pacific Affairs*, 2, 9 (June 1936), pp. 243-253.

Ronan, William J., 'The Kra Canal: A Suez for Japan?', *Pacific Affairs*, 3, 9 (September 1936), pp. 406-415.

Ruppel, Willy, *Genfer Götterdämmerung: Werden, Wirken und Versagen des Völkerbunds*, Stuttgart: Union Verlag, 1940.

Sayre, Francis B., *Experiments in International Administration*, London and New York: Harper & Bros., 1919.

—————, 'The Passing of Extraterritoriality in Siam', *American Journal of International Law* (January 1928), pp. 70-88.

————— (Phya Kalyana Maitri) (ed.), *Siam: Treaties with Foreign Powers, 1920-1927*, Bangkok: Royal Siamese Government, 1928.

Seidenfaden, Erik, *Guide to Bangkok with Notes on Siam*, 2nd ed., Bangkok: Royal States Railways of Siam, 1928 (Reprint Singapore: Oxford University Press, 1984).

Siam Directory, The Only Complete and Up-to-date Hand-Book of Siam, Bangkok: Siam Observer Press, 1922.

Sivaram, Madhvan, *The New Siam in the Making: A Survey of the Political Transition in Siam, 1932-1936*, Bangkok: Stationer's Printing Press, 1936 (Reprint New York: AMS Press, 1981).

Smith, Roger M. (ed.), *Southeast Asia, Documents of Political Development and Change*, Ithaca (NY) and London: Cornell University Press, 1974.

Souvenir of the Siamese Exhibition at Lumbini Park B.E. 2468, Bangkok: The Siam Free Press, B.E. 2470 (1927).

Statistical Yearbook of the Kingdom of Siam, ed. by Department of Commerce and Statistics, Ministry of Finance, Bangkok, 1916-1920; ed. by Department of General Statistics, Ministry of Finance, Bangkok, 1921-1930; ed. by Division of Central Service of Statistics, Department of the Secretary-General of the Council, Bangkok, 1933-1935; Statistical Yearbook Thailand, ed. by Central Service of Statistics, Bangkok, 1937-1950.

Vol. 12: B.E. 2469 (1926-27)

Vol. 13: B.E. 2470 (1927-28)

Vol. 20: B.E. 2480 (1937-38) & 2481 (1938-39)

Vol. 21: B.E. 2482 (1939-40) to 2487 (1944)

Sweetser, Arthur, 'The First Year and a Half of the League of Nations', *The Annals of the American Academy of Political and Social Science*, 96 (1921), pp. 21-30.

Thailand, Department of Publicity (ed.), *How Thailand Lost Her Territories to France*, Bangkok: Department of Publicity, 1940.

Thak Chaloemtiarana (ed.), *Thai Politics: Extracts and Documents, 1932-1957*, Bangkok: Social Science Association of Thailand, 1978.

Thompson, Virginia, *Thailand: The New Siam*, New York: Macmillan, 1941 (Reprint New York: Paragon, 1967).

Toynbee, Arnold J., '1. The Liquidation of Foreign Extra-territorial Privileges in Siam. 2. The Revision of the Régime along the Frontier between Siam and the French Possession and Protectorates in Indo-China', *Survey of International Affairs 1929*, London: Oxford University Press, 1930, pp. 405-421.

Trittel, Walter, *Thailand*, 2nd ed., Berlin: Junker & Dünnhaupt, 1943.

Vichit Vadhakarn, *Thailand's Case*, Bangkok: Thanom Punnahitananda, 1941.

Willoughby, Westel W., *Opium as an International Problem: The Geneva Conferences*, Baltimore: Johns Hopkins Press, 1925.

Wissler, Albert, *Die Opiumfrage: Eine Studie zur weltwirtschaftlichen und weltpolitischen Lage der Gegenwart*, Probleme der Weltwirtschaft, vol. 52, ed. by Bernhard Harms, Jena: Institut für Seeverkehr und Weltwirtschaft an der Universität Kiel, 1931.

Woods, Arthur, Dangerous Drugs: *The World Fight against Illicit Traffic in Narcotics*, New Haven (CT): Yale University Press, 1931.

Zimmerman, Carle C., *Siam Rural Economic Survey, 1930-31*, Bangkok: Bangkok Times Press, 1931.

E. Secondary Works

Alagappa, Muthiah (ed.), *Political Legitimacy in Southeast Asia: The Quest for Moral Authority*, Stanford (CA): Stanford University Press, 1995.

Aldrich, Richard J., *The Key to the South: Britain, the United States, and Thailand during the Approach of the Pacific War, 1929-1942*, South-East Asian Historical Monographs, Kuala Lumpur: Oxford University Press, 1993.

Aldrich, Robert and John Connell, *France's Overseas Frontier: Départements et terretoires d'outre-mer*, Cambridge: Cambridge University Press, 1992.

Allen, Richard, *A Short Introduction in the History and Politics of Southeast Asia*, New York: Oxford University Press, 1970.

Amrith, Sunil, *Decolonizing International Health: India and Southeast Asia, 1930-65*, Basingstoke: Palgrave, 2006.

Anuson Chinvanno, *Thailand's Policies towards China, 1949-54*, Basingstoke and London: Macmillan, 1992.

Apirat Petchsiri, *Eastern Importation of Western Criminal Law: Thailand as a Case Study*, Comparative Criminal Law Project, Wayne State University Law School, Publication Series, vol. 17, Littleton (CO): Rothman, 1987.

Asia Watch and the Women's Rights Project (eds), *A Modern Form of Slavery: Trafficking of Burmese Women and Girls into Brothels in Thailand*, New York et al.: Human Rights Watch, 1993.

Bachofen, Maja, *Lord Robert Cecil und der Völkerbund*, Zürich: Europa-Verlag, 1959.

Baer, George W., *Test Case: Italy, Ethiopia, and the League of Nations*, Stanford (CA): Hoover Institution Press, 1976.

————, *The Coming of the Italian-Ethiopian War*, Cambridge (MA): Harvard University Press, 1967.

Baker, Christopher and Pasuk Phongpaichit, *A History of Thailand*, Cambridge: Cambridge University Press, 2005.

Balinska, Martin A., 'Assistance and not mere Relief: The Epidemic Commission of the League of Nations, 1920-1923', in Paul Weindling (ed.), *International Health Organisations and Movements*, Cambridge: Cambridge University Press, 1995, pp. 81-108.

Bao, Jiemin, *Marital Acts: Gender, Sexuality, and Identity among the Chinese Thai Diaspora*, Honolulu: Hawai'i University Press, 2005.

Barandon, Paul, *Die Vereinten Nationen und der Völkerbund in ihrem rechtsgeschichtlichen Zusammenhang*, Abhandlungen der Forschungsstelle für Völkerrecht und ausländisches Öffentliches Recht der Universität Hamburg, vol. 1, Hamburg 1948.

Barmé, Scot, *Luang Wichit Wathakan and the Creation of a Thai Identity*, Singapore: Institute of Southeast Asian Studies, 1993.

————, *Woman, Man, Bangkok: Love, Sex and Popular Culture in Thailand*, Lanham (MD): Rowman and Littlefield, 2002.

Barros, James, *The Aaland Islands Question: Its Settlement by the League of Nations*, New Haven (CT): Yale University Press, 1968.

————, *Betrayal from Within: Joseph Avenol, Secretary-General of the League of Nations, 1933-1940*, New Haven (CT) and London: Yale University Press, 1969.

————, *Britain, Greece and the Politics of Sanctions: Ethiopia, 1935-1936*, London: Royal Historical Society, 1982.

————, *The Corfu Incident of 1923: Mussolini and the League of Nations*, Princeton (NJ): Princeton University Press, 1965.

————, *The League of Nations and the Great Powers: The Greek-Bulgarian Incident 1925*, Oxford: Clarendon, 1970.

————, *Office without Power: Secretary-General Sir Eric Drummond 1919-1933*, Oxford: Clarendon, 1979.

———— (ed.), *The United Nations: Past, Present, and Future*, New York: Free Press and London: Collier-Macmillan, 1972.

Bartlett, Christopher J., *The Global Conflict, The International Rivalry of the Great Powers, 1880-1970*, London and New York: Longman, 1984.

Bastin, John and Harry J. Benda, *A History of Modern Southeast Asia: Colonialism, Nationalism, and Decolonization*, Englewood Cliffs (NJ): Prentice-Hall, 1968.

Batson, Benjamin A., *The End of Absolute Monarchy in Siam*, Singapore: Oxford University Press, 1984.

————, 'The Fall of the Phibun Government, 1944', *Journal of the Siam Society*, 62, 2 (1974), pp. 89-120.

————, 'Phra Sarasas: Rebel with Many Causes', *Journal of Southeast Asian Studies*, 27, 1 (1996), pp. 150-165.

Baumgart, Winfried, *Vom Europäischen Konzert zum Völkerbund, Friedensschlüsse und Friedenssicherung von Wien bis Versailles*, Erträge der Forschung 25, 2nd ed., Wiesbaden: Wissenschaftliche Buchgesellschaft, 1987.

Beck, Peter J., 'The League of Nations and the Great Powers, 1936-1940', *World Affairs: Woodrow Wilson and the League of Nations, Part One*, 157, 4 (Spring 1995), pp. 175-189.

————, 'The Winter War in the International Context: Britain and the League of Nations in the Russo-Finnish Dispute 1939-1940', *Journal of Baltic Studies*, 12 (1981), pp. 58-73.

Bernatzik, Hugo Adolf, *Die Geister der gelben Blätter, Forschungsreisen in Hinterindien*, Gütersloh: Bertelsmann, 1951.

Bewley-Taylor, David R., *The United States and International Drug Control, 1909-1997*, London and New York: Pinter, 1999.

Bishop, Ryan and Lilian S. Robinson, *Night Market: Sexual Cultures and the Thai Economic Miracle*, New York: Routledge, 1998.

Booth, Ann E., *Colonial Legacies: Economic and Social Development in East and Southeast Asia*, Honolulu: University of Hawai'i Press, 2007.

Booth, Martin, *Opium: A History*, New York: St. Martin's Press, 1996.

Borg, Dorothy, *The United States and the Far Eastern Crisis of 1933-1938, From the Manchurian Incident through the Initial Stage of the Undeclared Sino-Japanese War*, Harvard East Asian Series, vol. 14, Cambridge (MA): Harvard University Press, 1964.

Boudreau, Frank C., 'International Civil Service', in Harriet E. Davis (ed.), *Pioneers in World Order: An American Appraisal of the League of Nations*, 2nd ed., New York: Columbia University Press, 1945, pp. 76-85.

Boyes, Jon and Piraban S., *Opium Fields*, Bangkok: Silkworm Books, 1991.

Brailey, Nigel J., *Thailand and the Fall of Singapore: A Frustrated Asian Revolution*, Boulder (CO): Westview Press, 1986.

Bristow, Edward J., *Prostitution and Prejudice: The Jewish Fight Against White Slavery 1870-1939*, Oxford: Clarendon, 1982.

Brook, Timothy and Bob Tadashi Wakabayashi (eds), *Opium Regimes: China, Britain, and Japan, 1839-1952*, Berkeley: University of California Press, 2000.

Brown, Andrew, *Labour, Politics and the State in Industrializing Thailand*, London and New York: Routledge Curzon, 2004.

Brown, Ian G., *The Creation of the Modern Ministry of Finance in Siam, 1885-1910*, Basingstoke and London: Macmillan, 1995.

————, *Economic Change in South-East Asia*, Kuala Lumpur: Oxford University Press, 1997.

————, 'The End of the Opium Farm in Siam, 1905-7', in John Butcher and Howard Dick (eds), *The Rise and Fall of Revenue Farming: Business Elites and the Emergence of the Modern State in Southeast Asia*, London and New York: St. Martin's Press, 1993, pp. 233-245.

————, *The Elite and the Economy in Siam, c.1890-1920*, East Asian Historical Monographs, Singapore: Oxford University Press, 1988.

Brown, Louise, *Sex Slaves: The Trafficking of Women in Asia*, London: Virago, 2000.

Brummelhuis, Han ten, *King of the Waters: Homan van der Heide and the Origin of Modern Irrigation in Siam*, Leiden: KITLV Press, 2005.

Bruun, Kettil, Lynn Pan and Ingemar Rexed, *The Gentlemen's Club: International Control of Drugs and Alcohol*, Studies in Crime and Justice, Chicago and London: University of Chicago Press, 1975.

Butcher, John and Howard Dick (eds), *The Rise and Fall of Revenue Farming: Business Elites and the Emergence of the Modern State in Southeast Asia*, London and New York: St. Martin's Press, 1993.

Cady, John F., *Southeast Asia: Its Historical Development*, New York: McGraw-Hill, 1964.

————, *The Southeast Asian World*, The World of Asia Series, St. Louis: Forum Press, 1977.

Castendyck, Elsa, 'Social Problems', in Harriet E. Davis (ed.), *Pioneers in World Order: An American Appraisal of the League of Nations*, 2nd ed., New York: Columbia University Press, 1945, pp. 229-239.

Chaiwat Khamchoo and E. Bruce Reynolds (eds), *Thai-Japanese Relations in Historical Perspective*, Institute of Asian Studies, Chulalongkorn University, Asian Studies Monographs, vol. 41, Bangkok: Innomedia, 1988.

Chaiyan Rajchagool, *The Rise and Fall of the Thai Absolute Monarchy: Foundations of the Modern Thai State from Feudalism to Peripheral Capitalism*, Studies in Contemporary Thailand, vol. 2, Bangkok: White Lotus Press, 1994.

Chalong Soontravanich, 'Siam and the First Hague Peace Conference of 1899', in Charit Tingsabadh (ed.), *King Chulalongkorn's Visit to Europe: Reflections on Significance and Impacts*, Bangkok: Centre for European Studies, Chulalongkorn University, 2000, pp. 31-44.

—————, 'Siam and the First World War: The Last Phase of Her Neutrality', *Nusantara*, 4 (July 1973), pp. 83-90.

Charit Tingsabadh (ed.), *King Chulalongkorn's Visit to Europe: Reflections on Significance and Impacts*, Bangkok: Centre for European Studies, Chulalongkorn University, 2000.

Charivat Santaputra, *Thai Foreign Policy, 1932-1946*, Thai Kadi Research Institute, Bangkok: Charoen Wit Press, 1985.

Charnvit Kasetsiri, 'The First Phibun Government and Its Involvement in World War II', *Journal of the Siam Society*, 62, 2 (1974), pp. 25-88.

Chatterjee, Syamal Kumar, *Drug Abuse and Drug-Related Crimes: Some Unresolved Legal Problems*, Dordrecht, Boston and London: Martinus Nijhoff, 1989.

—————, *Legal Aspects of International Drug Control*, The Hague, Boston and London: Martinus Nijhoff, 1981.

Chatthip Nartsupha, Suthy Prasartset and Montri Chenvidyakarn (eds), *The Political Economy of Siam, 1910-1932*, Bangkok: Social Science Association of Thailand, 1981.

Christie, Clive J., *A Modern History of Southeast Asia: Decolonization, Nationalism and Separatism*, Tauris Academic Studies, London and New York: I.B. Tauris, Singapore: Institute for Southeast Asian Studies, 1996.

—————— (ed.), *Southeast Asia in the Twentieth Century: A Reader*, London and New York: I.B. Tauris, 1998.

Chu Pao-chin, *V. K. Wellington Koo, A Case-Study of China's Diplomat and Diplomacy of Nationalism, 1912-1966*, Hong Kong: Chinese University Press, 1981.

Chula Chakrabongse, *Lords of Life: A History of the Kings of Thailand*, London: Alvin Redman, 1960.

Claude, Inis L. Jr., *Swords to Ploughshares: The Problems and Progress of International Organization*, 4th ed., New York: Random House, 1984.

Clyde, Paul H. and Burton F. Beers, *The Far East: A History of the Western Impact and the Eastern Response (1830-1970)*, 6th ed., Englewood Cliffs (NJ): Prentice Hall, 1975.

Colbert, Evelyn S., *Southeast Asia in International Politics*, Ithaca (NY): Cornell University Press, 1977.

Dahm, Bernhard and Roderich Ptak (eds), *Südostasien-Handbuch: Geschichte, Gesellschaft, Politik, Wirtschaft, Kultur*, München: C.H. Beck, 1999.

Darling, Frank C., *Thailand and the United States*, Washington D.C.: Public Affairs Press, 1965.

—————— and Ann B. Darling, *Thailand: The Modern Kingdom*, Singapore: Asia-Pacific Press, 1971.

Davis, Harriet E. (ed.), *Pioneers of World Order: An American Appraisal of the League of Nations*, 2nd ed., New York: Columbia University Press, 1945.

Davisakd Puaksom, 'Of Germs, Public Hygiene, and the Healthy Body: The Making of the Medicalizing State in Thailand', *Journal of Asian Studies*, 66, 2 (May 2007), pp. 311-344.

Delaye, Karine, 'Colonial Co-operation and Regional Construction: Anglo-French Medical and Sanitary Relations in South East Asia', *Asia Europe Journal*, 3 (2004), pp. 461-471.

Descours-Gatin, Chantal, *Quand l'opium finançait la colonisation en Indochine, L'élaboration de la régie générale de l'opium (1860 à 1914)*, Collection Recherches Asiatiques, Paris: L'Harmattan, 1992.

Dixon, Chris, *The Thai Economy: Uneven Development and Internationalism, Growth Economies of Asia*, London and New York: Routledge, 1999.

Dubin, Martin D., 'The League of Nations Health Organisation', in Paul Weindling (ed.), *International Health Organisations and Movements*, Cambridge: Cambridge University Press 1995, pp. 56-80.

Dülffer, Jost, Hans-Otto Mühleisen and Vera Torunsky (eds), *Inseln als Brennpunkte internationaler Politik, Konfliktbewältigung im Wandel des internationalen Systems, 1890-1984: Kreta, Korfu, Zypern*, Köln: Verlag Wissenschaft und Politik, 1986.

Egerton, George, 'Collective Security as Political Myth: Liberal Internationalism and the League of Nations in Politics and History', *The International History Review*, 4 (1983), pp. 496-524.

Emdad-ul Haq, M., *Drugs in South Asia: From the Opium Trade to the Present Day*, Basingstoke and London: Macmillan, 2000.

Emerson, Rupert, L.A. Mills and Virginia Thompson, *Government and Nationalism in the Southeast Asia*, New York: Institute of Pacific Relations, 1942 (Reprint New York: AMS Press, 1978).

Emmerson, Donald K., '"Southeast Asia": What's in a Name?', *Journal of Southeast Asian Studies*, 15, 1 (March 1984), pp. 1-21.

Farley, John, *To Cast Out Disease: A History of the International Health Division of the Rockefeller Foundation (1913-1951)*, Oxford and New York: Oxford University Press, 2004.

Farooqui, Amar, *Smuggling as Subversion: Colonialism, Indian Merchants and the Politics of Opium*, New Delhi: New Age International, 1998.

Fessen, Helmut and Hans-Dieter Kubitscheck, *Geschichte Thailands*, Bremer Asien-Pazifik Studien, vol. 7, Münster and Hamburg: Lit, 1994.

Finestone, Jeffrey (ed.), *A Royal Album: The Children and Grandchildren of King Mongkut (Rama IV) of Siam*, Bangkok: Loma, 2000.

—————— (ed.), *The Royal Family of Thailand: The Descendants of King Chulalongkorn*, London: White Mouse Editions, 1989.

Fistié, Pierre, *L'évolution de la Thaïlande contemporaine*, Paris: Armand Colin, 1967.

—————, *Sous-developpement et utopie au Siam: le programme de réformes présenté en 1933 par Pridi Phanomyong*, Paris: Mouton, 1969.

Fukada, Mahito H., 'Public Health in Modern Japan: From Regimen to Hygiene', in Dorothy Porter (ed.), *The History of Public Health and the Modern State*, The Wellcome Institute Series in the History of Medicine, Amsterdam and Atlanta: Editions Rodopi, 1994, pp. 403-423.

Ghosh, Lipi, *Prostitution in Thailand: Myth and Reality*, New Delhi: Munshiram Manoharlal, 2002.

Girling, John L.S., *Thailand, Society and Politics*, Ithaca (NY) and London: Cornell University Press, 1981.

Goldstein, Erik, *Winning the Peace: British Diplomatic Strategy, Peace Planning, and the Paris Peace Conference, 1916-1920*, Oxford: Clarendon, 1991.

Goodrich, Carter, 'The International Labour Organization', in Harriet E. Davis (ed.), *Pioneers in World Order: An American Appraisal of the League of Nations*, 2nd ed., New York: Columbia University Press, 1945, pp. 87-106.

Gräning, Bärbel, *Prostitutionstourismus in Thailand: Die sexuelle Verfügung über Frauen in ihrer historischen Entwicklung*, Bremen: Übersee-Musem und Geographische Gesellschaft Bremen, 1988.

Greene, Stephen L.W., *Absolute Dreams: Thai Government under Rama VI, 1910-1925*, Bangkok: White Lotus Press, 1999.

Grimm, Tillman, *China und Südostasien in Geschichte und Gegenwart*, Köln and Opladen: Westdeutscher Verlag, 1966.

Gronewold, Sue, *Beautiful Merchandise: Prostitution in China 1860-1936*, New York: Haworth, 1982.

Gupta, D.C., *The League of Nations*, New Delhi: Vikas, 1974.

Hall, Daniel G.E., *A History of South-East Asia*, 5th ed., London and Basingstoke: Macmillan, 1984.

Hanlon, John J., *Principles of Public Health Administration*, St. Louis: Mosby, 1950.

Hardy, Andrew, 'One Hundred Years of Malaria Control in Vietnam: A regional Retrospective, Part I, 1900-1945', *Mekong Malaria Forum*, 5 (January 2000), pp. 91-101.

—————, 'One Hundred Years of Malaria Control in Vietnam: A regional Retrospective, Part II, 1945-1999', *Mekong Malaria Forum*, 6 (April 2000), pp. 98-110.

Hasemann, John B., *The Thai Resistance Movement During the Second World War*, Bangkok: Chalermnit, n.d.

Headrick, Daniel R., *The Tentacles of Progress: Technology Transfer in the Age of Imperialism, 1850-1940*, New York and Oxford: Oxford University Press, 1988.

Hell, Stefan, 'Diplomatie gegen Opiumhöhlen: Siam und die Bemühungen des Völkerbundes zur internationalen Opiumkontrolle', Periplus 2000, *Jahrbuch für außereuropäische Geschichte*, pp. 154-175.

—————, *Der Mandschurei-Konflikt: Japan, China und der Völkerbund 1931 bis 1933*, Tübingen: Universitas, 1999.

—————, 'The Role of European Technology, Expertise and Early Development Aid in the Modernization of Thailand before the Second World War', *Journal of the Asia Pacific Economy*, 6, 2 (2001), pp. 158-178.

—————, 'Siam and the League of Nations, 1920-1946', in Franz Knipping, Piyanart Bunnag and Vimolvan Phatharodom (eds), *Europe and Southeast Asia in the Contemporary World: Mutual Influences and Comparisons*, Asia-Europe Studies Series, vol. 2, Baden-Baden: Nomos, 1999, pp. 151-163.

'Historical Survey', *UNODC Bulletin on Narcotics*, 3 (1953), <http://www.unodc.org/unodc/en/ data-and-analysis/ bulletin/bulletin_1953-01-01_3_page003.html>.

Hudson, Manley O., 'The World Court', in Harriet E. Davis (ed.), *Pioneers in World Order: An American Appraisal of the League of Nations*, 2nd ed., New York: Columbia University Press, 1945, pp. 65-75.

Hunter, Eileen and Narisa Chakrabongse, *Katya and the Prince of Siam*, Bangkok: River Books, 1994.

Ingram, James C., *Economic Change in Thailand since 1850*, Stanford (CA): Stanford University Press, 1955.

Iriye, Akira, *Global Community: The Role of International Organizations in the Contemporary World*, Berkley (CA), Los Angeles (CA) and London: University of California Press, 2002.

Jeffrey, Leslie Ann, *Sex and Borders: Gender, National Identity, and Prostitution Policy in Thailand*, Chiang Mai: Silkworm Books, 2002.

Jennings, John M., *The Opium Empire: Japanese Imperialism and Drug Trafficking in Asia, 1895-1945*, Westport (CT) and London: Praeger, 1997.

Jeshurun, Chandran, 'The Anglo-French Declaration of January 1896 and the Independence of Siam', *Journal of the Siam Society*, 58, 2 (1970), pp. 105-126.

Jha, Ganganath, *Foreign Policy of Thailand*, New Delhi: Radiant, 1979.

Kahn, Joel S. (ed.), *Southeast Asian Identities: Culture and the Politics of Representation in Indonesia, Malaysia, Singapore, and Thailand*, London and New York: I.B. Thauris, Singapore: Institute of South East Asian Studies, 1998.

Kennedy, Michael, *Ireland and the League of Nations, 1919-1946: International Relations, Diplomacy and Politics*, Dublin: Irish Academic Press, 1996.

Keyes, Charles F., *Thailand, Buddhist Kingdom as a Modern State*, Boulder (CO) and London: Westview Press, 1987.

King, Wunsz, *China and the League of Nations, The Sino-Japanese Controversy*, Asia in the Modern World, vol. 5, 2nd ed., New York: St. John's University Press, 1973.

Knipping, Franz, Piyanart Bunnag and Vimolvan Phatharodom (eds), *Europe and Southeast Asia in the Contemporary World: Mutual Influences and Comparisons*, Asia-Europe Studies Series, vol. 2, Baden-Baden: Nomos, 1999.

Kobkua Suwannathat-Pian, *Kings, Country and Constitutions: Thailand's Political Development 1932-2000*, London and New York: Routledge Curzon, 2003.

————, *Thailand's Durable Premier: Phibun through Three Decades, 1932-1957*, Kuala Lumpur: Oxford University Press, 1995.

————, *Thai-Malay Relations, Traditional Intra-regional Relations from the Seventeenth to the Early Twentieth Centuries*, East Asian Historical Monographs, Singapore: Oxford University Press, 1988.

————, 'Thai Wartime Leadership Reconsidered: Phibun and Pridi', *Journal of Southeast Asian Studies*, 27, 1 (1996), pp. 166-178.

Kullada Kesboonchoo Mead, *The Rise and Fall of Thai Absolutism*, London: Routledge Curzon, 2004.

Kuß, Susanne, *Der Völkerbund und China: Technische Kooperation und deutsche Berater 1928-34*, Berliner China-Studien, vol. 45, Münster: Lit, 2005.

Latimer, Dean and Jeff Goldberg, *Flowers in the Blood: The Story of Opium*, New York: Franklin Watts, 1981.

Lee, Marshall M., *Failure in Geneva: The German Foreign Ministry and the League of Nations, 1926-1933*, Ann Arbor: UMI, 1976.

Le Failler, Philippe, *Monopole et prohibition de l'opium en Indochine: Le pilori de Chimères*, Collection Recherches Asiatiques, Paris: L'Harmattan, 2001.

Likhit Dhiravegin, *Nationalism and the State in Thailand*, Bangkok: Thammasat University Press, 1985.

————, *Siam and Colonialism (1855-1909): An Analysis of Diplomatic Relations*, Bangkok: Thai Watana Panich, B.E. 2518 (1975).

Lindblad, J. Thomas, *Foreign Investment in Southeast Asia in the Twentieth Century, A Modern Economic History of Southeast Asia Series*, Basingstoke and London: Macmillan, New York: St. Martin's Press, 1998.

Lloyd, Lorna, 'The League of Nations and the Settlement of Disputes', *World Affairs: Woodrow Wilson and the League of Nations, Part One*, 157, 4 (Spring 1995), pp. 160-174.

Louis, William R., *British Strategy in the Far East, 1919-1939*, Oxford: Oxford University Press, 1971.

Lowes, Peter D., *The Genesis of International Narcotics Control*, Geneva: Librairie Droz, 1966.

Lumholdt, Niels and William Warren, *The History of Aviation in Thailand*, Hong Kong: Travel Publishing Asia, 1987.

Mackay, Derek, *Eastern Customs: The Customs Service in British Malaya and the Opium Trade*, London and New York: Radcliffe, 2005.

MacNair, Harley F. and Donald F. Lach, *Modern Far Eastern International Relations*, 2nd ed., Toronto, New York and London: Van Nostrand, 1955.

Manderson, Lenore, *Sickness and the State: Health and Illness in Colonial Malaya, 1870-1940*, Cambridge: Cambridge University Press 1996.

————, 'Wireless Wars in the Eastern Arena: Epidemiological Surveillance, Disease Protection and the Work of the Eastern Bureau of the League of Nations Health Organisation, 1925-1942', in Paul Weindling (ed.), *International Health Organisations and Movements*, Cambridge: Cambridge University Press 1995, pp. 109-133.

Manich Jumsai, M.L., *History of Anglo-Thai Relations*, Bangkok: Chalermnit, 1970.

————, *History of Thai-German Relations*, Bangkok: Chalermnit, 1978.

Marks, Sally, 'The Small States at Geneva', in *World Affairs: Woodrow Wilson and the League of Nations, Part One*, 157, 4 (Spring 1995), pp. 191-196.

Marushima Eiji, 'The Origin of Modern Official State Ideology in Thailand', *Journal of Southeast Asian Studies*, 19, 1 (March 1988), pp. 80-96.

Maule, Robert B., 'British Policy Discussions on the Opium Question in the Federated Shan States, 1937-1948', *Journal of Southeast Asian Studies*, 33, 2 (June 2002), pp. 203-224.

————, 'The Opium Question in the Federated Shan States, 1931-36: British Policy Discussions and Scandal', *Journal of Southeast Asian Studies*, 23, 1 (March 1992), pp. 14-36.

May, Herbert L., 'The Evolution of the International Control of Narcotic Drugs', *UNODC Bulletin on Narcotics*, 1 (1950), <http://www.unodc.org/unodc/en/data-and-analysis/bulletin/bulletin_1950-01-01_1_page003.html>.

May, Herbert L., 'Dangerous Drugs', in Harriet E. Davis (ed.), *Pioneers in World Order: An American Appraisal of the League of Nations*, 2nd ed., New York: Columbia University Press, 1945, pp. 182-192.

McAllister, William B., *Drug Diplomacy in the Twentieth Century, An International History*, London and New York: Routledge, 2000.

McCloud, Donald G., Southeast Asia: *Tradition and Modernity in the Contemporary World*, Boulder, San Francisco and Oxford: Westview, 1995.

McCoy, Alfred W., *The Politics of Heroin*, New York: Lawrence Hill, 1991.

Meienberger, Norbert, *Entwicklungshilfe unter dem Völkerbund: Ein Beitrag zur Geschichte der internationalen Zusammenarbeit in der Zwischenkriegszeit unter besonderer Berücksichtigung der technischen Hilfe an China*, Winterthur: Keller, 1965.

Meyer, Kathryn and Terry Parssinen, *Webs of Smoke: Smugglers, Warlords, Spies, and the History of the International Drug Trade*, Lanham (MD): Rowman & Littlefield, 1998.

Miller, Carol, 'The Social Section and Advisory Committee on Social Questions of the League of Nations', in Paul Weindling (ed.), *International Health Organisations and Movements*, Cambridge: Cambridge University Press, 1995, pp. 154-157.

Moffat, Abbot Low, *Mongkut, The King of Siam*, 3rd ed., Ithaca (NY): Cornell University Press, 1962.

Moore, Frank J. and Clark D. Neher, *Thailand: Its People, Society and Culture*, New Haven (CT): Human Relations Area Files, 1974.

Muscat, Robert J., *Development Strategy in Thailand: A Study of Economic Growth*, Praeger Special Studies in International Economics and Development, New York, London and Washington D.C.: Praeger, 1966.

Nagazumi, Akira, 'Toward the Abolition of the Unequal Treaties: The Cases of Japan and Thailand', in Carl

A. Trocki (ed.), *The Emergence of Modern States, Thailand and Japan*, Thailand-Japan Studies Program, Conference Proceedings, March 19-20, 1976, Bangkok: Institute of Asian Studies, Chulalongkorn University, 1976, pp. 45-58.

Neher, Clark D., 'The Foreign Policy of Thailand', in David Wurfel and Bruce Burton (eds), *The Political Economy of Foreign Policy in Southeast Asia*, London: Macmillan, 1990, pp. 177-203.

——— (ed.), *Modern Thai Politics: From Village to Nation*, Cambridge (MA): Schenkman, 1979.

Neher, Clark D. and Ross Marlay, D*emocracy and Development in Southeast Asia: The Winds of Change*, Boulder (CO): Westview Press, 1995.

Nicol, Gladys, *Thailand*, London: Batsford, 1980.

Nish, Ian, *Japan's Struggle with Internationalism: Japan, China, and the League of Nations, 1931-33*, London and New York: Kegan Paul, 1993.

———, 'Research Notelet: Thailand, Japan and the League, 1933', in Suntory and Toyota International Centre for Economics and Related Disciplines (STICERD), London School of Economics (ed.), *Japan-Thailand Relations*, International Studies Discussion Paper no. IS/91/228, London: STICERD, September 1991, pp. 77-80.

Northedge, Frederick S., *The League of Nations, its Life and Times 1920-1946*, 2nd ed., Leicester: Leicester University Press, 1988.

Nuntana Kalipalakanchana, Phuangphet Suratanakawikun and Supatra Nilwatchala, *The Relationship between Japan and Thailand 1932-1945*, Bangkok: Institute of Asian Studies Chulalongkorn University, 1978.

Oblas, Peter B., '"A Very Small Part of World Affairs", Siam's Policy on Treaty Revision and the Paris Peace Conference', *Journal of the Siam Society*, 59, 2 (1971), pp. 51-74.

———, 'Treaty Revision and the Role of the American Foreign Affairs Adviser, 1909-1925', *Journal of the Siam Society*, 60, 1 (1972), pp. 171-186.

Office of the National Culture Commission (ed.), *The Centennial of H.R.H. Prince Wan Waithayakon Krommun Naradhip Bongsprabandh*, Bangkok: National Culture Commission, 1991.

Owen, Norman (ed.), *Death and Disease in Southeast Asia: Explorations in Social, Medical, and Demographic History*, Singapore: Oxford University Press, 1987.

Pantip Paribatra, M.R. (ed.), *H.H. Prince Traidos Prabandh: His Life and Works, In Commemoration of the Centenary of His Birth*, Bangkok: Craftsman Press, 1983.

Pasuk Phongpaichit, Sungsidh Piriyarangsan and Nualnoi Treerat, *Guns, Girls, Gambling, Ganja: Thailand's Illegal Economy and Public Policy*, Chiang Mai: Silkworm Books, 1998.

Peleggi, Maurizio, *Lords of Things: The Fashioning of the Siamese Monarchy's Modern Image*, Honolulu: University of Hawai'i Press, 2002.

Pensri Duke, 'Historical Perspective', in Wiwat Mungkandi and William Warren (eds), *A Century and a Half of Thai-American Relations*, Bangkok: Chulalongkorn University Press, 1982, pp. 1-57.

Petersson, Niels P., *Imperialismus und Modernisierung: Siam, China und die europäischen Mächte 1985-1914*, Studien zur internationalen Geschichte, vol. 11, München: Oldenbourg, 2000.

———, 'King Chulalongkorn's Voyage to Europe in 1897', *Journal of European Studies at Chulalongkorn University*, 3, 2 (1995), pp. 1-27.

Pfeil, Alfred, *Der Völkerbund: Literaturbericht und kritische Darstellung seiner Geschichte*, Erträge der Forschung, vol. 58, Darmstadt: Wissenschaftliche Buchgesellschaft, 1976.

Pluvier, Jan, *South-East Asia from Colonialism to Independence*, Kuala Lumpur: Oxford University Press, 1974.

Pauline Poon Pui-ting, 'Political Manoeuvrings in Early Twentieth Century Hong Kong: The Mui Tsai Issue', *E-Journal on Hong Kong Cultural and Social Studies*, 3 (June 2004), <http://www.hku.hk/hkcsp/ccex/ehkcss01/issue3_ar_pauline_poon.htm>.

Porter, Dorothy, *Health, Civilization and the State: A History of Public Health from Ancient to Modern Times*, London: Routledge, 1999.

——— (ed.), *The History of Public Health and the Modern State*, The Wellcome Institute Series in the History of Medicine, Amsterdam and Atlanta: Editions Rodopi, 1994.

———, 'Introduction', in Dorothy Porter (ed.), *The History of Public Health and the Modern State*, The Wellcome Institute Series in the History of Medicine, Amsterdam and Atlanta: Editions Rodopi, 1994, pp. 1-44.

Ramaer, R., *The Railways of Thailand*, Bangkok: White Lotus Press, 1994.

Ray, Jayanta Kumar, *Portraits of Thai Politics*, New Delhi: Orient Longman, 1972.

Ray, Kabita, *History of Public Health: Colonial Bengal 1921-1947*, Calcutta: K.P. Bagchi, 1998.

Reeve, Wilfred D., *Public Administration in Siam*, London and New York: Royal Institute of International Relations, 1951 (Reprint New York: AMS Press, 1975).

Reid, Anthony (ed.), *Slavery, Bondage and Dependency in Southeast Asia*, St. Lucia, London and New York: University of Queensland Press, 1983.

Renard, Ronald D., *The Burmese Connection: Illegal Drugs and the Making of the Golden Triangle*, Studies on the Impact of the Illegal Drug Trade, vol. 6, Boulder (CO) and London: Lynne Rienner, 1996.

Renborg, Bertil A., 'The Grand Old Men of the League of Nations', *UNODC Bulletin on Narcotics*, 4 (1964), <http://www.unodc.org/unodc/en /data-and-analysis/bulletin/bulletin_1964-01-01_4.html>.

Reynolds, Craig J. (ed.), *National Identity and Its Defenders, Thailand, 1939-1989*, Monash Papers on Southeast Asia, no. 25, Clayton (Victoria): Centre of Southeast Asian Studies Monash University, 1991.

Reynolds, E. Bruce, '"International Orphans" – The Chinese in Thailand During World War II', *Journal of Southeast Asian Studies*, 2 (1997), pp. 365-388.

————, *Thailand and Japan's Southern Advance, 1940-1945*, Basingstoke: Macmillan, 1994.

Riggs, Fred W., *Thailand: The Modernization of a Bureaucratic Polity*, 2nd ed., Honolulu: East-West Center Press, 1967.

Roemer, Milton I., 'Internationalism in Medicine and Public Health', in Dorothy Porter (ed.), *The History of Public Health and the Modern State*, The Wellcome Institute Series in the History of Medicine, Amsterdam and Atlanta: Editions Rodopi, 1994, pp. 403-423.

Rong Syamananda, *A History of Thailand*, 7th ed., Bangkok: Thai Watana Panich, 1990.

Rothermund, Dietmar (ed.), *Aneignung und Selbstbehauptung: Antworten auf die europäische Expansion*, München: Oldenbourg, 1999.

————, *Asian Trade and European Expansion in the Age of Mercantilism*, Perspectives in History, vol. 1, New Delhi: Manohar, 1981.

————, *The Global Impact of the Great Depression, 1929-1939*, London and New York: Routledge, 1996.

Rothstein, Robert L., *Alliances and Small Powers*, New York and London: Columbia University Press, 1968.

Royal Danish Ministry of Education (ed.), *Thai-Danish Relations: 30 Cycles of Friendship*, Copenhagen: Royal Danish Ministry of Education, Bangkok: Pigkames Press, 1980.

Royal Thai Embassy, Berne and Federal Department of Foreign Affairs of Switzerland (eds), *Siam-Swiss Centenary: The Growth of a Friendship*, Bangkok: Amarin and Berne: Royal Thai Embassy, 1997.

Rush, James R., *Opium to Java: Revenue Farming and Chinese Enterprise in Colonial Indonesia, 1860-1910*, Ithaca (NY) and London: Cornell University Press, 1990.

Saitip Sukatipan, 'Thailand: The Evolution of Legitimacy', in Muthiah Alagappa (ed.), *Political Legitimacy in Southeast Asia: The Quest for Moral Authority*, Stanford: Stanford University Press, 1995, pp. 193-223.

Sar Desai, Damodar Ramaji, *Southeast Asia, Past and Present*, 4th ed., Boulder (CO): Westview Press, 1997.

Schmidt, Jan, *From Anatolia to Indonesia: Opium Trade and the Dutch Community of Izmir, 1820-1940*, Leiden: Nederlands Instituut voor het Nabije Oosten, 1998.

Schofield, Richard (ed.), *Reference of the Shatt al-'Arab Dispute to the League of Nations and Subsequent Bilateral Negotiations in Teheran and Geneva, 1934-1935*, The Iran-Iraq Border 1840-1958, vol. 8, Durham: Archive Editions, 1989.

Seefelder, Matthias, *Opium, Eine Kulturgeschichte*, 3rd ed., Landsberg: Ecomed, 1996.

Schendel, Willem van and Henk Schulte Nordholt (eds), *Time Matters: Global and Local Time in Asian Societies*, Amsterdam: VU University Press, 2001.

Shimazu, Naoko, *Japan, Race and Equality: The Racial Equality Proposal of 1919*, London and New York: Routledge, 1998.

Shotwell, James T., 'Security', in Harriet E. Davis (ed.), *Pioneers in World Order: An American Appraisal of the League of Nations*, 2nd ed., New York: Columbia University Press, 1945, pp. 26-41.

———— and Marina Salvin, *Lessons on Security and Disarmament from the History of the League of Nations*, New York: King's Crown Press, 1949.

Siam Society (ed.), *Collected Articles in Memory of H.R.H. Prince Wan Waithayakorn*, Bangkok: Siam Society, 1976.

Siffin, William J., *The Thai Bureaucracy: Institutional Change and Development*, Honolulu: East-West Center Press, 1966.

Siriporn Skrobanek, Nataya Boonpakdee and Chutima Jantateero, *The Traffic in Women: Human Realities of the International Sex Trade*, London and New York: Zed Books, 1997.

Skinner, George William, *Chinese Society in Thailand, An Analytical History*, Ithaca (NY): Cornell University Press, 1967.

————, *Leadership and Power in the Chinese Community of Thailand*, Ithaca (NY): Cornell University Press, 1958.

Sompop Manarungsan, *Economic Development of Thailand, 1850-1950, Response to the Challenge of the World Economy*, Bangkok: Institute of Asian Studies, Chulalongkorn University, 1989.

Songsri Foran, *Thai-British-American Relations during World War II and the Immediate Post-war Period, 1940-1946*, Thai Kadi Research Institute Paper no. 10, Bangkok: Thammasat University Press, 1981.

Sparrow, Gerald, *Land of the Moonflower*, 2nd ed., London: Elex Books, 1955.

————, *Opium Venture*, London: Hale, 1957.

Spencer, Chistopher P. and V. Navaratnam, *Drug Abuse in East Asia*, Kuala Lumpur: Oxford University Press, 1981.

Sri Kunht-Saptodewo, Volker Grabowsky and Martin Großheim (eds), *Nationalism and Cultural Revival in Southeast Asia: Perspectives from the Centre and the Region*, Wiesbaden: Harrassowitz, 1997.

Stevenson, William, *The Revolutionary King: The True-Life Sequel to The King and I*, London: Constable, 1999.

Stoffers, Andreas, *Im Lande des weißen Elefanten: Die Beziehungen zwischen Deutschland und Thailand von den Anfängen bis 1962*, Schriften der Deutsch-Thailändischen Gesellschaft e.V., vol. 22, Bonn: Deutsch-Thailändische Gesellschaft, 1995.

Stowe, Judith A., *Siam becomes Thailand: A Story of Intrigue*, Honolulu: University of Hawaii Press, 1991.

Suntory and Toyota International Centre for Economics and Related Disciplines (STICERD), London School of Economics (ed.), *Japan-Thailand Relations*, International Studies Discussion Paper no. IS/91/228, London: STICERD, September 1991.

Supaporn Jarunpattana, *Siam-Japan Relations 1920-1940*, Visiting Research Fellow Monograph Series, no. 159, Tokyo: Institute of Developing Economies, 1989.

Swan, William L., 'Thai-Japanese Relations at the Start of the Pacific War: New Insight into a Controversial Period', *Journal of Southeast Asian Studies*, 18, 2 (1987), pp. 270-293.

Swanson, Herbert R., 'Advocate and Partner: Missionaries and Modernization in Nan Province, Siam, 1895-1934', *Journal of Southeast Asian Studies*, 13, 2 (September 1982), pp. 296-309.

Tagliacozzo, Eric, *Secret Trades, Porous Borders: Smuggling and States Along a Southeast Asian Frontier, 1865-1915*, New Haven (CT): Yale University Press, 2005.

Tan, Antonio S., 'The Philippine Chinese Response to the Sino-Japanese Conflict, 1931-1941', *Journal of Southeast Asian Studies*, 12, 1 (1981), pp. 207-223.

Tarling, Nicholas, *Britain, Southeast Asia and the Onset of the Pacific War*, Cambridge: Cambridge University Press, 1996.

————— (ed.), *The Cambridge History of Southeast Asia*, vol. 2: The nineteenth and twentieth centuries, Cambridge: Cambridge University Press, 1992.

—————, *Imperial Britain and Southeast Asia*, Kuala Lumpur: Oxford University Press, 1975.

—————, *Imperialism in Southeast Asia: A Fleeting Passing Phase*, London and New York: Routledge, 2001.

—————, 'King Prajadhipok and the Apple Cart: British Attitudes towards the 1932 Revolution', *Journal of the Siam Society*, 64, 2 (1976), pp. 1-38.

—————, *Nations and States in Southeast Asia*, Cambridge: Cambridge University Press, 1999.

—————, 'Rice and Reconciliation: The Anglo-Thai Peace Negotiations of 1945', *Journal of the Siam Society*, 66, 2 (1978), pp. 59-111.

Tate, D.J.M., *The Making of Modern South-East Asia*, vol. 1: The European Conquest, Kuala Lumpur: Oxford University Press, 1971.

—————, *The Making of Modern South-East Asia*, vol. 2: The Western Impact, Kuala Lumpur: Oxford University Press, 1979.

Tej Bunnag, *The Provincial Administration of Siam, 1892-1915*, Kuala Lumpur: Oxford University Press, 1977.

Terwiel, Barend J., 'Acceptance and Rejection: The First Inoculation and Vaccination Campaigns in Thailand', *Journal of the Siam Society*, 76 (1988), pp. 183-201.

—————, 'Asiatic Cholera in Siam: Its First Occurrence and the 1820 Epidemic', in Norman Owen (ed.), *Death and Disease in Southeast Asia: Explorations in Social, Medical, and Demographic History*, Singapore: Oxford University Press, 1987, pp. 142-160.

—————, 'Bondage and Slavery in Early Nineteenth Century Siam', in Anthony Reid (ed.), *Slavery, Bondage and Dependency in Southeast Asia*, St. Lucia, London and New York: University of Queensland Press, 1983, pp. 118-137.

—————, 'The Bowring Treaty: Imperialism and the Indigenous Perspective', *Journal of the Siam Society*, 79, 2 (1991), pp. 40-47.

—————, 'Civilising the Past: Nation and Knowledge in Thai History', in Willem van Schendel and Henk Schulte Nordholt (eds), *Time Matters: Global and Local Time in Asian Societies*, Amsterdam: VU University Press, 2001, pp. 97-111.

—————, 'The Development of Consensus Nationalism in Thailand', in Sri Kunht-Saptodewo, Volker Grabowsky and Martin Großheim (eds), *Nationalism and Cultural Revival in Southeast Asia: Perspectives from the Centre and the Region*, Wiesbaden: Harrassowitz, 1997, pp. 133-143.

—————, *A History of Modern Thailand, 1767-1942*, Histories of Southeast Asia, St. Lucia, London and New York: University of Queensland Press, 1983.

—————, *Thailand's Political History: From the Fall of Ayutthaya in 1767 to Recent Times*, Bangkok: River Books, 2005.

—————, 'Thai Nationalism and Identity: Popular Themes of the 1930s', in Craig J. Reynolds (ed.), *National Identity and Its Defenders, Thailand, 1939-1989*, Monash Papers on Southeast Asia, no. 25, Clayton (Victoria): Centre of Southeast Asian Studies, Monash University, 1991, pp. 133-154.

—————, *A Window on Thai History*, 2nd ed., Bangkok: Duang Kamol, 1991.

Thak Chaloemtiarana, *Thailand: The Politics of Despotic Paternalism*, Bangkok: Tammasat University Press, 1979.

Thamsook Numnonda, 'The American Foreign Affairs Advisers in Thailand, 1917-1940', *Journal of the Siam Society*, 64, 1 (1976), pp. 75-96.

—————, 'The Anglo-Siamese Secret Convention of 1897', *Journal of the Siam Society*, 53, 1 (1965), pp. 45-60.

Thawatt Mokarapong, *History of the Thai Revolution: A Study in Political Behaviour*, Bangkok: Chalermnit, 1972.

Thomas, Gordon, *Enslaved*, 2nd ed., New York: Pharos Books, 1991.

Thomas, R.T., *Britain and Vichy: The Dilemma of Anglo-French Relations, 1940-42*, The Making of the 20th Century, London: Macmillan, 1979.

Thongchai Winichakul, 'The Quest for "Siwilai": A Geographical Discourse of Civilizational Thinking in Late Nineteenth and Early Twentieth-Century Siam', *Journal of Asian Studies*, 59, 3 (August 2000), pp. 528-549.

—————, *Siam Mapped: A History of the Geo-Body of a Nation*, Honolulu: University of Hawai'i Press, 1994.

Thorne, Christopher, *The Limits of Foreign Policy: The West, the League and the Far Eastern Crisis of 1931-1933*, London: Hamish Hamilton, 1972.

Tilman, Robert Oliver (ed.), *Man, State, and Society in Contemporary Southeast Asia*, New York: Praeger, 1969.

Torunsky, Vera, 'Der Korfu-Konflikt von 1923', in: Jost Dülffer, Hans-Otto Mühleisen and Vera Torunsky (eds), *Inseln als Brennpunkte internationaler Politik, Konfliktbewältigung im Wandel des internationalen Systems, 1890-1984: Kreta, Korfu, Zypern*, Köln: Verlag Wissenschaft und Politik, 1986, pp. 60-96.

Trocki, Carl A., 'Drugs, Taxes, and Chinese Capitalism in Southeast Asia', in Timothy Brook and Bob Tadashi Wakabayashi (eds), *Opium Regimes: China, Britain, and Japan, 1839-1952*, Berkeley: University of California Press, 2000, pp. 79-104.

276

————— (ed.), *The Emergence of Modern States, Thailand and Japan*, Thailand-Japan Studies Program, Conference Proceedings, March 19-20, 1976, Bangkok: Institute of Asian Studies, Chulalongkorn University, 1976.

—————, 'Opium and the Beginnings of Chinese Capitalism in South-East Asia', *Journal of Southeast Asian Studies*, 33 (2002), pp. 297-314.

—————, *Opium, Empire and the Global Political Economy, A Study of the Asian Opium Trade*, London: Routledge, 1999.

Tuck, Patrick, *The French Wolf and the Siamese Lamb: The French Threat to Siamese Independence, 1858-1907*, Bangkok: White Lotus Press, 1995.

United Nations (ed.), *The League of Nations 1920-1946, Organization and Accomplishments, A Retrospective of the First Organisation for the Establishment of World Peace*, New York and Geneva: United Nations, 1996.

————— (ed.), *The League of Nations in Retrospect, Proceedings of the Symposium, Geneva 6-9 November 1980*, Berlin and New York: De Gruyter, 1983.

United Nations Information Service (ed.), *United Nations in Thailand*, Bangkok: ECAFE, 1971.

United Nations Information Service Bangkok (ed.), *United Nations and Thailand*, Bangkok: United Nations Information Service, 1964.

United Nations Information Service, ECAFE (ed.), *Thailand and the United Nations*, Bangkok: United Nations Information Service, 1966.

Van Luijk, Eric W. and Jan C. van Ours, 'The Effects of Government Policy on Drug Use: Java, 1875-1904', *Journal of Economic History*, 61, 1 (2001), pp. 1-18.

—————, 'The Effects of Government Policy on Drug Use Reconsidered', *Journal of Economic History*, 62, 4 (2002), pp. 1122-1125.

Veatch, Richard, *Canadian Foreign Policy and the League of Nations, 1919-1939*, Toronto and Buffalo (NY): University of Toronto Press, 1975.

—————, 'The League of Nations and the Spanish Civil War, 1936-9', *European History Quarterly*, 20 (April 1990), pp. 181-207.

Vella, Walter F., *Chaiyo! The Role of King Vajiravudh in the Development of Thai Nationalism*, Honolulu: University of Hawaii Press, 1978.

—————, *The Impact of the West on Government in Thailand*, Publications in Political Science, vol. 4, no. 3, Berkeley: University of California Press, 1955.

Verma, Dina Nath, *India and the League of Nations*, Patna: Bharati Bhawan, 1968.

Vichitvong Na Pombhejara, *Pridi Banomyong and the Making of Thailand's Modern History*, Bangkok: Chaiwichit Press, 1983.

Walker, William O. III., *Opium and Foreign Policy: The Anglo-American Search for Order in Asia, 1912-1954*, Chapel Hill (NC) and London: University of North Carolina Press, 1991.

Walters, Francis P., *A History of the League of Nations*, 5th ed., London, New York and Toronto: Oxford University Press, 1969.

Warren, James Francis, Ah Ku *and* Karayuki-san, *Prostitution in Singapore, 1870-1940*, Singapore: Oxford University Press, 1993.

Wathinee Boonchalaksi and Philip Guest, *Prostitution in Thailand*, Salaya (Nakhon Pathom): Institute for Population Research, Mahidol University, 1994.

Weindling, Paul (ed.), *International Health Organisations and Movements, 1918-1939*, New York: Cambridge University Press, 1995.

Wenk, Klaus (ed.), *Die Verfassungen Thailands*, Die Staatsverfassungen der Welt in Einzelausgaben, vol. 5, ed. by Forschungsstelle für Völkerrecht und ausländisches öffentliches Recht der Universität Hamburg, Frankfurt a.M. and Berlin: Metzner, 1964.

—————, 'The Relations Between Germany and Thailand', in *Southeast Asia and the Germans*, Tübingen and Basel: Erdmann, 1977, pp. 145-165.

Williams, Phil (ed.), *Illegal Immigration and Commercial Sex: The New Slave Trade*, London and Portland (OR): Frank Cass, 1999.

—————, 'Trafficking in Women and Children: A Market Perspective', in Phil Williams (ed.), *Illegal Immigration and Commercial Sex: The New Slave Trade*, London and Portland (OR): Frank Cass, 1999, pp. 145-170.

Wilson, Constance M., 'Revenue Farming, Economic Development and Government Policy during the Early Bangkok Period, 1830-92', in John Butcher and Howard Dick (eds), *The Rise and Fall of Revenue Farming: Business Elites and the Emergence of the Modern State in Southeast Asia*, London and New York: St. Martin's Press, 1993, pp. 142-165.

Wilson, David A., 'The Military in Thai Politics', in Robert Oliver Tilman (ed.), *Man, State, and Society in Contemporary Southeast Asia*, New York: Praeger, 1969, pp. 326-339.

—————, *Politics in Thailand*, Ithaca (NY): Cornell University Press, 1962.

Wiwat Mungkandi and William Warren (eds), *A Century and a Half of Thai-American Relations*, Bangkok: Chulalongkorn University Press, 1982.

Wright, Joseph J. Jr., *The Balancing Act: A History of Modern Thailand*, Bangkok: Asia Books, 1991.

Wurfel, David and Bruce Burton (eds), *The Political Economy of Foreign Policy in Southeast Asia*, London: Macmillan, 1990.

Wyatt, David K., *Thailand, A Short History*, 2nd ed., Bangkok: Silkworm Books, 1984.

Young, Edward M., *Aerial Nationalism: A History of Aviation in Thailand*, Smithsonian History of Aviation Series, Washington D.C. and London: Smithsonian Institution Press, 1995.

F. Unpublished Papers, Manuscripts, and Theses

Chalong Soontravanich, 'Siam and the First Hague Peace Conference of 1899: A Preliminary Note', Unpublished Manuscript, 1996.

Copeland, Mathew P., 'Contested Nationalism and the 1932 Overthrow of the Absolute Monarchy in Siam', Ph.D. Thesis, Australian National University, 1993.

Darmp Sukontasap, 'The Third World and the United Nations Security Council: The Thai Experience, 1985-1986', Ph.D. Thesis, Fletcher School of Law and Diplomacy, Tufts University, 1993.

Flood, Edward Thadeus, 'Japan's Relations with Thailand, 1928-1941', Ph.D. Thesis, University of Washington, 1967.

Guénel, Annik, 'The Conference on Rural Hygiene in Bandung of 1937: Towards a New Vision of Health Care?', Paper Presented at Conference on 'History of Medicine in Southeast Asia', Center for Khmer Studies, Siem Reap, Cambodia, January 9-10, 2006.

Hart, Keith, 'The Military Participation of Siam in the First World War (1914-1918)', unpublished document, Thailand Information Center at Chulalongkorn University Main Library, n.d.

Hell, Stefan, 'Southeast Asia in Early International Organization: The League of Nations' Activities in the Region before the Second World War', Paper Presented at 'The 16th Conference of the International Association of Historians of Asia (IAHA)', Kota Kinabalu, Malaysia, 27-31 July 2000.

Highley, Albert E., 'The Actions of the States Members of the League of Nations in the Application of Sanctions against Italy, 1935/1936', Ph.D. Thesis, University of Geneva, 1938.

Hong Lysa, 'The Evolution of the Thai Economy in the Early Bangkok Period and its Historiography', Ph.D. Thesis, University of Sydney, 1981.

Likhit Dhiravegin, 'Political Attitudes of the Bureaucratic Elite and Modernization in Thailand', Ph.D. Thesis, Brown University, 1973.

Link, Willi, 'Die Interessenlage zwischen Großmächten und Kleinstaaten auf den beiden Haager Friedenskonferenzen', Ph.D. Thesis, Tübingen University, 1948.

Montri Supaporn, 'The Role Performance of Prime Ministers in the Thai Political System: Styles of Military and Civilian Rule, 1932-1983', Ph.D. Thesis, Case Western Reserve University, 1984.

Nambara, Makoto, 'Economic Plans and the Evolution of Economic Nationalism in Siam in the 1930s', Ph.D. Thesis, School of Oriental and African Studies, University of London, 1998.

Oblas, Peter B., 'Siam's Efforts to revise the Unequal Treaty System in the Sixth Reign, 1910-1925', Ph.D. Thesis, University of Michigan, 1974.

Orasa Thaiyanan, 'Die Beziehungen zwischen Thailand (Siam) und Österreich-Ungarn (1869-1917/19)', Ph.D. Thesis, University of Vienna, 1987.

Patcharee Thawonphayak, 'Die Entwicklung des staatlichen Schulwesens in Thailand 1851 bis 1997, Eine Studie zur historischen Entwicklung des staatlichen Schulwesens in Thailand', Ph.D. Thesis, Passau University, 1997.

Pracha Guna-Kasem, 'Thailand and the United Nations (1945-1957)', Ph.D. Thesis, Yale University, 1960.

Seksan Prasertkul, 'The Transformation of the Thai State and Economic Change (1855-1945)', Ph.D. Thesis, Cornell University, 1989.

Sogn, Richard R., 'Successful Journey: A History of United States-Thai Relations, 1932-1945', Ph.D. Thesis, University of Michigan, 1990.

Swan, William L., 'Japanese Economic Relations with Siam: Aspects of Their Historical Development 1884 to 1942', Ph.D. Thesis, Australian National University, 1986.

Vikrom Koompirochana, 'Siam in British Foreign Policy, 1855-1938: The Acquisition and Relinquishment of British Extraterritorial Rights', Ph.D. Thesis, Michigan State University, 1972.

Index